The Islands of Western Scotland

D1346982

THE REGIONS OF BRITAIN

Previous and forthcoming titles in the
series include:

The Pennine Dales Arthur Raistrick
The Upper Thames J. R. L. Anderson
The Lake District Roy Millward and Adrian Robinson
The Scottish Border and Northumberland John Talbot
    White

North East England Arthur Raistrick
East Anglia Norman Scarfe
The Cotswolds H. P. R. Finberg
Pembrokeshire John Barrett
The Peak District Roy Millward and Adrian Robinson
Cornwall W. G. Hoskins

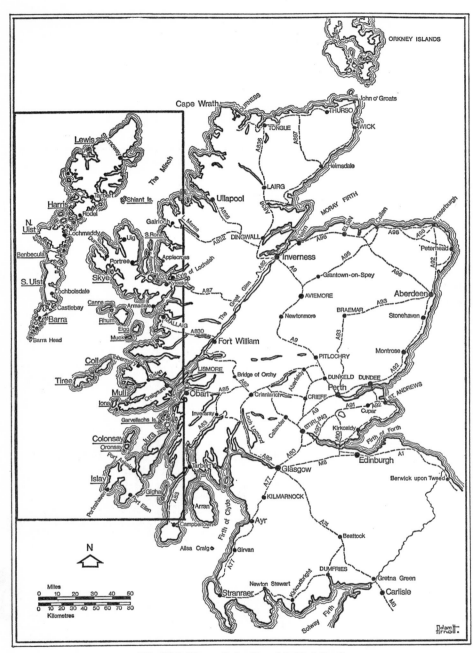

The Hebrides and the Scottish Mainland

W. H. MURRAY

The Islands of Western Scotland

The Inner and Outer Hebrides

EYRE METHUEN . LONDON

First published 1973
© 1973 W. H. Murray
Printed in Great Britain for
Eyre Methuen Ltd
11 New Fetter Lane, London EC4P 4EE
by Cox & Wyman Ltd
Fakenham, Norfolk

SBN 413 26100 x (hardback)
SBN 413 30380 2 (paperback)

The Islands of
Western Scotland

Contents

The Islands of
Western Scotland

Illustrations

MAPS

Acknowledgements

It will be evident that no man can write on subjects so diverse out of his own research and knowledge. This book has been made possible only by the literary work of men over a space of more than 2,000 years, in particular since AD 1500. I have read or consulted more than three hundred books and papers, which I list at the end, and like me their authors have been indebted in turn to innumerable others. The correct interpretation of studies so specialized as the many branches of geology, ecology, archaeology and the historical record, is hardly possible to a writer untrained in their separate disciplines, therefore I asked and received help from men and women who were expert. Despite the pressures of their work, they gave me time, information, criticism, and correction with unexpected generosity. I have in particular a need to express my indebtedness for advice on geology to George Scott Johnstone of the Institute of Geological Sciences at Edinburgh; on ecology to J. Morton Boyd, director of the Nature Conservancy in Scotland; on wintering geese to Malcolm A. Ogilvie of the Wildfowl Trust; on prehistory to Euan W. MacKie of the Hunterian Museum at Glasgow University; on Gaelic literature to Professor Derick S. Thomson of the Celtic Department at Glasgow University; on Hebridean history and language to Graham Donald, the head of the House of Islay; and on Pictish art and exhibits at the National Museum of Antiquities to the curator, R. B. K. Stevenson.

There are many others to whom I give thanks for assistance. Among these are Miss Helen C. Nisbet for archaeological references; the officers of several branches of central and local government; the Highlands and Islands Development Board, the Department of the Environment, the Department of Employment, the Forestry Commission (West and North Conservancies), the

Meteorological Office at Edinburgh, the Department of Agriculture and Fisheries, and the counties of Argyll, Inverness, Ross, and Sutherland.

The men and women most knowledgeable on their subjects frequently disagree on the interpretation of facts. I have given opposing views where they can be given concisely, but when (as most often happens) they involve lengthy expositions beyond the scope of this book, I have chosen the opinion that appears to me to be backed either by the better evidence or common sense. If I should have fallen into error, ascribe it to me and not to the experts whose advice I did not invariably take; had they been writing, they would have entered the numerous qualifying factors to which I have rarely been able to give space.

Footnote references in the text are to the entries in the Bibliography under date and author.

Acknowledgements and thanks for permission to reproduce photographs are due to Planair, Edinburgh, for plates 1, 3a, 10, 19b, and 20a; to A. D. S. Macpherson for plates 2a, 4a, 5, 11, 14a, 15a, 16b, 20b, and 23; to the Institute of Geological Sciences, Edinburgh, for plate 2b; to Noel Habgood for plates 3b and 4b; to Audrey Holmes for plates 6, 15b, 17a, and 19a; to Tom Weir for plates 7 and 17b; to J. Allan Cash for plates 8a, 12b, 14b, 18b, and 24; to Donald B. MacCulloch for plates 8b and 12a; to the Hunterian Museum and the University Court, Glasgow, for plate 9a; to the National Museum of Antiquities, Edinburgh, for plates 9b, 13b, 21, and 22b; to the Universitetets Oldsaksamling, Oslo, for plate 13a; to the Royal Commission on Ancient and Historical Monuments, Scotland, for plate 16a; and to Trinity College, Dublin, for plate 22a.

I should also like to give thanks for permission to use the following drawings, diagrams, and plans: to Graham Donald for Frank Newall's ground plan of Dun Fhinn, which appears in *Foundations of Islay*, Part II, 1970; to Euan W. MacKie for his drawing and ground plan of a broch on Tiree, which appeared in the magazine *Gairm*; to the Glasgow Archaeological Society for the ground plan of Breacacha Castle on Coll, which appeared in their *Transactions*, New Series, Vol. X, 1941; and to the Institute of Geological Sciences for the diagram of Volcanoes and Dyke Swarms, based on the Crown Copyright Geological Survey diagram and reproduced by permission of the controller of H.M.S.O. These were all re-drawn by Adam Arnott, who also drew the rest of the maps and diagrams.

Acknowledgement and thanks for permission to use the song *Seagull of the Land-Under-Waves* from *Songs of the Hebrides* is due to the Trustees of the Estate of Marjory Kennedy Fraser and Boosey and Hawkes Music Publishers Ltd, and thanks is due to Professor Derick S. Thomson for his poem *The Herring Girls* from *Eadar Samhradh is Foghar*.

The Islands of
Western Scotland

Introduction

On a cloudless morning of early June, 1936, I climbed on to the summit of Sgurr Alasdair in the Cuillin of Skye, and for the first time saw the Hebrides whole, as an archipelago fringing the North Atlantic. I could not see them all, of course – they stretch 240 miles north to south – but fully half their length lay clear to the west. At that time of year Scotland's west seaboard has a peculiar clarity of atmosphere seen only during the three months following the spring equinox. The sea then can take on a deeper, more brilliant blue than I have ever seen on the Mediterranean, distances shrink, and the excess of ultra-violet light burns the skin. From my 3000-foot stance I looked forty miles across the channel of the Minch to the long, lilac spine of the outer isles, which did not, as in other months, line the horizon, but was close enough to let me see, far across the back of North Uist, the black dot of St Kilda, a hundred miles away on the broad Atlantic. By a trick of light the sea appeared to slope down from the horizon, in a flat calm so very like polished ice that I imagined the isles like curling stones about to slide in to the mainland. Their fabled mystery, which they commonly owe to haze or light cloud, was no less marked in that crystal air, for their edge of the ocean site was made so plain. A realm of several hundred islands lay awaiting discovery. I felt, in anticipation at least, some of that exploratory excitement that the first Scandinavians and Scots must have felt more than 1,500 years before me, and the Bronze Age and Neolithic seamen still earlier.

Thirty years later, I had come to know the Hebrides in all their parts from their sea-channels and cliffs, their sandy bays with marram dunes and flower-starred machair, up to their brown moors and rocky mountains. Like most people I was captured by their beauty of wild land and wild-life, their natural architecture and Atlantic setting, and by their people of mixed Gaelic and Norse stock.

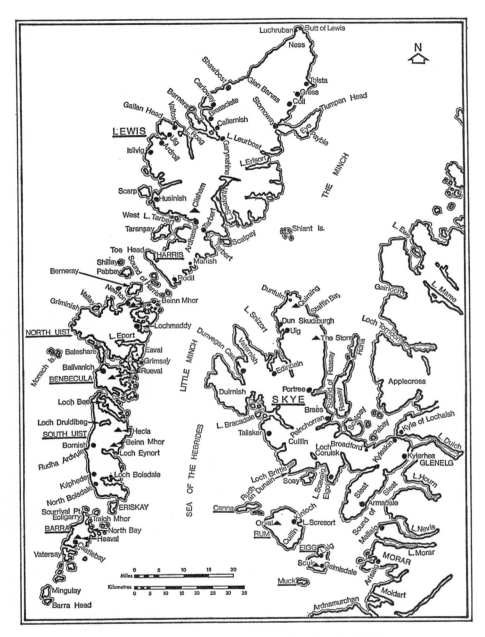

Map 1a *The Hebridean Islands (Northern Section)*

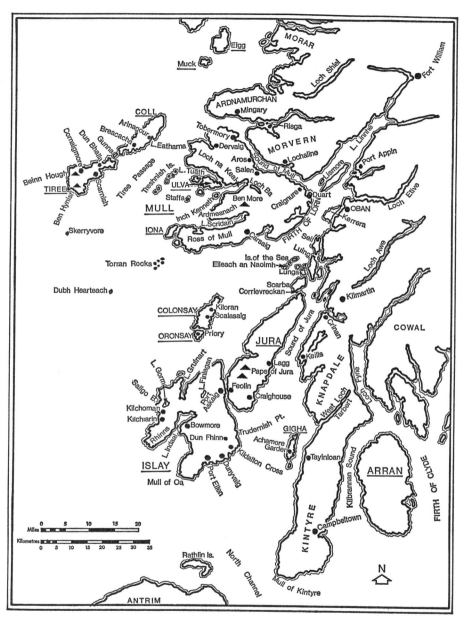

Map 1b *The Hebridean Islands (Southern Section)*

My first love was romantic, which had the merit of stirring me to find out the sterner, less delightful realities. I wanted to know the islands in depth, but soon learned that this was far from easy. Many books and papers have dealt in recent centuries with special aspects of the Hebridean record: the geology, ecology, prehistory, the political and social history, economy, and Gaelic culture – but none brought these six phases together in one volume. If I wanted such a book, it seemed that I would have to write it myself. I did want, for I believed that the Hebrides could be properly understood only in the round, and when Eyre Methuen invited me to write in their *Regions of Britain* series, I seized the chance.

While trying to get at the truth, my account is far from complete, for that would need a dozen volumes. There are so many differences in life and living conditions, often subtle but important, within the individual islands, that I can hardly make a statement without realizing that several qualifications ought to be made. My tale too takes a wide sweep, omissions of detail being necessarily numerous. For example, to leave room for other things, the geology has been much simplified and has nothing on the Moine Thrust, which gave schist to a coastal strip of south Mull; the archaeology has next to nothing on Bronze or Iron Age pottery; the ecology little on seaweeds, more fully treated in their economic context; and Celtic literature no examples (save by reference) of classical Gaelic verse, for I felt it more important to give the space to a live poet.

My plan (chapter 2 onwards) has been to engage with the Hebrides prenatally, when the land was one with Greenland and the Eurasian continent, in order to show the earth and sea movements by which the land was built up and the islands formed, the means by which they were shaped and the ways they were sculpted by over-riding ice, the pageant of their first colonization by plant and animal life, and then by man, and how these feats were achieved. I give much space to the enterprise on land and sea of the Stone, Bronze, and Iron Age peoples, for their abilities were extraordinary. In describing the first arrival of the Scots and their union with the native Picts under pressure of Norse invasion, I have shown the settlement life of all three so far as that can be known – how they worked, dressed, fed, were housed, worshipped, thought, and played – emphasizing that they lived and ruled themselves by original, democratic ideals.

My tracing of the mistakes the people made, their exploitation of the islands' resources, the challenges to survival they overcame or failed to meet, and the growth of trade and arts, discloses several ironies of history. Many readers may be surprised to know that in the golden age of the thirteenth to sixteenth centuries, the entire Hebrides and Highland coast formed one Atlantic principality, self-supporting, powerful, and independent, whose ambassadors dealt direct with the kings of Scotland, England, and Europe. But the seeds of decline had already been sown. The strength of Hebridean democracy and its Gaelic culture had been undermined by the imposition from Lowland Scotland, against the isles-men's will, of a foreign feudalism. The most cruel irony was this, that when the light of democratic ideals later dawned on the Lowlands, the Hebrides were left in feudal dark. This led to successive collapses of the political, social, and econo-mic structures, and of cultural tradition. The reconstitution of these over the last hundred years is a work still continuing, and a story often grim, sometimes heroic, but always lively.

I

Physical Description

An island is defined, in the Scottish census report of 1861, as 'any piece of solid land surrounded by water, which affords sufficient vegetation to support one or more sheep or which is inhabited by man'. Applied to the Hebrides, this definition helpfully excludes unnumbered skerries,* and gives a count on Scottish seas of 787 islands, 589 of which – more than two-thirds – lie off the west coast. The Hebrides in turn may be loosely defined as Scotland's western isles, by long custom and general consent excluding numerous islands that lie deeply within the arms of the mainland. Thus the islands of the Firth of Clyde and those that have no Atlantic outlook in the great sea-lochs, are not in the Hebrides. So many islands remain marginally placed, both in site and size, that the test for inclusion becomes a matter of opinion, and no precise figure can be given. In my opinion, there are approximately 550 islands in the Hebrides, of which 64 are inhabited, including lighthouses.

The main body of the Hebrides takes clear shape as two archipelagos lying parallel to the coast, the outer overlapping the inner for sixty miles. The Outer Hebrides, thirty-five to fifty miles from the mainland, form a compact line 130 miles long. The Inner Hebrides, bigger and more scattered in a double rank 142 miles long, lie close in to the coast. Together they shield the west coast against the full assault of Atlantic seas. Skye and the Small Isles, at the north end of the Inner Hebrides, receive a like benefit, but south of the overlap, Tiree, Coll, Iona, the Ross of Mull, Colonsay, and Islay, are every bit as exposed as the outer isles, and like them are lined to the west by sandy beaches. Shell-sand is a natural resource of great importance to island agriculture and Skye pays for its protection by the lack of it.

* Rock islets and reefs.

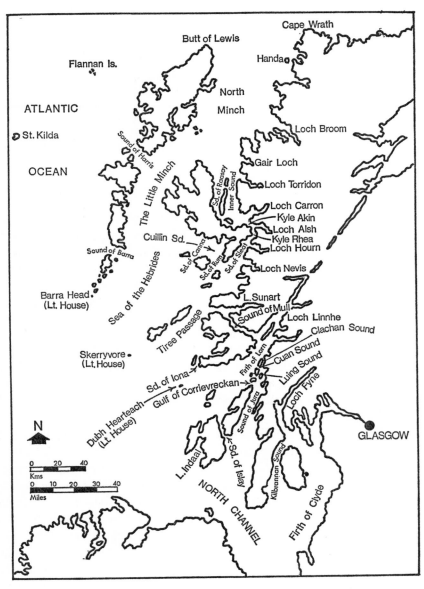

Cape Wrath

Butt of Lewis

Handa

Flannan Is.

North
Minch

ATLANTIC

Loch Broom

St. Kilda

Gair Loch

OCEAN

Loch Torridon

Sound of Harris

The Little Minch

Loch Carron
Kyle Akin
Loch Alsh
Kyle Rhea
Loch Hourn

Sd. of Raasay

Inner Sound

Cuillin Sd.

Sound of Barra

Sea of the Hebrides

Sd. of Canna

Sd. of Rum

Sd. of Sleat

Loch Nevis

Barra Head.
(Lt. House)

L. Sunart

Sound of Mull

Loch Linnhe

Clachan Sound

Tiree Passage

Skerryvore
(Lt. House)

Firth of Lorn

Cuan Sound

Luing Sound

Sd. of Iona

Dubh Hearteach
(Lt. House)

Gulf of Corrievreckan

Loch Fyne

Sound of Jura

N

L. Indaal

Sd. of Islay

GLASGOW

Kilbrannan Sound

0   20   40
Kms

0   10   20   30   40
Miles

NORTH CHANNEL

Firth of Clyde

Map 2   *The Sea Channels*

The broad channel between the Inner and Outer Hebrides is to the north of Skye called the Minch, to the west of Skye the Little Minch, and south-west of Skye, the Sea of the Hebrides.

The Inner Hebrides have a land area of more than 1,000,000 acres, and the Outer 716,000 acres. Together they carry a population of 46,000, of which two-thirds live on the Outer Hebrides. Last century, when the population was twice as large, two-thirds lived on the Inner Hebrides.* The people support themselves by crofting, sheep- and cattle-farming, fishing, seafaring, Harris tweed-weaving, and a host of smaller industries.

The main islands of the Inner Hebrides fall naturally into three groups around Skye, Mull and Islay. Skye belongs to Invernessshire, but the two others to Argyll. From north to south they are:

		Acreage	Population
1. SKYE, Raasay, Rona, Scalpay, Pabay, Soay, and outliers		428 998	7 481
The Small Isles of Rum	30 000		
Eigg	5 000		
Muck	1 586		
Canna	2 880	39 466	150
2. MULL, Iona, Inch Kenneth, Ulva, Gometra, Staffa, the Treshnish Isles and other outliers		224 788	2 170
Lismore		10 000	120
Coll		18 316	1 054
Tiree		18 896	
3. ISLAY		150 585	3 875
Gigha and Cara		3 622	140
Colonsay and Oronsay		11 075	381
Jura and Scarba		93 794	
		999 540	15 371

The Outer Hebrides fall into three groups around Lewis, the Uists, and Barra. Lewis belongs to Rossshire and all the others to Invernessshire. After 1974 they

* The ways in which that transposition occurred and numbers were halved will be discussed in later chapters, for they cannot be ascribed solely to sheep-farming clearances without over-simplification.

will become one regional authority named the Western Isles. From north to south they are:

	Acreage	Population
1. LEWIS with HARRIS (one island), Bernera (Loch Roag), Scarp, Taransay, Berneray (Sound of Harris), Ensay, Killegray, Scalpay, the Shiant Isles, and the Flannan Isles	528 165	23 702
2. The UISTS: North Uist, Pabbay, Boreray, Vallay, Kirkibost, Baleshire, the Monach Isles	75 513	1 807
South Uist, Benbecula, Eriskay	90 093	3 799
3. BARRA, Vatersay, Fuday, Hellisay, Gighay, Flodday (north), Flodday (south), Sandray, Pabbay, Mingulay, and Berneray (Barra Head)	22 222	1 159
	715 993	30 467

To these must be added the very numerous outliers, some close, some far-flung, not listed above. Special attention is due to St Kilda, forty miles west of the Outer Hebrides, and to Sula Sgeir and North Rona equally far north; these, with the Shiant Isles close to east Lewis, and Handa on the Sutherland coast, are all important wild-life stations. There are many others. The farthest outlier, Rockall, 300 miles west of the mainland, is by definition no island, but the Gaelic-speaking Scots gave it a better name, *Sgeir Rocail* (pronounced Rawcal), the Sea-rock of Roaring. The Inner Hebrides include a Firth of Lorn group, Seil and Luing, which are nearly part of the mainland, with Lunga and the Isles of the Sea (the Garvellachs) offshore. The latter have some of the oldest monastic remains in Scotland. On Luing are bred some of the best cattle of the West Highlands. And around them lurk notorious tide-races, most notably the Grey Dog and the whirlpool of Corrievreckan.

All six inhabited groups have steamer and air services from the mainland. BEA operate daily flights from Glasgow to Tiree, Barra, Islay, Benbecula, and Lewis (Stornoway), the two latter also with daily flights to and from Inverness. Loganair have augmented these services with daily flights from Glasgow to Benbecula and Stornoway, weekend flights to Mull and Coll (May to October), and thrice weekly flights to Skye from Inverness and Glasgow.

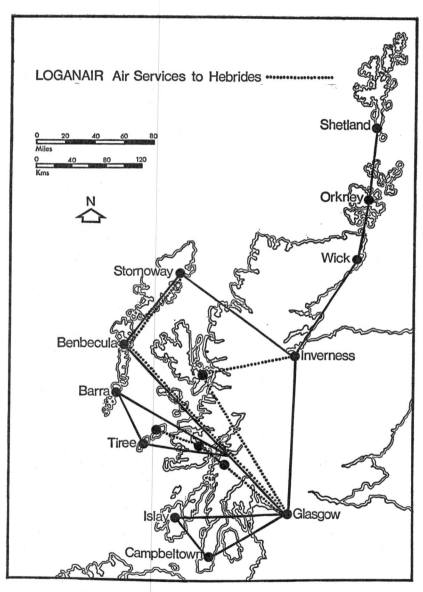

LOGANAIR Air Services to Hebrides ·············

Shetland

Orkney

Wick

Stornoway

Benbecula

Inverness

Barra

Tiree

Islay

Glasgow

Campbeltown

N

0   20   40   60   80
Miles

0   40   80   120
Kms

Map 3 *BEA flights from Glasgow and Inverness*
to The Hebrides, Orkney, and Shetland

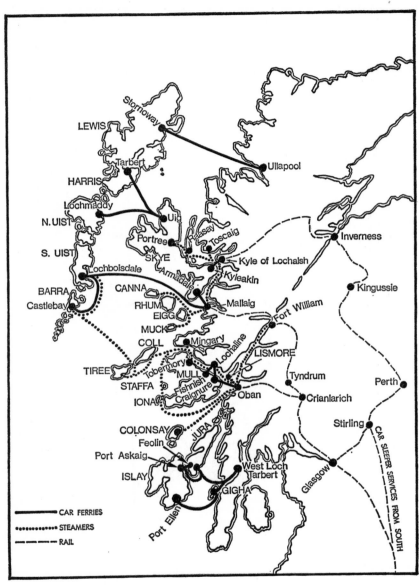

Map 4a *Car ferry, steamer and rail services*

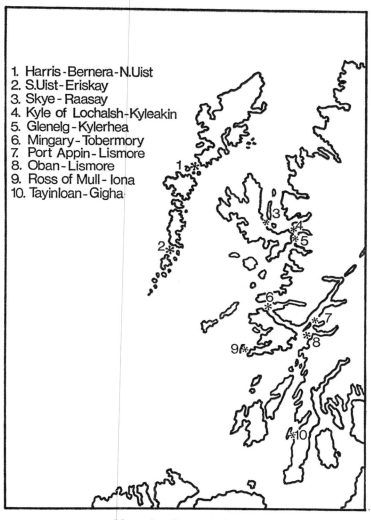

1. Harris-Bernera-N.Uist
2. S.Uist-Eriskay
3. Skye-Raasay
4. Kyle of Lochalsh-Kyleakin
5. Glenelg-Kylerhea
6. Mingary-Tobermory
7. Port Appin-Lismore
8. Oban-Lismore
9. Ross of Mull-Iona
10. Tayinloan-Gigha

Map 4b *Passenger ferries*

The principal steamer and car-ferry services are operated by David Mac-Brayne Ltd, who are subsidized by central government, and car-ferry services (unsubsidized) by Caledonian MacBrayne Ltd. Car-ferries run from Glenelg and Kyle of Lochalsh to Skye. Ferries for passengers only run daily from Kintyre (Tayinloan) to Gigha, from Lorn (two miles south of Oban) to Kerrera, from Port Appin to the north end of Lismore, from Ardnamurchan (Mingary) to Tobermory in Mull, from South Uist (Ludag) to Eriskay, and from North Uist (Newton) to Berneray and Harris (Leverburgh). Motorboats may be privately hired at the island and mainland ports.

Since the Hebrides stretch 240 miles through three degrees of latitude, air travel best reveals something (but only something) of their pattern. The Outer Hebrides from aloft can look like a barrier reef, surprisingly inhabited, edging a vast Atlantic. The Inner Hebrides look from there more like a mainland fringe. Such impressions are too remote. The more intimate approach is by sea, either by public services or better still, if you seek a wide, general impression, on one of the National Trust for Scotland's spring or autumn cruises, which go through the length and breadth of the Isles. Land-travel is finally all-important, because first impressions from seaward can be quite misleading. Approach by ship is made to their eastern sides, where the ports lie for protection, and with few exceptions that aspect is forbidding. They present their welcoming faces most usually to the west, where flower-covered machair spreads at the back of the bays.* Even that sight is from seaward too distant, for a belt of shallow water to the islands' west keeps big ships well out.

The islands seen in silhouette from the sea take every shape, from fangs of rock 600 feet high, like St Kilda, to flat pancakes like Tiree; from close-packed mountains that tower out of the water, like Rum or Skye, to the low monotonous line of Coll. Between such extremes of the flat and vertical, the islands undulate, swelling and sinking from 3000 feet to 50. All share a brown heathery colour, for their bare moorland backs screen the lower varieties of life. Between the Inner and Outer Hebrides there are two clearly marked distinctions in relief. The outer isles throughout their long length are so narrow and compact that they appear, even to the geologically ignorant, as if they might at one time have been one island, like the crest of a mountain ridge, and that in fact is what they were and are. Whereas the inner isles are by comparison very widely scattered. Again, the outer isles keep low to the water, rising briefly to 2600 feet on Clisham in Harris, and only once again to nearly 2000 feet on the Hecla range of South Uist. Grace-

---

* Machair is the grass sward on calcareous ground behind beaches.

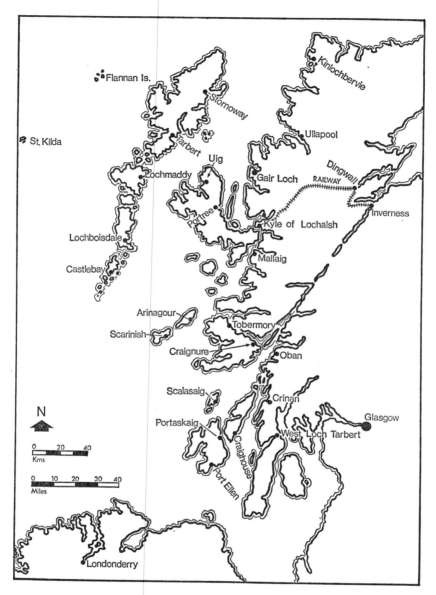

Map 5 *Ports*

ful in outline as seen against the sky, hilly in part, they roll gently down the horizon from the Butt of Lewis to Barra Head. Most of the inner isles stand much higher out of the water, leap and fall in height, and are much more heavily bayed on Skye, Mull and Islay.

These differences of form are due to differences of rock. Writers on the Hebrides say that the outer isles are called the Gneiss Islands and the inner the Trap Islands. Such titles are confined to books. I have never heard them used. The Outer Hebrides are often called the Long Isle, sometimes the Western Isles (especially since they became a parliamentary constituency), but not Gneiss Islands. Yet that word says as much as the others. The Long Isle is made of gneisses. They are incredibly hard and tough, resisting erosion better than other island rocks. Therefore the Long Isle's back does not drain well and is almost uninhabited peat-bog. Trap, as a term loosely used for volcanic rocks, could fairly be applied to most of the inner isles, except Coll, Tiree, Iona, and islands south of Mull. In general, the more brittle or softer rocks have been hugely eroded, and the relatively greater heights to which some attain were once greater by far.

However widely the islands differ, there are several qualities they share, even if they do not share them equally. The foremost, because it most impresses an incomer, is a lightness and freedom of atmosphere. He feels that he can breathe as if for the first time fully. His sense of freshness comes of the wide open skies and vast expanse of light-reflecting sea; from the stir of air, which is always cooler than the mainland's. Colours share a luminous quality, which is less noticeable close into the mainland than farther out – less marked in central Mull than Iona, but not less in Iona than in outer isles. The islands share too a strange combination of starkness and Atlantic mildness. They are windy, but in favoured places, where folds and hollows give soil and shelter, rich in flowers and trees. Plants may grow low to the ground to escape continuous wind, but, if they have soil, grow they will in this mild climate even on the most exposed machairs, where July grass often disappears under the top-load of blossom. Bare of trees for the main part, the islands offer startling contrasts in nakedness side by side with lush growth. A famous example is Colonsay, where the farmland, and the exotic garden of Kiloran valley with its palm trees, eucalyptus, magnolia, rhododendrons, azaleas, and flame trees (*embothrium longifolium*), contrast with bleak outlands to north and south. All larger islands offer contrasts both within themselves, with one another, and between groups. While sharing the qualities of Atlantic insularity, all are different.

If you sail from the Clyde round the Mull of Kintyre and move north-west up the North Channel, a most remarkable feature of Islay at once appears – a feature caught by Ptolemy in his second-century map of the Five *Ebudae*. Seen from south or north between Ireland and Iona, Islay appears as two distinct islands with no visible link. The ground between the eastern and western hills is so flat and low, and so heavily bayed to north and south, that it vanishes. Ptolemy names each part separately as *Ebuda* (which possibly indicates that he was aware

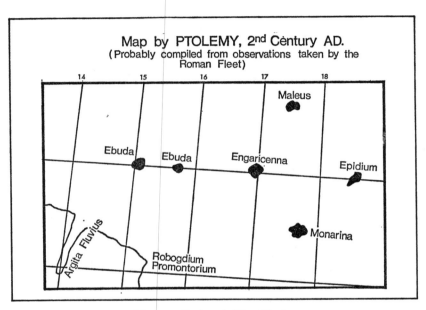

Map 6 *Ptolemy's Five Ebudae*

of the link and was representing appearances only). His map, however regarded, is incorrectly oriented, but if allowance is made by aligning his north-east point of Ireland with *Maleus* as true north, the five 'islands' fall fairly correctly into place with *Maleus* as Mull, *Engaricenna* as Jura, *Monarina* as Arran, and *Epidium* (between Arran and Jura) as the Kintyre peninsula, which would naturally be thought an island and was occupied by the Epidii. Island shapes could not be known, so the map-maker has represented them as blobs indicating relative positions according to prominent hill-clusters.★

Ila is an old Gaelic word meaning the Island Bent like a Bow, and Islay seen

★ Skene (1876) guesses the two *Ebudae* as Islay and Jura, *Engaricenna* as Scarba, and *Epidium* as Lismore, but he was unaware of Islay's twin aspect.

closer bends in just this way around Loch Indaal. The eastern mountains are a heathery quartzite desert rising to 1600 feet, but the fertile inner and central area is mica-schist with limestone, bearing several hundred farms that look like a slice out of Ireland only forty miles south. Bowmore on Loch Indaal is the island's heart with eight hundred people, a hospital, a school for three hundred children, and shops. The chief ports are Port Ellen on the south coast and Port Askaig on the north-east.

Jura, separated from Islay by the narrow Sound of Jura, can muster barely two hundred people for all its twenty-seven miles' length, for its long back is again barren quartzite, almost nipped in two by a central isthmus at Tarbert. A narrow strip of schist runs down the east side, where the people live in half a dozen villages, with a pier at Craighouse in the south. The entire western half is uninhabited by man, is roadless and trackless, stony and cave-bitten along the coast, but adorned by three hills named the Paps of Jura. They rise to over 2500 feet and dominate every view within a radius of thirty miles or more. Once there were wide cattle grazings on Jura, with green grass spreading deep into present moorland (like northern Ireland), but now the island has reverted to red deer (4,000 head) as in Viking days, when it was named *Dyr Oë* (pronounced Joorah), meaning Deer Island.

Colonsay was two islands when man first arrived there, for the Kiloran glen was then a strait. Measuring eight miles by three, with the tidal island of Oronsay tacked to its south end, its rock is a low strata of Torridon sandstone containing lime. Good soil, and the alignment of low hills reaching 470 feet, which protect the glen from east and west winds, allow Colonsay to hold a range of plant and animal life matched by no other island.

Gigha, three miles off the coast of Kintyre, surpasses Colonsay in the fertility of its grassland. Gigha (old Norse *Gudey*,* meaning Good Island) measures six miles by one and a half. It takes the shape of a sea serpent, long and humpy. A spinal ridge of epidiorite runs through from north to south, and rising to 300 feet protects and nourishes a dozen farms on 900 acres of arable land. The soil is rich, the land green, and dairy farming the rule. In summer, nearly 1,000 gallons of milk go daily to the creamery at Achamore for cheese-making. The garden at Achamore House rivals in beauty those of Colonsay and Inverewe. Gigha is reputed to be Scotland's most productive island in proportion to land area.

Across the Firth of Lorn towards Mull, island landscape becomes Highland. Mull is mountainous, rising on Ben More to 3170 feet, to which the big hills

* Haco's Expedition, 1263: Flatigan and Frisian MSS.

are concentric. The west side is so deeply indented by the sea-lochs of Scridain and Keal that a big head and tail have been left projecting north and south-west. The head is gentler, lower moorland, and the sixteen-mile tail is the Ross of Mull – a bare peninsula, but hilly with sheltered glens. It ends a mile short of Iona, to which it was formerly joined. Mull almost lost its head to a glacier, which left on withdrawal only a narrow neck about sixty feet above sea-level. The main mass of Mull is volcanic rock – Tertiary lavas piled on top of earlier Moine schist, between which lies a thin spread of Cretaceous and other sediments, deposited there when shallow seas spread over this land before Mull was an island. The friable rock has given Mull well-drained soil, much of it ranking with the most fertile in the Highland area.* The primary industry is sheep- and cattle-farming, but production is a fraction of what it should be. The land has never recovered from the exploitation of the nineteenth century.

The east coast channel, the Sound of Mull, is only two miles wide and the land there of South Highland character – well-wooded on the coastal strip, above which rise grassy hill-slopes with neither heather nor big cliffs. The ports on this coast, at either end of the sound, are Craignure, served from Oban (ten miles) by a car-ferry, and Tobermory, which is, in appearance, the finest small town of the Hebrides, with a population of 650. Its bay is circled by steep slopes wooded in sycamore. Modern houses ring the upper slope, but down on the main street, which curves around the water's edge, are stone houses of the eighteenth century, built in two or three storeys with pointed attic windows. Walls are painted black, white, pink, and cream, with windows picked out in other colours. The harbour, guarded by Calve Island, is one of the safest anchorages in the Hebrides.

The west coast is a bay twelve miles wide at the mouth, divided behind by the Ardmeanach peninsula and sprinkled with islands – the Treshnish, Ulva, Gometra, Staffa, Little Colonsay, and Inch Kenneth. This is coastal landscape on the grand scale. Although the country is bare, there is much roadside oak and hazel, meadowsweet and iris, and some luxuriant fuchsia heavy with red and purple blossom. The seascapes change from headland to headland where the lochs bite in or cliffs project. The landward feature is the terraced formation of the hill-flanks; and seaward, when the sun is out, the water-colours spreading green, blue, and purple among scattered islands.

Tiree, twenty miles west, seems the most oceanic of all the inhabited islands, being unprotected even within itself. The land lifts only a few feet above sea-level except at the western extremity, where two hills rise to 460 and 388 feet.

* 1955: Darling.

35

Tiree is eleven miles long and half a mile to six miles wide, for a dozen bays sculpt the perimeter. The soil on the gneiss is heavily sanded from the beaches. The island is wholly crofted, and the work concentrated on stock-raising with a sheep-to-cattle ratio of three to one (as against sixteen to one on Mull). Two gains from sea-level flatness are a moderate rainfall and much sun. In St Columba's time, this was *Tir Iodh*, the Land of Corn, later known as the Granary of the Isles, until land-use began to change to cattle-rearing in the seventeenth century. There is a pier and tiny harbour at Scarinish.

The sister island of Coll is only two miles away across the Sound of Gunna. Of the same size and same rock as Tiree, but shaped like a seal heading north, it has only an eighth of Tiree's population, this for reasons mainly physical and partly historical. A broad moorland 200–300 feet high, peaty and stony, occupies too much ground. On the western and southern machairs, crofting has been largely replaced by farms ranching store-cattle. The population could be doubled by reversion to dairy farming.* The only big inlet is Loch Eatharna, where there is an exposed pier and small village, called Arinagour.

Eigg, Muck, Rum, and Canna, known collectively as the Small Isles (from the name of their parish), lie ten to twenty-five miles out from Mallaig, between Coll and Skye. They are eye-catching landmarks, each of distinctive shape. Canna, five miles long by one mile wide, is a high lava platform of 400–500 feet. Rum takes diamond-form, eight miles by eight between its points, fringed by great sea-cliffs and heaving up in the south to gabbro peaks of 2500 feet. Eigg has a kidney-shape. Its chief feature, as seen from the north, is a V-shaped glen notching the middle of its five-mile back. Its south end bears a great tusk of 1289 feet called the Scuir. This spectacular monument to the forces of erosion and uplift has for its summit a 300-foot block of pitchstone lava resting on an old river-bed, in which driftwood fossils have been found.† Muck, three miles to its south, is like a flat piece of shrapnel with torn edges. A hill of 451 feet sticks up at the west end. All except Rum are fertile islands. Muck and Canna both have some of the earliest ground of the West Highland area, producing saleable potatoes by the end of May, for the Tertiary tuff‡ on east Canna gives soil even more productive than the basalt, and on Muck the basalt has been helped by sand-blow. Eigg is the chief island, carrying half the parish population on its 5,000 acres, whereas Rum, with 30,000 acres, has only forty (most of whom are

* *The Coll Report, 1947*, in 1955: Darling.
† 1964: Richey.
‡ Lavas pulverized by explosion within a volcano and discharged as coarse ash and dust, which on falling to the ground consolidate in beds.

employed by the Nature Conservancy). The northern part of Rum is Torridon sandstone, and the southern gabbro. This basically poor land has, since the nineteenth century, been given over first to sheep and then to deer, with consequent deterioration. The island was bought in 1957 by the Nature Conservancy for biological research. The Small Isles have one good harbour and pier on Canna. Landings on the others are made by ferry between ship and shore.

Skye, by far the largest inner isle, is laid out spread-eagle over the sea, with more limbs than a starfish. Although sixty miles long and twenty-five wide at widest, it has no land more than five miles from a shore. More than twenty other islands lie close by, but only three of these (Raasay, Soay, and Rona*) are now inhabited. The Sound of Sleat separates Skye from the mainland by only a quarter of a mile at Kyle Rhea, but the principal crossing point is the half-mile channel at Kyle Akin, which has better road-approaches, harbours, and a rail-head at Kyle of Lochalsh. Despite the southern facilities, the majority of the people live in the north and west, for south Skye has poor soil from its Torridon sandstone, and from the granite and gabbro of the Cuillin, whereas the northern two-thirds have a good brown soil from basalt, and a lower rainfall than the mountain-dominated south. Skye is heavily crofted, therefore bare of trees except on local plantations. But bareness is a relative term. The north Trotternish peninsula is much barer than south Skye, but when you arrive there at Uig, after a spell on the oceanic decks of the Long Isle, you will (if a mainlander) at once sense your home-coming to the shelter of land rising high out of the water, with lush grass, fox-gloves and roses by the roadside, bigger fields of corn or potato, and gardens around houses. On the other hand, no ground in the outer isles is barer than the Cuillin. Useless as these hills are for any primary industry, they sit on Skye like a crown, giving the island a majesty. Their twenty rock peaks circle Loch Coruisk to a height of 3200 feet, and have, since the early nineteenth century, drawn more visitors to Skye than any other of its features.

The most varied scenery that Skye can offer is not here, but to the north-west around Dunvegan, where mountain, moor, and water are fringed by woods and seen across islanded bays with craggy shores. White houses or thatched steadings stand on green crofts. Dunvegan Castle, built on a rock by the shore, is still the home of MacLeod after seven centuries. It lends an air, and gives the district a focusing point. The island's principal villages on the east coast are Kyleakin and Broadford; on the west, Dunvegan – with Uig growing in importance as a fishing port and car-ferry terminal. The only town is Portree, with a good

* Lighthouse keepers only on Rona.

natural harbour screened by Raasay. This is the administrative centre, with a population of approximately two thousand.

The Outer Hebrides, being set close and almost entirely gneiss, might be thought of uniform character. Yet they differ widely. Lewis, forty miles long by twelve to twenty-four, is the largest and most heavily populated island of all, and with the least arable ground. Its broad back swells in low peat-lands called the Black Moor. From this distinctive feature the word Lewis derives (from *Leogach*, pronounced Looach, meaning marshy). The Ness district to the north is much flatter and greener, if still more wind-blasted, while the south end around the Harris border lifts to hills of 1500 feet. Crofting townships spread all round the coastal strip. The word township in the Hebrides means a very different thing from a Lowland village. It means a collection of houses whose tenants gain subsistence in whole or part from the land or crofts on which the houses stand. They may be grouped or lineal in pattern according to the lie of the land, and vary in size from only four families to a population of five hundred or more – Tolsta in north-east Lewis has nearly one thousand. Stornoway, a burgh with a population of 5,280, is the only town of the Outer Hebrides. Its excellent harbour, two miles long by a mile wide under the wing of the Eye peninsula, gave it a natural advantage for development. Southern Lewis is penetrated by half a dozen long sea-lochs and is much more deeply bayed than the northern half. The west side has few sandy beaches, the best of which lie around Uig and Valtos. Loch Roag on the west and Stornoway on the east are the two fishing centres.

Harris is divided from Lewis only by a broad rampart of hills, which reach 2622 feet on Clisham, the highest hill of the Outer Hebrides. This mountainous north land is pinched off from south Harris by an isthmus half a mile wide, and here is the true frontier. North Harris is much like Lewis, but south Harris seems another island – more sheltered, with gentler land and milder atmosphere. The village of Tarbert on the east shore of the isthmus even has flower gardens. The entire west side is a chain of eight sandy beaches, divided by rocky spurs, lying at the back of a great bay between north Harris and Toe Head. Every beach is backed by machair leading on to grassy hills behind. The east coast by contrast matches the Black Moor as a Long Isle freak – a desert of bare gneiss indented by thirty bays (the district is called Bays), most of them with a township at their head. They give lobster boats good anchorage. The fishing centre for Harris is in East Loch Tarbert, where the island of Scalpay harbours twelve modern boats and has a population of 444. Tarbert itself is not a fishing port. Its pier takes the Harris passenger and cargo trade.

The Sound of Harris is the first of several straits that split the Outer Hebrides, and the most decisive one. It separates the northern isle of Lewis-with-Harris from the southern isles, which are more thoroughly agricultural.

There are in the south isles two main physiographical differences between east and west, which determine a fish-based economy for one and an agricultural-based economy for the other. First, only the west has the machair, which is almost continuous. Second, the west dips gently to shallow water and is unindented, while the east dips more steeply to deeper water, is rocky instead of sandy, and is much indented. Thus the west has nearly all the arable and pasture, the inner machair is ploughable, and reapers can be used; whereas the eastern inlets give good shelter for fishing boats, but the tillage on the crofts has required a special development of lazybeds built up on the rocks. Lazybeds are a system of tillage used to provide drainage and soil where either are insufficient. Narrow strips, not less than three feet wide nor more than eight, are made by digging trenches alongside and throwing the earth on to the beds. Their Gaelic name is *feannagan* (from *feann*, to scarify), and the more recent English name is from ley, meaning untilled ground. The east coast of Harris has no soil, and the lazybeds there have had to be constructed by building up beds of peat between the rock-ribs and piling seaweed on top.

North Uist measures twelve miles by sixteen. The eastern part has half its land area under innumerable freshwater lochs behind a heavily shattered coast. Little can be done with such land. There is a good harbour and pier at Lochmaddy, which has a population of nearly four hundred, with shops, bank, hotel, and cottage hospital. The croft-land on the west is excellent.

Benbecula, about six miles in diameter, is linked to North and South Uist by long bridges. It lies almost as low in the sea as Tiree, and is even more wind-smitten. There is no large township or harbour, but the north-western flats at Balivanich carry an airstrip, now of much value to life on the Uists. Just north of centre, the hill of Rueval, 409 feet, is worth climbing for its view to St Kilda on one side and the Cuillin of Skye on the other.

South Uist, twenty miles long by six wide, is ranged down its east side by the sharp hill-ridges of Hecla and Beinn Mhor, 2000 feet. The island is given its peculiar character by a host of lochs that spreads down its whole western length at the back of an unbroken machair. They are famous for their bird-life and fishing. A large part of the machair is now given over to a rocket range, which was set up in 1961 by the Ministry of Defence to test-fire the *Corporal* missile, for which an observation post was also set on St Kilda. When the *Corporal* became obsolete in 1968, four new rockets were installed, two of them for weather research (from one hundred miles up in the stratosphere they release instruments

39

floated on parachutes). A labour force of two hundred men was recruited in 1970 to build permanent barracks and housing at a cost of £6½ million. In 1972, the Ministry announced a plan to spend a further £20 million in extending the range. The islanders fear that so huge an extension will damage the natural resource of the island – the machair – and that firing will interfere with lobster fishing, these being primary industries, to which temporary work on buildings is very much secondary. The island's main population lives south in the townships of Daliburgh and North Boisdale. The harbour, pier, hotel, and a village, lie at the head of Loch Boisdale, which runs four miles into the land.

Access to Eriskay is from Ludag in South Uist, from which a passenger ferry plies one and a half miles across the Sound of Eriskay. Eriskay is less than three miles long by one and a half wide. It lacks soil. All its north, east, and south parts are rocky moorland, and its central parts occupied by two bare hills, Ben Scrien, 609 feet, and Ben Stack, 403 feet. Between the two, the east coast has a deep bay with harbour, pier, and township. The north coast with a smaller harbour and quay has the principal township of stone-built houses, some white-washed, some thatched, or with roofs slated dark blue or painted red. There is more brightness and colour here than in any South Uist township. The land is everywhere ribbed by projecting rock, but with grassy hollows between, often striped by lazybeds of oats and potatoes. A population of over two hundred lives on the prawn, herring, and lobster fishing. The women knit gossamer shawls and fishermen's jerseys, the latter in patterns unique to Eriskay (sails, waves, harbour-steps, and others), which are sold on the mainland.

Across the Sound of Barra from Eriskay, twenty islands of the Barra group trail south. They, with Eriskay, are patterned like a twenty-five-mile tail to the South Uist spine, broad based but thinning to a tip. Barra, eight miles long by four wide, is larger than all the rest of its parish. Its hill-filled interior rises south of centre to 1260 feet on Heaval. The coasts keep true to type, from rock-girt east to sandy west. A north-eastern feature is the narrow peninsula of Eoligarry, which shoots out to Scurrival Point. The east side of its isthmus, which is only three hundred yards wide, contains one of the famous beaches of the Isles, the Traigh Mhor (Great Strand), better known as the Cockle Strand. A mile wide and a mile deep, it provides between tides the landing ground for BEA aircraft. The succulent cockles are said to be the best in Britain, and the shells are crushed at a local factory for harling-grit and poultry-feed. Only a thin line of disintegrating dunes divides the Traigh Mhor from the Traigh Eais on the west side. The collapse, caused by erosion of the marram-bondage by livestock rutting and wind, has postponed the building of a new airstrip. The east coast township of Northbay has lobster boats moored in its nearby creeks, and lazybeds built up on the rocks. Castlebay on the South coast is the island's capital, with a big harbour and pier screened by Vatersay. Substantial stone houses front the main road. Castlebay has played a great part in the fishing industry, to which derelict quays bear witness, and could still have a promising future.* The village is given distinctive character by the islet castle of Kisimul, standing on its rock 150 yards offshore. Like Duart and Dunvegan, it is still inhabited, after being restored in 1959.

The dozen islands south of Barra are uninhabited, except for Vatersay, which is the second largest and still has ninety people. Mingulay, near Barra Head, is known for more than its boat-song. Ornithologists make annual expeditions to the western sea-cliffs, 750 feet high, which are a main breeding station for auks and kittiwakes. Close offshore stand three big stacks, one with a natural arch through which boats can sail. The name Mingulay appropriately means Bird Island.

Half a mile south across the Sound of Berneray lies the last outpost, Barra Head. A tall lighthouse sits on top of its south butt, which fronts the Atlantic with a 630-foot cliff. From there to Labrador there is no more land for two thousand miles.

* See chapter 9.

2

Rock and Water

The rocks building the Hebrides tell a story of renewal and demolition in unending cycles through vast periods of time, accompanied later by a slow, persistent progress of organic life, leading finally to the islands' inhabitation by man. It is the story of the earth in miniature. When man travels through the Hebrides, he is in the close and constant company of those elements of earth basic to life on its surface – rock and water. Rock springs pinnacled from the sea, crouches in reefs, stretches skeleton-like along the horizon, lifts in mountains. Everywhere the bare bones of the land show through. When he looks around, questions arise involuntarily. How does this scoured land sustain life? What is all this rock, and how has it come to be carved into this pattern of inner and outer isles?

The Outer Hebrides being almost entirely of gneiss, and the Inner Hebrides from Skye to Mull largely volcanic lavas, we have here lying side by side, divided only by the Minch, two extremes of the geological record, for the gneiss is Archaean rock, nearly three thousand million years old, while the lavas are Tertiary, formed only fifty million years ago, which by geological reckoning is new rock.

One of the best places to look at gneiss is the west coast of Coll, where the hills grip the beaches in strong pink talons, dividing them into coves. Here different kinds of gneiss alternate. The colour is fresh, the grain either compact or coarsely crystalline. The rock sparkles. You might feel a momentary awe at its age, but will at once understand why geologists feel affection for rock so easy on the eye, and call it the Old Boy.

Hebridean gneiss is of two main kinds, which take origin one from sedimentary and the other from igneous rock. Both have been metamorphosed deep in the earth by heat and pressure, their ingredient minerals being often converted into others (like pyroxene to hornblende), which can be seen running through the gneiss in bands. Slow cooling has given the crystalline texture. The colour can be pink or grey, and the glitter given either by quartz granules or mica. The sedimentary rock was born as sand or mud laid down in water, then metamorphosed into the schist called paragneiss. It makes Coll, Tiree, and Iona in the inner isles. The igneous rock, distinguished by the name orthogneiss, makes almost the whole of the outer isles. These broad terms cover a highly variable complex of rocks, usually called Lewisian after the Isle of Lewis. Only on Harris does it lift to mountain height on Clisham. Famous among the numerous ingredients of Lewisian rock are the limestone outcrops of Tiree and Iona, whose marble has been used for ornamental stones.*

If you take a piece of pink gneiss in the hand, you may think it impossible to distinguish from granite. Like granite it may be largely composed of quartz, with felspar, mica, and hornblende. It seems possible that some true gneiss has been made out of granite by shearing, that is, been subject to such stress by movements in the earth's crust that the granite has been made to flow like liquid and been foliated, which means that the minerals are squeezed into parallel ranks, streaked by the lines of flow. Shearing can be so intense that the structure of a rock is wholly obliterated. It is then called mylonite or flinty crush. The east coast of the Outer Hebrides gives Scotland's classic example. More than one thousand million years ago a long belt of gneiss was thrust north-westward on to the gneiss now forming the Long Isle. This thrust-plane – the plane of separation between the moved and unmoved rock – extends 120 miles from near the Butt of Lewis to Barra. Immediately east of this line the gneiss is crushed and sheared, but on the thrust-plane itself the rock must have been liquefied, for the flinty crush there is like black glass up to 100 feet thick.†

Observe again this fragment of gneiss, how clean and fresh it looks. You might be tempted to think it had seen the light of day only yesterday. In a relative sense your thought could be near the truth. Lewisian gneiss may span the two geological aeons of earth's history, but for much of that time it has lain deeply buried. Equally prolonged denudations were required to lay it bare.

The Outer Hebrides emerge out of time as an ancient splinter of Europe, or rather of an early continent of which Europe is a shrunken remainder, and which once spread west and north across the Atlantic to embrace the British Isles, Iceland, and Greenland.‡ Everywhere on earth the oldest known rocks are found to be

---

* The quarries are no longer worked, and the 'Iona' marble sold on the mainland, and in Iona itself, comes from Connemara in Ireland.
† 1948: Phemister.
‡ 1897: Geikie.

43

gneisses. In Europe, they range from the Urals to Finland; but it is in Scandinavia, where they spread over wider tracts, that most evidently they belong to that old continent with which the Hebrides were one.

Still standing on Coll, turn from the low gneiss islands to face the Inner Hebrides. The contrast startles. On Skye, Rum, and Mull, are mountains 3000 feet high. The Inner Hebrides have little gneiss apart from Coll, Tiree, and Iona, but small areas appear at the north tip of Raasay and South Rona, at the south-east fringe of Skye on the Sleat peninsula, and the Rhinns of Islay. Islay and Jura are mostly Dalradian quartzite and schist of late-Cambrian age. Torridonian sandstone makes Colonsay. The rest of the Inner Hebrides, their main bulk from Mull to Skye, is igneous rock. And the greater part of that is basalt lava.

Basalt varies in colour from green to pale brown and black. The purer the basalt the blacker it is. Compact and heavy, it splits with a conchoidal fracture (like the curved shell of a conch). The rock is too fine-grained for its minerals to be seen without a microscope, but it sometimes holds big crystals (olivine, augite, or plagioclase). In its coarser varieties like dolerite the minerals can be recognized by eye. True basalt exposed to weathering tends to split into long columns, often hexagonal, which are the outstanding feature of Fingal's Cave in Staffa, and of the Shiant Isles off Lewis, where the columns on Garbh Eilean's north face are almost six feet in diameter. They are caused by the vertical jointing given to the basalt when it contracted during cooling. The Vikings gave the name Staffa, which means Stave Island, from their own houses, which were built from tree-logs set vertical.

Between pure basalt at one end of the scale and coarse gabbro at the other, there are numerous degrees of crystalline igneous rock giving a variety of rocks called peridotite, eucrite, andesite, rhyolite, and so on, which again may be metamorphosed into something else, from an original gabbro or dolerite. These igneous rocks are simply magma in different degrees of crystallization due to differences of cooling rate, or of changes due to heat, stress, or pressure. The two main kinds of igneous rock most worth noting in the Inner Hebrides, because they have given rise to differing landscapes, are the plutonic and plateau lavas. The plutonic rocks were cooked deep in the crust; they build the Cuillin of Skye and Rum and the pinnacles of St Kilda. The plateau lavas were poured at the surface and build the more gently curved hills and moorland, but also the great sea-cliffs.

Basalt and gneiss. Two archipelagos so different, so close, one so old, the other largely new, joined by land until recent times, yet now separated by sea; what and when were the earth-movements, how did they happen, and how do we know when?

It becomes necessary here to take a much wider view than the Hebridean. The gneiss goes back to the beginnings of geological time, but the earth is at least one thousand million years older. The method used for measuring age, discovered since the achievement of atomic fission in the 1930s, is radio-active dating from both metallic and non-metallic elements. If an element is radio-active it decays at a fixed rate, turning slowly into a more stable element as its radio-active store falls. For example, carbon 14 absorbed from the air by all living things begins on their death to convert into nitrogen, losing half its radio-active store in approximately 5,730 years. In each succeeding 5,730 years its radio-active content again drops by half until nothing measurable is left. For the archaeologist this makes a good measuring tool, with a useful limit of around 45,000 years (or 70,000 using a difficult technique). But the geologist's time-scale requires a radio-active element with a longer half-life than carbon. He finds this in uranium, rubidium, thorium, potassium, and others, which can be widely traced in rocks throughout the earth, and have half-lives of thousands of millions of years. Radio-active dating is not free of error. Valid experimental results given by physicists are occasionally anomalous in their geological context, meaning that something is wrong, not necessarily with the process, but with the specimen.

An approximate age for the earth presently acceptable to most geologists has been reached by radiometric-dating meteorites, on the assumption that all bodies of the solar system had a simultaneous creation, for astronomers mostly agree that sun and planets probably condensed out of a cloud of interstellar gases. Thus the meteorites proved to be 4·5 thousand million years old. The basic assumption is still, however, beyond man's power to prove.*

Earth and sun alike, cool at first, grew hot on reaching densities that induced interior nuclear reaction. The sun shone and the earth turned molten. As contraction slowed down and radio-active content decayed, the earth began to cool again. A crust slowly formed and is still only three miles thick under ocean floors, although twenty miles thick on average under continents. Beneath that thin rock shell lies a hot mantle 1,800 miles deep, surrounding a molten core (probably iron) of 4,350 miles' diameter. The story of the Inner Hebrides gives spectacular evidence of the heat generated in the upper mantle and the closeness of its magma to the crust. The earliest rock yet found on earth is a gneiss of Tanganyika, radio-dated to 3·6 thousand million years. Lewisian gneiss is of two age groups, the first

* 1964: Beiser.

Geological Time Scale

From the scale currently in use by the Institute of Geological Sciences. The older dates cannot be considered precise. (They can vary $\pm$ 10m in the 500 m.y. range depending on the values chosen for half-lives of strontium.)

Era	Period	Age (m.y.)	Hebridean Events
Pre-Cambrian		3,000–600	Gneiss: 2600–1200m Torridonian: 800m
Lower Palaeozoic	Cambrian	600–500	Cambro-Ordovician shelf-sea over NW Scotland and geosynclinal sea over South Highlands
	Ordovician	500–440	CALEDONIAN OROGENY Dalradian schists, S. Highlands: 470–420m
	Silurian	440–400	Caledonian granites: 400m
Upper Palaeozoic	Devonian	400–350	END OF CALEDONIAN OROGENY Metamorphic block, uplifted, weathers and deposits Old Red Sandstone in shallow seas, estuaries, and mountain basins. Late Caledonian granites (Ben Nevis, Glencoe, etc). Great Glen Fault
	Carboniferous	350–270	Deposits in the sea of the

2,600–2,200 million years, found in North Uist, Benbecula, and South Uist (north half), and the second 1,600–1,200 million years throughout the rest of the gneiss islands.*

Turning now to the north-west Highlands and Hebrides, we find that much of the first gneiss land must have sunk under the sea, for it became overlain by Torridonian sandstone formed from eroded gneiss about eight hundred million years ago. This dull red sandstone is named after the Torridon district of

* 1965: Craig.

Era	Period	Age (m.y.)	Hebridean Events
			Hebrides and Loch Linnhe. Climate tropical
	Permian	270–225	Intrusion of many dykes in Isles
Mesozoic	Triassic	225–180	Shallow seas invade Inner
	Jurassic	180–135	Hebrides: sedimentary
	Cretaceous	135–70	rocks of Skye, Eigg, Raasay, and Mull
Tertiary	Eocene	70–40	Volcanoes build basalt tableland. Gabbro and granite intrusions: 60–50m
	Oligocene	40–25	Subtropical climate, cooling
	Miocene	25–11	Elevation of Scotland 30–20m. Subsidence of North Sea basin and
	Pliocene	11–1	Atlantic seaboard with separation of Hebrides from mainland: 15–10m
Quaternary	Pleistocene	600th. – 10,300	ICE AGE
	Holocene	10,300	Post-glacial period opens. Rising sea divides Outer Hebrides transversely c.8000 BP, and Straits of Dover open Mesolithic man enters the Hebrides c.6,600 BP

Wester Ross, where it forms distinctive, pyramidal mountains. Ripple marks, rain-pits, and sun-cracks, and the overlapping of the strata, show that the sand was deposited in shallow seas from land to the north-west, which was then desert: only micro-fossils of plankton have been found. The sea-floor continued to subside, for Torridon sandstone still reaches a thickness of 8000 feet. After their deposition, the Torridonian rocks were heaved up by crustal warping, then so vigorously eroded that large tracts were completely swept away, exposing the old gneiss once again, which then itself came under attack. In the Hebrides, no Torridonian survives in that monolithic mountain form peculiar to Ross and Sutherland, but its strata covers large tracts of Skye in the Sleat peninsula and satellite isles, the north half of Rum, all of Colonsay, and a bit of north-west Islay.

All this northern land was reduced to a sea-level plain, which at last sank under the Cambrian sea. The sea covered Britain and Norway. Its floor sank slowly while at least 16,000 feet of sand and mud accumulated. The fossils in this sediment were to bring the first evidence of well-organized fauna on earth and give name to the first geological era – the Palaeozoic (from the Greek, ancient life).

Scotland and the Hebrides lay under the Cambrian sea for 150 million years. Out of it rose a huge mountain chain called the Caledonian. It must have been of Alpine scale, possibly Himalayan. On a broad front it extended from Scotland through Norway to Spitzbergen. Its ribs have been traced running north up the east coast of Greenland, and from Newfoundland south to New York. This great uplift began about 500 million years ago and continued through the Ordovician period into the early Devonian.*

The Caledonian mountains were constructed out of the old sediments of the Cambrian sea-floor, probably including the underlying Torridonian rocks. Their deep burial and heat and stresses in the earth had transformed the soft sands and mud into the quartzite and crystalline schists found in the Scottish Highlands today, but the once-flat beds were thrown into gigantic overfolds and intensely contorted. In the hottest regions in the core of the new mountains, enormous masses of granite were formed by crystallization. The Cairngorms and Cruachan are examples of this granite. The Hebrides have one splendid exhibit at the west end of the Ross of Mull, facing Iona. Its pink rock was used to build Iona Abbey, the piers of Blackfriars Bridge, and the Albert Memorial.

As the mountain chain rose from the sea it was barren land without protective vegetation, and suffered severe attacks by weather. Torrential rains caused floods, which formed huge boulder-beds later consolidating as cliffs of puddingstone. On the way to the isles at Oban, you may see the cliffs at the back of George Street.

Giant volcanoes like Glen Coe and Ben Nevis broke out during these millions of years of crustal folding, but of all the lavas they poured over the land only a little appears on the Inner Hebrides, much of which had yet to be built. Meantime, the Caledonian mountain-building period gave the Highlands and Islands their prevailing north-east to south-west grain. Later earth movements were to shape the land, and erosion to determine its present-day relief, but that north-east

* Ibid.

48

1. Saligo Bay, west coast of Islay. West coasts are deeply bayed and sandy.

2a. Folded gneiss, Carloway, Lewis.

2b. The Carsaig Arches, Ross of Mull. Tunnels bored by
the sea through columnar basalt.

3a. Isle of Staffa, Argyll, showing hexagonal columnar basalt caused by the vertical jointing given to the basalt when it contracted during cooling. The columns stand on a tufa basement with a cap of amorphous basalt. Fingal's Cave is the rightmost (south face). On Ulva behind (*right*) may be seen the terrace formation caused by lava flows.
3b. Raised Beach, north-east Skye, at Culnacnock, east coast of Trotternish peninsula.

4a. The eastern corrie of the Storr, 2358 feet, in the Trotternish peninsula, Skye. The slopes beside the great cliff have a rich soil growing a wealth of arctic plants.

4b. The Red Cuillin of Skye – granite.

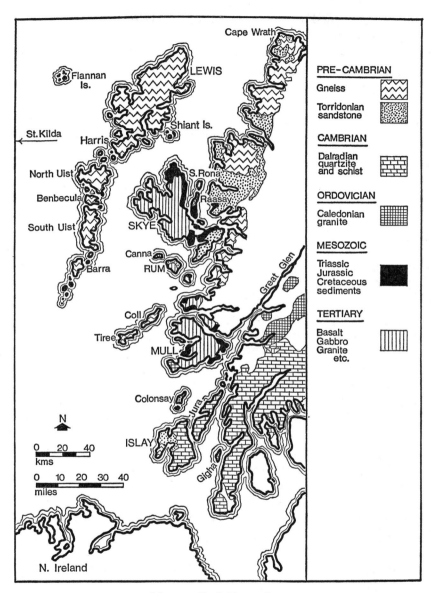

Cape Wrath

Flannan
Is.

LEWIS

Shiant Is.

St. Kilda

Harris

S. Rona

North Uist

Raasay

Benbecula

SKYE

South Uist

Canna

Barra

RUM

Coll

Tiree

MULL

Colonsay

N

ISLAY

Gigha

kms
0   20   40

miles
0   10   20   30   40

N. Ireland

Great Glen

Jura

PRE-CAMBRIAN

Gneiss

Torridonian
sandstone

CAMBRIAN

Dalradian
quartzite
and schist

ORDOVICIAN

Caledonian
granite

MESOZOIC

Triassic
Jurassic
Cretaceous
sediments

TERTIARY

Basalt
Gabbro
Granite
etc.

Map 7   *Rock Formations*

to south-west grain had been imparted by Caledonian folding. The alignment of the Outer Hebrides and parts of the Inner seems to be related on such a trend.

Scotland again weathered down to an almost sea-level plain. Volcanoes erupted near the sites of Glasgow and Edinburgh, tropical jungles and coral reefs flourished. To the south of England the Hercynian mountain chain rose across central Europe into Russia, and that too was reduced to sea-level. The Hebridean area was partially invaded by shallow seas of the Mesozoic era, which laid down sediments of the Jurassic and Cretaceous periods (fringes of Skye, Eigg, and Mull), but the old northern land still rose over the region of Scotland. A long period of dormancy was now approaching a violent end.

In Tertiary times, when the Hebrides were enjoying the sub-tropical climate of the Eocene period, there broke out the most prolonged and intense volcanic activity of Britain's history.* This outbreak had long been dated to seventy million years ago, then fossil pollen found at the base of lavas in Mull and Ardnamurchan suggested that eruptions had begun not earlier than forty-five million years ago, and now radio-active tests on gabbro and granite intrusions date them between sixty and fifty million years.† Seven centres of eruption were St Kilda, Skye, Rum, Ardnamurchan, Mull, Arran, and north-east Ireland. There must have been others near and afar, now hidden under the sea, for the Tertiary igneous province extended north-west across the Arctic circle to embrace Iceland and Greenland.

Volcanic action developed in two main phases. First came the outpouring of plateau lavas. From vents and fissures they rolled out in flows up to fifty feet thick, or rarely to a hundred feet, spreading far and wide across the land, piling one above the other over millions of years to reach mountainous height. They built a tableland of which Skye, the Small Isles, and Mull are vestiges, heavily dissected.

Secondly, upwelling magma exploded through the crust in volcanoes of large vent, and they were sometimes preceded, sometimes followed, by an uprise of subterranean plutonic masses like big blisters, which remained deeply buried. There has been lack of agreement among geologists whether the first outpourings of plateau lavas erupted from fissures or through volcanic vents, but in 1924 a crater six miles wide was found in Mull, seven miles east of Ben More, and has been dated to the lava plateau phase.

The explosion vents and plutonic intrusions were all accompanied by a shat-

* 1964: Richey.
† 1965: Craig.

50

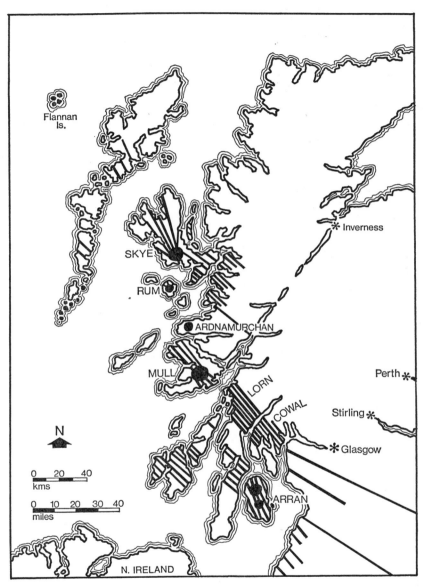

Flannan
Is.

Inverness

SKYE

RUM

ARDNAMURCHAN

Perth

MULL

LORN

Stirling

COWAL

Glasgow

N

0   20   40
kms

0   10   20   30   40
miles

ARRAN

N. IRELAND

Map 8 *Tertiary Volcanoes and Dyke Swarms*

tering of the earth's crust. From each centre, linear dykes swarmed out exactly as in glass shattered by a bullet hole. From the Mull volcano the swarm goes thickly through Lorn and Cowal to the Clyde, continuing more sparsely into Yorkshire and the Northumberland coast. All take north-west and south-east courses. Those from Skye cross the Outer Hebrides at Harris and the mainland at Morar. These dyke-swarms came too late to be feeders for the laval plateau. The likelihood is that lava issued mainly from craters rather than dykes even at an early stage, clear trace of the craters being largely wiped out through the later rise of plutonic rock and erosion.

Much has been learned from visible evidence about the conditions of eruption. That the lavas erupted quietly is shown by the rarity of interbedded ash. That eruptions recurred intermittently and shifted from one centre to another is shown by the red soil and clay that had time to form in normal terrestrial conditions between flows, and they bear evidence of forests, while the pillow-lavas of central Mull show that lakes had gathered. Near Ardtun in the Ross of Mull, two miles north of Bunessan, the basalt encloses leaves of oak, hazel, plane, and maidenhair tree. The pollen of plants and conifers indicate a climate similar to Europe's Mediterranean coast today. The fossil of a whole tree trunk engulfed by columnar basalt was found early last century on a sea-cliff in Mull on the Ardmeanach peninsula. The trunk is forty feet high and five feet wide. The coastal strip there is named the Wilderness – a wilderness of stone fallen from the 1200-foot cliff above. The cast has been almost wholly picked away, perhaps by visitors, but fragments of charred wood remain on ledges.

The basalt plateau in its prime stood taller than the rest of Scotland, complete with volcanic cones. And all that prolonged upbuilding was followed by erosion so fierce and dissection so long continued that its chain of extinct volcanoes was laid bare, each to its cauldron foundations; and even those most deeply buried plutonic rocks, covered by thousands of feet of basalt, stood clear on Rum, Skye, and St Kilda. Their rock had become tough gabbro. Beside them, likewise revealed and likewise forged close to the volcanic furnaces, appeared massive granite hills. They build the Red Cuillin, the Orval hills of west Rum, and Conachair of Hirta, 1397 feet, the latter giving St Kilda the highest sea-cliff in Britain. Since all these hills owe their emergence to the stripping away of the less resistant basalt, it must seem an anomaly that much of the Black Cuillin ridge, including the Inaccessible Pinnacle at the summit of Sgurr Dearg, is basalt. The reason is that the plutonic mass, while still under cover, was itself intruded by

* 1964: Richey.

molten magma, which, trapped in dykes, was baked at great heat and much altered, becoming harder than plateau basalt.* The striking difference in shape between the rounded Red Cuillin and the pointed Black, has been largely caused by the dense swarm of more brittle dykes cutting the tougher gabbro north-west and south-east, and these weathered out as gullies and notches, leaving free-standing towers.

The plateau rock too has taken mountain form in Mull, but the more typical scenery is of broad, undulating hills and moors rising to 1000 feet or more. The surface of the lava-sheets breaks down into good soil, well-drained and grassy. Their successive flows give to the Inner Hebrides two distinctive features, one in terraced hill-flanks, displayed at their best along the west side of Mull, the other their truncated edges, which are the sea-cliffs, some clearly displaying the fifty-foot flows, and a few the hundred-foot. Such giant cliffs cannot fail to excite wonder, but here they emphasize that a once-great plateau survives only as island fragments.

Towards the end of the Tertiary era, between thirty and twenty million years ago (Oligocene-Miocene periods), when Scotland by vast denudations had been yet again reduced to a peneplain, the earth reawoke. In repeated upheavals it raised the Alps. At the same time a series of upward pulses raised Scotland, but this time as a solid block free of folding. The land stood far higher than now and extended westward to the continental shelf beyond St Kilda. It remained one with Scandinavia.

The new tableland dipped from north-west to south-east, and the new rivers ran down the slope. They dissected the Hebridean region and carved Highland glens. But these rivers were intercepted by others following the north-east to south-west grain of the old Caledonian structure, like the Great Glen (Inverness to Loch Linnhe) and perhaps the Minch. Some of the Caledonian grainlines were faults, hence these rivers eroded their beds faster than the rivers running on solid rock, whose waters were finally captured and redirected. Thus the land and its river-systems were broken up, several hundred mountains were carved where none had been, and the landscape relief came gradually towards the shape of today's. Two events were still necessary to make it recognizable as 'Scotland' and to sever the Hebrides.

The first of these was the foundering of the continental margin of Eurasia. It came at the close of the Miocene period or perhaps early in the Pliocene between fifteen and ten million years ago. By the end of it, the old lowland plain

* Ibid.

linking Scotland with Norway had sunk under the North Sea; and Britain had become a European peninsula with Scotland as its north-westerly promontory. At much the same time, the western half of the Scottish land-mass also subsided. The Atlantic flooded in among the farther mountain tops, isolating them as islands. The valley of the Minch was filled, while the sea ran thirty or forty miles into westward-running glens of the mainland. Scotland had taken its widely indented coastline with several hundred western isles. The Hebrides were born.

The second event was the Ice Age. The hot dry climate of Mesozoic times had been slowly but steadily cooling through the Tertiary era, and the cause of that is still under discussion. Geophysicists believe that the earth's crust was now moving on its mantle,[*] for there is good evidence, from the magnetization of minerals in rock, that the North Pole was over Hawaii in Cambrian times, then nearer Japan in Silurian, thereafter continuing to move across the North Pacific – placing the Hebrides within twenty degrees of the equator in Permian times[†] – and so to the Arctic. The South Pole likewise shifted out of the Atlantic, finally to cover Antarctica's sub-tropical vegetation under a glacial waste. There is no reason to believe that the earth's axis had changed. It was the crust that moved. While the Poles were at mid-ocean warm water would repress any big-scale development of ice. But when Siberia, Alaska, Northern Canada, and Greenland became snowbound, too much land formerly absorbing sun-heat became heat-reflecting and cold. The Arctic glaciers advanced.

The Ice Age began in the Pleistocene period about 600,000 years ago, and if the polar-wandering theory is correct we are still in the middle of it. Thus far there have been four great glacial advances, all followed by retreats and by long-lasting interglacial periods of climate no less warm than now, when the earth could return to its life-encouraging self. This temperature cycle within the Ice Age was explained by Milankovitch, the Serbian physicist of the 1920s, in calculations showing that deviations in the orbit and rotation of the earth should every 40,000 years bring cool summers discouraging glacial melt, and mild arctic winters encouraging heavy snowfall. His findings obtain support from recent American work.[‡]

The four ice ages have left records of themselves in rocks striated and smoothly ground, and in moraines and detritus of earths, gravels, and boulder-clays. Evidence of repeated advance and retreat comes from the intercalation of stratified material like peat and the remains of plants, trees, and animals between the

* 1964: Bullard. 1964: Beiser.
† 1967: Rayner.
‡ Harold Urey on fossils.

deposits of each advance. From these can be read that changes of temperature over the land caused emigrations across Europe into Britain of Arctic fauna and flora; when cold increased they moved south to France. When warm interglacials approached a climax, African lynx, leopard, elephant, and hippopotamus crossed the Sicilian and Gibraltar land-bridges into Europe. The most important immigrant to Britain was man. His remains dating to an early interglacial have been found in the upper Thames valley, and in beds earlier than the last glacial deposit in England. But not in Scotland.

Little is known of the duration of the first three glaciations or of the landscaping achieved. Each advance so fouled the evidences of its predecessors by stripping moraines and channels, and each retreat caused such changes in sea-levels, that in Scotland none of the three earlier deposits has been identified. Only the last ice age has left clear traces. Its important effects on the Hebrides and their sea-channels are best considered as two phases, that of maximum glaciation, and that of more recent.

The warm interglacial ended 70,000 years ago. The climate grew steadily colder reaching two maxima of glaciation, the first 55,000 years ago, and the last (from radio-carbon tests of sediments) only 20,000–17,000 years ago.* Between these dates, numerous Arctic animals occupied Scotland. Their remains include woolly rhinoceros, hairy mammoth, reindeer, elk, giant deer, lemming, bear, and northern lynx. These animals may well have reached Scotland direct from Scandinavia, for the North Sea basin had again become dry land by withdrawal of water locked in polar ice. The plain grew forests before it was finally drowned in post-glacial times, and mammoth bones have been dredged from its bed. Animals would enter the Inner Hebrides across the Skye, Mull, and Jura isthmuses. A woolly rhinoceros that roamed the site of Glasgow (Bishopbriggs) has been carbon-dated to 27,500 years.† Two thousand years later the last glaciation was in full swing.

At the first onset, northern Europe was overwhelmed by an ice-sheet 5000 feet thick over Scandinavia and Scotland, thinning to the south and east where it spread deep into France and Germany. All of that ice-flood was in continuous motion. The Scottish Highlands were a glacial centre. Rock-striae and boulder-transport show that this Scottish ice poured east, west, and south. The eastern current met close offshore with the big Scandinavian ice-barrier, which deflected one branch south to help fill the North Sea basin as far south as London, and

* 1969: Pennington.
† 1967: Sissons.

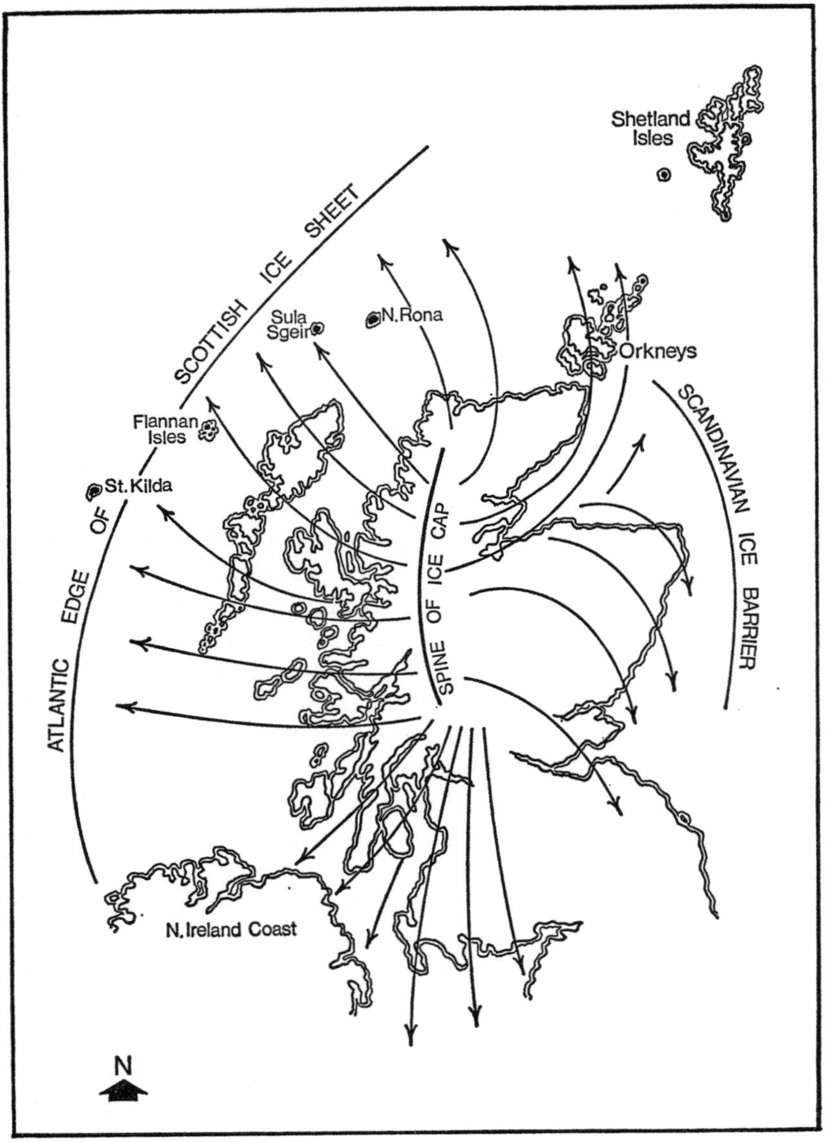

Shetland Isles
SCOTTISH ICE SHEET
Sula Sgeir
N.Rona
Orkneys
Flannan Isles
St.Kilda
SCANDINAVIAN ICE BARRIER
ATLANTIC EDGE OF
SPINE OF ICE CAP
N.Ireland Coast
N

Map 9 *Direction of Ice Flow at Maximum Glaciation*

another branch north across the Orkney Islands. The south stream flowed down the Clyde valley to fill the basin of the Irish Sea as far as Cork, maintaining a thickness of 1800 feet along the flanks of the Wicklow hills, carrying sea-shells to 1350 feet on Welsh hills, and thrusting a great spur through the Cheshire gap between Wales and the Pennines to deposit Ailsa Craig granite in the English Midlands. The west stream rolled on a broad front across the Minch and Sea of the Hebrides to bury the entire Outer Hebrides. Only the mountain of Clisham stood out as nunatak from a 2000-foot ice-cap.

Had man been able to sail a boat off the coast, the scene might have appeared not unlike North Greenland today – except that the edge of the ice-cap was of far greater extent, say two thousand miles from south of Ireland to Norway's North Cape. This Atlantic edge must have fronted the sea with a precipitous wall several hundred feet high, discharging icebergs.

When Scotland's maximum glaciation was achieved, the great thickness of the ice-cap allowed glacier-flow to be independent of the underlying land, which was not sculpted. At earlier and later stages, the ice had sufficient scouring power to deposit 600 feet of detritus in the North Sea basin.

As the start of the more recent phase, Scotland's single glacial centre had become two. One covered the high west-coast spine from Sutherland to Argyll; the other, farther east, the high Grampian spine. At the peak of this glaciation all of southern Scotland still lay under the ice-sheet, which was 3000 feet thick where it crossed the Highland line.* On the West Highland axis the ice reached 3600 feet near Glen Coe, and 1600 feet on the Hebrides. Western snowfalls were then much heavier than eastern (as rainfall is now), hence the western hills became more dissected by a more powerful ice-action.

At the Inner Hebrides, the westward-flowing glaciers from the mainland were partially deflected by the Tertiary volcanic mountains. These were high enough to own their own ice-caps and glacier-systems. The Cuillin glaciers were powerful enough to nudge the big Loch Alsh glacier north up the Inner Sound of Raasay, and those of Mull to split the Loch Linnhe glacier, sending one stream across northern Mull and the other over the Ross of Mull and Iona, beyond which they reunited to over-ride Coll and Tiree. Rum and Jura both had independent glacier systems.

The old north-east to south-west fault lines of Caledonian origin that run between the Inner and Outer Hebrides, from the Great Glen to either side of Colonsay, through the Sound of Sleat and Tiree Passage, and from Loch Fyne to

---

* 1956: Charlesworth, modified by Sissons in 1967: Craig.

the Firth of Clyde, were now used by the big ice streams to exploit every weakness in their beds and in flanking islands. It seems possible that Arran was part of Kintyre until Argyll ice, which had greatly deepened Loch Fyne, cut the Kilbrennan Sound. A long peninsula of the Lorn coast apparently ran south-west parallel to Kintyre until the Firth of Lorn glacier sliced it into the seven islands of Islay, Jura, Scarba, Lunga, Luing, Shuna, and Seil. Mull was part of mainland Morven when the Loch Linnhe ice, forced north, cut the Sound of Mull, and very nearly cut Mull in two at the Salen-Loch na Keal breach. Skye was joined to the mainland at Glenelg and Balmacara until the Loch Alsh glacier cut the land links at Kyle Rhea and Kyle Akin.

Glacial deepening of Hebridean sea-channels became most emphatic where mountains rose to baffle the main ice-streams, and to add their own ice, thus forcing the main streams through island passages.* Rock basins were thus excavated in the Sound of Rum, deepening the floor to 500 feet; in the Sound of Jura to 720 feet; between Rum and Canna to 780 feet; and in the Cuillin Sound between Rum and Skye to 834 feet. In these basins fissures go beyond 1200 feet. The greatest depths in British coastal seas are recorded in the Inner Sound of Raasay, where the Loch Alsh glacier cut down to 1062 feet and fissures go beyond 1500. Other basins or deep trenches exceeding 700 feet appear between Lismore and Mull, in the middle of the Firth of Lorn, and along the whole eastern fringe of the Outer Hebrides. They reach 800 feet south-east of Barra Head. Soundings of 1200 feet off Barra Head, and of 1300 feet off south Harris, have been recorded.

In the Outer Hebrides, the main legacy from the ice-streams has been erosion, not deposition, although boulder clay appears in north Lewis. Erratic boulders are rare and mainly of Torridonian and Cambrian rock from the mainland. A strange lack is of Inner Hebridean rock; not even Skye erratics have ever been found in outer isles. Geikie explains this by suggesting that only the upper clean ice-sheet over-rode the isles, while the lower, carrying ground moraine, deposited in the Minch.

The retreat began with the break up of Scotland's two main ice-sheds into numerous independent centres. More and more lower mountains projected as nunataks. Warmer summers brought a gradual rise in snow levels across the country from east to west. When the snow-line had risen to 2000 feet in the Cairngorms, it was still at 1000 feet on the Inner Hebrides and 750 feet in the Outer. Retreat was slow in the west. The hills of south Lewis, and their neigh-

* 1967: Sissons.

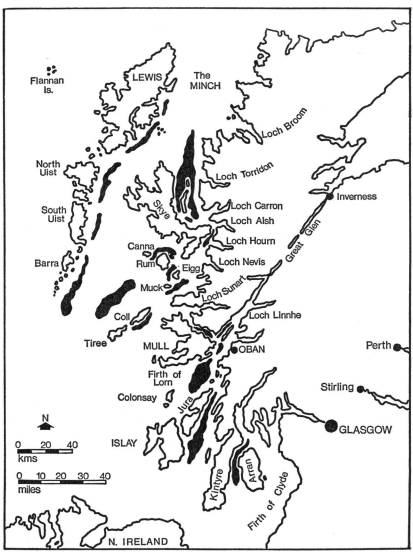

Map 10 *Glacier Basins cut in Sea Channels*

Flannan
Is.

LEWIS

The
MINCH

Loch Broom

North
Uist

Loch Torridon

Skye

Loch Carron

Inverness

Loch Alsh

South
Uist

Loch Hourn

Great Glen

Canna

Barra

Rum

Loch Nevis

Eigg

Muck

Loch Sunart

Coll

Loch Linnhe

Tiree

MULL

OBAN

Perth

Firth of
Lorn

Colonsay

Jura

Stirling

GLASGOW

N

0   20   40
kms

0   10   20   30   40
miles

ISLAY

Kintyre

Arran

Firth of Clyde

N. IRELAND

bour Clisham of Harris, bore a central ice-cap, sending well-developed glaciers radiating in every direction. In South Uist, minor glaciers were established on the 2000-foot hills of Hecla and Beinn Mhor, and in North Uist on Eaval, 1138 feet.* The mainland ice-sheet had never reached St Kilda, which ran its own valley glacier at Village Bay.†

The dissolution of the great mainland ice-caps came in two stages.‡ The first was the formation of confluent glaciers, when the ice was still thick enough to flow across the water-sheds between glens, seeking outlets in different directions at once. The distinct signs of confluence are the moraines left on cols and ridges. On high mountain flanks, lateral moraines were now forming terraces. Their summit ridges and peaks, exposed to prolonged frosts, began to break up. Nowhere is that disintegration presented better than in Skye. The Cuillin ridges were chiselled into thirty splintered peaks bearing vast screes on their flanks and tumbled blocks in their corries. No climber who has laboured up the Great Stone Shoot of Sgurr Alasdair, or up Garsbheinn by its western corrie, will ever forget the toil exacted; nor forget the elation of his plunge down the An Stac scree-run to Coire Lagain. All the debris remaining today on this and other island hills is only a portion of its earlier mass, for the glaciers carried much of it into the sea.

In the main glens, the ice had begun widening and straightening the walls, truncating lateral spurs, often to leave hanging valleys (many with waterfalls later), and grinding V-shaped ravines into U-section. These effects, with the erosion of corries at the valleys' heads, and the overdeepening of their floors, were continued into the next stage, that of valley glaciers.

The diminishing volume of ice allowed the flow to be entirely directed by the glens' walls, which became striated. Earlier moraines were largely removed from upper slopes and naked rock exposed. In mainland glens, terminal and lateral moraines are the most conspicuous evidence of valley glaciers. They are less evident in the Hebrides, where the glaciers retreated later than those of eastern Scotland, but when they did, melted faster and tended to leave surface stone unmarshalled. The moors around Sligachan at the north side of the Cuillin are much hummocked by drift where the great Sligachan glacier died in its tracks. A good example of a horse-shoe moraine lies at the mouth of Coire a' Ghrunnda, the highest corrie of the Cuillin where the ice lasted longest.

Coire a' Ghrunnda's glacier has left some of the best Scottish exhibits of scored and polished rock. The gabbro slabs in the corrie-bed have been smoothed and

* 1956: Charlesworth, and Sissons in 1965: Craig.
† 1948: Phemister.
‡ Ibid.

rounded to immense boiler-plates, which are almost unclimbable, so that access up the bottom half of this long corrie is confined to an exceedingly narrow line. The bed shows also how efficient ice-falls were in excavating steep drops.

The more dramatic landscape carvings are 'overdeepenings' of valley floors. Small-scale examples are in high mountain corries, close under the peaks. The ice scouring these hollows not only gouged their bottoms but plucked out the rocks at the back. Formerly down-sloping hollows were thus scooped out as deep bowls, the raised outer lips often retaining lochans in their floors, while the peaks or ridges circling behind were thinned back and made sharper. The big-scale examples are down at the mountains' bases, especially on the west coast where steeper glaciers ran faster. These gouged many of the sea-lochs, often giving them a deeply trenched or over-deepened inner loch separated by narrows from a broad outer loch. The process is similar to a river's where it comes over a fall on to more level ground. The waterfall scoops a pool, shifting forward and depositing gravel on to an outer lip or shallows. A glacier-made lip may become a high and dry moraine-barrier impounding a loch, like Loch Ba in central Mull.

The most impressive witness in Britain to the power of a valley glacier is Loch Coruisk in Skye, where the great basin of Coir' Uisg is ringed by a nine-mile horse-shoe of gabbro peaks from Garsbheinn to Sgurr na Stri. The Coir' Uisg glacier, which swept out to sea as far as the island of Soay, cut the rock basin to a depth of 100 feet below sea-level. Loch Coruisk is thus 125 feet deep.* Its water escapes through a moraine-barrier by the Scavaig Burn, then tumbles white across a broad gabbro sill into the green sea of Loch Scavaig. The sill itself is a famous example of glacier striation. The Coruisk scene has international renown. A man who penetrates the great corrie on foot is given a sense of adventure into wild land still in primitive state, unspoiled as yet despite the large number of summer tourists, who visit by steamer from Mallaig and by motor-boat from Elgol.

When Scotland reached (and passed) the valley glacier stage, its land, so long depressed under the weight of the ice and now released from that enormous burden, lifted up in several movements of isostatic recovery. These left their mark in old shore lines, now raised high above the sea. The centre of uplift appears to have been Rannoch Moor.† The Outer Hebrides, being one hundred miles out from that centre (of an oval ring), rose too little to match the rise in sea-level caused by melting ice, so that old shore lines were drowned. Each rise of the Inner Hebrides and Highland coast was followed by an equally spread period of

* 1941: Harker.
† 1967: Sissons.

rest, long enough for beaches to become established. Such equal and simultaneous rises are accounted for by the theory of isostasy – that big land masses float on the earth's mantle.

Raised beaches are to be found in England and Wales, but in Scotland are naturally much more plentiful. Throughout the Inner Hebrides they appear at heights of 100 feet, 50 feet, and 25 feet above present sea-level,* the last rise being post-glacial. Such round figures are traditional. They are loose expressions, and correct heights vary twenty feet to either side of them. Beaches at twenty-five feet need not even be of the same age.† The real isostatic movements have been veiled by great rises in post-glacial sea-level during the years 8500 BP to 5500 BP, and are nearly double what the raised beach figures indicate. Neighbouring Scandinavia, since losing its heavier load, has risen nearly 1000 feet, is still rising, and has probably 650 feet to go to attain equilibrium.‡ The Hebridean rise is therefore modest, but the raised beaches can be eye-catching.

They appear throughout the inner isles in a large variety of forms: boulder-fields of quartzite pebbles, sea-worn to an eggshell smoothness, but as big as tennis balls, found along the west coast of Jura and Colonsay; shelves at the back of bays, like Oban, or the one at the back of Loch na Keal in Mull; sandy grassland, like the western machair of Iona; flat-topped headlands and cliffs, like those of south-east Skye between Kyleakin and Broadford; wide, almost unbroken flats bordering Loch Indaal in Islay; erosion platforms like Tiree, almost all of which lies at the twenty-five and fifty-foot levels; wave-cut rock-shelves, like the pre-glacial brim of the Dutchman's Cap in the Treshnish Isles, where Atlantic seals haul out to breed (pre-glacial in this context means before the last glaciation); valley floors, where once separate islands have become joined, as in Colonsay – the Hebrides have thus lost islands to the mainland, for example, the Mull of Kintyre; and most spectacular of all, those long terraces cut along Rum's western precipice, with sea-cliffs below and more ancient sea-cliffs above, buttressing a mountain-face.

Hundred-foot beaches are the least numerous, and often absent where they might be expected because valley glaciers were still reaching the sea at the time of the first uplift. Deposits on these beaches may be fluvioglacial sands and gravels from melt-water. Some deposits may thus resemble beaches, yet not be so. When they are extensive, the beaches and their deposits make a valuable contri-

* 1948: Phemister.
† 1967: Sissons. In dating events, I use the term BP, before present, reserving BC dating for use in chapters relating to man.
‡ 1964: Beiser.

bution to island life in their provision of well-drained ground for crops and grazing. This is true of all inhabited inner isles, particularly Skye, where crofts thus sited are most numerous, for example at Broadford. An oddity on Colonsay is the Uragaig headland to the west side of Kiloran Bay. Between its lower and upper cliffs a broad beach platform has been cut in pre-glacial times about 135 feet above the sea. And there perches Uragaig croft.

When raised beaches are backed by cliffs, the former sea-caves, arches, blow-holes, and stacks, are left high and dry to puzzle mainland visitors ignorant of the cause. A splendid sandstone arch, through which one can walk, was bored by the post-glacial sea near the north end of Eileach an Naoimh, in the Isles of the Sea. It is named A 'Chlarsach, the Harp. An old sea-stack may be visited on the way to the isles near Oban. It stands by the roadside a few hundred yards short of Dunollie Castle. Its tall pillar was eroded by the sea out of a puddingstone cliff, and is named Clach a' Choin, the Dog Stone (where the legendary hero Fingal tethered his hunting dog Bran). Caves are numbered by the hundred. They have sheltered man and beast in the Hebrides since early post-glacial days, and not only in prehistoric times. They have been used as chapels, like the Cathedral Cave in south Eigg; as tombs, and as staging posts for funeral parties taking coffins to Iona (north and south Jura); as prisons (Idrigill in Skye); as hermits' cells, illicit stills, forts, fishermen's quarters for sleeping, net-drying, and fish-curing, as refuges during the Clearances, and as hiding places for all men from prince to robber.

The Outer Hebrides have a different post-glacial history. From Barra Head to the Butt of Lewis they had formed a single island until the west-to-east valleys were invaded by the sea after the Ice Age.* Not only are raised beaches absent, but submergence without re-emergence has been the rule since the ice-sheet vanished.† Tree trunks, roots, and peat are frequently exposed by wind and sea on the west coast sands below high-water mark, and at lower levels by low spring tides. The sites of some exposures are found at five points on Lewis; on Pabbay in the Sound of Harris; on Benbecula at Borve; on South Uist at Loch Eynort, the west coast strand, and Lochboisdale; on Eriskay, Colonsay, Tiree, and Coll.‡ The submerged peat has been radiocarbon-dated to 5700 BP in Benbecula. Continued drowning is shown in North and South Uist by Neolithic chambered cairns and Iron Age duns now partly submerged. Deep peat has been found in Stornoway Bay, and ships' anchors have fetched up peat a few miles west of

* 1967: Sissons.
† 1948: Phemister.
‡ 1967: Sissons.

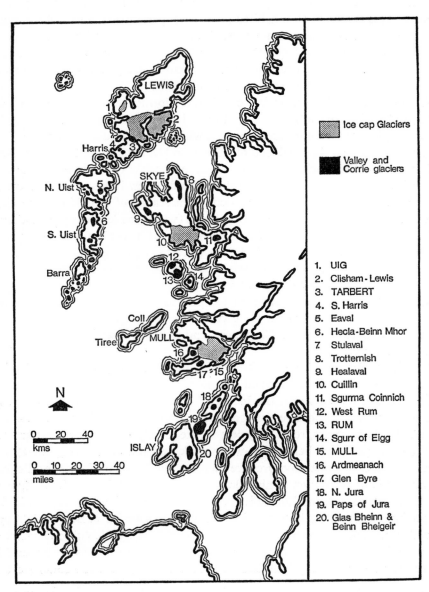

Map 11 *Late Glacial Centres*

5a. Machair and sand dunes eroded by wind-blow after rutting by vehicles and rabbits, at Luskentyre, Harris.

5b. The Black Cuillin of Skye. The head of Coir' Uisg from Sgurr Dearg. On the left is Sgurr na Banachdich, on the right Sgurr a' Ghreadaidh. The head of the corrie was plucked out by glaciers.

6. Machair of South Uist, with spring flowers.

North Uist. These Holocene sinkings are thought to have been induced by the mainland uplift and the new weight of water coming on the peripheral seabeds, which had long been dry land.

The final phase of the Ice Age was slow withdrawal of glaciers into high mountain recesses. Retreat was not a steadily continuing event. There were three important re-advances of valley glaciers with warmer spells between.* Before the second re-advance the hairy mammoth had already been able to return to Scotland, where his tusks, left in Ayrshire, have been carbon-dated to 13,700 BP. Ben More in Mull, the Cuillin, and Clisham in Harris, held their ice longest; their dwindling corrie glaciers probably lingered to a late period, until, one day some 8,000 years ago, the last ice had gone.

The Ice Age was such a dramatic event in the history of the northern hemisphere, and its sculpting of surface features in the Hebrides so strong, obvious, and interesting, that it may be well to recall the more important and prior action of running water. In earlier times the land had been stripped down to its most ancient rocks and plutonic masses. Several thousand feet of solid rock had been taken off in the process. The new Miocene tableland had been cut up in turn; its rocks, glens, hills, and the islands of the Hebrides, had been shaped by water before the ice. Ice gave emphasis, refined form, added important touches, and swept a landscape already carved from the mass.

Many events, marine, crustal, and volcanic, had given birth to the constituent rocks of the Hebrides, but to none is topography more directly due than to falling and running water.

* 1965: Craig.

3

Climate and Life

When the last great ice-sheet withdrew from the Hebrides, life was extinct. Buried for thousands of years, the islands emerged flayed. Not only had the skin of vegetable and animal life been shorn off, but on eastern slopes that had taken the main brunt, the soil too. On some islands, spectacularly on Harris, the rock surfaces have stayed bare to this day, and on many other eastern faces only a thin vegetation grows out of a thin peat. Conditions were better on the west side of each island's central spine, and in the hollows, glens, and inland flats. In general, however, the islands were without notable deposits of the alluvia that covered the mainland's low country, for such deposits had been largely sunk in the sea.

Had man been able to survey the scene (as he could the European), prospects for renewal of life might have looked remote. The Outer Hebrides were at obvious disadvantage in relation to the Inner. The sea made a wide, stormy barrier, which all incoming plant and animal life would have to find means of bridging. Gneiss would not weather so rapidly as the rocks of most inner isles, and was short of the minerals that make for good soil. The same could be said for the quartzite areas on Jura and Islay, and the Torridonian on Rum and Sleat. The Outer Hebrides, lying exposed at the edge of a great ocean, were probably as they are today, the most windswept region of Britain, but then ringed by pack-ice in winters longer-lasting than now, their snow-line 1000 feet lower than the Cairngorms', their summer rainfall likewise heavier. Such wind, cold, and wet inhibit life.

The recolonization of the isles was to be a long process achieved within severe limits. Grim as these handicaps might appear, they were to carry their compensations, and to be less severe than at first might seem likely. To appreciate what

66

these compensations were during 10,000 years of post-glacial changes in climate, we must take stock of conditions affecting the British peninsula.

Much has been learned through the technique of pollen analysis about the order of recolonization. The technique was introduced to Britain in the 1930s by Sir Harry Godwin at Cambridge. Much work has still to be done in Scotland, and the technique itself may be in need of refinement, hence nothing that is said on the basis of pollen analysis need be accepted uncritically.

Renewal of plant and animal life in Britain was made easier by three fortunate accidents.

First, England south of the Thames had not been glaciated, and from that base arctic life could begin to creep north as soon as ice vacated the ground. It is one of the merits of a post-glacial period that in its early part the soils are rich in life-encouraging minerals ground from the rocks by the ice.* As soon as temperatures rise above 6 °C. (42·8 °F.), a rapid spread of vegetation is to be expected. The retreat of southern ice began nearly 20,000 years ago, and although Scotland was then under deep glaciation, which continued several thousand years longer than in England, the northward migration of life was under way. By 14,000 BP the tundra of south Scotland was feeding mammoth, which probably ate substantial quantities of lichen, sedges, and several of the plants on which deer can feed in the Highlands and Islands today. Such gains were in part wiped out 500 years later, and again 2,000 years later, by two large advances of the Scottish ice, called respectively the Perth and Lomond Readvances. But much low country remained unglaciated, there were considerable areas where arctic plants could survive, and among these were the Hebrides.

Second, Britain remained part of Europe, with the River Thames a tributary of the Rhine, until c.8000 BP. The date of the Dover cut is not yet known, nor whether it was due more to downwarping of the land than to eustatic change (change of sea-level), but we do know, from the carbon-date of peat taken from the bed of the North Sea, that the southern part of that basin was dry around 8425 BP.† Till then, at least, plants and animals were able to migrate direct into Britain. The first colonizers from Europe were lichens, mosses, mountain dryas, sedges, dwarf birch, various willows – species characteristic of today's arctic regions and of Scotland's hill-tops.

Third, world sea-levels were at least 400 feet lower than now at the time of maximum glaciation.‡ At the end of the Ice Age, so much polar ice remained un-

* 1969: Pennington.
† 1967: Sissons.
‡ 1969: Pennington. 1967: Sissons.

melted that slow eustatic change left land-bridges within the British Isles where none are today. An estimate of sea-levels made in 1961 by R. W. Fairbridge gave the following results:

17000 BP sea-level 225 feet below present
12000 BP sea-level 150 feet below present
9000 BP sea-level 120 feet below present
8000 BP sea-level 75 feet below present
6000 BP sea-level 25 feet below present
1000 BP sea-level approximately as now

Thus towards the close of the Hebridean glaciation, north-west Ireland was probably linked to the Argyll islands. The Outer Hebrides were certainly one long island until a late stage. There is a tradition in Harris that open land once extended to St Kilda, but that seems unlikely, even allowing for subsequent downwarpings – the sea-charts give soundings of 360 to 480 feet for all sea outside St Kilda's ring of seven islets. At the Inner Hebrides, the calculation of land-links is confounded by the difficulty of relating sea-level change to the isostatic rise in land. It seems likely that Islay, Colonsay and Jura were part of the land-bridge between Ireland and the Argyll mainland, having an isthmus at Craignish. Coll and Tiree were one island. Mull was linked to Morvern. Skye was a mainland peninsula linked to Glenelg and Balmacara. There were others, and all such links were an aid to the free immigration of species.

Failing land migration, plants and animals have other means of bridging sea-barriers. Seed-dispersal mechanisms are efficient and varied. Many seeds and fruits depend on aerial distribution, some being splendidly equipped for the purpose with wings and parachutes. Here the Hebrides gain advantage from their frequent gales, which carry seeds enormous distances. St Kilda was later to have birch and hazel scrub from seed blown at least fifty miles from the Outer Hebrides – or eighty from the mainland. Other seeds are swallowed by birds and sown from excreta (birds on migration usually fly with their crops empty). Waterside plants and others produce seed with a buoyant structure and a case resistant to sea-water, so that streams and ocean currents can float them to new habitats. Frequent testimony to the efficacy of this means is borne by South American seeds deposited in viable condition along the shores of the Hebrides, and indeed the whole seaboard of West Europe. Some plants use animals for dispersal, producing burr fruits that become attached to their coats by hooks.

European plants and animals came into Britain by three land routes. From the west, Lusitanian plants appear to have migrated from Spain and Portugal round the Bay of Biscay into west Ireland (e.g. Mediterranean heather and saxifrage),

68

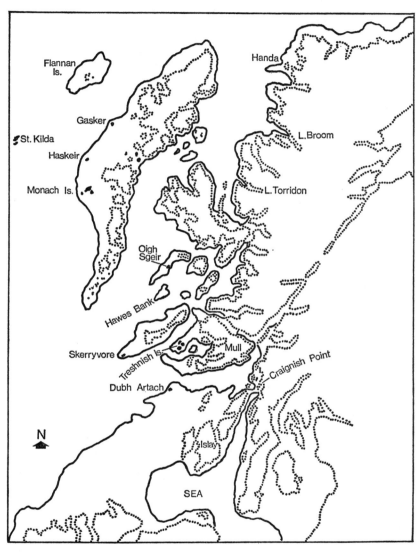

Map 12 *Land-form, 14,000 BP*
(sea-level 30 fathoms [180 feet] lower than now)

and to the Hebrides (e.g. pale butterwort and moneywort). The main colonization came from the east and south-east. Pioneer plants for the tundra were moss and lichen, sedges, dwarf willow, juniper, dwarf birch, and crowberry heath. The tenacity and swift spread of plant species in a harsh sub-Arctic climate is shown by deposits in Loch Droma, at 900 feet on the western spine of Rossshire. These have been carbon-dated to 12,800 BP immediately after the Perth re-advance.* The vegetation on patches of calcareous soil was richly varied, with a general plant cover of crowberry heath type, and of birch copses on ground otherwise treeless. The Hebrides, lower and warmer with a longer growing-season, would carry vegetation at an earlier date.

By 12,000 BP temperatures in south Scotland had risen to 10 °C. (50 °F.) in July, and –7 °C. (20 °F.) in January – figures lower than today's by 2·78 °C. and 12 °C. respectively. Glaciers were decaying and the open tundra was dominated by heather and crowberry. Then the cold returned for the final Lomond re-advance, which lasted 1,600 years. The ice-sheet was local, intense cold general. Throughout Britain, little pollen is found in deposits of the period. The sea-level was 150 feet lower than now: there would still be direct migration of plants and animals to some of the Inner Hebrides towards the close of that cold spell.

The glaciers of the Lomond re-advance began to decay around 10,300 BP, and this date marks the start of the post-glacial period for Scotland, often called the Holocene. Five distinct climatic changes occurred in the next 8,000 years, which largely determined the character of Hebridean and West Highland life. Dates and weather have been established by radiocarbon test and pollen analysis.†

10000 BP	Pre-Boreal	Subarctic
10–7000 BP	Boreal	Dry and warmer
7–5000 BP	Atlantic	Warm and wet: climatic optimum
4–3000 BP	Sub-Boreal	Warm and dry: climatic optimum
2500 BP	Sub-Atlantic	Wet and cool, continuing

While the Hebrides were growing new vegetation during the 4,000 years and more preceding 10,000 BP, they fringed an Arctic region; their seas were encumbered with winter ice, and their land was partially snow- and ice-covered. They would then receive in summer large flocks of breeding birds of the species that migrate today to the Arctic from tropical and temperate zones:‡ the sandpiper family – knots, bar-tailed godwits, purple and curlew sandpipers, turn-

* 1967: Sissons.
† 1969: Pennington.
‡ 1969: Fitter.

stones, sanderlings and perhaps the little stint – and other water birds like pomarine and long-tailed skuas, grey phalaropes, little auks (which winter at sea near the pack ice), and the great northern diver. Among Arctic birds, then breeding and resident in the Hebrides, would probably be king eiders, ivory gulls, and gyr falcons, which would make irregular flights southward. Birds that would fly north to breed in the Hebrides in summer, instead of flying south from the Arctic to winter in the Hebrides as at present, would be barnacle, white-fronted and greylag geese, and whooper swans. On the other hand, many sea-birds that now breed in the Hebrides, like auks, petrels, and the cormorant, would then be summer migrants from breeding stations farther south.

While the last ice-sheets were melting off the mainland around 10,000 BP, the tundra there was invaded by sparse forests of birch, pine, and hazel. Many earlier plants killed by cold were now able to re-enter and spread rapidly. They would easily reach the Inner Hebrides, where Islay-Jura-Colonsay had become one island, separated from the mainland by a narrow channel, and Skye still remained a peninsula.

The first mammals must long since have been crossing to both inner and outer isles on the winter pack-ice. Polar bears would be early visitors from the north. Later mainland immigrants would include wolf, brown bear, fox, blue hare, and others, which today are often seen above 20,000 feet on Himalayan snow and ice. They are, like man, adventurous. The sea-level ice-bridges of the Hebrides would extend to such animals a positive invitation. It seems possible that in this way the wild cat reached Lewis, where the bones were found in an Iron Age midden, and the pine marten reached Harris, where they survived till the 1870s. Some animals, such as hare and deer, have been introduced to particular islands by man (reaching others without his aid), but wild cats would not be candidates for an assisted passage. The fox, whose bark today raises lingering echoes around Loch Coruisk at dawn, certainly crossed to Skye on foot. The wild bear, wild ox, and wolf have all left their bones on inner islands. The wolf may have been widespread in the Hebrides, for as late as 1549 Donald Monro, the Dean of the Isles, remarks in his *Description of the Western Isles* that there were no wolves on Harris, implying that other islands still had them. Other incomers to the islands, a few to become extinct in Scotland within the next 5,000 years, but some long-lasting, were reindeer, lemming, northern lynx, beaver, elk, horse, and the giant Irish elk that stood six feet tall bearing 90lb antlers, which spread up to eleven feet wide.* Fauna that could tolerate the subarctic weather of the pre-Boreal

---

* 1964: Stephen.

period, and would closely follow the retreating snows, would include ptarmigan, snow-bunting, grouse, dotterel, golden plover, and black- and red-throated divers, all of which are present in the Hebrides today.

A growing warmth over the next 3,000 years allowed mainland Scotland (except the north-west) to grow a closed forest of birch, pine, and hazel, in which the birch and pine canopy was sufficiently open to allow the hazel scrub abundant increase to the exclusion of heath.* During the Boreal period, the Inner Hebrides became heavily wooded on their eastern flanks, while their western, and the Outer Hebrides, carried sparser cover. Oak and elm were spreading well on favourable ground, but were never able in Scotland to achieve their south of England status. Small song-birds, like the tits, wren, hedge-sparrow and others were spreading through the new forests. The greylag goose perhaps bred for the first time in the Outer Hebrides, and the osprey in the Inner. The giant elk had proved too bulky to survive the change from the early, rich vegetation of open pasture to forest. A few may have found temporary respite in western Islay, Mull, and Skye, and the north-west Highlands, but all had died out before man could see them.

The climate was not sufficiently warm and dry to discourage peat-formation, which began around 9500 BP,† but temperatures had risen high enough in the northern hemisphere to cause a rapid melt of polar ice. Sea-level now rose much faster – almost fifty feet in one thousand years – and the North Sea basin again subsided. The Dover strait opened. Flora that had already dispersed into Britain before that event is called native.

Granted the boldness of animals and efficiency of plants in bridging sea gaps, we must not underestimate the barriers. Following the swift spread of cold-tolerating species, the spread of varied warmth-loving species was slow. When the English Channel opened, numerous flowering plants and land animals, slower-moving than the others, were stopped at the gulf. Britain received only two-thirds of the species of mammal that were able to migrate into Scandinavia, and the Hebrides only half those of Britain. Some animals would swim out to the islands in summer. Deer will swim from one island to another when the urge takes them, and do so annually today, for example, between Jura and Islay, Mull and Morvern, and Rum and Canna. A wild-cat kitten has been caught swimming the strong tidal waters between Glenelg and Skye.‡ The brown she-bear would swim in autumn to an offshore island to hibernate and to cub, as she does

* 1962: McVean.
† 1967: Rayner.
‡ 1960: Maxwell.

today in northern Norway. Several species were able to reach one island, but unable to spread to others. For example, there are no squirrel in the Hebrides and now no badger or wild cat. The hare reached inner isles, but not outer except by introduction. The result is that the balance of nature on some islands has an accidental bias: Gigha, Coll, Tiree, and the outer isles have no fox, stoat, or weasel, hence the rabbit finds a paradise there (except Tiree, which has none). By the end of the Boreal period, the Hebrides had received the greater part of its population of mammals from red and roe deer down to the common vole.

Around 7000 BP an extraordinary climatic change caused European temperatures to jump 2 °C. (3·6 °F.) above present. Heavier rainfall accompanied the warmth, and the two had strong but diverse effects on the new forests. On the one hand, the whole country including the Hebrides grew tree-cover to 2000 feet, which in the Outer Hebrides would be reduced to lower height by wind. On the west Highland coast, mild damp favoured dense forest, especially on well-drained ground. On the other hand, heavy rain began to leach the Highland and Island soils. Pine and birch, tolerant of acid conditions, continued to provide the Highland forest. On the islands around 5000 BP, birch and hazel spread to their greatest extent since post-glacial times began, with willow now gaining in prominence. The wren, song thrush, and sparrow must by now (if not earlier) have entered the Outer Hebrides and St Kilda.

The rapidly increasing alder of the Lowlands failed to gain ground northward or out to the Hebrides, where a fast and wide spread of hill peat was developing. Ling heather invaded the leached ground. 'The growth of sphagnum moss,' remarks Fraser Darling, 'under optimum conditions has felled forests as surely as fires and axes.' That is what happened now. Moss destroyed much scrub hazel, while accumulating peat robbed the birch and high-level mainland pines of soil for regeneration. The tree-line was again cut back.

In the mid Atlantic period the first Mesolithic men arrived in the Hebrides, followed in the late Atlantic by Neolithic. The climate of the Atlantic period had caused little destruction of animal life. The lemming and northern rat-vole were the only mammals unable to adapt. But from now on, man was to be the principal destroyer of animal species.

Between 5000 and 4000 BP the rainfall eased off and the warmth continued. This dry optimum of the sub-Boreal period lasted fifteen hundred years. Trees again won over the peat bog and the Highland forest mounted to a maximum height of 3300 feet (2000 feet is today's limit). The forests of the Inner Hebrides received additions of alder, oak, pine, ash, and elm. The same trees spread an extensive scrub through the Outer Hebrides. Their pollen in St Kilda peat* is thought to have come on aerial plankton from the Outer Hebrides (perhaps with some from the mainland). On the mainland, forest clearance for grazing and cultivation began around 3000 BP, but not in the Highlands till Roman times, more than a thousand years later. In the Hebrides, man must have been felling and burning trees, for the bigger islands were inhabited by organized communities by 3600 BP.

Bird-life in the sub-Boreal phase was far greater in density than now.† The Atlantic period had established a basic pattern of woodland: when that tree-cover was finally lost through man's action, land birds of woodland type still held to their ground.

The dry and sunny days of the sub-Boreal drew to a close around 2500 BP, when a wet and cold climate enveloped the British Isles. Lowland summer temperatures fell 2°C. (3·6°F.). In the Islands and Highlands, clouded skies deprived the land of sun, checked evaporation, and caused a resumption of peat growth. The tree-line again receded; heather advanced, allowing a spread of moorland birds. This wet cold has lasted to the present day with three marked oscillations.

At the beginning of that sub-Atlantic period, continuous primeval forest had covered the mainland and most of the Inner Hebrides, except Coll, Tiree, Iona, and the open hill-tops, and so it would have continued till now, for that is the natural condition of the country, had man not intervened. His fire and fellings of the last 2,500 years have brought the Highlands their vast expanses of open moorland, and they cleared the islands. Much Hebridean woodland was stunted and sparse, except in favoured sites, compared to its mainland growth and density, and when Iron Age man appeared in the Hebrides around 400 B.C. a quick clearance of tree-cover became possible – and seemed likely, for the Celts kept big herds of cattle and used metal axes to clear forest for grassland. But 1,400 years later, Lewis was still well-forested, according to Viking reports. Conservation was practised by inner island chiefs, who employed foresters. Hazel and rowan were specially conserved, the hazel for its value in making fishing rods, creels, and hoops, and the rowan for its fruit and as a charm against evil. The history of woodland varied according to each island's internal economy, its population, and control. Under clan control, islands like Skye and Mull were well-wooded in birch and oak in the sixteenth century,‡ and were still forested a hundred years

* 1961: McVean.
† 1969: Fitter.
‡ 1577: An account written for James VI.

later.* Lismore was so well covered in oak that in 1596 the sea could not be seen from the interior except at two named places.† Now its back is bare. After the clan system had been rejected by the chiefs from 1763 onward, the island estates began to change hands, the woods were exploited and vanished. Large quantities of timber were felled on Mull and other islands to make charcoal for export to England's iron furnaces.‡ Wholesale felling and burning was then stimulated by the switch from cattle- to sheep-farming, and by the population explosion of 1800–41 (an increase from 60,000 to 93,000), when the need for timber for house- and boat-building, casks, furniture, and fuel, became acute. But the principal destroyer was the flockmaster's fire.

In both Outer and Inner Hebrides, scrub would spread rapidly today if allowed, for willow, juniper, rowan, and birch can be seen to grow well on islets in freshwater lochs, like Loch Druidibeg in South Uist, where they have protection from grazing animals. The quality of tree-growth has inevitably deteriorated with the climate and the advent of man. Their combined work in exposing soil to the elements has leached the plant nutrients, increased acidity, encouraged bog, and denied trees regenerative opportunity. That is not the whole tale: gales and man have both done much to make islands fruitful, as will appear later.

Two important oscillations in the sub-Atlantic climate came in the periods A.D. 1000–1200, and 1430–1850.§

The first brought a new climatic optimum to western Europe. Vineyards were able to move three hundred geographical miles farther north and six hundred feet higher above sea-level. In south Greenland, the temperature rose 2–4 °C. (nearly 4 °F. to 7 °F.) higher than now, so that plants grew on land now permanently frozen, and drift ice disappeared from the seas south of Norway's North Cape. Such warm conditions greatly aided the Vikings' occupation of the Hebrides, and their explorations of Greenland.

The second oscillation brought an advance of Alpine and Scandinavian glaciers in the greatest cold since the Ice Age, and was thus named the Little Ice Age. It reached its worst between 1550 and 1700. Eighty years after that maximum, sea temperatures recorded in British latitudes were still 1 °C. to 3 °C. (nearly 5 °F.) below present. A huge expansion of Arctic pack-ice had occurred, allowing polar bears to reach Iceland. On Scotland's Atlantic coast, eye-witness reports were of

---

* 1938: MacLeod.
† 1947: Carmichael.
‡ 1775: Pennant.
§ 1966: Lamb.

storm damage by spray, bitter summers, the failure of harvests, and the whole-sale destruction of woods on exposed land. The Hebrides were most vulnerable, but the woods destroyed would be mostly scrub. Early in the seventeenth century there was a considerable reafforestation movement in Scotland, with plantations of native birch and pine, sycamore from abroad, and beech from England. Syca-more has proved to be a most successful tree on nearly all inhabited islands.

A third, much briefer oscillation is recorded for the forty-odd years between 1890 and c.1938. World air temperatures rose 0·5 °C, and the growing season lengthened by two weeks in Britain. Enormous quantities of Arctic ice had broken up after the Little Ice Age, and now, between 1918 and 1938, the sea-ice area shrank twenty per cent, which meant that the shipping season to Spitz-bergen and Greenland doubled to seven months. Prophets warned that if these apparently happy conditions continued indefinitely the Arctic might be clear of ice by the end of the century, and rising sea drown much of the Hebrides (and coastal cities like London). In fact, there was no appreciable rise in sea-level during these twenty years, and sub-Atlantic weather returned.

In the Hebrides today, mean summer temperatures range from 12·78 °C. (55 °F.) in the north to 13·89 °C. (57 °F.) in the south. These are approximately half a degree (or 1 °F.) lower than Scotland's east coast. The winter temperatures are more important. They are 5 °C. (41 °F.) to 5·56 °C. (42 °F.) for the whole length of the Hebrides, and these are 1·66 °C. (3 °F.) higher than the east coast. The large winter difference is caused by the North Atlantic Drift of the Gulf Stream, prevailing westerlies, and the fact that the islands are small. The Drift closely envelopes them. The temperatures given are for sea-level, but there is an abrupt drop in temperature for mountain heights above sea-level. For example, the highest west-coast mountain, Ben Nevis, 4406 feet, has a mean annual tem-perature below freezing point. At the same time, the coastal strips and low inner islands are milder than anywhere in Britain except the south-west of England and the west fringes of Wales and Ireland. Thus the Hebrides are virtually free of snow except on the mountains, where it never lies as long or as heavily as on mainland hills. North-westerly blizzards are brief. Scotland's principal snowfalls come on easterly or south-easterly winds, which discharge over the Highlands before reaching the Hebrides. Snow comes on to low ground lightly and infre-quently. Frost is neither prolonged nor extreme, say 1 °C. or 2 °C. (or 2 °F. or 3 °F.) below freezing for at most a few days in the year. Exceptions are rare and never of mainland severity. The result is that in sheltered positions exotic shrubs and trees like palms and figs are able to grow in the open on the southmost islands of Gigha, Islay, and Colonsay. Gigha and Colonsay each have one of the

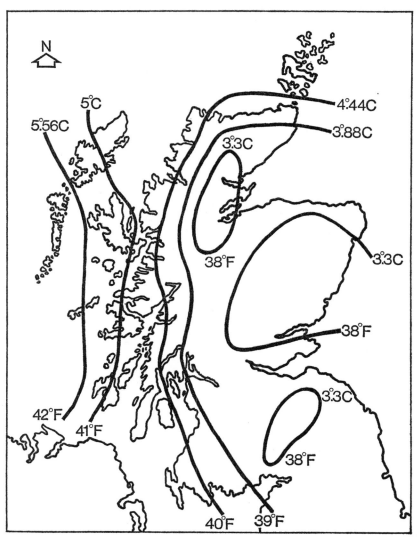

Diagram Ia *January Isotherms*
(layered West to East in response to N. Atlantic Drift and West Winds)

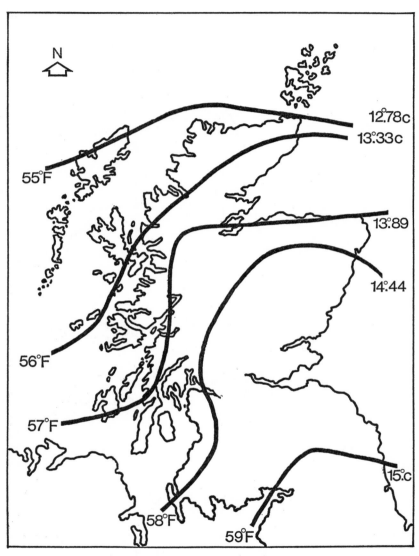

Diagram 1b *July Isotherms*
(layered South to North)

four famous gardens of the Scottish west coast, the others being Crarae and Inverewe.

The West Highlands are the wettest region of Europe. But the high rainfall of 120 inches or more comes not on the coast but several miles inland along the high mountain spine on which the ice-cap had once been centred. Precipitation is almost as closely related to land-height as temperature; a few miles from the base of a mountain the rainfall may be only half that of the summit. The Hebrides lie well beyond the heavy rain belt. They have a fall of 40 to 60 inches, except on the mountains of Harris, Skye, Rum, and Jura, where it rises to 60 to 80 inches, and to 120 inches on central Mull. Two points of great importance are that the Outer Hebrides are excessively windswept, and that in most of the Inner Hebrides evaporation is never likely in any month of the year to keep pace with rainfall, so that the regenerative power of many plants is reduced by water-logging of the ground. The former condition so increases the plants' transpiration by ventilation of the leaves that these become parched and fall early, while the latter overworks the plants in transpiring activity (giving off water). Both stunt growth. Bog and marsh plants thrive, as do willows. The very heavy rain of central Mull is in part offset by the porosity of the lavas, which allows a natural drainage so good that few lochs have formed.

The climatic feature of the Hebrides, the outstanding feature, is wind, strong and persistent. It comes in off the Atlantic laden with moisture, and although the rain clouds continually renew themselves out of the west, the wind drives them across the low islands to precipitate mainly on the Highlands. Thus the Outer Hebrides, and the Inner too where low-lying, have long hours of sunshine, especially in April, May, and June. The long-term average for May sunshine is 234 hours on Tiree, 200 hours on Skye at Trotternish, and 195 hours on Lewis at Stornoway. It might seem from these figures that the sandy beaches of the isles must be idyllic holiday resorts. The great strands have in fact finer quality scenery and sand than anything of the kind fringing the Mediterranean. That they remain relatively unused is due to wind. Calm spells occur, even on outer isles; one may enjoy a day's sunbathing or several if lucky. Yet as a general rule wind is incessant. Living on an outer island is like living on the deck of a ship. The mainland Highlander has more shelter from his hills than he realizes; the outer islesman has little or none. If you ask him for a weather forecast, he will not, like the mainlander, answer dry, wet, or sunny, but quote you a figure from the Beaufort Scale, say Force 3 or Force 10. He listens to the shipping forecast. Wind is what matters here.

Townsmen generally have little conception of the violence of Hebridean wind.

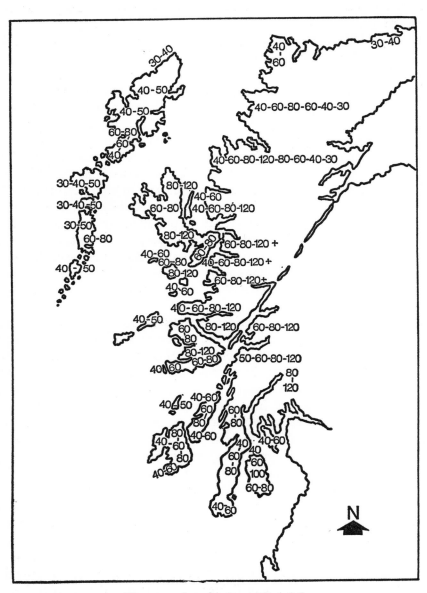

Map 13 *Average Annual Rainfall*
(in inches)

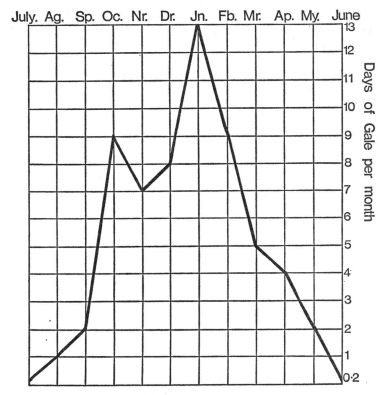

July. Ag. Sp. Oc. Nr. Dr. Jn. Fb. Mr. Ap. My. June

Days of Gale per month

Diagram 2 *Gale record for the Butt of Lewis averaged monthly over 6 years 1930 to 1936*

Note: The low gale record for mid-summer does not imply lack of wind.

Days of gale (when average wind speed reaches 34 knots or more) number one in six at the Butt of Lewis,* and one day in eight on the relatively sheltered east coast at Stornoway.† These figures are annual averages. Winter gales blow one day in three at the Butt. At Barra Head, where there is no shallow water to break the gigantic storm-seas, surf and small fish are blown over the 630-foot cliff on to the grass on top. Sir Archibald Geikie, when Director General of the Geological Survey, recorded from Barra Head a hurricane that moved a 42-ton block of

* Recorded by Coastguard Station, 1930–6.
† 1970: Ritchie and Mather.

gneiss, dislodging it five feet. On St Kilda, the army have in recent years recorded gusts of 130 mph. One gust, unmeasured, bent an angle-iron gantry 90° from the vertical. These are records from the more exposed positions, yet one would have to be cautious in declaring, from pollen analysis on a particular site, that Neolithic man felled Hebridean forests as he did English. In 1968, a night's storm felled more trees in West Scotland than man could harvest in ten years. But a stricken forest will regenerate. The wholesale disappearance of island trees is undoubtedly man's work through the centuries. The wind stunts rather than eliminates.

The wind gives useful service to the Hebrides in dispersing seed and pollen, but in addition it gives one other benefit of paramount importance. It blows sand, blows it far and wide, and on that vital office the economy of many islands has been built up and still depends.

The western shores of the Hebrides are open to the full battering power of an Atlantic ocean stretching uninterrupted 2,200 miles to Labrador. They lie in the track of North Atlantic storms. They are widely bayed, with arms stretching out to receive what the ocean may give, and the sea has given them sand. It has given prodigiously, for the slight post-glacial sinking of the Outer Hebrides, and the eustatic rise, have left several miles of shallow water to the west, on which sand can accumulate and be retained. Gneiss produces poor and acid soil, but the sand of the gneiss islands is not of pulverized rock (as on Skye it is pulverized basalt); the sea has freely provided the needed sands out of its own lime-concentrating organisms.

The west coast of the Outer Hebrides is lined for nearly one hundred miles with shell-sand. The lime content of sand-samples taken from seventy-six beaches and machair varies from 16% to 84%, with an average of 48%.* The same favour has been shown to Coll, Tiree, and Iona, to the south half of Colonsay, and to lesser extent to other islands. Some of these beaches are vast in length or breadth; many are small coves linked in a series of half a dozen together. All are backed by a strip of marram grass, usually narrow but sometimes expanding in dunes. Behind that again lies the calcareous machair, forming a strip of grassland from two miles deep down to a few hundred yards. On this the islander grazes his cattle and sheep in large number. Between the machair and moor lies a fourth strip, this one of mixed sand and peat humus, giving arable land for crops of hay, corn, barley, oats, and potatoes, and possessing many base-rich lochs with fine trout.

---

* 1970: Ritchie and Mather. 1971: Ritchie.

The whole interior of each island is moorland. Tiree has less than most in proportion to size and no peat-bog. It offers an example of the way that high winds work salvation for gneiss islands. Its windswept erosion platform has been made fertile by the lime blown in from its ring of huge beaches. A gale blows one day in eleven, and so thorough has been the sanding that good loam has built up on top of the gneiss. The ground has been transformed into a calcareous plain, not only draining well but ploughable, and carrying, far from the shores, a machair vegetation pre-eminently suitable for stock-raising. The island is heavily crofted.

Stock-raising is the principal land-industry of the isles. It depends on their chief asset, the machair, which in turn depends on a seaward belt of marram grass. This spiky bent grows two or three feet tall, pale green in colour, tending to yellow at the tips. Its tough creeping roots bind the sand, stabilize the ground, and stop erosion. It is accompanied by a small fore-dune community of ragwort, sandwort, couch-grass, and others, but were it not for the marram the wind would create dune-deserts by blowing out the sand. Many acres have been lost to cultivation in the past by human carelessness, like rutting the marram with wheeled vehicles, over-cutting it for thatching, and over-grazing by sheep and rabbits. It used to be stated in the duke of Argyll's Tiree leases that a farmer who found a hole in the marram dunes must plant marram to fill it. Without such preservation in the nineteenth century, when population was high, the economy of the gneiss islands might well have collapsed.

Protected from erosion by the marram belt, the machair is developed by a first colonization of flowering plants like the clovers and trefoils, which fix nitrogen and create the conditions that allow seventy or eighty different plants to strike root. Until a man has seen good machair, like that of Berneray, of the Monach Isles, or of Tiree, he may find it hard to realize that although the crofters call it 'gress' it grows not grass but flowers. Among the most common of the four-score plants are buttercup, red and white clover, daisy, blue speedwell, dandelion, eyebright, birdsfoot trefoil, hop trefoil, harebell, wild thyme, yellow and blue pansy, and silverweed.*

One plant or another may be dominant on a particular machair, like bloody cranesbill reddening the August dunes behind Hogh Bay on Coll; or primrose at Eoligarry in Barra, where a hillslope of 300 feet becomes in May one of the wonders of the Isles – perhaps the most dense pack of primrose in Scotland. A few plants, not on Morton Boyd's list of typical flora, may yet be abundant on some remote machair, like scarlet pimpernel at the Ross of Mull; or appear as

* For a full list see *The Highlands and Islands* by F. F. Darling and Morton Boyd.

strays, like purple loosestrife, rare in the Isles, whose bright red spikes appear at the Rudha Ardvule of South Uist; or pink sea-convolvulus, *Calystegia soldanella* found only in Eriskay and Vatersay, and alleged to have been sown by Prince Charles Edward Stewart when he landed on Eriskay from France in 1745. The prince's flower has a small, heart-shaped leaf and large trumpet, blooming in June at the marram fringe.

In May, the main body of the machair puts out its flowers in annual order, daisies first, buttercups soon after, then blue speedwell and yellow birdsfoot trefoil, the others following till the green turf is almost lost to sight under blossom. In their season or at periods in a cycle of years, one or two species may take over most of a machair. I have been to Toe Head isthmus in Harris when it was wholly under daisies; it blazed like a snowfield, and half an hour later flushed pink as the cups closed in response to cloud and a sharpening wind. In July, the Berneray and South Uist machairs are a rolling sea of buttercup, clover, and daisy, each massing separately in the wide troughs but merging on the green billows. The wind is charged with clover-scent. This can be strong enough on Tiree to carry seaward to an approaching steamer. When the cows are first turned on to well-flowered machair, they can soon have scented breath and their milk a flower-sweet taste. June and July is the time to see and scent this dense blossom, for the machair is heavily grazed. By August, most has been cropped short (save on a few machairs kept for wintering) and green is the only surviving colour.

Lewis has relatively little machair, for its west coast is rocky. The few sandy coves like Dalmore and Dalbeg are ringed by cliffs that prevent the inblowing of sand. South of Gallan Head, where the sands of Valtos and Camus Uig are of very pure shell, inblowing is again checked by hills. Instead, the island is famed (or notorious according to one's point of view) for that extraordinary feature of the Outer Hebrides, the Black Moor of Lewis. It occupies the whole interior except the north point of Ness. It is not habitable ground: people live on the coastal fringe. The broad back of the island has been gouged by glaciers into innumerable shallow hollows, now filled by many hundred of lochs and by peat-bog. The whole of the Long Isle, especially the Uists, suffered the same gouging. The moors are blanketed in peat and so congested by freshwater lochs that nearly one quarter of the land-area is under water. The Black Moor is distinguished by its dark brown colour, by its great area, by its grimness under cloud when the lochs lie black, and by its untold wealth in peat. The latter has made an important contribution to island life.

The deep peat of the interior has been measured across a 10,000-acre tract:

maximum thickness 19½ feet, average 7½ feet.* This enormous deposit is an accumulation of 9,000 years, starting in the Boreal period. The Hebrides gave its formation ideal conditions – a hard acid rock and high humidity with cool summers, giving a low evaporation rate. Cold, wet, and acid ground thus inhibited the micro-organisms that ought to have caused the decay of withered vegetation, which instead built itself up year by year as a thickening mat. (This suppression of bacterial activity has given peat its preservative qualities, most useful to the biologist and archaeologist.)

The plant communities that develop on peat-bog are classified as basin bog, raised bog, and blanket bog according to the ground they inhabit and their way of growth.† Basin bog forms in depressions where the water draining off acid rock stagnates. It depends on bad drainage rather than high rainfall. The dominant plant is sphagnum, and the bog produced is limited to the wet area. Raised bog builds up on top of basin bog until it fills the basin and may even rise above the surrounding moor. The upper layer thus becomes independent of the parent basin, so that it requires rain and humid air to maintain growth. Blanket bog is so named because it spreads over land as a continuous cover, except on rock outcrops and steep hill-slopes. The first growth, unlike the others, does not depend on local drainage water, but on frequent rain and constant humidity, and given that climate it will continue to build up. Glacier-scooped gneiss exhibits all three kinds of bog in plenty, but the distinction between raised and blanket bog is often blurred. The vegetation growing on top varies from one part of the country to another, especially from east to west Scotland. The typical western plants are a poor type of ling and bell heather, cotton grass, bog-myrtle, cross-leaved heath, bog-asphodel, sundew, blue moor grass, deer's hair grass, and many others, amongst which sphagnum moss grows rampant in the wetter places. Some lochans may be broadly rimmed with bog-bean, which in bloom looks like soap-suds, for the white petals have a feathery edge.

To appreciate fully the difference between moor and machair, and between Lewis and the isles to its south, it is best to climb a hill. A hill with a good view for the purpose is Beinn Mhor in North Uist. It rises only 625 feet above Newton and may be climbed in about thirty-five minutes. From its top, the eastern moorland of North Uist looks like a battle-field from the First World War – a shell-cratered morass, ten miles by six. At the middle is a watery maze named Loch Scadavay, unique in Scotland for the relation of its 50-mile shoreline to a total

* 1965: Craig.
† 1949: Tansley.

water-area of only 1¾ square miles. Tortuous spits and 125 islets dotting the surface cause the freak figures. On the island's west side, by contrast, bay after bay of white sands scallop a sea of peacock greens and blues, bordered inland by miles of cattle-thronged machair.

The sight must drive home to anyone not dull-witted that if land can be so transformed by the wind-spread of lime, then if man spreads it where wind cannot, much moorland can be reclaimed. Such reclamation with fertilizers added, has been extensively practised since 1956.

Much land has been reclaimed in Lewis by centuries of peat-cutting where boulder-clay has been exposed under the banks. The glacial deposit thus laid bare is called skinned ground. It may become part of the common grazing, but if mixed with some peat and grass and fed with seaweed and shell-sand it becomes good soil. Examples may be seen near Stornoway on the Eye peninsula.

The Black Moor is not sterile. Cattle can be grazed on its summer shielings, which are its dry hillocks and green hollows. Some of the tiny huts on the shielings can be seen from the roadways, but most are lost to sight in the moor's immensity. Many of the lochs give indifferent trout fishing. The scene can be grim in foul weather, but when sun floods over its back and cloud-shadows from a windy sky race across switchback hills, the lochs flash blue or white and the moor comes alive. The vast sweep of its landscape is unique in the Isles.

The moors of the Inner Hebrides have better soil, at least on the basalt of Mull, Skye, and the Small Isles. Better drainage leaves them dryer despite greater rainfall, and the grazing is good. The soil of Muck and Canna is particularly rich: the islands are famed for their May potatoes, grown on beds of glacial drift. Even the quartzite moorlands of Jura and Islay – the largest expanse of the poorest rock in the Highlands and Islands – have in the past grazed large stocks of beef-cattle compared with those of today. The past century has seen a great deterioration in the quality of Hebridean moorland caused by the displacement of cattle by sheep.

Almost all woodland and sizeable trees are confined to the east sides of the islands, away from westerly winds. Exceptions to the rule are found on the Inner Hebrides, but such western sites are well in from the open coasts at Dunvegan in Skye, or Bridgend in Islay, or Gruline in Mull, and woods like these were planted by landowners, who gave the young growth protection; now they are tall, full-grown trees – beech, elm, chestnut, oak, sycamore, cherry, and pine, spruce, larch, and cypress. At Dunvegan Castle, Colonsay, and Gigha, the woods are open to the public. The owners have given to the people of the Isles, and to visitors, a rare pleasure – the chance to walk among broad-leaved trees and scented conifers. The only other opportunities are in east-coast woods at Stornoway Castle and Kinloch Castle on Rum. The Forestry Commission have planted large areas of central Mull, Skye, and Jura. These are commercial plantations of exceeding monotony. Other plant life in their interiors is suffocated.

The Outer Hebrides have more natural scrub than will ever meet the eye until one explores. Beinn Mhor of South Uist has a shallow glen on its southern slopes above Loch Eynort, called the Allt Volagir. There you will find hazel and birch woods, where the ground is carpeted in spring with bluebell, wood-sorrel, primrose, and violet, replaced in summer by foxglove, herb-robert, bugle, and wild thyme. Near the Traigh Mhor of Barra, a tiny glen is crowded with pine, sycamore, and chestnut. There are numerous little communities like this throughout the isles, and many small plantations intended either for shelter-belts or amenity, which have remained stunted or taken wind-tormented shapes. Nearly eight hundred species of plants have been listed in the Outer Isles, including a surprisingly large number of native trees. Statistics prove that the islands are very far from treeless, yet, like all statistics, they require field knowledge for their interpretation. Thus the list includes apparently common plants like honeysuckle, roses, aspen, holly, foxglove, and silver birch; but you may journey from the Butt to Barra and see none from the roadways. Somewhere in the Hebrides most British plants can find a home, but the sites are by mainland standards severely restricted.

Some of these sites are of rare kind, if not unique. A pair with double interest, geological and botanical, occur on Skye's Trotternish peninsula. At the north end is the Quiraing (pronounced Kooraing, from the old Gaelic Cuith-raing meaning Pillared Stronghold); at the south end is the Old Man of Storr, a huge basalt pinnacle that can be seen from Portree outlined against the sky. Both have origin in landslips before the Ice Age, on the most impressive scale to be seen in Britain. They occurred along the Trotternish spine and were caused by the collapse of Jurassic sedimentary rock under the great weight of Tertiary lava-flows resting on top, with spectacular results. Glaciers removed the earlier slipped debris, but post-glacial slipping has continued to the present day.*

The Quiraing is a corrie at 500 feet between the summit cliffs of Meall nan Suireamaich, 1779 feet, and a wall of rock-towers on its eastern side. Entry is gained past a 100-foot obelisk called the Needle. At the corrie's centre is a crag called the Table with a flat top 100 yards long by 40 wide, set as though in the great hall of a fortress. The narrow gaps between the outer towers are like

---

* 1964: Richey.

windows, opening on to the sea and the mainland mountains. On the inner cliffs grow a great variety of arctic and rock plants.

The Storr, twelve miles south, is the highest point of Trotternish, 2358 feet, from which 600-foot cliffs drop to an eastern corrie deeply sculpted. This corrie is one of the most freakish of Scottish rock-scenes, for its lower rim bears a dozen basalt pinnacles of weird shape – one is a thin corkscrew 100 feet high with three tall arch-holes punched through its pillar. Over them all towers the Old Man, 160 feet high and precariously balanced, for it leans out from its rock-plinth.

The Gaelic *Stor* means either high cliff or decayed tooth, and both are appropriate, for the Old Man is a fallen block that has been weathered to fang-like shape. Ravens and buzzards fly among the pinnacles, which startle the eye all the more for their springing out of a corrie-floor of bright green grass. The main hill-slope beside the great cliff has rich soil growing a wealth of arctic plants like purple saxifrage, Alpine lady's mantle, hairy rock cress, saw wort, rose-root, globe flower, and others including the smallest and also most rare of British plants, Iceland purslane (*Koenigia islandica*). It has oval leaves and minute white flowers of three petals. It appears on no other site in Britain.

4

Sea and Wild-life

Hebridean seas are in a sense richer in plant life than their islands. At sea as on land, the entire animal population depends for its food on plant life. Plants and only plants can use the energy in sunlight to convert elements otherwise locked in water, soil, and air into the proteins, sugars, and starches on which animals live. In the sea this plant life is nine-tenths plankton, drifting mostly in the upper 100-foot layer penetrated by sunlight. Plankton includes both plant and animal organisms, at least three-fifths of which are a plant-form called diatoms. These single-celled algae feed on minerals and salts. Several million may be present in a quart of water. They are the sea's pasture, providing grazing for thousands of animals from copepods to whales. Copepods are the world's most numerous multi-celled animal – a crustacean no bigger than a pinhead, but devouring 130,000 diatoms for a day's meal. A herring may have in its stomach 7,000 such crustaceans, thus nearly a million diatoms are required to feed one herring for a few hours. The Hebridean seas, being rich in plankton, are rich in fish, and in the sea-birds and mammals at the top of the food chain.

Plankton thrive in cold or temperate water; in tropical seas they are relatively scarce. No one who has swum in the icy waters of the Hebrides has ever thereafter been able to feel impressed by the tale of the Gulf Stream 'warming our shores'. At this point we have to make a clear distinction between the Gulf Stream and the North Atlantic Drift.

The Gulf Stream is a great clockwise whirl in the North Atlantic basin between the bulge of Africa and the Gulf of Mexico; its cause, a combination of sun-heat, wind, and the spin of the earth. The eastward spin of 1,000 mph at the equator tends to leave the sea behind, and to cause winds and currents in the northern hemisphere to move in a clockwise direction. The north-east trades

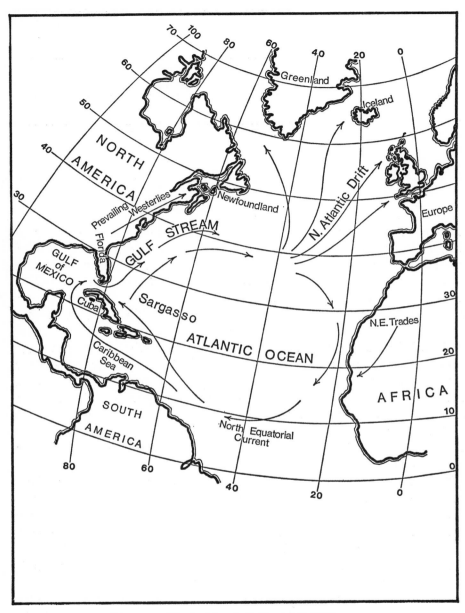

Map 14 *North Atlantic Drift and Gulf Stream*

blow diagonally down from North Africa towards the equator; deflected there by sun-heat and spin, they curve northward, and from North America prevailing westerlies blow diagonally east to north Europe. Thus the Gulf Stream starts as an equatorial current running west before the trade winds. The main stream goes through the Caribbean, and baffled there by the Yucatan peninsula and then by the cul-de-sac of the Gulf of Mexico, is spun sharply east between Florida and Cuba. At this point it bursts back into the Atlantic, an ocean river 50 miles wide, 1500 feet deep, and racing at 5 mph. Its temperature is 26·6 °C. (80 °F.).*

Out in the cold Atlantic the stream widens, steadily losing depth, speed, and heat. Half way to Europe, above latitude forty, the stream is carried on by the prevailing westerlies, but here a large part of it drifts off north, no longer river-like but spreading as a great fan-shaped drift of surface water impelled by the westerly winds towards the British Isles. The North Atlantic Drift helps the climate of north-west Europe by raising water-temperature. But that is an over-simplification. On a cold January day, when an easterly air stream from the continent was giving the Hebrides midday frost with an air temperature of minus 1·1 °C. (30 °F.), the sea temperature taken from an incoming tide (feeling colder to my hand than the air) was 8·8 °C. (48 °F.). Thus the warming influence of the North Atlantic Drift on the Hebrides and north-west Europe largely depends on the help of prevailing westerlies.

An unseen aid to keeping these cool Hebridean seas as warm as they are (surface temperatures vary from 8 °C. in winter to 12 °C. in summer) is the submarine ridge linking north Scotland to Iceland and Greenland. Submerged though it be, it prevents the southward flow of the near zero bottom layers of the Arctic Ocean.

The great event of the sea year is the spring explosion of vegetable and therefore animal life. In the mid-winter months plankton is scarce, lacking sunlight, but in March and April the huge increase in sunlight, and perhaps the very slight rise in sea temperature, triggers off a reproduction of life so rapid that a diatom in one month may have one thousand million progeny. At the same time the host of marine animals from minute crustaceans to big fish spawn their eggs into the water, each kind by the thousand, or hundred thousand, or big fish by the million. Only by such boundless fertility can the various species survive. The eggs drift with the plankton and hatch larvae that feed on plankton, while fish feed on both. And the fish, from small fry to adults of herring size, are devoured by bigger fish and by vast numbers of nesting gannets, fulmars, puffins, guillemots,

* 1962: Engel.

razorbills, kittiwakes, terns, shags, and numerous duck and other sea-birds, which find on the Hebrides their ideal breeding stations.

Hebridean waters hold a huge variety of species from the common herring to the rarely seen giant squid, sixty feet long, and exotic reptiles like the loggerhead turtle,* a large Mediterranean species, remarkable for the great size of its head. The fish important to man, bird, and mammal are herring and mackerel, and then the white fish (fish with white flesh, not oily), which include cod, coalfish, ling, haddock, whiting, flounders, halibut, and skate. Salmon lack the numbers inshore that make them so important to West Highland fisheries. The shellfish of greatest value to island fishermen are lobster and prawn: the prawn catch landed at Stornoway now equals that of herring in money-value.

The Hebridean herring, about twelve inches long, are of the finest quality fished in European waters. They feed principally on crustaceans, which they sieve from the sea through gill-rakers. The female lays 30,000 eggs, which do not drift on the surface but become attached to stones and seaweeds. Of all the fish in the sea, the herring have been in the past the most important to man in the Hebrides owing to their great abundance and nutritious flesh. They have made possible the habitation of islands like Eriskay, too rockily barren to support live-stock, and have, with mackerel, sustained in the eighteenth and nineteenth centuries an island population that the land alone could not have fed. The great-est herring shoals, the best quality fish, and often the best fishing, are found to the west of the Outer Hebrides. The priest on Eriskay (himself a fisherman) told me of sighting and following a shoal seven miles long near St Kilda. Despite the enormous depredations by man (the Scottish fishery alone takes nearly 600 million herring annually),† and the far greater toll taken by other predators, the fertility of the fish is such that Hebridean herring are so far maintaining their numbers.

Not so long ago, it was believed that herring shoals made a clockwise migra-tion around the British Isles, moving as a cohesive body. This idea is now abandoned. Instead, the shoals are believed to come and go, concentrating here and there round the coast, so far inexplicably. Off the Hebrides they are taken at all seasons by trawlers using drift, seine, purse, and ring nets.

Mackerel are caught in the same way in prodigious number. They lay ten times as many eggs as the herring, but these float more vulnerably on the surface and therefore hatch in less time (seven to ten days). They are migrant fish, appearing off the Hebrides from July to September.

* 1969: Darling and Boyd.
† 1971: Herring Industry Board, Report.

The cod family includes saithe (coalfish), ling, lythe (pollack), haddock, whiting, hake, and the common cod. The latter shares with herring first place as nutritious food. The female lays between three and nine million eggs, which can locally cloud the sea in March, but few reach maturity. Saithe and lythe are exceedingly numerous, and these with mackerel are fished in summer and autumn by the islanders from their own rowing boats and from rocks, using rod and line. The main catches of ling, hake, and haddock are in deep water beyond the Outer Hebrides, but haddock and whiting are taken locally on inshore lines. The ling is the most prolific fish in Hebridean waters: the female produces up to thirty million eggs. They used to be an important fish in the inner isles, but there they have almost disappeared. They remain numerous west of St Kilda, where they are fished from Norway. Their liver oil is used as a substitute for cod liver oil.

Cod fishing has suffered great injury from the use of the trawl, which destroys immature fish. The whole of the cod tribe are best taken on small or great lines, not only for reasons of conservation but because the fish are less bruised and better fit for market. Small (inshore) lines are up to 12,000 feet long with hooks set four feet apart and baited with mussel, cockle, crab, limpet, worm, or herring fragments. The lines are run out from a metal cylinder and shot across the tide two or three miles from land. The ends are weighted with stones below and buoyed above. Half an hour to an hour later they can be harvested. Great-line fishing works on the same principle with stronger gear and much longer lines to fish deeper water for bigger fish of the same cod tribe, and also halibut. Halibut, the biggest of the flat fish, sometimes attaining seven feet but usually four or five feet, are taken along the continental shelf.

Salmon feed largely on herring, but the ocean feeding grounds for Scottish salmon are not certainly known. It must be hoped that they never will be. There is a current belief that the grounds lie off south-east Greenland. The Outer Hebrides may lie on their route to the mainland coast, but have too few rivers of good size to draw them in quantity. As in most of the Inner Hebrides, rivers tend to be too short and steep. Skye has the best salmon rivers of the Isles, and Skye and Mull have the only sea-salmon fisheries. These appear on the Staffin sea-cliffs of Trotternish, where the nets are set seaward in parallel rows, and on Mull at the south, west, and north-east coasts.

A number of different sharks cruise annually through the Hebrides. An occasional appearance is made by the thrasher (fifteen feet), which eats herring and appears to round them up with the extraordinary upper lobe of the tail. Its blue colour makes it easily mistaken for the much more dangerous blue shark (twelve to fifteen feet), which is a regular summer visitor to the English Channel but is only rarely seen off west Scotland. Tope (six feet) are probably common, for they are caught often enough, but are not seen, being bottom feeders. The common shark of the Hebrides is the basking shark (thirty feet), which appear in fairly large numbers each summer. There is only one bigger fish in the sea, and that is the whale-shark (sixty feet) of the Indian and Pacific oceans. Since the basker's liver can yield a ton of oil it was much hunted twenty years ago in its chief grazing ground, the Minch. Baskers are quite harmless, feeding on plankton sieved through gill-rakers. They are very common in the Firth of Clyde in July, and up to twenty years ago would cruise round the sea-lochs within a few feet of the shore rocks if the water were deep. I have had to ship my oars while one nosed alongside my boat, less than a hundred yards from my house. These days have gone. They are rarely seen now in the lochs, but remain common between the Inner and Outer Hebrides for a short period each year.

Most of the mammal species other than seals are summer visitors only. These are dolphins and whales. Since they all have to surface to breathe, they are very much in evidence from June and July onward, or as early as April on occasion, throughout the sea-channels of the inner isles. The whales are of two groups, the toothed and the toothless, the latter called baleen whales. The toothed species include sperm whales, and the dolphins and porpoises that are the common species of the Hebrides. Three dolphins, the common, bottle-nosed, and Risso's (eight to twelve feet) abound, to the damage of herring and mackerel fisheries. They appear in schools of a dozen to twenty, which will often follow a boat while they frolic around. To anyone not in the fishing trade they make a joyful sight at play. They leap exuberantly out of the water. The bottle-nosed schools can jump ten feet vertically. Risso's, larger and more sedate, are reported as a rarity on other British coasts. In the Hebrides the fishermen call them 'dunters' from their habit of leaping at random. Porpoises (six feet) are by comparison shy. They too move in schools and will sport on the surface, but without leaping clear. Their circular motion through the water makes the reappearing fin look as though set on the rim of a slow catherine wheel. In Elizabethan times they were prized as a royal dish, said to taste like pork.

The dolphin tribe include the twenty-five-foot killer whales of global range. They have been reported around the Inner Hebrides hunting either alone or in small packs of up to five in number (in high latitudes they have been sighted in herds of forty, and even of hundreds). Warning of their presence is given by the five to six feet of dorsal fin, curved back like a broad sabre. The upper body is black, the under, white. The killer is a most ferocious animal with a large appetite – the remains of thirteen porpoises and fourteen seals were found in the stomach of an immature specimen.* They will sometimes attack their own kind, and are known to have ganged up to savage the great whales, seeking only the tongue, which they tear out and devour.† The occasional disappearance of small boats and their crews has been blamed on the killer, but in all the history of the Hebrides there is only one recorded instance of attack on man. This occurred in 1680 when a killer overturned a fishing boat off west Lewis and killed three of the four crewmen. Another boat's crew, who witnessed the attack, saved the fourth man.‡

The pilot whale (twenty-eight feet) visits the Hebrides in herds of several hundred. The herds will come close inshore and this in the past has led them into trouble. Between the seventeenth and nineteenth centuries the men of Lewis used to pursue them in boats off Gallan Head and Stornoway. They herded them into a bay, wounded one mortally, and when it ran ashore the rest would follow, up to fifty being finally stranded. In 1629, one hundred were killed off Stornoway with swords, and bows and arrows.§ In 1873 a herd tried to pass through the Clachan Sound between Seil and Luing – a passage navigable only at high tide. They stuck where the water shallowed, had no room to turn, and 192 were stranded. One of the great fin whales taken in the same trap two years earlier measured seventy-eight feet.

Occasional sperm whales (sixty feet) pass the Isles in summer. They are deep divers, able to sound for an hour, and when they surface spout twenty to forty times while they repay the oxygen-debt to their muscles.‖ They yield whalers ambergris and spermacetti. The latter is an oily wax stored in a cavity of the square-fronted head, and valued for machinery oil, ointments, and candles. The ambergris taken from the stomach may be worth £10,000 as a perfume stabilizer. This waxy ooze is formed round the undigested beaks of giant squid, on which the whale largely lives, feeding along the hundred-fathom line west of St Kilda. The great whales normally (but not invariably) hold their course to this line, which is the continental shelf. During the first half of this century, they were hunted from a Hebridean whaling station on Harris – Ardhasig on the north shore of West Loch Tarbert – operated by Norwegians. Sperm and blue whales

---

* 1929: Harmer.
† 1962: Engel. 1968: Matthews.
‡ 1695: Martin. (No evidence that he had interviewed witnesses.)
§ 1919: MacKenzie (quoting Dymes MS in British Museum).
‖ 1968: Matthews.

were the quarry. The station was reopened in the 1950s, but after some whales were taken it closed again. No whales are now hunted off the Hebrides.

Except for the sperm, all the great whales are baleen, or whale-bone whales, so named because they sieve plankton and krill through a whalebone filter of seven hundred blades, which can be as long as fifteen feet. The blades hang from the palate and have the inner side hairy, like a sheepskin rug. The enormous tongue, which can weigh a ton, ejects each mouthful of water through the sieve, when the rakers flick the food back into the gullet. As well as for oil and meat, they used to be hunted to provide women with corsets and towns with fuel for street-lighting. The baleens seen off the Hebrides are blue whales (a hundred feet), which are the world's biggest animals, weighing 150 tons, fin whales (eighty feet), Atlantic right whales (sixty feet), humpback whales (fifty feet), Rudolphi's rorqual (fifty feet), and lesser rorqual (thirty-three feet). The blue, fin, and right whales are now few in the northern hemisphere, for they are slow breeders (one calf in two years) and man has butchered more than a million since 1920. The blue whale is now in great danger of extinction: the 10,000 survivors* may be too few to find mates while they range for food over the world ocean. The passage of most of the great whales through Hebridean waters occurs largely unnoticed on their migrations between tropical and polar waters: in the one they breed, and in the other feed for nearly six months on rich plankton, for the richest plankton of the world ocean is found not in temperate seas like the Hebridean, but along the borders of the polar seas when the spring thaw is melting the pack-ice. The wealth of arctic sea-life is then incredibly great, the spring explosion far excelling that of British coastal waters. The surface sea so teems with plant life that diatoms often tinge the water bright green.

The truly Hebridean mammals are seals: the common seal and the grey or Atlantic seal. The common seal is most numerous in the Firth of Lorn, with colonies in the sea-lochs from Loch Nevis southward. In the Outer Hebrides, they chiefly frequent the quiet eastern rocks and bays, or the sounds between islands, but appear too on the west side at sheltered places. They bear their young in June, and the calves are much less open to accident than grey seals', for they can go to sea almost at once and be suckled there. Crofter-fishermen shoot them in the Firth of Lorn and elsewhere to reduce damage to fisheries. Their stomach contents when examined are surprisingly modest and weigh only 10 lb.

The grey seal is one of the world's rarer seals, and the Scottish stock the world's biggest. The principal Hebridean stations are North Rona, used by

---

* Estimate given at U.N. Stockholm Conference, 1972.

7a. St Kilda. The gannetry on Stac Lee and Stac an Armin.

7b. Gannet with young.

8a. Kittiwakes.

8b. Puffins.

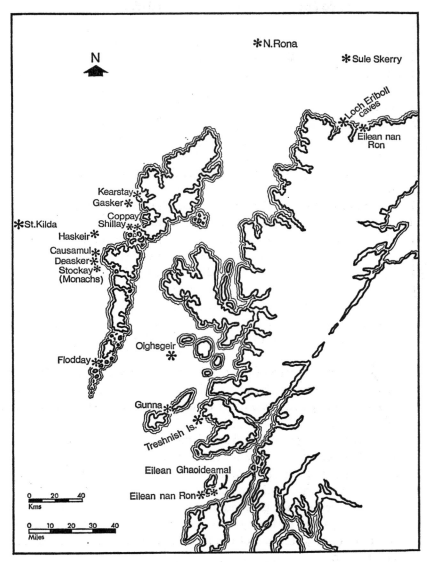

Map 15 *Grey Seal Breeding Stations*

7,500 seals in autumn, followed by Gasker with some 2,000, then Shillay, Haskeir, Monach, Treshnish, the skerries off Oronsay, and St Kilda, each with approximately 1,000 or less down to a few hundred. A dozen smaller stations are found on islets off the outer and inner isles. None in the Hebrides breed on islands inhabited by man. Grey seals concentrate at all these islands or skerries during the last four months of the year, but mostly in October, to calve and to mate, and later to change their coats. Copulation follows the calving after an interval of approximately three weeks. By this time the calves are weaned, but do not go to sea before shedding their first white fur and growing their sea-going coat – blue-grey for the female and grey-black for the male – and this takes two or three weeks from birth. Deserted by their parents, but endowed with a huge store of food in their fat, the pups have to make their own way to the sea, and when they finally do, range widely in the next few months between Ireland and Iceland – at the two extremes.*

Grey seals are six to eight feet long and weigh up to 560 lb. From prehistoric times until last century, they have given islanders a natural resource, providing food and sealskin clothing for home use and export, and oil for light. Being so vulnerable at breeding time, when they have to spend such a long time ashore in a small space, they were too easily killed by man. By the end of last century the Scottish population was alleged (without proper count) to be down to five hundred. In 1914, Parliament passed a protection Act, but the grey seals were saved less by law than by economic factors affecting man – the production of rubber boots and paraffin oil from 1850 onward, and the depopulation of outlying islands.

The boundless providence of the sea, its warmth, its inexhaustible plant and animal life, even the vast sands of its shelled animals, have nourished the islands directly and indirectly and given other benefits still to be reckoned, such as seaweed and sea-birds.

In winter storms, immense quantities of tangle-weed (laminaria) are cast up on western beaches. From earliest known times, the islesmen have gathered this tangle for fertilizing the machair. Whole communities used to come down with their horses and carts, pitchforks and creels, to gather this manna for manure, and in the eighteenth century for the manufacture of kelp, then a most remunerative industry. Nowadays they gather by lorry, and since much of it goes to the alginate industry (see chapter 9) instead of the land, more use than hitherto is made of chemical fertilizer.

* 1969: Darling and Boyd.

The sea's destructive powers, gradually eroding the gneiss and more swiftly the basalt, have not been without aid to wild-life, and therefore to man. A cruise by boat around the western cliffs of Rum can be enlightening, for seen at close quarters they show the sea in process of carving the solid rock. The waves seize upon faults and excavate creeks, tunnels, and caves by compressing air into every cleft – these big Atlantic rollers can fall upon rock with a blow measured at three tons to a square foot. Alternating compression and expansion of air loosens the rock so that caves or tunnels are drilled, often to either side of more resistant rock that becomes first a small headland, then a natural arch, and when the bridge falls, a stack. Spouting caves are formed by the enormous inner compression exploding through a weakness in the roof. A spouter easily seen is on the south-west coast of Iona, but a better example of such a sea-bore is at Islivig on the west coast of Lewis, seventy-five yards in from the open shore. Explosions in a tunnelled cave may bring down the roof, leaving a big inland cauldron. A good example is at the Griminish headland of North Uist, which is also bored 150 yards from side to side by a big arch. The Hebrides abound in natural arches, caves, and stacks. Great arches through which boats can sail are found in the Shiants at Garbh Eilean, at Sula Sgeir, and Mingulay. The finest stacks are St Kilda's Stac Lee (544 feet) and Stac an Armin (627 feet), the latter the highest in the British Isles, and the Great Stack of Handa. One of the longest caves is MacKinnon's Cave near Gribun on Mull, about two hundred yards in length with three chambers. The sea also quarries cliff-faces high above sea-level by hurling at them boulders, blocks, and stones. Thus hewn out by winter storm-seas, the cliffs, stacks, and skerries of the Hebrides provide in autumn breeding-platforms for grey seals, and in spring ideal sites for nesting sea-birds.

Gannets, petrels and auks are the sea-bird groups for which the Hebrides are best known. The gannet or solan goose is Britain's largest sea-bird with a wing-span of six feet. When seen diving it cannot be mistaken for any other bird: wings folded to shape an arrowhead, it plummets from a hundred feet or more. The world's greatest gannetry is St Kilda. The gannets concentrate on three gabbro islands four miles north of Hirta (the main island): Boreray, which is cliffed to 1245 feet, and its two sea-stacks, Stac Lee and Stac an Armin. A count in 1959 showed 45,000 pairs – nearly half the British population, and nearly forty per cent of the world's population. Another big gannetry is on Sula Sgeir, an oceanic rock forty miles north of Lewis. Gannets have been eaten by islanders from earliest times, and over the last four centuries the men of Ness have made annual expeditions to Sula Sgeir to harvest the birds in early September. The Sula Sgeir gannetry is now the only one from which birds are culled today, this

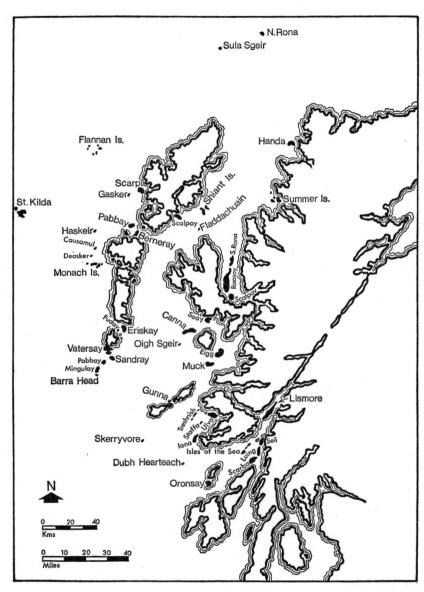

Map 16 *Principal Islets, Skerries, and Outlying Isles*

by special legislation under the Bird Protection Act of 1954. The men take some 3,000 young birds or 'gugas' while they are still on the nest but deserted by their parents. Last century the men would spend a fortnight on the island (now only a few days), taking the birds as they 'ripened', and salting them in the barrel before return to Lewis. They were exported all over the world to emigrants, mostly in Australia, North America, and New Zealand. They are clearly an acquired taste, for while one islander extols them to me as 'not unlike good kippers', Dr Morton Boyd finds them 'more akin to a rather tough goose that has been pickled in cod liver oil for at least a year'.

The Hebrides have four species of petrel – the fulmar, Manx shearwater, storm petrel, and Leach's petrel. St Kilda again has Britain's biggest fulmar colony, 20,000 pairs nesting on the great face of Conachair on Hirta, to which must be added 10,000 non-breeding birds. James Fisher thought that these accounted for only half the total on the seven St Kilda islands. St Kilda held the only British colony until 1878, when fulmars from the Faeroes came south to Shetland, then to Orkney and North Rona, spreading from there southward along the British coasts, until now there are five hundred colonies totalling 100,000 breeding pairs. This spectacular advance, all the more remarkable for the bird's laying only one egg annually, has been aided by the increase of trawlers jettisoning fish-offal. Fulmars at first required for their nest site the top parts of tall cliffs, but now they accept almost anything. I have found them on North Uist on easily accessible rocks twenty feet above the sea, and Darling and Boyd report them from sand dunes on the Monach Isles. They are truly oceanic birds. The young range in winter at least as far as the Barents Sea and the Newfoundland Banks.

Manx shearwater especially favour the Inner Hebrides on Rum, Eigg, Canna, and the Treshnish Isles. On Rum they burrow into grassy ledges on the cliffs and into the open mountain slopes above 2000 feet on Allival. At the back of the hole they lay (like all other petrel) only one egg, after which they feed by night and stop flying by day. I recommend the ascent of Allival at midnight in May. The hill-top seems to be alive, burbling underfoot from the subterranean chirping and screeching of many hundreds of birds. As their mates come and go you will hear the swish and whirr of wings but will never glimpse them in the air. Over the sea they fly low in stiff-winged glides, banking to expose alternately the black upper- and white underparts, shearing the wave-caps with their wing-tips. Like other petrels they never go ashore except to breed.

Storm petrels and Leach's breed on most outlying islands, like St Kilda, the Flannans, Sula Sgeir, North Rona, Shillay, and others. Large numbers use

North Rona, but the bigger St Kilda islands are the principal breeding ground in Britain for Leach's.

The auk family are heavily represented throughout the Isles by guillemot and razorbill, and by puffin north and west of the Treshnish. Great auk bred on St Kilda until 1840. They stood $2\frac{1}{2}$ feet high, with vestigial wings like the penguin's, for they had totally adapted to sea-surface life. They ranged across the North Atlantic and were ruthlessly killed by fishermen for feathers, food, and bait. Egg collectors paid as much as 315 guineas for one egg. The bird was doomed. Its rarity became such that when the last was taken on St Kilda the men, not recognizing it, killed the bird out of fear. Four years later the world's last was killed off Iceland.

The puffin is the most numerous auk of the Hebrides. They choose nesting sites on the turfy tops of sea-cliffs, into which they burrow. Basalt islands with friable soil therefore suit them best. There are large colonies on the Treshnish Isles, Eigg, Canna, the Ascribs and Fladda-chuain off Skye, and the Shiants, especially the latter. Rum and Handa have small colonies. Gneiss islands have puffinries on Barra Head, Mingulay, Gasker, and Haskeir (the two latter west of Harris and North Uist respectively). On St Kilda they outnumber all other birds. No count has been made, but estimates indicate several hundred thousand. They disperse in winter over the North Atlantic, by which time they have shed the red-blue-yellow sheath of the bill, which has become dull in colour.

Guillemots and razorbills breed far more widely than puffins. The two birds are usually but not always associated, with the razorbills lesser in number. They are ledge-nesters, laying pear-shaped eggs to prevent rolling, but since the razorbill prefers niches or tufts to open ledges its single egg is shaped less acutely than the guillemot's. Guillemots have nested on Rockall, three hundred miles out from the mainland, and 13,850 pairs breed on St Kilda, but they seem to find granite and gabbro less to their liking than Torridonian sandstone, for the relatively small cliffs of Handa carry double their number.

Handa lies half a mile off the Sutherland west coast. It measures $1\frac{1}{2}$ miles by 1 mile. At the north end the sandstone cliffs rise sheer out of the sea to 300 feet. They are cut by a geo (from the Norse gja, a creek) where the Great Stack has been chiselled out of the main cliff. The walls of the geo are the sea-bird metropolis of the north-west seaboard. In May and June, a visitor approaching the edge is prepared for a memorable sight by the birds' wild clamour. The ledges are so packed with brown guillemots and black razorbills that their glossy backs hide the rock. Puffins whirring off the top of the Stack splay out scarlet legs behind. Kittiwake colonies build their seaweed nests lower down the face. A count in 1962 by the Royal Society for the Protection of Birds (who from that year have managed the island as a bird sanctuary by agreement with the owner), gives 800 puffins, 4,000 fulmars, 12,000 razorbills, 14,000 kittiwakes, and approximately 60,000 guillemots.

The Treshnish Isles are a string of eight basalt islets and numerous skerries four miles out from north-west Mull. The southmost is the Dutchman's Cap. Two miles to its north, the isle of Lunga carries a multitude of nesting auks, petrels, shags, and kittiwakes. They richly manure the grass on top, to which a thousand barnacle geese fly in winter, together with hundreds of thrushes, blackbirds, and starlings. This fertilizing service by sea-birds has provided pasture on large numbers of rocky islets, which although uninhabited by man are grazed by his ferried sheep, and were formerly grazed by his cattle too, which would be swum across where the passage was not too wide.

One of the more splendid sights of the Hebrides in late September and early October is the vast migration of geese to the empty flats of western Islay between Gruinart and Loch Gorm. At sundown, if the weather is fine, the gaggles fly in against luminous skies: Greenland white-fronts, barnacles, and greylags, day after day they come, until the machair and arable land, and offshore islands, have many thousands. Wedges of whooper swans come down on Loch Gorm, their trumpet call sounding over the moorland and their wings thrashing. Fifty have been counted in the air together. The water meadows and stubble at the Gruinart flats are the favourite feeding places for the barnacle geese. If you try to make a close approach, the birds will cloud the sky and nearly deafen the ear, although the more musical *kow-yow* of the white-fronts can always be distinguished from the gruff yapping of the barnacles. A count of barnacle geese on Islay in March 1971 (by Malcolm A. Ogilvie of the Wildfowl Trust) gave a total of 15,100 – more than two-thirds of Britain's population – an extraordinary increase since March 1961, when the number was 5,500. The cause has not been established but may be due to an increase in population following a succession of good breeding seasons, and to a redistribution, rather than to any change in the farming regime on Islay. White-front numbers over the last decade have varied from 1,500 to 3,000, while greylags have decreased from 600 to 200, for there has been a general withdrawal of the species from outlying wintering areas to the lusher farms of lowland Scotland. The migration of geese and swans back to the Arctic breeding grounds starts around Easter.

These are only a few of the breeding and wintering stations of the Hebrides. There are smaller ones on well nigh every island, and these have been increasingly used as the human population has dwindled. Birds or any other animals

that must congregate in large number in small space, whether to rest on migration, or to winter, or to breed, are at dire risk from man's hand. Large passages of
snipe, variable in number, come down on the marshes of Tiree in October – so
Tiree, it has been claimed, has the best snipe-shooting in Europe: four guns in
November may shoot six hundred birds in a week. The most vulnerable are
breeding sea-birds and grey seals, hence their concentration in such large number
on a small number of outlying or inaccessible rocks. It is ironical that Handa and
St Kilda were thus made habitable for man, who but for that harvest could not
have lived there. On South Uist, the duck and barnacle geese flying in to Loch
Ardvule draw the fire of wildfowlers. Yet for all instances of the kind, the
Hebrides remain for the sea-bird true sanctuary.

Like the herring gull, the dark green shag is one of the most rapidly increasing
sea-birds of Britain. Confining itself to rocky coasts, it is more abundant along
the eastern shores of the islands than along the sandy west. Cormorants, though
less numerous, may appear anywhere. They are the only webbed bird without a
mechanism for oiling their feathers, and so draw attention by spreading their
wings to dry each time they come to land, or to perch on a buoy. The cormorant
is one of our deepest diving birds and has been caught in the fishermen's nets
more than 130 feet below the surface.*

Many land and freshwater birds adapt to island life by becoming partially
marine in feeding habit, like the redshank and greenshank. Herons have made a
home on the sand-swamped reefs of the Monach Isles, eight miles west of North
Uist, where they nest in an empty house. The beaches have all the usual summer
birds, dunlin, ringed plovers, oystercatchers, sheld-ducks, curlews, sandpipers,
and many others. Of these, the most gorgeous is the sheld-duck: plumage white,
but with a broad orange band across the chest and shoulders, a dark green head
with a crimson beak, and black wing-tips. Common as they are in spring, in
July they migrate to Heligoland to moult, thus are often never seen by holidaymakers, who tend also to miss many of the temporary or winter visitors to beach,
bay, and machair, such as whooper swans, mergansers, long-tailed duck, brent
geese, scoters, turnstones, redshanks and greenshanks, sanderlings, and bar-
tailed godwits.

The three latter waders prefer the long open beaches to the small ones favoured
by most birds. All have their preferences for one site or another. Machair and
grassland draw large flocks of golden plover in spring and autumn, geese in
winter. But from May to mid-summer, the machair belongs to the lark and pee-

* 1969: Fitter.

wit, to the lark especially if we grant command by sheer volume of sound: rising at half-past three in the morning from dew-drenched machair, they sing on and on, eighteen hours a day in May and more in June. If instead we judge by visible presence, the peewits are the possessors, always crying and falling out of the sky, and frolicking over the land: no bird seems to enjoy a machair more than they.

The starling is the common bird of the crofts. Wherever the ruin of some old blackhouse offers a roost, a few starlings will use it, but the large flocks use the cliffs and caves. On Lewis, the fields at the back of bays may be blackened by starlings. On the Harris machairs, where six big bays scoop the west coast, they abound in small flocks of a dozen to twenty. In north-west Coll and all over Tiree, larger flocks of starlings and sparrows appear together. Nearly all the starlings on Tiree roost in caves at the south-west headland of Caenn a' Mhara. The machairs everywhere are alive with sound and movement, as well as colour.

The Hebrides offer an immense variety of habitat, especially to water-birds. Throughout the Long Isle, the thousands of lochs and lochans have an extremely wide range of site and shape, able to accommodate most birds' preferences: lochs set on machair, arable ground, moorland, and rock; lochs peaty and shingly, deep and shallow, islanded and open, twisty and straight, many crowded with water-lilies, and some fringed by reeds. Nesting or feeding on these are swans and geese, coot, teal, sheld-ducks, eiders, mallard, mergansers, black-throated divers, red-necked phalaropes, tufted ducks, herons, and many others.

An excellent example of this varied habitat is in South Uist at Loch Druidibeg, which in 1958 was made a Nature Reserve under the Nature Conservancy. Wildly convoluted, heavily islanded, it measures two miles by one. Beinn Mhor and Hecla tower craggily out of the moor behind. Massive clumps of golden whin and red rhododendron fringe the north shore between spruce, pine, and, most oddly, a few monkey-puzzles. The loch is Britain's chief breeding ground for the native greylag goose, which on the mainland is rare as a breeding species, and elsewhere on the Hebrides breeds only in small numbers on Lewis, Benbecula, North Uist, and perhaps on south Coll. Here, on Loch Druidibeg, the geese nest on the islets, so that sight of them is lost in spring; but in June, when the goslings are hatched and in the water, the geese lead them out to the machair lochans that shine along the buffer-strip of inbye croftland between machair and moor. In autumn, the September sky can be noisy with young and old flying to and fro in family parties. In winter, they share the machair with barnacle geese and white-fronts flying in from Greenland and Iceland.

Islay is more richly stocked with birds than the other islands. More than 180 species (half the British breeding species) have been recorded, nearly a hundred of which stay to breed.

Among the larger birds, the heron is plentiful, sea-fishing along the sheltered lochs, sounds, and channels. Pheasants, introduced to Britain by the Romans, are found on most of the Inner Hebrides, notably Islay, Colonsay, Gigha, and Jura. On Islay their hard *korr-kok* is heard everywhere except the Rhinns, and the bird constantly seen. Black grouse are present on Islay and Mull, and red grouse common though not plentiful on Hebridean moors. Kestrels are common but merlin few. Golden eagles range through all the Hebrides. They build eyries on hill-country from 1000 feet down to very low levels – I have visited an eyrie built in the gully of a 50-foot sea-cliff in Mull. Peregrine falcons are now rare, yet they range from Islay to Handa and out to St Kilda.

The bays and beaches of Skye are much poorer in bird-life than any other large island, but the mountains and moors are relatively rich in birds of prey. On the summit of Sgurr Alasdair in June I have watched four eagles, harassed by ravens and gulls, circle the peak. Buzzards are present on all large islands, numerously on Mull, where on the forested east side they perch on posts alongside the road.

The white-tailed sea-eagle bred throughout the isles, including St Kilda, until last century, when like the osprey they were killed out by sportsmen, keepers, shepherds, and by nest robbers. Final extinction came during the period 1879 to 1890. The peregrine and golden eagle have in turn been put in danger by the widespread use of persistent organo-chloride pesticides. The predators are most vulnerable, for while their prey may be only slightly contaminated, they, at the top of the food chain, receive a concentration of poison. The result has been a disastrous decline in breeding success. A high percentage of eggs laid are infertile, and have thin shells that break too easily. The chemicals found in eagles' eggs have been dieldrin, aldrin (now withdrawn from the market but persisting), endrin, keptachlor, DDT, and BHC. The osprey, since its return as a breeding bird to the Cairngorms in 1952, has suffered likewise. Ospreys have in recent years been reported from the inner and outer isles, but are not as yet known to nest. In the isles they might have a better chance of survival than on the more heavily contaminated mainland.

A rare British bird shot nearly to extinction in Scotland is the chough, now making a slow recovery in the Hebrides. Like a smaller, more elegant raven, it has the same glossy blue-black plumage, but a bright red beak and wings. It nests, and may readily be seen, at the most southerly cliffs of the Hebrides – the Mull of Oa and the Rhinns on Islay.

The isolation of land birds and mammals on the islands has caused several species to differentiate. It seems doubtful if any existing bird-species have been longer than 12,000 years in the Hebrides, except as summer visitors before the Lomond readvance, when July temperatures reached 10 °C. (50 °F.) – the same as Iceland's today. Later cold may again have put the islands out of bounds. If land birds other than arctic did not move in until around 10,000 BP, we may think this a short period for evolutionary change, yet some British birds have differentiated from European in that time; in still less, five Hebridean birds have differentiated from British: hedge sparrow, song-thrush, wren, stone-chat, and rock pipit. These had probably all reached the Hebrides around 7000 BP, when birch and hazel had spread across the isles at the close of the Boreal period. Their changes have been mostly in feather pigments, giving a darker colour (in response, it has been doubtfully suggested,* to wetter climate and cloudier sky; but Hebridean skies are in fact brighter than the mainland's).

In St Kilda, changes have gone further in the wren: it is slightly larger, has a greyer head, whiter eye-stripe, lighter underparts, more strongly marked wing-bars, and a different song. When the bird was proclaimed a new species (it is really a sub-species) in 1884, it came under such persecution by egg and skin collectors that an Act of Parliament for its protection had to be passed in 1904. The wren's present population on St Kilda is thought to be around two hundred pairs. They may be seen and heard behind Village Bay of Hirta, but their real home is the puffinries of the cliff-edges, where manure provides insect food.

Several land mammals have also differentiated. Apart from introduced species, it seems unlikely that any of the present mammals entered the Hebrides later than the Atlantic period 7,000 to 5,000 years ago.† Twenty-four species of wild land-mammal are now distributed unequally over hundreds of islands. They are shrew (common, pygmy, and water), hedgehog, mole, bat (pipistrelle and long-eared), hare (brown and blue), rabbit, vole (short-tailed and bank), mouse (house and long-tailed field), brown rat, stoat, weasel, pine marten, otter, fox, and deer (red, roe, and fallow). Four domestic animals have long since gone wild – sheep, goat, ferret, and cat. Sub-species have evolved mostly from the insectivores and rodents.

Common shrews are present on Gigha, Jura, Mull, Raasay, and South Rona, with a sub-species on Islay differentiated by size and colour. There are none in the outer Hebrides. Pygmy shrews are on all main islands, but water shrews are recorded only from Mull, Skye, and Raasay. Hedgehogs are found only on some

* 1969: Fitter.
† 1968: Matthews.

inner isles, notably Mull. The Hebrides had no moles till 1800, when they were introduced to Mull by a ship dumping earth-ballast from Morven. They have since spread to all parts of the island.

The brown and blue hares are on both inner and outer isles, with Scottish and Irish sub-species restricted to Islay, Jura, and Mull. Rabbits were introduced to all larger islands in medieval times, and by 1549 had become numerous .* Later they were taken by lighthouse keepers to many islets like the Flannans. They continue to thrive on most islands despite reduction from pest-proportion by myxomatosis.

Short-tailed voles have a Hebridean sub-species *Microtus agrestis exsul*, which is the common vole of the islands except Lewis, with further sub-species on Islay, Gigha, Eigg, and Muck. Bank voles are absent from the Hebrides except Raasay and Mull, where they are darker and heavier than mainland voles (Raasay voles are twice their weight) and are thought to be possibly not a sub-species but survivors of an original Scandinavian race.†

No harvest mice are now recorded for the Hebrides, although present in Lewis in 1903.‡ Skye has the long-tailed field mouse, *Apodemus sylvaticus sylvaticus*, but all other islands have the Hebridean sub-species, *A.s. hebridensis*, which is the common field-mouse of the Isles and differs from *sylvaticus* by its larger size, greater weight, longer feet, and shorter ears. Rum and St Kilda have sub-species of their own. The St Kilda field-mouse of Hirta, *A.s. hirtensis*, is related to the Hebridean mouse but is again distinguished by larger size on all points noted above. Matthews (1968) suggests that it may have been introduced by man, but Darling and Boyd (1969) consider that it differs from mainland mice in ways that may be too distinct to have arisen in the short period that has allowed other Hebridean mice to differ in size and colour from the mainland species. If they are right, St Kilda may have the only mammal of Scotland that has survived the Ice Age – a feasible survival since the island lay beyond the edge of the great ice-cap.

Stoats and weasels are confined to inner islands. Jura and Islay have a sub-species of stoat, smaller than the mainland breed and closer to the Scandinavian. Stoats were one of the earliest immigrants after the Ice Age,§ and therefore are present on most inner isles; weasels were late-comers, and so are present on few. Other early immigrants were pine martens and otters. The pine marten, which has been absent from the Hebrides for a hundred years, reappeared on Raasay in

* 1549: Monro.
† 1968: Matthews.
‡ 1903: Mackenzie.
§ 1968: Matthews.

1971, when a single specimen was identified beyond doubt.* This confirms other recent sightings there. The otter is a powerful swimmer able to go anywhere, and thus the only carnivore now inhabiting the Outer Hebrides. The fox now appears only on Skye, although it was abundant on Mull† and probably other islands until around 1800. Polecats once had a thin spread through the Hebrides even to Lewis, but died out early in the twentieth century. They were reported from Mull in 1950,‡ but this report on investigation has proved to be of feral ferrets (numerous, some large with a black muzzle and a dark stripe down the back).

Fallow deer are found on Mull, and in the woodlands of south Islay, to which they were introduced in the fourteenth century by John, the Lord of the Isles.§ They are natives of the Mediterranean coasts and may have been first brought to Britain by the Romans. Roe deer are native to Britain, but now their only island habitats are in Islay and Seil. Red deer in the Outer Hebrides are concentrated on the Clisham hills of Harris and Lewis, with small herds in North Uist and Pabbay in the Sound of Harris. On the Inner Hebrides they are much more widespread and numerous, especially on Jura (4,000 head) and Rum (1,500), the latter stock being managed by the Nature Conservancy, who acquired the island as a Nature Reserve in 1957. Since 1954, deer have become an increasingly valuable crop for export to Germany, the annual value to exporters of Scottish venison being estimated in 1970‖ at one million pounds sterling, which equals the value of the salmon catch. (The landowners receive only half that figure, to which must be added the sporting value, worth quarter of a million.)

Two domestic animals now feral come close to being wild animals in the true sense. These are the Soay sheep of St Kilda and the goat. Soay is a small island 1100 feet high to the north-west of Hirta. Its sheep have dark brown coats (some light brown) of short wool. The rams' horns take a wide curve. They are agile rock-climbers and cannot be herded: on any attempt to work them with a sheep-dog they scatter and make for the cliff-ledges. They may well have been brought in by Neolithic man. Evidence on the ground shows that St Kilda was inhabited before the Vikings settled there a thousand years ago, and Soay sheep appear to be the same as those of Neolithic farmers in Britain. When St Kilda was evacuated in 1930, 107 Soays were transferred to Hirta. They have increased tenfold in thirty years, but numbers fluctuate steeply according to weather and pasture.

* 1972: Alison Lambie, *Scotsman*.
† 1695: Martin.
‡ 1970: Macnab.
§ 1967: Donald.
‖ Red Deer Commission.

Goats descend from the wild goats of Asia and the Greek islands, and their bones have been found in the Mesolithic caves at Oban (*c*.6500 BP). Goats revert to the wild state within a very short time of escaping domestication. In Scotland only the fittest survive, for the kids are born in the harsh winter weather of January and February. They are found on Islay, Jura, Mull, Rum, Eigg, South Rona, and Harris. From isle to isle they differ widely in size, colour, and horn-curve. Their spectacular grazing grounds are the coastal cliffs. Always they move with an unhurried deliberation. On Islay at the Mull of Oa, a troop of brown goats daintily pick their way round the base of the cliffs, cropping gullies and grassy bowls. Rum has over a hundred black and white goats, large hairy animals, which graze on the high terraced sea-cliffs. But the most splendid goats known to me in the Hebrides are those of the Ross of Mull. They graze the high-angle talus slopes that fall to the sea from a long line of cliffs near Malcolm's Point. They are white, a herd of forty pairs, and the males have the longest horns I have seen on goats except alpine ibex.

Rum supports a score of free-running ponies, smaller and hardier than mainland breeds. There is no evidence of their origin. The traditional story, that they swam ashore from a wrecked galleon of the Spanish Armada, has to be discounted through lack of evidence of the wreck. In earlier centuries they were dun-coloured with a black eel-stripe down the back, but the use of different stallions has produced white, black, grey, and chestnut animals. Since 1957, the Nature Conservancy have been re-establishing the early type. They maintain the stock to perpetuate a breed of national repute, and to provide pack-animals for transport of deer carcases. Surplus stock is sold.

The reptiles of the Hebrides are slow-worm, common lizard, and adder. All of them can swim, and the adder's ability is shown by the discovery of one specimen many miles out at sea.* The slow-worm (eight inches) of the inner and outer isles is the only reptile of the Outer Hebrides, where it has local distribution. The common lizard (five inches) and the adder (twenty to thirty inches), fare no farther than larger inner islands. The diamond pattern down the adder's brown back conceals it well in its moorland habitat, but not on the marram dunes, where it likes to bask in the sun. Some have differentiated from mainland species by less emphatic marking with lighter colour. Widespread as they are, the reptiles are not often seen.

Outer Isles have no amphibians. All the inner have frog and toad. The common (smooth) newt is recorded only from Skye, Rum, and Tiree: the palmate newt

---

* 1964: Smith.

(Scotland's most common) only from Skye, Mull, and Rum. Since the amphibians' skin cannot endure salt water, they were presumably introduced to the isles in their tadpole stage.

An insect that brings notoriety to the wetter Inner Hebrides (but not to the windy Outer) is the ubiquitous midge. On Rum they are such a scourge that earlier this century estate workers in summer were paid midge money to subsidize the tobacco they needed for smoke-screen. Recent research on midge-control has brought no useful result. Bees, dragonflies, flying ants, certain flies, ticks, and spiders make rewarding studies, and still more so the lepidoptera.

A surprising feature of exposed islands like Barra and Tiree in mid-summer is the profusion of common blue butterflies seen flitting over the machair. That creatures so weightless and delicately made can survive outer island wind seems to border on the miraculous. Their evolutionary trend,* one might think, must be towards small size; any butterfly of large wing-span is in great danger of being blown seaward. Obvious as this may seem, there has evolved throughout the Hebrides one of the larger British butterflies – the sub-species, *scotica*, of the dark green fritillary *Argynnis aglaia*. The ordinary dark green appears on nearly all islands, with the darker and larger Hebridean variety on many of them. Both have managed to live by avoiding windswept localities. One particularly interesting exception is found on the low, shelterless island of Flodday, south-west of Barra, where the dark green (*A. aglaia*) has evolved an exceedingly small form of paler colour.

The Hebrides have several other fritillaries: the pearl-bordered, found only on Rum; a sub-species of the small pearl-bordered found on Rum, Soay, Skye, Scalpay, and outer islands; marsh fritillary only on Islay, Jura, Mull, Rum, Tiree, and Gunna; and the green veined on St Kilda.

The Hebrides have two arctic butterflies that must have entered Scotland before the end of the Ice Age. These are the Scots argus of Skye, Scalpay, and Raasay, and the large heath of both inner and outer isles. The meadow brown is common, but has produced a handsome sub-species, *Maniola splendida*, larger and more richly brown with brighter orange, on Barra, Vatersay, and South Uist. Most islands are likely to have peacock, grayling, small heath, small white, green veined white, and small tortoiseshell, and the inner to have clouded yellow. Several moths of the Inner Hebrides are rare: transparent burnet on Skye, Rum and Gunna; belted beauty on Rum and the machair of inner isles; the grey moth, death's-head hawkmoth, and convolvulus hawkmoth on Canna. All

* 1957: Ford.

islands with much heather have magpie moth. No full record of Hebridean lepidoptera has yet been made, and those named above are only a few selected from the many species to be seen.

My aim in the last three chapters has been to show in broad outline, with salient features, how the Hebrides were formed, and although isolated as islands were related to Britain and Europe; and how on the retreat of the Pleistocene ice their land and sea became warmed and populated until their endowment of plant and animal life had grown rich enough to support man. When he began to arrive in the Hebrides 6,000 years ago, his heritage was prepared and waiting. He came to islands stocked with natural resources beyond his basic needs, but not to an Eden where fruit might be plucked from the bough. Man would need strength, resourcefulness, ingenuity, and tenacity to win a living and to get leisure for a life above an animal plane. And these qualities he had. To conserve and enrich his land, rather than to exploit and desolate it, he also needed wisdom and knowledge. But these were not powers that he possessed in sufficient degree.

5

Man: the Distant Past

Scotland has no record of man until post-glacial times around 6400 B.C., but since that is a carbon date for the first deposition of alluvial clays under which a dug-out canoe was found in the Tay valley near Perth, not for the canoe itself, it carries an element of doubt. The first firm dates are from Fife. Ten readings from charcoal found in hearths range from 6100 ± 255 B.C. to 4165 ± 110 B.C. In southern England, small numbers of men had appeared during the Old Stone Age, coming and going over several hundred thousand years as glaciation waned or waxed. If ever they reached Scotland during the warm interglacials, all trace has been wiped out by the last big advance of ice. The first known men in Scotland were Mesolithic, or Middle Stone Age men, so named to indicate a chronological succession, and not because they represented a cultural advance on the Old Stone Age of Britain or Europe. In fact they fell far short of the standards in art and artifact achieved by the earlier Magdalenian people. The Hebrides received their first men later than the mainland, around 3800 B.C. (carbon date) in the mid-Atlantic period, when temperatures were 4°F. above present. Forests of birch and hazel heavily covered the islands, and wild-life abounded in mainland woods.

Mesolithic men kept no domestic animals and sowed no crops. They were nomadic hunters and fishermen, living in tiny groups usually of a single family, each one of which could have been responsible for many of the one hundred site-deposits that have so far been found in Scotland.* Thus their total number may not have exceeded a few dozen, or at most a few hundred. They dispersed widely along the coasts of Ayrshire, the Clyde, Argyll from Kintyre to Ardnamurchan, and the Hebrides. This western pattern of dispersal suggests that they came from

* 1962: Atkinson.

Ireland, and some confirmation is given by their stone artifacts, which are of the same very primitive character found at Larne on the coast of Antrim. Life for these people must have been most precarious, both by lack of community strength and craft-knowledge, and by chance of accident to their strongest members.

In choosing ground on which to live, the Mesolithic men showed a marked preference for islands, or caves, and everywhere for open shores, which are now raised beaches at the twenty-five- and fifty-foot levels, for the land was then taking its last isostatic rise. They chose sites very much as experienced campers might choose today – on dry ground with natural drainage, close to fresh water, and sheltered from wind. Other important needs were shore rocks from which shell-fish could be gathered, and ground that was clear of undergrowth and lurking wolves. The brown bear, later to win fame as *Ursus Caledoniensis* in the Roman circus, was plentiful on the mainland. I know from travel in the central Himalaya, where women go daily to the woods to gather firewood (and brown bear are probably less numerous than they were in Scotland) that few upper villages are without women scarred by accidentally panicked bear. The Meso-lithic man's choice of island and beach sites would be based on more than shell-fish supplies.

Artifacts of the Mesolithic people have been discovered throughout the Hebrides, most notably on Colonsay and Oronsay, Islay, Tiree, Coll, Skye, and Lewis. Associated with these finds are several caves in a cliff at the back of Oban Bay, and a raised beach site on the island of Risga on Loch Sunart. The Oronsay, Risga, and Oban sites were excavated last century, but thus far radio-carbon tests have been given only to an Oronsay midden, where a piece of bone has been dated 3800 B.C., and an oyster shell 3065 ± 210 B.C. The earlier figure when corrected becomes 4600 B.C.

On Oronsay and other Argyll islands, large conical mounds on otherwise flat ground between beach and machair had long aroused curiosity. In Gaelic legend they were known as sitheans (pronounced sheeans), or fairy knolls. Three of these were opened on the eastern side of Oronsay in the early 1880s.* They were found to be sandhills covering huge dumps of limpet shells and other kitchen refuse of Mesolithic families. The dumps had been made in hollows, but the shifting of sand by wind had raised them high. It has been estimated† that ten people could have built such a dump in seven years.

At Oban, when the new town was rising in the period 1869 to 1894, and quarry-

* 1954: Lacaille.
† R. J. C. Atkinson.

Correction of Radiocarbon dates

Radiocarbon dates are only approximately correct, but are valuable as holding a constant relationship to each other. Comparison of C14 dates with tree-ring dates, which are exact, shows that C14 dates for the particular period 5000–1000 B.C. are too young on the following scale:

> 200 years at 1000 B.C.
>
> 350 years at 2000 B.C.
>
> 500 years at 2500 B.C.

a maximum of 800 years at 4000 B.C.

When the carbon dates for man's first arrival in Scotland and the Hebrides are converted to real or calendar years, the result is:

MESOLITHIC MAN	carbon date	real date	climate
Fife: charcoal in hearth	6100 B.C.	6100 B.C.	Boreal
Isle of Oronsay: bone	3800 B.C.	4600 B.C.	Atlantic
NEOLITHIC MAN			
Isle of Arran: charcoal	3160 B.C.	3800 B.C.	late Atlantic

As new discoveries are made, these figures are likely to be further back-dated.

ARCHAEOLOGICAL TIME SCALE
(dates are approximate, not precise,
and calendar, not carbon)

Age	Hebrides	Scotland	England
Palaeolithic	No record	No record	400,000 B.P.
Mesolithic	4600 B.C.	6100 B.C.	7000 B.C.
Neolithic	3800 B.C.		4200 B.C. (C14 = 3500)
Bronze	1600 B.C.	1700 B.C.	1700 B.C.
	to	to	to
Iron	400 B.C.	450 B.C.	500 B.C.
	to	to	to
	A.D. 400	A.D. 400	A.D. 400

men were working on low cliffs along the edge of a fifty-foot raised beach, where George Street now runs, they discovered seven caves. Three of these had deposits of stone and bone artifacts and animal debris, similar to those of Oronsay and Risga.*

* Ibid.

At all sites the stone manufactures were extremely primitive: narrow pebbles mostly under four inches in length, much abraded at the edges and perhaps used for scraping flesh off bone and shell; chisels, picks, and choppers of flaked stone; heavier cutting stones, given their edge by flaking and grinding, and apparently used on an anvil to cleave bone; and hammer stones of varied size. There were no arrowheads, although these have been found at other Mesolithic sites. Oronsay had only a hundred poor-quality flints, Oban none. The men had not yet discovered the nearest flint beds at Carsaig in Mull, and in Morvern and Ardnamurchan.

The bone tools were barbed harpoons, a fish hook, an axehead cut out of red deer antler, one needle, numerous spikes, awls for piercing hide, pins of polished bone and antler, and slivers of bone that might have been used for flensing and polishing. One Oban cave had the broken-up skeletons of a man and child, which have not yet been carbon-dated.

The shell debris was limpet, whelk, mussel, cockle, solen (razor-shell), scallop, oyster, crab, snail, and cowrie. The cowries were each pierced in two places, and were clearly meant to be strung as necklaces. The greater bulk of the debris was limpet, a most nourishing food, valued in historical times and still eaten today in the Outer Hebrides. (I have shared a plateful with crofters of west Lewis.)

The bird bones were great auk, guillemot, razorbill, gannet, shag, cormorant, sheld-duck, merganser, gull, tern, ringed plover, water-rail, goose, and swan. They reveal a sea-bird life unchanged to the present day. The absence of woodland birds seems surprising, although sea-birds would be more plentiful, and larger.

The fish debris was tope (the six-foot shark), saithe, haddock, skate, grey mullet, wrasse, sea-bream, dogfish, angel fish, thornback ray, and conger eel. The absence of mackerel is surprising, but many of the bones could not be identified. All harpoons were pierced at the handle to take line, which may have been of spun gut, but not all the fish were speared. Hooks were made, but only one has been found (on Risga). No wooden spears have survived, although they must have been used, their tips hardened by fire, to take mammals.

The mammal bones were wild ox, red and roe deer, goat, boar, wild cat, pine marten, otter, badger, fox, weasel, hare, vole, and bat. The sea-mammals were grey and common seal, rorqual, and dolphin. Dog bones appeared in an Oban cave, but the signs were that this had been a late intruder. Notable absentees are bear and wolf with whom man was clearly not trying conclusions. The smaller pelts when stitched would serve for clothing, and the larger hides for bed, tent, and coracle.

The coracle, made of hides stretched over a light wooden frame, would certainly be used in preference to the dug-out canoe, which was too heavy and far too narrow in the beam to survive in Hebridean waters, where it would be quickly swamped. The light-weight, more easily managed coracle would much better serve man's nomadic needs. He must certainly have come by coracle from Ireland – eighteen miles to Kintyre by the shortest crossing, and twenty-five or thirty to Islay and Ayrshire. This same course and design of boat were to serve immigrants to the Hebrides over the next 3,500 years.

By what route, devious or direct, these Mesolithic men of the Hebrides first reached Ireland is uncertain. Archaeologists at first thought their culture was Azilian, thus named from a cavern of Le Mas d'Azil in the French Pyrénées, where harpoons of flat antler were taken as the type product. Those of Oban and Oronsay seemed to match them. It has since been shown that Azilian dispersal to west Scotland cannot be upheld.* The Hebridean harpoons have a more convex shape than the Azilian, and the culture as a whole is more likely to be late Larnian. The men of Larne had a true Mesolithic culture, which dispersed in the stone industries of the Firth of Clyde and Kintyre before the colonists reached Oban.

Ireland had been uninhabited through the Ice Age, and the first ground that man occupied was the raised beach at Larne and other coastal sites of Antrim. By deduction from the shape of choppers and picks on these sites, archaeologists conclude that Larne had a double immigration of men, one group from Spain across the Bay of Biscay (Asturian culture), and another from north Europe; and this latter group may have reached Larne by way of Cresswell Crags in Derbyshire. A direct migration from north-west England by sea to Argyll, omitting Ireland, remains a possibility, for a Mesolithic cave was discovered in 1959 on the west coast of Argyll at Kilmelfort, with flints and other deposits more akin to Cresswellian than Larnian.†

The Mesolithic culture in the Hebrides did not remain static. Sites on Coll and Tiree, and sitheans at Balnahard in north Colonsay, which have yielded a Larne pick, flint blades, stone cores and axes, and an arrowhead barbed and tanged, show distinct advances on the earliest work in the isles. Mesolithic men must have received a stimulus from Neolithic when these arrived several hundred years after them. A carbon date of 3160 ± 110 B.C. has been received for charcoal from a Neolithic chambered cairn of Monamore in Arran.‡ The tomb itself had

---

* 1954: Lacaille.
† 1962: Atkinson.
‡ 1964: MacKie.

been built earlier, perhaps around 3300 B.C., and when that date is corrected in light of tree-ring counts it becomes 4000 B.C. No Hebridean sites have yet been dated, but when they are it would seem unlikely that they will be much later than the Arran site.

The Neolithic or New Stone Age people had arrived in south Britain two or three hundred years earlier. Their appearance in Scotland from Ireland and England was perhaps the most important event in the history of the Isles. Neolithic stone work was certainly to become spectacular, but the important points are that these were the first men to bear promise of civilization; that they were farmers with arts and crafts ready for development; and that colonization from Europe was now to be a continuing process as men moved in over a period of 3,000 years, less in waves than in slow streams, constantly bringing in new skills in stone and metal, which have caused them to be rather arbitrarily (but necessarily for analysis) divided into Neolithic, Bronze, and Iron Age peoples. It is important to realize that these were not large, sudden influxes of new peoples, but seepages of men with acquired arts, crafts, and knowledge into the human dough of Britain, which they leavened. The armed invasions were to come later. Meantime, there was land for everyone and no cause for wars.

The early Neolithic people left their artifacts over most of the sands and shores of the Inner and Outer Hebrides, where they are still being discovered today. Their monuments in stone, and those of their Bronze and Iron Age successors, are likewise so numerous in the Highlands and Islands that excavation and field research has been negligible in proportion to the work waiting to be done. The consequence is that archaeologists, requiring to distinguish theory from fact in writing prehistory, use a scholarly austerity that may, despite its virtue, tend sometimes to blind the layman's eyes. Readers should accept much of Scottish prehistory with minds open to the chance of new discoveries leading to conclusions different from those presently held.

Among the first Neolithic sites found in the Hebrides was a cave at Kiloran Bay in Colonsay. It contained the flint tools and bones that distinguish Neolithic industries from Mesolithic. The typical Neolithic tools throughout Britain were axes ground and polished; leaf-shaped arrowheads chipped from flint; picks, knives, and scrapers, ground so that they could be used for working wood; and sickle-blades for reaping. Experiment has shown that the axes were efficient in felling trees and clearing ground for pasture. The people were the first to breed animals in captivity. The bones of the Colonsay site were of ox, sheep, and horse, to which other sites add dog, goat, and pig. The cereals grown were barley and a primitive form of wheat. A final distinguishing feature was the first earthenware pottery made by man – thick, coarse, and at first crudely shaped.

It is believed that the Neolithic peoples had their origin in Asia near the Caspian Sea, and spread from there up the Danube to central and north Europe and along the shores of the Mediterranean to Spain. Their immigration to the Hebrides came by way of Spain to Ireland. The Hebrides and Ireland always tended to receive most immigrants by the Atlantic seaways, being without the North Sea link more important to the colonization of the British mainland. Skeletons found show that men were of short stature and long-headed.

In the course of their long migration from east to west they had become expert seamen and boat-builders. They found Scotland covered in primeval forest and virtually uninhabited. Their travel up the west coast would go entirely by sea: travel by foot remained notoriously difficult far into historic times, from roughness of ground, the tremendous forest, and the land's heavy indentation by sealochs. They arrived in the middle of the warm Atlantic period when birch and hazel had spread through the Hebrides to their greatest extent, but were now suffering a set-back from the spread of moss and hill peat. They came first to the Argyll islands, direct from Ireland and also by way of the Kintyre and Knapdale isthmuses at Tarbert and Crinan. The great number of chambered cairns at Crinan show that the settlement there became a large one, having quick access to the Clyde lochs on one hand and the Atlantic seaways on the other.

The people spread in time to all islands, and perhaps to the farthest outlier, St Kilda. Around 3000 B.C. they would become much encouraged by the advent of the warm, dry sub-Boreal period. They came with their livestock. Few in number though their animals were, their boats (like miniature Noah's arks) must have been substantial to take such freight in rough tidal waters. Their skin boats of oxhide were probably large. The Arctic Eskimoes until recently used sea-going skin boats (umiaks) up to sixty feet long for transporting heavy goods, and up to thirty-five feet long for whaling. Neolithic boats may have been equally large. It has been estimated* that a thirty-two-foot coracle could have carried over three tons of cargo, including eight rowers, one steersman, passengers and stores, two cows carried thrown, and two calves or six pigs or ten sheep. Such a coracle would be stable, yet quickly responsive to the crew in treacherous water. The Hebridean tides taken at the flood would greatly aid the crossings from north Ireland. The main stream goes north up the Hebridean channels at two knots, increasing to seven and eight knots around certain points or through

---

* 1969: Case.

narrow straits like the upper Sound of Jura, the Dorus Mor off Crinan, the Sounds of Luing, Sleat, and others.

Helpful as the tides can be, they lay traps for the unwary. Where islands are close-set and intersected east to west, the flooding tide picks up speed and swings west between them, giving dangerous passages like the Gulf of Corrievreckan (north of Jura) and the Grey Dog (north of Scarba). Admiralty charts show a nine-knot race for the Corrievreckan, where a great whirlpool is caused by a hidden rock-pyramid. When a strong westerly wind opposes the spring flood, the commotion is such that the roar of the overfalls can be heard along twenty miles of the mainland coast. Many other tide-races give turbulent seas, navigable if taken with a fair tide or at slack water. Several passages open to the west can have dangerous breaking seas over hidden banks. The expert seamanship required for safely helming a deep-keeled ship in such waters would be less necessary to the crew of a shallow-draft coracle. Drawing perhaps six inches of water, they could hold as close to the shore as they wished and often ignore tide-races by keeping inside them.

At the Outer Hebrides, tides flood in from east and west together, and the safety or danger of a given course varies widely according to wind, time of day, and even the season of the year. In short, sea-passages for a small boat are complicated, but these Neolithic sailors mastered them, and that must have meant repeated reconnaissances of islands and channels before final moves were made. They occupied all larger isles, at first in small numbers but by 2000 B.C. in substantial ones. Their number for all Scotland has been estimated as 10,000.* Coracles must in time have become a common sight in the island bays and sounds when the men went out to fish and explore. This design of boat lasted thousands of years, was used by Picts and Celts far into the first millenium A.D., and brought the Irish missionaries to Iona and Lismore. All were skilled and daring seamen.

Nothing of intimate kind has survived from Neolithic life except in stone or pottery. Saddle querns were in use before 2000 B.C. for grinding grain by the backward and forward motion of an upper stone on a lower, but wooden utensils, baskets, bows and arrow-shafts, hide clothing and the first fabrics woven from wool, all have gone. So too have the homesteads of wood and wattle thatched with marram, turf, and heather. The earliest immigrants may have been nomadic at first, clearing ground and settling for a few seasons, then moving on from isle to isle, but by 2000 B.C. they had settled in numbers sufficiently large to raise a multitude of chambered cairns.

* Ian Grimble.

Neolithic cairns are of two main kinds:* gallery graves, which are long cairns, like the English Long Barrow, covering a rectangular chamber; and passage graves, which are huge round cairns covering a round chamber entered by a low passage, which in the Hebrides is usually set in the sheltered east side. Every kind of modification between passage and gallery graves, and between round and long cairns, is found in the Hebrides, but with the passage grave in a round cairn everywhere predominating. Most have been long robbed of their stone for building in historic times, and the sites have become so derelict by increase of peat that only a few reward inspection. They are still numerous on all large islands. Islay, for example, has at least fourteen.

The average round cairn has a diameter of fifty feet, and the long cairn a length of sixty feet; heights are normally six to ten feet. But much bigger ones are plentiful.

Examples are:

Barra.   Dun Bharpa (Mound of the Cairn). 2¼ miles north of Castlebay. Diameter 85 feet. Circled by vertical slabs up to 7 feet high. Inner chamber capped by a slab 10 feet by 6.

Lewis.   Gress cairn, 7 miles north of Stornoway. 92 feet by 77.

Mull.   Port Donain, 5 miles south of Craignure. 100 feet by 50. Chamber 14 feet long.

North Uist.   Barpa nam Fiannay (Cairn of the Warriors of Fionn). 4 miles west of Lochmaddy. 165 feet by 46 – one of the longest in the isles.

      Barpa Langass, on the lower slopes of Beinn Langass, near the head of Loch Eport – one of the best preserved round cairns in the isles. Entrance under a big lintel to eastern passage, which leads to a chamber 9 feet by 6, height 7 feet. Relics found include pottery, a disc of pierced talc, a scraper, and a barbed arrow.

The funeral rites practised at chambered cairns were both cremation and inhumation, the burial of animals alongside the human bodies, and the deposit beside them of pottery and ornaments. The use of the tombs may have been reserved to the islands' leaders and their families, for carbon dates from Arran show that the Monamore cairn was in use for a thousand years – much too long a period to accommodate a community's dead.†

In Scotland, Wales, and England, but especially in Ireland, the megalith builders raised many burial chambers without a covering mound. These are

* 1963: Feachem. 1962: Pigott.
† 1964: MacKie.

called dolmens, of which Ireland has nearly a thousand. Some of their cover-stones are immense – one near Carlow weighs a hundred tons. But many of the largest chambers made of huge stone slabs were given a complete cairn-covering. One at New Grange near Drogheda is forty feet high and covers an acre of ground. There is nothing of that size in the Hebrides. Yet the handling and erection of great stone masses, even to the islanders' smaller scale, shows much art and the presence of large numbers of men in efficient social organization. The logs required to roll the big stones were probably the precursor of the wheeled cart.

Megalith building was not only a fashionable art, but clearly involved a belief in life after death, for which provision was made by interment of grave-goods with the bodies. The cairns and dolmens would therefore become the scenes of ceremonial rites. From 1800 B.C., the people's inherited skill in stone-moving was used for new developments in megalith building – henges, avenues or align-ments, monoliths or standing stones, and stone circles. Their standing stones have remained vertical for at least 3,600 years, although some are sunk only $2\frac{1}{2}$ to 3 feet in the earth, and that alone is an extraordinary engineering feat. The developments appear to have spread across the Channel from Brittany to south-west England, Wales, and Ireland, and so to Argyll, Islay, and the Hebrides. The apparent facility with which an exceptional skill in manipulating and erecting heavy standing stones spread through the Hebrides and the other countries *en route*, where the communities might be thought unlikely to have found time to learn the art for themselves, has brought the theory* that the original builders were not the native people but a missionary community who directed their megalithic work while they moved northward. They may very well have shared with the people a common or similar tongue.

Among the most impressive monuments raised were henges, of which there are five hundred in Britain, and the stone circles with alignments. Henges (from old English hengen, to hang) are named from the horizontal lintel stones, which at Stonehenge (and there only) bridge the gap between tall standing stones. A distinguishing feature of henges is their encirclement by an earthwork bank, some three hundred feet or less in diameter, which is ditched on the inner side. Scottish henges do not extend to the Hebrides, but the stone circle with align-ment reached its fullest development at Callernish in west Lewis – the most im-portant of its kind in Britain, as Stonehenge is of henge structure.

The Callernish site was first excavated in 1857–8 by Sir James Matheson, an

* 1923 and 1924: Perry. 1957: Bibby.

East India merchant who had bought Lewis from the MacKenzies in 1844. The stones were deep-sunk in peat, many almost covered, and five feet of this peat had to be dug out to reveal a roofless chambered cairn between the central monolith and the eastern arc of an inner circle. Careless work caused the displacement of several stones on this eastern arc, and some have since vanished. Below the base of the cairn were two stone chambers of beehive shape containing minute pieces of human bone, apparently the remains of a cremation. A passage six feet long gave entrance from the east side of the circle. The chambers were topped by the four pillar stones of a dolmen, the table-stone of which lay in the passage. Callernish has thus a unique combination of chambers, dolmen, cairn, circle, avenue, and cruciform lines.

The site is a windy and sun-flooded headland thrusting out into East Loch Roag. To its south, the Harris hills run east to west in four great waves, each topping 2000 feet, and westward lie the islands of Loch Roag. On the flat top of the headland, the forty-eight stones forming the circle and avenue look at first like a petrified copse. Originally there were probably seventy-five stones, but nearly thirty have been carried away, or been overthrown and engulfed in surrounding peat. As they stand today, they clearly mark the once-great avenue, ninety yards long and nine yards wide, aligned north to south.* Its west side is marked by ten stones about six feet high, the east by nine stones. The north end gives entrance. At the south end stands the circle of thirteen monoliths, of average height ten feet, around a central monolith of fifteen feet seven inches. Two other stones to the south-west and south-east of the circle show that the circle and the south pointer were formerly double. The outer circle was confluent with the avenue. The inner circle remains intact with a diameter of thirty-seven feet, while that of the outer is sixty-three feet. Beyond the outer circle, single lines of standing stones radiate east and west, each of four stones. The south line of five stones ends ninety feet from the inner circle and is twice the length of the other two.

The purpose for which the people used the carefully aligned avenue, pointers, and circle has been the subject of much speculation. The structure appears to have gone askew, presumably by drift of the peat during 3,600 years. The south line, for example, is now aligned with the west side of the avenue. Professor A. Thom† does not accept drift, for he cites this skew pattern as evidence that the alignments were for astronomical purposes. He suggests that the avenue could have been used in both directions for sighting on the moon to the south and

* 1928: Royal Commission.
† 1967: Thom.

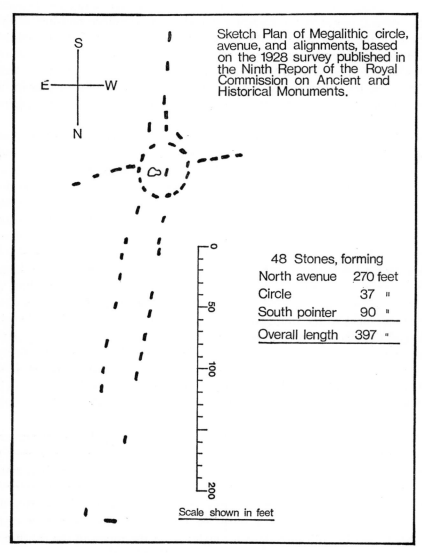

Sketch Plan of Megalithic circle, avenue, and alignments, based on the 1928 survey published in the Ninth Report of the Royal Commission on Ancient and Historical Monuments.

S

E———W

N

48 Stones, forming

North avenue	270 feet
Circle	37 "
South pointer	90 "
Overall length	397 "

0

50

100

200

Scale shown in feet

Diagram 3 *Callernish, Island of Lewis*

Capella rising to the north in 1800 B.C. The line running west from the main circle points to the setting-point of the equinoctial sun. The east line shows the rising point of Altair in 1800 B.C. The south line is set accurately in the meridian (azimuth 180°·1).

His findings agree in large part with earlier calculations by the astronomers Boyle Somerville† and Sir Norman Lockyer. Somerville notes that the central pillar casts its shadow exactly along the line of grave and passage at sunset on the day of the equinox, that west and south lines are accurate cardinal points, and that the difference of 1⅓ degrees in the orientation of the two avenue lines gave positive aid in observing Capella successively along each alignment. Lockyer and Somerville arrived independently at the conclusion that the avenue had been aligned on Capella from the azimuth (direction) of the line of stones, the angular height of the horizon on that line, and the Callernish latitude. From these data their calculations produced a declination for a star (its distance from the equator) that could refer only to Capella rising in 1800 B.C. (give or take two hundred years). Stellar observations would be preferred to solar for determining dates because a star's periodic shifts in position are greater than the sun's. Lockyer argues that the purpose of the dolmen would not be to cover the grave but to give a dark room for better observation along the sight-line. Three facts support him: (1) the centre of the avenue is in exact line with the centre of the cairn; (2) before the cairn was built, the dolmen exactly faced the avenue; (3) Martin Martin reported in 1695 that a single stone then stood at the centre of the avenue's north end. Therefore, an observer lying in the dolmen would look to Capella as if from the backsight of a gun through the foresight of the north-centred stone. Somerville adds that of fifty-five megaliths examined by him in Scotland and Ireland, only six had lacked evidence of orientation. The cruciform shape of the Callernish structure has been explained by no theory other than the astronomical. The circle, it has been guessed, was made around 1600 B.C., two hundred years later than the great lintelled circle of Stonehenge.

The single standing stones and circles of the Hebrides are likewise thought to have been erected from 1600 B.C. onwards. They so abound that no complete list has been made, and islesmen accept them unthinkingly as part of the natural scene. The biggest monolith is the Clach an Trushal, thirteen miles north-west of Stornoway in the township of Ballantrushal. It stands nineteen feet high, six feet wide, and nearly four feet thick. South Uist has one of seventeen feet on a hillside eight miles north-west of Lochboisdale. The smaller stones of the Inner

† 1912: *Journal of the Anthropological Institute of Great Britain and Ireland,* vol. xlii.

Hebrides have more deeply impressed me by the singular beauty of their settings and the wide views they command. The purpose of all of them is not certainly known, but that many were aligned to give calendar dates seems beyond dispute. Professor Thom has shown that four standing stones of the Outer Hebrides are aligned on the St Kildan peak of Boreray, 1245 feet, which projects from the horizon more than fifty miles distant. They are Clach Mhic Leoid on a headland of Harris above the Sound of Taransay; a stone on Benbecula west of Beinn Rueval; An Carra (sixteen feet high and five wide) on South Uist west of Beinn Mhor; and Clach an t-Sagairt on North Uist. As seen from these stones, the sun sets behind Boreray to give primary calendar declinations. From his study of many other stones and circles and their alignments, Professor Thom concludes that their builders had a thorough knowledge of practical geometry, achieved a skill in measurement equalled today only by a trained surveyor, and were so well acquainted with the small amplitude ripple on the moon's declination that they left definite indicators by which men today can determine its magnitude. He demonstrates in addition that the solar markers divide the Megalithic year into eight parts, with evidence for a further division into sixteen parts, and that the common unit of length throughout megalithic Britain was 2·72 feet (which sounds like an average pace).

Such early knowledge of astronomy in the Hebrides need not be thought surprising – its elements were indispensable to all primitive peoples trying to improve on their way of life. Primitive men were not, because they were illiterate, less intelligent than modern men. They had to sow and reap, hunt and fish, in immediate response to season. Having no printed calendars or mechanical clocks, they turned to the face of the sky, especially the night sky, where the stars were their almanac. It is natural in man to feel wonder when he watches the stars, and for systematic observation of their movements to be allied to divination, or study of their supposed influence on man's destiny. This double role was later, if not in Megalithic times, that of the Druids. They were capable of bold original thought as well as close calculation. Plutarch, in *De Facie et Orbe Lunae*, writes 'The Druids celebrate the feast of Saturn once every thirty years because they contend that Saturn takes thirty years to complete his orbit round the Sun'. In postulating an orbit round the sun, not to mention calculating the exact time taken, the Druids were fully 1,500 years in advance of Copernicus, whose publication of *De Revolutionibus Orbium Coelestium* in 1543 presented an idea – that earth and planets revolved round the sun – so incredible to thinkers of the time that only men with much knowledge of astronomy could entertain it for one moment.

From the completed structures and the great abundance of Megalithic works in the Hebrides, the prehistorian infers peaceable times, tolerable freedom from want, an organized society of considerable numbers with strong leadership, and thus, for a minority of their number, freedom from the need to hunt or grow their own food. A widespread division of labour had become possible. To some this meant leisure to think, plan, and direct labour and trade; to others, the chance to specialize in crafts and develop trade skills. The high quality of later Neolithic tools and weapons indicates professional work at factories. There was early barter trade between Scotland, England, and Ireland, with Langdale axes and Irish gold ornaments coming into Argyll and the Clyde estuary. By the second millennium there was a far-reaching trade in raw metal sea-borne from Ireland. Copper and bronze had come into use (a use limited at first to the communities' leaders) along trade lines that must have been sparse but important. Scotland, but not the Hebrides, had copper and gold of her own, obtainable south of a line between the firths of Lorn and Tay. There were large copper deposits on the Ayrshire coast at Kaim, where the famous Gavilmoss bronzes were found – now in Kelvingrove Museum, Glasgow. These are thought to be the finest axe and spear heads discovered in Britain. The manufacture of bronze implements, requiring an alloy of copper with tin, developed in Scotland from bronze ingots imported from Ireland, and probably from tin brought direct from Cornwall, which would account for the later settlement in Ayrshire of the Cornish Damnonii tribe. These wares, with copper ore and bronze ingots, were traded with north-east Scotland by way of the Great Glen, with the Hebrides, and with England.

Ireland was rich in copper and gold, and by trading for tin with Cornwall held precedence over Britain in the production of bronze ware until the mid-Bronze Age. Her copper hatchets, dagger-axes or halberds, and spearheads, spread across Europe; amber, jet, and copper articles came in exchange from the Baltic and Spain, together with less durable material not known, but which would certainly include flax for rope and cord (essential to the erection of megaliths, and to sailing and fishing), grain, salt, and hides. The Hebrides, so easily accessible from North Ireland and with traditional links there, received some of this trade, as also from the mainland, and would be open to the ideas that traders bring.

The introduction of metal so hugely overlapped continued stone-working that dates for the start of the Bronze Age are hard to fix within several centuries. In England an acceptable date is 1700 B.C., earlier in Ireland and later in the Hebrides. Ore smelting and the change of technique from stone to metal working required long experiment and practice, and involved too the acquisition of new knowledge in field geology. Long after the Bronze Age began in each country, stone- and bone-work reached the culmination of their own techniques. A remarkable illustration comes from a bay of west Lewis, near the village of Valtos on Loch Roag, about six miles west of Callernish. The islanded bay, backed by machair and low hills, has a mile-long sweep of sand named the Traigh Beiridh. On this beach, only thirty feet above the sea, has been found the working floor of an Iron Age stone factory, with hut circles and middens in hollows.* Using local gneiss, mylonite, and red deer horn, the industry had had a large production of heavy choppers, of scrapers and flakes made on the anvil, and of knives and hammer blades. Here Mesolithic techniques had persisted through four millennia because the people found the product useful. The site's late date was revealed by Samian ware and other Iron Age pottery.

Early Bronze Age immigrants from the Rhine, who had valuable contributions to make to island life, were the Beaker Folk, named from their distinctive pottery. Their graves on the mainland have the body buried in the crouch position within a stone cist, accompanied by a beaker.† The skeletons were of round-headed men of robust build, five feet eight inches tall. In the Hebrides crouch burials have rarely been found – one was discovered at Sanaig in Islay in 1959 – but many beaker sherds have been discovered in Islay, Mull, Coll, Tiree, Skye, and North Uist. The Beaker Folk seem to have travelled freely along the European coasts, acquiring much knowledge on the way. Although not at first metal workers – their manufacture of flint arrowheads, thin, sharp, barbed, and tanged, shows a fine technique – they knew the use of bronze, and some of their stone blades seem to have been designed from bronze prototypes. Their stone axes were ground to a high polish, and were most effective in tree-felling.

The Bronze Age people left no record of religious belief or practice other than that to be read from the megaliths. The Callernish avenue and circle is thought to have served two ends. The first was sun worship, and the idea gains support from written records. Herodotus in the fifth century B.C., referring to an exchange of visits between leaders of thought in Greece and Ireland, especially mentioned the visit made to Greece by a philosopher named Abaros from a Winged Temple of the Northern Isles, and that report is recorded by Eratosthenes and later Greek writers. Diodorus Siculus states that Abaros visited Pythagoras, which has interesting implications in light of Professor Thom's finding that the megalith builders had been working towards the Pythagorean theorum a thousand years earlier. The only winged temple in northern latitudes was Callernish.

* 1954: Lacaille.
† 1962: Pigott.

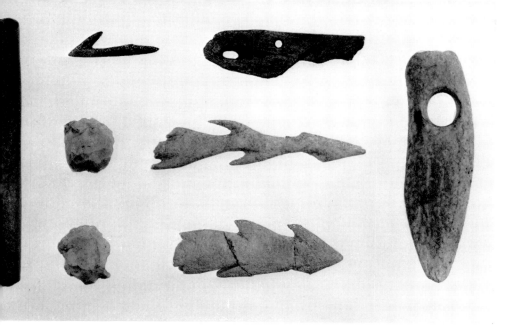

9a. Mesolithic implements. The fishhook is from Risga, the others from Oronsay.
Left : stone limpet hammer (4⅜ inches); *Top :* bone fishhook (1½ inches) and harpoon butt
with hole for line; *Centre and bottom :* flint scrapers and barbed harpoon tips in bone
(centre harpoon, 3⅝ inches); *Right :* antler mattock (4⅛ inches).

9b. Neolithic axes from Kiloran Bay, Colonsay.

10. The Gulf of Corrievreckan, between Scarba (*bottom*) and Jura. The tide race taken at the flood, with overfalls and great whirlpool near centre.

The oral record passed on from the early Celtic occupation is that Callernish was a Teampull na Greine, or Temple of the Sun. Sun-circles are numerous in the Isles. Two of the larger are in west Lewis: one near Barynahine, on Cnoc Fillibir, has concentric circles of twenty-eight and fifty-three feet diameter; another by Loch Roag is of sixty-five feet. Many other clues in language, stone, and custom, point to the same conclusion.* Islay has a big stone circle on the Rhinns near Cuiltuinn, which means the Back of the Fires. Some of these circles are known in the ancient Gaelic as Bel Beachd, meaning the Circle of Bel, the Celtic sun god.† It would appear that much Bronze Age tradition is embodied in the Gaelic glossaries. Forms of sun-worship persisted in the Isles through 1,700 years of the Christian era. Their trace was recorded by Martin in 1695 – boats heading to sea were always rowed sunwise to court good fortune; men walked sun-wise around cairns and monuments; the poor on receiving alms would make three turns sunwise around their benefactor. The celebration of Beltane continued to be observed in remote areas as late as the eighteenth century.‡

The second end served at Callernish, that of seasonal calendar, could not have been the only purpose, for it would not have required a design in stone so elaborate. The truth must surely be that both opinions are correct. If a primary purpose were determination of seasonal change, the ceremonial rites and a form of worship or sacrifice would inevitably develop. If the primary purpose were sun worship, or fertility rites, or offerings arising out of the sense of seasonal need and change that all human races experience given a natural environment, then the more precise dating of season by these alignments would follow. The two purposes lead to complementary events.

Events of that kind need leaders. The Irish tradition is that the later Celtic Druids were preceded by a class of Bronze Age seers from whom, in Ireland, Druidism developed under the Celts. That such a class must have evolved in the Hebrides, that they were powerful and knowledgeable, and were respected as sages, could not by any writings be so emphatically stated as by the solid evidence on the ground. One cannot say more with certainty.

Later cairns and circles had no burial chambers. By 1000 B.C. burial customs had changed to cremation, with the ashes preserved in urns, or to burial in unmarked pits. Not even the most important dead were henceforth commemorated in raised stone, and this new humility (if such it was) lasted nearly 1,000 years.

Cup-and-ring marks are a Bronze Age mystery as yet unsolved. These are

---

* 1919: MacKenzie.
† 1949: Dwelly.
‡ See below, pp. 153–4.

cup-shaped hollows measuring one to three inches across, punched out by pick and hammer on standing stones, grave-slabs, rock-faces, boulders, flat stones – wherever a stone surface offered an invitation. Some are ringed with grooves, a few with two or three concentric rings, which may be crossed by radial grooves. They are found in the Hebrides, the Orkneys, Highland and Lowland Scotland, Ireland, north England, and Spain. Their purpose has defeated archaeologists, whose suggestions range from mere ornamentation to religious or sexual symbols. Professor Thom deduces from them a geometry similar to that found in the stone circles, and a unit of length equal to 1/40th of his megalithic yard.* Some of their dense clusters around a central cup-and-ring suggest a sun or moon circled by a pack of stars. Two examples, in Ayrshire and Islay, define the shape of the Great Bear. This could be accidental, although Graham Donald† notes that in Islay, at Kilchiaran, the two stars α and β Ursae Majoris, which point at Polaris, have been carved with the first to the left of its present station, and thus more in accord with its station of several thousand years ago.

During the last few millennia B.C., most of Europe had been occupied by Indo-European-speaking peoples, who appear to have migrated originally from the highlands south of the Caspian Sea. It is not known at what early date the Celtic language separated from the closely-related Indo-European. The Celts were a pastoral, nomadic people, forming not a single nation but a confederacy of tribes of similar speech. From the Stone Age they had occupied the Danube and the Alps; from the Bronze Age, Spain, France, and parts of Italy. Around 900 B.C. they developed the use of iron at Hallstat in Austria and spread their culture, religion and speech among the peoples north of the Alps from the shores of the Black Sea to the Atlantic. During their wars of the fourth century B.C., when they invaded Italy and sacked Rome, Europe was in ferment. Long before then, small bands of the Celtic tribes known to the Romans as Galli (from the word Gael, romanized as Gall) had begun to cross the Channel into Britain and Ireland.

The Celts were tall, strongly-built men with red hair and blue or grey eyes. They brought to Britain the use of iron and new arts and crafts of La Tène culture, named from the types of ornaments and weapons discovered at La Tène in Switzerland (near Lake Neuchâtel). They were to revolutionize life in the British Isles, and great landscape changes date from their arrival. In the last century B.C., a Celtic tribe called Belgae, whose territory lay north and east of the Seine and Marne, arrived in south Britain as colonists. They came under the pressures of Roman and tribal aggressions, and brought with them the use of heavy ploughs,

* 1968: Thom.
† 1964.

which speeded the cultivation of land cleared by felling. They minted gold coins, introduced the pottery wheel and new decorative arts, and organized a kingdom with a thriving export trade in corn, cattle, metal, and slaves.

The Celts wanted the best land they could get. From 500 B.C. or earlier they were moving north through Britain to Scotland, their numbers swollen by tribes displaced in the south, and later by refugees from West Gaul, when that country came under Roman attack in the last century B.C., until their over-running of mainland Scotland forced the settled inhabitants to build great numbers of hill-top defences and forts. The invaders too required strongholds, and the result was a new stone age in wall-building.

In Ireland, the Celts formed small states ruled by kings. And the states for their own protection grouped in five large hegemonies. The territory of the northern group was Ulster, from which the Scots' historic settlement of the Hebrides and Argyll was later to come.

The Celts, prior to their immigration, had known the inhabitants of Britain and Ireland under the name Pretani. To the Greeks, Albion and Iverna were the Pretanic Islands. Caesar spelt the name Brittani. Following Agricola's invasion of Scotland in A.D. 79, the Romans described the principal Highland tribe as red-haired and large of limb and named them Caledonii,* probably from the Gaelic *Caile-daoine*, meaning Spearmen, and pronounced Caledoyni. Their territory was the central Highlands. Several other named tribes occupied the west coast, but which if any of them controlled the Hebrides is not known. From A.D. 297, all of them were named Picti or Pictones by Roman writers, who applied the name to the whole confederation of Highland tribes united by the need to oppose Rome. The name did not necessarily belong to any one of the tribes, but the con-federacy adopted the name and the Pictish kingdom became the sole nation north of the Highland Line until the sixth century.

Historians thus date the Picts from A.D. 300 onwards, and to avoid confusion most archaeologists reserve the adjective Pictish for reference to the five hundred years following that date. The question remains, who were the people whom the Romans named Picts? The only language records to survive are place-names, brief inscriptions on stone, and a list of Pictish kings. From these it is evident that their law and speech were Celtic. Succession to the throne was governed by the Celtic law of Tanistry, which did not recognize the principle of primogeni-ture. The Celtic language has three groups: the classical or continental Gaelic of greater Gallia, which was the parent of the two others – Goidelic, which is Irish,

* Tacitus, A.D. 93.

Scots, and Manx Celtic – and Brittonic, which mainly developed after the sixth century A.D. as Welsh, Breton, and Cornish Gaelic. Pictish is thought to be a Gallo-Britonnic language. Its race and place-names, taken as classical Gaelic, translate accurately.*

The earlier, prehistoric Picts may have been the ancient people of the land, that slow stream of exploratory colonists who had been entering Scotland, Ireland, and the Hebrides from early Bronze Age times. There seems to be no good reason why such people should not have been early Celts, since their tribes came to possess the greater part of Europe and were penetrating its farthest corners. Alternatively, the Picts may have been the earliest of the Celtic immigrants moving in from 500 B.C. More likely they were both, for the indications are that the prehistoric Picts were no single race but a heterogeneous people.†

Iron was scarce in the last few hundred years B.C., but the incoming Celts and settled inhabitants felled the forests of south Scotland and built large numbers of homesteads, both in timber and stone, of which a few hundred remain as monuments in the Southern Uplands. A considerable skill in masonry was displayed in the larger walled settlements. In the Lowlands, palisaded sites have been carbon-dated to the seventh and sixth centuries B.C.;‡ these and hill-top earthworks enclosed as many as ten acres with up to fifteen circular houses before the Roman invasion of A.D. 79. They were the first villages. Ploughshares were in use, although most cultivation was by hoe. Chariot gear, swords, and scabbards show that trade with Ulster continued. The times, if troubled, were of social advancement and the tribes flourished. As in Ireland, they grouped in ever larger petty kingdoms, until by the time the Romans arrived they had formed into two main groups: the Britons south of the Forth-Clyde line, and the Picts (not yet historic Picts) to the north.

The first walled buildings, all in drystone, had begun to appear in Scotland from the seventh century B.C. onwards, and by A.D. 100 were exceedingly numerous and widespread throughout all inhabited islands. They took three principal forms with variations: (1) hill forts, (2) small stone forts (duns and brochs), and (3) domestic structures (wheelhouses, round stone huts, and souterrains).

The first hill forts were simply defensive walls strengthening a natural fastness and protecting the living quarters inside, which were timber round-houses and lean-to huts. Walls were made double to a thickness of eight to forty feet, their interior space being filled with stone rubble. They were often built around a

* 1970: Donald.
† 1955: Wainwright.
‡ 1970: Mackie.

timber framework, as shown by socket-holes in the outer walls. More than seventy such forts in Scotland have vitrified walls, whose stones have been cemented by heat. There are no vitrified forts in England or Wales. East- and west-coast sites have received carbon dates of 590 B.C. and 490 B.C. respectively. These vitrified forts are most numerous around the sea-lochs of the Firth of Clyde, and at either end of the Great Glen. Only two or three have been found in the Hebrides, the best one at Trudernish point in south Islay. This small fort is placed on the hillock between the bays of Aros and Claggain, with splendid views far up the Sound of Jura to craggy isles and thirty miles eastward over Kintyre to the Arran mountains. The low, crumbled walls have been heavily fused by heat. That fusion of silicious rock-rubble is easy has been repeatedly demonstrated in recent years. When peat, kelp, and wood, in which sand and soda are present, are burned with stone rubble in a strong wind, they form a slag-like cement. Stones could thus be aggregated to form strong ramparts. There appear to be good arguments both for and against intentional vitrifaction. Gordon Childe demonstrated by experiment that vitrifaction could be caused by attackers firing the wooden framework in the walls, and most archaeologists accept his theory. On the other hand, there are difficulties in applying it to Craig Phadrig at Inverness, and Dun Mhic Uisneachain on Loch Linnhe, where the vitrified ramparts are continuous, double, and concentric along the top edges of steep defensive slopes.

The classic mainland examples of hill forts are Dunadd near Crinan, which became the capital fort of the first Scots kingdom, and Craig Phadrig at Inverness, which may (not proven) have become the capital fort of Pictland. A Hebridean hill fort of this kind is Dun Cholla, on the south moorland of Colonsay, but the greatest hill fort of the Highlands and Islands is on Islay, where Digh Mhor (the great Mound) encloses 2·9 acres behind triple terraced walls. This fort is believed to have been the base for an Irish expeditionary force of the third century A.D.*

Settlement walls, and refuge walls for emergency use only, are common in the Hebrides. An example of refuge type is the summit of the Scuir of Eigg, 1289 feet, where a ten-foot thick wall on the west side joins two cliffs standing eighty yards apart. All other approaches are naturally barred by pitch-stone crags, which rise four hundred feet from the lower hill-slopes. Nine acres of the summit are thus enclosed. Settlement walls might be on open ground, as in Skye at Dun Gerashader, north of Portree, where an oval enclosure, 170 feet by 100 feet, has a wall fourteen feet thick; or set on a hillock, like Dun Skudiburgh in Skye, near

---

* 1971: Donald.

Uig, where a wall ten feet thick encloses an oval of 150 feet by 120 feet. In the Outer Hebrides, such walls were often built across the isthmuses of peninsulas. The Griminish headland of North Uist is thus defended by a wall 360 feet long, and one across the rocky headland of Rudha na Berie in Lewis, near Carloway, is twenty-three-feet thick. In a much later example from Skye, the wall has an internal gallery. This wall, twelve feet thick and nine feet high, cut off the promontory of Rudh' an Dunain of Loch Brittle. There are very many others.

During the period 200 B.C. to A.D. 200, duns so multiplied in the Hebrides that no one has yet found time to trace and number them. All told there must be many hundreds. Islay alone has more than 124,* and fresh discoveries are still being made. The word dun (pronounced doon) originally meant a mound, the word being transferred to the fort or strong house built on top. Nearly all have been reduced to rubble, usually with little more than a foot of stone to mark the outline. Much has been learnt from the ruins. The duns were built circular, oval, and oblong; some have galleries between the walls, some were ringed by outer defensive walls; and on Lewis many were insular, built on the islets of freshwater lochs.

The typical dun has walls ten to twenty feet thick and rarely more than fifty feet in diameter. They are sometimes hard to distinguish from settlement walls except by site or the small area enclosed. Thus Dun Cul Bhuirg, built on top of a tall rock on Iona's west coast, had two platforms inside with evidence of timber-framed houses, one with a central hearth, and a large quantity of Iron Age pottery. The huge number of small duns built along the coast on rocky points are unexplored and unexcavated. Few are worth visiting for their own sakes, but almost all for their views. They so invariably command the widest prospect available on a given stretch of coast, and are so often visually interlinked, that strategic siting as watch-posts under an island plan, perhaps with signal beacons made ready alongside, seems likely. Excavations may show that they were lived in; most are too small to have withstood siege or attack by a large force.

Insular duns are a feature of the Outer Hebrides, where they are sited on freshwater islets to take full advantage of an abundant natural asset. Sometimes they are ringed by an outer defensive wall, which may be a settlement wall to which the dun has been added for final retreat. An example is Dun Buidhe in north Benbecula. The duns were linked to the shore by a causeway, an example of which can be seen on the Eye peninsula of Lewis near Lower Bayble, where the causeway is nine feet wide and ninety feet long.

Galleried duns, having a passage within the walls, were a later development of

* 1971 figure.

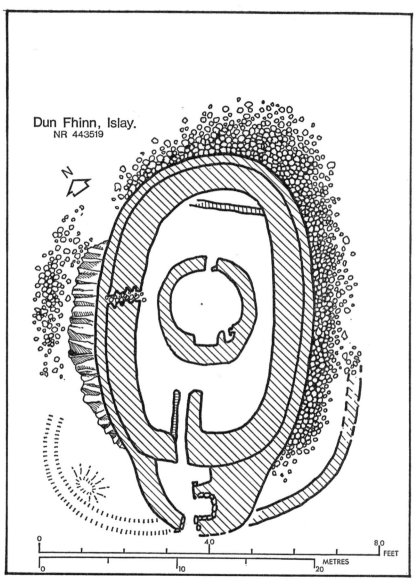

Dun Fhinn, Islay.
NR 443519

Diagram 4 *Iron Age Fort*

solid-walled duns. Access to the top was by stone steps on the face of the inner wall or else from the lower passage. The areas enclosed, up to fifty feet in diameter or seventy by forty feet if oblong or oval, have signs of timber lean-to and round-houses. One of the largest is Dun Liath in Skye, north-west of Uig, measuring 150 feet by 80 feet. Where their walls have an upper as well as a ground-level gallery they are called semibrochs, and the assumption that brochs proper were evolved from them seems to be confirmed by a carbon date from Dun Ardtreck, a semibroch in Skye, showing that it had probably been built in the second century B.C.*

The brochs are the most interesting and sophisticated buildings of the early Iron Age. They are circular towers, peculiar to Scotland, originally named from the Gaelic word bradh (pronounced brawgh), meaning any round object (variant forms in ancient Gaelic are burg, brog, and borg). Nearly five hundred appear on the northernmost coasts and islands, and in the Hebrides, where the best preserved example is at Carloway in Lewis. Carloway broch, like all others, has been robbed of much stone, but still stands impressively to thirty feet, bearing a dull green patina and displaying, in half-section, galleries between hollow walls.†

The brochs were cleverly planned by professional builders, who made full use of a remarkable advance in masonry skills to provide secure refuge in time of danger. The double walls were built forty to fifty feet high from base diameters of fifty or sixty feet. Within their thickness of fifteen feet or more, they were ringed by a series of four to six galleries, which narrowed as they rose to the top. Short stone stairs linked each to the one above. The gallery floors were simple slabs that served also to bind the two walls together. The stones of the main walls were square-cut and closely laid, yielding no toe-hold. A few of these surfaces were to remain unbroken by weather for two thousand years. The outer wall was built concave, sloping gently inward to the vertical middle part, and then outward to the light overhang of the upper (the latter feature seen only at Mousa, in the Shetland Isles). No window or other opening pierced the outer wall, except for a narrow fifty-foot-high entrance passage, which was closed by a massive wooden door and had a guard-chamber set in the wall to one side. The door swung on a stone pivot and was barred by a beam housed in wall sockets. The tower was left unroofed. The inner wall had windows. These lit the galleries and commanded the courtyard, the diameter of which varied from nineteen to forty feet. Excavations have revealed post-holes, which are interpreted as supports for the raised wooden floor of a gallery resting on a scarcement ledge of the inner wall.

* 1970: MacKie.
† Plate 126.

The intermural galleries, which sometimes had one or more tiny chambers shaped like beehives with vaulted roofs, were too narrow to have been used as living quarters. They gave only standing ground and access to the wall-top. The courtyard was certainly not big enough to enfold a community's livestock, which would be driven off to hill or moor before an attack. Brochs were clearly not intended to withstand a long siege, for wells have not often been found in them – although in Shetland the Mousa broch, which has a well, withstood siege by the earl of Orkney as late as 1154. Their purpose was temporary refuge, to give time while the larger community of an island or district could gather to expel intruders, and their design to that end faultless. The smooth concavity of the outer wall made it unscaleable, and at the same time allowed the besieged to overlook the gateway from the wall-top. If the gate were forced, the unlucky raiders would find themselves penned in the interior yard as if at the bottom of a well, and the greater their number the more casualties they would suffer from defenders above. No matter what the odds in the attackers' favour, only one man at a time could try to fight his way into the intermural gallery. In short, brochs were impregnable.

The history of a Hebridean broch-site over a six-hundred-year period has been revealed by Euan W. MacKie of the Hunterian Museum at Glasgow University.* Tiree has more than twenty prehistoric forts, all ruinous, and unexplored until the years 1962–4, when MacKie dug Dun Mor Vaul on the northeast coast. Dun Mor crowns a knoll between the rocks of Vaul Bay and farmland behind. Its original height was thirty feet at least, with perhaps four internal galleries. Now it stands only to six feet, but the walls are twelve feet thick, enclosing a courtyard of thirty-two-feet diameter.

MacKie reconstructed the history of the site by careful excavation of several thick floor-deposits and by radiocarbon dating of material found. The first settlers arrived in the fifth century B.C. and lived for two hundred years in wooden huts. The broch was built during the first century B.C., when a new group of men arrived, identified by pottery and other relics as Celts from southern Britain, perhaps forced out from their home ground by Belgic colonists. Their speech would be Brittonic. Since they had been able to engage professional builders to erect Dun Mor, they had probably migrated with all their possessions and livestock and been affluent for their time.

Among their possessions was the rotary quern, one of the first to be introduced to the Hebrides, where the use of such querns was to continue far into the nineteenth century. The broch appears to have been built as a communal refuge rather than one family's fortified homestead, for the first-floor deposits show

* *Antiquity*, December 1965.

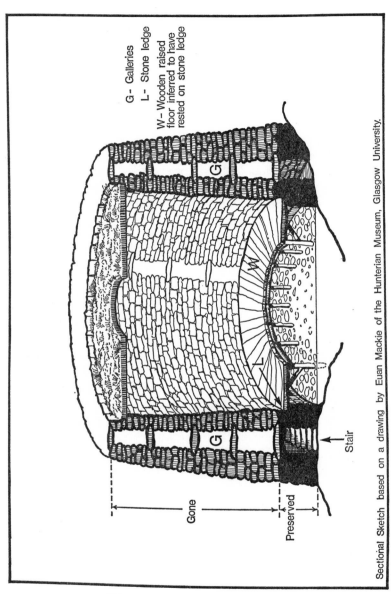

G - Galleries
L - Stone ledge

W - Wooden raised
floor inferred to have
rested on stone ledge

G

W

L

G

Stair

Gone

Preserved

Sectional Sketch based on a drawing by Euan Mackie of the Hunterian Museum, Glasgow University.

Diagram 5a *Dun Bhalla, Tiree*

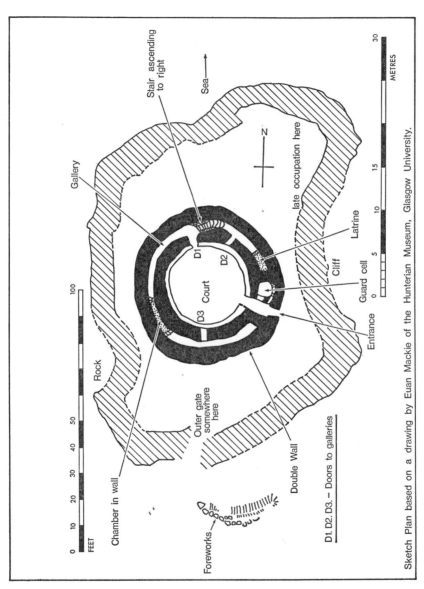

Stair ascending to right

Sea →

Gallery

late occupation here

N

D1

D2

Latrine

Court

Cliff

Guard cell

D3

Entrance

100

Rock

Chamber in wall

0 5 10 15 30
METRES

0 10 20 30 40 50 100
FEET

Outer gate somewhere here

Double Wall

Foreworks

D1. D2. D3. – Doors to galleries

Sketch Plan based on a drawing by Euan Mackie of the Hunterian Museum, Glasgow University.

Diagram 5b *Dun Bhalla, Tiree*

numerous patches of peat ash but no single hearth. A circular wooden gallery six feet wide was built around the inner wall. The gallery's inner edge rested on a ledge five feet above the floor, the outer edge being supported by wooden posts. When danger threatened, the women, children, and stores could be moved up there to leave the ground uncluttered. Bone debris of cattle and sheep was found in great quantity, and this, with the querns, show that farming was mixed.

In the second century A.D., a rectangular stone hearth was laid at the yard's centre, and the broch converted to a farmhouse. This change of use from a communal refuge to private ownership has been approximately dated from fragments of Roman glass and pottery. Tiree enjoyed more peaceful times in the third century, for the wooden gallery was taken down and the walls were reduced to a level approaching their present six feet and given a wooden roof. The farmhouse stood for another century while hundreds of shattered potsherds, many stone hammers, broken querns, and bits of iron tools, accumulated on the floor. The farm was prosperous. Among the many activities carried out on the site were iron smelting, as shown by slag, bronze casting, for which crucibles and bronze tongs were used, grain-grinding, spinning and weaving, and pot-making. The lack of intrusive pottery in the topmost levels suggests that the principal family had already gone or died when the farm was suddenly abandoned in the third century.

The cunning design of the brochs had been evolved to meet a threat to life raising in the Hebrides during the last few hundred years B.C. The great care and thought given to their planning and building, and the uprush of earlier defences on all islands, marked an end to three thousand years of peace. There had plainly arisen a need of defence learned from repeated harsh experience. Raids must have been frequently expected. From where did the enemy come?

The distribution map shows a dense concentration of brochs in the Shetland and Orkney Islands, on the coasts of Caithness and Sutherland, and in north Skye, and their relative scarcity in the southern Hebrides. Two explanations have been offered. The first, acceptable to many archaeologists, is that from 500 B.C. Scotland was increasingly overrun by the Celtic immigrants already mentioned, whose arrival had brought the need of forts and of fortified settlements. Later migrants, native or immigrant, had to move out to the isles and up to the farthest north mainland to find land, where the pre-existing communities to get protection employed professional broch-builders. MacKie's survey of all the brochs of Atlantic Scotland has led him to suggest a Hebridean origin of broch development, for which the prototypes were the semibrochs.*

The alternative opinion offered is that since brochs were concentrated in the

* 1970: MacKie.

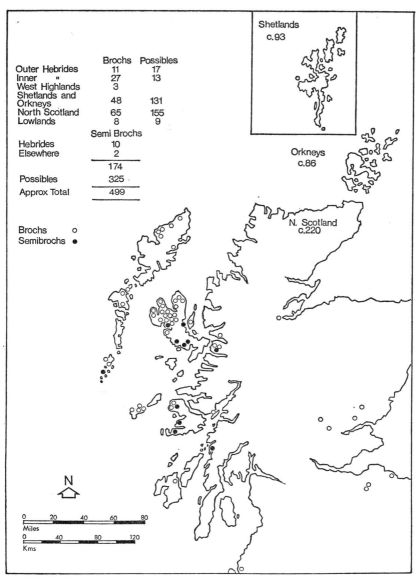

Shetlands
c.93

	Brochs	Possibles
Outer Hebrides	11	17
Inner "	27	13
West Highlands	3	
Shetlands and Orkneys	48	131
North Scotland	65	155
Lowlands	8	9

	Semi Brochs
Hebrides	10
Elsewhere	2
	174
Possibles	325
Approx Total	499

Brochs   ○
Semibrochs ●

Orkneys
c.86

N. Scotland
c.220

N

| 0 | 20 | 40 | 60 | 80 |
Miles

| 0 | 40 | 80 | 120 |
Kms

Map 17 *Broch distribution 100 B.C.–A.D. 100*

north, they in particular were built not against landseekers from the south but sea-borne raiders from the north, which means Scandinavia. The first lands subject to raid from Scandinavia would be these northern coasts and islands. Norway did not then exist as a nation, nor (so far as is known) were there Vikings sailing under that name, but Bronze Age rock-carvings in Scandinavia, dated to 1000 B.C. or earlier, depict longships capable of deep-sea voyaging.* Viking raids on Scotland are not recorded in writing till the eighth century A.D., but during the last two hundred years B.C. Scandinavian sea-rovers were engaging in commercial adventure abroad. Longship-building had all the while been advancing. Specimens found in peat bog at Nydam and dated to the third century A.D. were clinker-built in oak and red pine and seventy-five feet long. That such ships and men should fail to explore the coasts of Scotland for so long as 1,800 years is too hard to believe.

Scandinavia was prosperous in the last two centuries B.C., trading freely with Mediterranean countries and importing manufactures of good quality. In exchange, the seamen would certainly barter slaves, who formed the basis of most early Iron Age societies (including British and Irish) and of all Mediterranean countries. The demand for agricultural labourers, galley oarsmen, and servants, was huge. Norway itself had established slave-markets where Picts and Scots were bought and sold.† Scandinavian slavers would therefore have excellent cause to raid the coasts of Scotland.

No Scandinavian relics datable to that time have been found in Scotland – but even the four hundred years of historical occupation have yielded only a score of finds in the Hebrides. Supporters of the theory have to look to evidence other than archaeological, and their findings are of great interest. The Sagas report that Norse ships were using the isles for rendezvous long before permanent settlements, and Saxo Grammaticus, the Danish historian, regards these Norse incursions as occurring long before the eighth century. Boece (*Scotorum Historia*) says that Scandinavians were in Scotland at the time of Agricola. Irish historians record the raising of an expeditionary force in the third century A.D. under Fionn MacCoul to drive the men of Lochlann – Scandinavian pirates – off the Hebrides and mainland seaboard. Such an expedition would be raised as a matter of self-interest in aid of Picts then fully committed to resisting Roman power, which threatened both countries. The Hebridean base for this expedition may have been south-east Islay, on the plain of Tallant near Kildalton Chapel, where a concentration of nine forts and three weapon forges has recently been

* 1957: Bibby.
† 1903: Mackenzie.

explored and sketched by Frank Newall and Graham Donald.* The siting of these forts, it is argued, could have no strategic or defensive reason other than that of being the headquarters and training ground of the Irish expedition. One of these Islay forts is named Dun Fhinn; another, Burg Coul; and a third, Dun Charmaic (after Fionn's father-in-law Cormac). The main fort is Digh Mhor (pronounced Gee Vore), and the building here of Scotland's biggest hill fort would again seem inexplicable unless to serve that expedition. Success brought more peaceable times, and the dismantling of the plain of Tallant forts together with Hebridean brochs.

The probability that longships were present in Hebridean waters gains support from the circumnavigation of Britain by a small Roman fleet in the period A.D. 80–85. The Romans brought back a name for the Hebrides, which Pliny (first century) spelt Hebudes and Ptolemy (second century) rendered in Greek as Epoudai. The name, meaningless in itself, appears to be a phonetical rendering, naturally softened by the southern tongue, of the Norse Havbredey, pronounced Haubredey. *Hav* means sea; *bred*, edge; and *ey*, island. In the plural it translates as Isles on the Edge of the Sea – a good description of the Outer Hebrides. That the Romans picked up the name, perhaps while in harbour in Lewis or the Orkneys, seems likely. It has a typically Norse ring – the men gave their longships names like *Horse of the Gull's Track*, *Raven of the Sea*, and *Elk of the Fiords*.

Despite the widespread use of stone for defence, the main body of islesmen still lived in wattled huts, roofed with boughs and thatched with heather, pine-branch, turf or marram – a type of house that continued to be built in the Highlands until the late eighteenth century. Around A.D. 200, stone was used in the outer isles to build wheelhouses, which structurally were partly derived from brocs. Pre-broch primitive examples appear in the Shetland Isles, but these are much simpler than the classic wheelhouses, which are found only in North and South Uist and Shetland – it may be that others have been lost under drifting sand. Few have been excavated. The best-preserved example is on South Uist, on the Askernish machair near the township of Kilpheder. This wheelhouse is sunk in flat ground between dune-hills. It appears now as an open pit, seven feet deep and thirty feet in diameter, with walls standing six feet high. A central living space of eighteen feet diameter is given its own perimeter by the butt-ends of eleven pillar walls, which radiate like short wheel-spokes to the outer wall without joining the latter. A series of narrow chambers are thus formed by pillars that supported a timber and thatch roof. The entrance passage of twenty-four

* 1970: Donald.

feet is set, as is usual in the isles, on the east side, away from the shore wind. Stone steps lead down, showing that the house had been partially sunk for wind-protection, or concealment, or wall-support.

Wheelhouses were occupied till the fourth century and perhaps till the seventh. Their contents in North Uist included a wide range of whalebone tools, red and brown pottery decorated with impressed patterns, Samian ware of the second century, a Roman coin of Constantius II (A.D. 337–61), finger rings carved out of antler, combs and pendants of antler and whalebone, jade necklaces probably imported from the north of England, and bone dice for gambling. The people used both saddle and rotary querns, and carding combs to prepare wool for spinning and weaving. Although they worked metal, as shown by a furnace, iron slag, and stone and clay moulds and crucibles, there was a marked lack of bronze and iron objects, and spears were tipped with whale-bone. One whale-bone knife-handle carried a name, probably the owner's, MAQUNM DENCOT, carved in Ogham script.* The Scots had introduced Ogham to Dalriada in the fifth or sixth centuries. The script spread to Pictland, where it continued in occasional use for fifty years, mainly for the purpose of carving names on memorial stones.† The letters of the alphabet were represented by twenty straight lines incised on or across a long stem line.

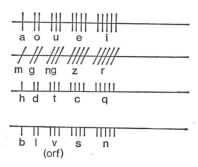

Diagram 6 *Ogham Alphabet*

The direction of writing was either horizontal or vertical starting at the bottom left-hand corner. The only other Hebridean Ogham is carved on a stone on Gigha. (400 inscriptions have been found in Britain – 315 in Ireland, 25 in Scotland, and 2 in the Hebrides.)

* 1931: *Proc. Soc. of Antiquaries, Scot.* LXVI, p. 56.
† 1962: Pigott (K. H. Jackson).

Earth-houses or subterranean chambers, and crannogs or artificial islands on freshwater lochs, were made in the Hebrides in small numbers from the early Iron Age far into historic times. Earth-houses were long narrow passages, roofed and walled with stone slabs, ending at an inner room. They were more numerous in Skye and the Small Isles, where they were tunnelled into the flanks of hills. Their largest concentration and most substantial construction appears in the heart of Pictland at Aberdeen and Angus, where the passages, six feet wide and high, were curved sharply to a terminal bulge and driven to a maximum length of eighty feet; whereas Hebridean examples reach ninety feet but are too low to allow an upright stance. The most elaborate, at Vatten in Skye, has offsets from the main passage. They were most likely used by the prehistoric Picts as refuges, and certainly by historic Picts as granaries, for which there is internal evidence. The Hebridean crannogs were of two kinds: one of stone foundation, either built on a low island or piled on shallows to the surface; the other of wooden piles driven into a loch's bottom, framed with lashed logs, and filled with rubble, stone, and brushwood. Some of these islands are fifty feet in diameter, and one in Mull is over eighty feet long. Enormous quantities of material had to be rafted out to build such crannogs. The wooden houses set on top often had a planked balcony round the outer wall, and projected over the water on piles supporting the outer edge. Some had a dock for canoes, and all had access to land by a submerged, zig-zag causeway. Crannogs are most numerous on Mull. A good specimen of the stone-built type on Loch Sguabain may be seen from the roadside in Glen More. Others have been found, with dug-out canoes, on Loch na Mial near Tobermory, Loch Frisa, Loch Ba, and in the Ross of Mull at Lochs Assapol and Poit-i. The dates of occupation and re-occupation are debatable, and range from 1000 B.C. to the Middle Ages.*

During the third century A.D. the Picts were receiving Irish help against the Romans. The Romans had been unable to penetrate to the West Highland coast or Hebrides, for the Picts, although narrowly defeated in A.D. 84 at Mons Grampius,† north of the Tay, maintained for three hundred years a successful guerrilla warfare, which held the Romans first to Hadrian's Wall between the Tyne and Solway, then to the Antonine Wall between the Forth and Clyde. Both walls were taken by the Picts, and retaken by the Romans. In the third and fourth centuries, the Picts were increasingly helped by Irish tribes named by the Romans Scotti, and their joint raids by sea on Roman territory intensified as

---

* 1963: Feachem.
† Tacitus. Modern scholars spell it Graupius, but *Gruaimpeinnean* (old Gaelic), meaning dark or grim mountains, gave the word Grampians: 1970, Donald.

Roman power weakened. Before the Romans finally abandoned the walls in A.D. 388, Irish settlers were occupying Britain's west seaboard from Devon to Argyll. And the Irish tribe that began to colonize Argyll's peninsula of Kintyre and the isle of Islay from around A.D. 220 were the Scots of Dalriada, a province of Antrim in Ulster. They came in peace as Celts to a Celtic land – Kintyre was held by the Epidii – where their Gaelic would be understood, where an understanding between the peoples had been established by trade and had been strengthened by action against common enemies.

They held their small settlements as part of their home-country, thus the colony was also named Dalriada (the Portion of Riada). The main settlement, on the flat isthmus of Crinan between Loch Fyne and the Sound of Jura, was, three hundred years later, to become the capital of an independent kingdom of Scots. For the present, the Picts saw no threat.

6

Colonization by Scots and Norsemen: 220-1500

The settlement of the Scots in the Hebrides, from their first arrival in the third century A.D. to the founding of Somerled's Kingship of the Isles in the twelfth century, falls within the Dark Age of Hebridean history, when little can be known from contemporary records. But much can be learned about the Picts and Scots from at least a dozen Greek and Roman historians writing between the first century B.C. and the fourth A.D.; from Adomnan, the abbot of Iona in the seventh century; the Venerable Bede of the eighth century; and finally from the early Irish MSS, principally the Annals of Ulster, of Tigernach (Abbot of Clonmacnoise), the Duan Albanaich, Leabhar Breac, and several others, which although not contemporary, being written between 1000 and 1550, present traditional accounts – copies of older documents and oral records. These sources, when sifted by the historians, give a general impression of the way the Island and Highland people dressed, fought, lived, and organized their communities in the pre-Christian era.

The first name and voice that history allows us to hear out of Scotland is that of Galgacus,* the King of Galloway. Under his command the Picts had made a well-organized defence against Roman invasion. Agricola's son-in-law, Tacitus, gave to Galgacus words that have sounded down the centuries: 'They make a wilderness, and call it peace.'† The voice rings out, as true of twentieth-century aggression as of Roman.

The early Celts, according to Roman records, all had red or fair hair, which the

---

* *Galgach* is the Gaelic word for warlike, and *Galgadh* means champion.
† 'Ubi solitudinem faciunt, pacem appellant', *Life of Agricola*.

Caledonians wore flowing over the shoulders. Only slaves had the hair cut short. Round bonnets were worn and skull-caps by fighting men. On a fragment of carved stone from the Antonine wall, the Picts, like all other Celts, are shown wearing the sagum, which was either a skin or a coarse woollen blanket thrown over the naked shoulders and fastened by a wooden pin or a brooch. The Romans were impressed by the Celts' skill in weaving and dyeing. At the time of the occupation, the striped sagum woven in several colours was commonly worn (and later adopted by the Saxons and Franks). In the Hebrides and Highlands there gradually evolved patterns of striping peculiar to districts and islands, so that a man's home territory could be told by the colour-design of his dress. The derivation of 'tartan' is from the old Scots and Irish Gaelic: *Tuar*, colour, and *Tan*, district. *Tuartan* meant district colour before it came to mean clan colour. The Senchus Mor refers also to laws of the B.C. era that a king's tartan could have seven colours, a Druid's six, and a noble's four.

Undressed sheepskins were popular clothing, being easily produced, and thus were worn as late as the sixth century by the lay monks of Iona, although they also had linen. The Celts were celebrated for their production of linen. They pounded the spun flax in a mortar filled with water, and to soften it again after weaving beat the cloth with clubs on a smooth stone. Such linen was probably worn only by the rich, like the tunic, which the Britons called 'cota'. The sleeved tunic as worn by Scots and Britons was close-fitting and reached below the thigh, hence was left open at the front or sides to allow freedom of movement, for kilt-pleating had not yet been invented. It was belted round the waist and never fell below the knee. The legs were usually bare but breeches (trews) were sometimes worn. The Scots, and probably the Picts too, wore untanned skins tied to the feet with thongs, hairy side out for good grip, or hairy side in for warmth. They were called *brog* when they covered only the foot; when they reached higher they were *cuaron*, which were of shaped cow-hide drawn by thongs neatly around the foot and pierced by holes to let water escape. Women's dress appears to have been much the same as men's – the sagum and cota, but the latter worn without sleeves and cut lower at the breast.

By modern standards, dress was scanty, but Marcellinus reports that 'the lusty youth had their limbs hardened with frost and continual exercise'. In battle the Picts and Scots threw off all clothing. They stripped for identification, for most Celtic warriors had their district colours tattooed or painted on their bare skins.* The chiefs wore helmets, shields, and breast-plates, but the main body

* Caesar. 1964: Donald.

of Picts and Scots affected no luxuries. Both Dio and Solinus have them fighting naked in the third century, but in the sixth Gildas gives them a loin-cloth.

The chiefs of Picts and Scots rode to battle on two-horse chariots, which had spoked wheels with hubs showing a high degree of carpentry skill. The horses were as small as Shetland ponies, and not normally given battle-action. The Pictish arms were the short spear, an oblong or circular shield, and the long, two-handed sword with a two-edged blade as broad as a hand and unpointed. Such swords were only slashers, and this limitation had caused the defeat of the Caledonian warriors at Mons Grampius. The legions had recoiled before the fury of their first charge; thereafter the short gladius or thrusting sword had played havoc with them at close quarters. The Scots sword had the blade and hilt cast in one piece in bronze, the blade being eighteen to twenty-eight inches long,* but when iron became readily available, they adopted the Pictish broadsword as their *claidheamth-mor*, or great sword, which they always used with a dirk for in-fighting. It remained an island weapon of renown until late in the seventeenth century, when its place was taken and its name usurped by the short, single-handed claymore with basket hilt. The Scots won Roman admiration for the dexterity with which they used small round targets covered in leather to receive and elude missiles.† They carried small bows with birch arrows only twenty-two inches long. This was not an effective weapon: nor in later years, when the bow and arrow became the principal weapon of the Gaels, was long-bow archery developed to the formidable scale of English arms.

That all principal islands were populated by the Picts would seem certain, for the mainland population must have been considerable to field 30,000 men (*sic*) for Mons Grampius,‡ and to contain 40,000 Roman troops early in the fourth century. The Picts built their huts of wattle and fed mainly on the meat and milk of their flocks, and on game won by hunting. Solinus avers that Hebrideans did not cultivate the land (a wrong impression gained from seaward) and the abundance of querns refutes him. The Scots were cattle-men, but like the Picts they also herded sheep of the four-horned species similar to those of St Kilda. They secured their beasts in earthwork enclosures, palisaded against wolves. Goats and horses – the horses small but fast-moving and high-spirited§ – wandered wild in large number.

Among the Picts and early Scots there was no family life in the narrow sense,

* 1896: W. Drummond-Norie.
† Tacitus.
‡ Ibid.
§ Ibid.

for the sanction of marriage was unknown. Men and women had a free sexual relationship, and the children of each community were reared as joint offspring.* The social unit was thus the larger family of the tribe, and children were well cared for. A boy won freedom from parental control at the age of fourteen, but did not receive tribal privileges, such as a share of land and a separate house, until a full circle of beard had grown at the age of twenty.† Since descent could not be traced with certainty through the father, succession to office, chiefship or kingship was through the mother. A father became the head of his own family in Erin only after the adoption of Christianity from the fourth century onwards, when marriage became obligatory. Right of succession through the mother then gradually died away, although retained by the high Kings of Alban (to keep royal blood pure) until the tenth century.

The full members of the Scots clans were equal and classless. Each man had a right to his share of arable land and of pasture for cattle, but inevitably there were some more equal than others. An able man who managed to increase his herd won an increase in his allotment, and of status within the clan. The owner of twenty cows or more was known as Bo-Aire, or Cow Lord.‡ The full members were called *saor* or free, but there were others named *daor* or unfree, and these were either wrongdoers sentenced to slavery or else incomers not of the tribe, such as mercenaries seeking employment, bondsmen who had come into Erin or Dalriada, or the native inhabitants of conquered land.§

Around 220,‖ the Scots colony of Dalriada, in Kintyre and the Argyll islands, came under the rule of Cairbre Riada.¶ He was the son of Conari II, the reigning High King of Erin (212–20). Under the Celtic law of Tanistry, which did not recognize succession by primogeniture and was at that time strictly observed, he could not succeed his father. The northern boundary of his territory was traditionally Glen More in Mull, marked on its south side by a cairn called *Carn Cul ri h'Iar-Inn* (Cairn with its back to the Western Isles, in reference to the south Hebrides), and on its north side by a *Carn ri h'Alban*. These Cairns were marked on Blaeu's map, surveyed by Timothy Pont around 1608, and are still there today. (Iar-In, Western Island, was the original form of Erin.)**

Julius Solinus, writing in the third century, presumably of Cairbre Riada,

---

* Ibid. 1877: Skene. 1955: Chadwick.
† 1877: Skene.
‡ 1949: Dwelly.
§ 1877: Skene.
‖ 1970: Donald. (Skene gives date, incorrectly, as 258.)
¶ Bede, and *Leabhar Breac*.
** 1970: Donald. 570 B.C.: *Argonautica*.

says, 'The King of the Hebudae was not allowed to possess anything of his own lest avarice should divert him from truth and justice'. His observation goes to the heart of the clan system of government, which although aristocratic was the antithesis of feudalism. Gaul had been regulated by clanship before the Romans, who found it prevalent throughout Britain and Ireland. A clan (Gaelic *clann*, children), was a tribe claiming common ancestry, which the chief represented. They acknowledged no private property in land, which belonged to the clan. Chiefship and kingship were subject to salutary democratic controls. Office was hereditary, but not to a person, only to a family from which the king or chief was elected. On his succession he was invested with cattle, grain and land to maintain his family and the dignity of office. He held all such property in trust for his people. The clansmen gave their chief obedience and, in the Christian era, the respect due to a father by his family. The chief in turn managed the clan's land for his people's good. He had the right of jurisdiction, yet could be deposed if found wanting. Every man's first duty was to clan and chief, wherever he might be, and the chief was responsible for every member. The close mutual trust and dependence thus engendered was almost wholly good. The full members of a Celtic clan, virtually classless, enjoyed from their leaders a respect unknown to the men of most other countries, where peasants were dealt with as livestock attached to the land. The clansman followed his chief by choice, not compulsion, and could feel himself to be of consequence in a society whose every commitment was his, and on which he could speak his mind without his loyalty being questioned. One product of the system had potential danger. Tacitus remarks that the Celts adopted all enmities as well as friendships. This meant that an injury suffered by one man was an injury to a whole clan, and that could lead to endless feuding unless the chiefs had commonsense.

The chain of command in the tribe was set up by the chief's appointing his relations as chieftains, giving each land in accord with his rank. And each of these leaders had his own following of relations, who were under his command in battle. All were in some degree related to the chief and felt pride in sharing his blood. The chief in his own lifetime appointed his successor or *Tanistear* (second person) to prevent an interregnum or minority, and such succession by Tanistry went to the oldest and most worthy, for the Celts, as shown by the Brehon laws, preferred experience and ability in their leaders to strength and youth. The chief had to obtain his clan's consent to any such appointment, and the new chief had to receive the sanction of his people before taking office, if only to acknowledge that his power was from theirs. In practice, the choice of the clansmen usually coincided with the wish of the chief, and the man with the best right to succession might sometimes be the king's son, or chief's son. A chief remained subject to dismissal, of which there are recorded instances. The law of Tanistry applied not only to clan government but to the Pictish and Scottish thrones until 1056. The lack of it thereafter led to weak kings, minority rules, and much misgovernment. Adomnan records that both the Picts and the Hebridean chiefs chose their king, and appointed a 'council of the wisest' to advise him.

Law was administered by judges known as Brehons (later as brieves), who gave their name to the laws, often described as 'of Ireland' because they were codified there in the Senchus Mor around A.D. 438. They were older than the Roman laws and common to the Celts. The Brehons were given farms for their support and allowed a proportion of the fines imposed. Almost every crime was punished by a fine of cattle, which went to the plaintiff or the chief. In Britain as a whole the chief riches of the people were cattle, according to Caesar, but in the Islands cattle were the only riches. Courts were held in the open air, where justice might be seen and heard to be done. Celts guilty of great crimes were impaled on stakes and burned.* A death sentence by the Caledonians could mean burning between two fires, which gave rise to the saying *'Edir da teine Bheil'*, 'He is between the two fires of Bel' (the sun god).† Such harsh laws were modified by St Patrick in the fifth century. An Islay site, where the Brehons held court, may be seen today 1¼ miles south of Bowmore, close to the right-hand side of the road. This is a semicircular knoll called *Torr a' Breithimh* (Judgement Mound), standing on open ground overlooking Loch Indaal. It is topped by a low wall of turf and stone, believed to be the dock, where defendant, judge, and plaintiff were in full sight and hearing of all clansmen present.

The religion of the Hebrides and Highlands beyond Dalriada was Druidism until after the coming of the Irish missionaries of the sixth century. The Greek and Roman historians give much fragmentary information about the Druids, whose essential doctrine, they say, was the immortality of the soul and its reincarnation. Julius Caesar thought that this belief might account for the Celts' extraordinary bravery in battle. He perhaps forgot that they fought for liberty. Little more is known of their faith or rites, for there is no record of a particular religion. They are recorded more as students of mathematical and scientific knowledge – of the movements of sun and stars, of the form and measurement of the earth, the history of men, and the law. On the subjects of law and divination

---

* Diodorus Siculus.
† 1831: Logan.

they were accepted authorities. Caesar tells of the remarkably long educational course undertaken by the Gallic Druids – twenty years of instruction given orally. He adds that they adjudicated on all territorial disputes and the inheritance of livestock. Diodorus reports that they were respected in peace and war and by enemies and friends alike.

The displacement of Pictish Druidism by Christianity, which had begun in the third century,* continued in the fifth when St Ninian, a Briton of Strathclyde who had been trained at Rome, preached Christianity to the southern Picts.† This would have little direct influence in the Hebrides, but shortly after Ninian's death, St Patrick, also a Briton, began in 432 his successful mission in Ireland. From Ireland the final conversion of the Hebrides and north Pictland was to come 130 years later, largely through the work of St Columba and St Moluag, but there were many others before and after. Christianity had certainly reached Ireland long before Patrick, for in 431 Palladius had been sent as bishop 'to the Scots believing in Christ'. There can be little doubt that Christian doctrine would by then have reached the Scots colony in Kintyre and Islay.

Centuries after the missionaries' work had been done, and the Druids were seen no more, Druidical festivals and rites continued to be observed in the Isles. One of these was the lighting of the Bealltuinn fires on May Day – named in Gaelic *Là Buidhe Bealltuinn*, the Yellow Day of the Fires of Bel. On this day all hearth fires were extinguished in the houses, and new sacrificial fires kindled on the hill-tops, where cattle were driven between the fires of Bel to keep them free of disease in the coming year.‡ From these purifying flames the hearth fires were relit. A Gaelic prayer was offered, *Beannachadhe Beothaidh*, or Blessing the Kindling.§

Dhé fadaidh thusa am chridhe steach
Aiteal graidh do m' choimhearsnach,
Do m' nàmh, do m' dhaimh, do m' charaid,
Do 'n t'saor, do 'n daor, do 'n traille —
O Mhic na Muire minghile,
Bho 'n ni is isle crannachaire
Gu ruig an t'Ainn is Airdre.

* Tertullian.
† Bede says the southern Picts received Christianity long before Ninian.
‡ 1695: Martin. 1949: Dwelly.
§ 1930: Nicolson. The prayer was first written down around 1650.

O God, kindle in my heart
A glimmer of the sun's warmth towards my neighbour,
Towards my enemy, towards my kindred, towards my friend,
Towards the free, towards the slave, towards the bondsman –
O Sons of the Earth soft and fair,
From the lowest created thing
Up to the Circle Most High.

The prayer uses very old words of double meaning. *Graidh* (now rendered as love) meant 'heat of the sun after bursting out from behind a cloud', and *Muire* (which may now be rendered as Mary) strictly means Earth. The Great Earth-Mother (spouse of the Sun) was *Gé*, partly *Muir*, the Sea, and partly *Muire*, the Earth. The name *Mairi* could mean Daughter of the Sea and Earth.*

On this day also the young folk met on the moors, where they cut a round ditch enclosing an area big enough to hold them all in the middle. They lit a fire, cooked and ate a custard of eggs and milk, then made a big oatcake which they broke into a bonnet. One piece was blackened with charcoal. Each person drew his portion blindfolded and whoever drew the black became the sacrifice, which he symbolized by leaping three times through the flames.† The purpose of the rite was to implore Bel's favour, that the year might be productive. The circle was the symbol of Bel, and after the Scots Christians came to the Isles the Druidic circle became incorporated in the sculptured cross – a design known thenceforth as the Celtic Cross. St Martin's Cross, encircled by its 'glory' in front of Iona Abbey, is especially appropriate to the site, for Iona was reputedly a Druidic centre long before the coming of Columba.

When the Romans abandoned Britain in the early fifth century, the Picts and Scots combined to plunder the Britons as far south as London. The arrival of Anglo-Saxon colonists in Britain halted these excursions in mid-century. The Picts turned their energies to home affairs, where the Angles and Britons were firmly established in the Lowlands, and the stream of Scots colonists to the coasts of Argyll was quickening (Argyll – Gaelic *Earra-ghaidheal*, pronounced Er-a-gyl – means Coastland of the Gael). The main phase of Scots colonization began around 500, when Fergus, Angus, and Lorn, the sons of Erc, the king of Dalriada in Ireland, crossed the sea to Argyll,‡ which their people had now been holding for almost three hundred years.

* Graham Donald of Islay.
† This latter rite was observed until the 1930s at Tarbolton, in Ayrshire – but only for the fun of commemoration.
‡ *Annals of Tigernach* and *Duan Albanaich.*

The records are not contemporary, therefore not fully historical, and they differ in detail, but there is no reason to suppose them incorrect in broad outline. Angus, Fergus, and Lorn would be barred from succession to the throne of Irish Dalriada by the law of Tanistry. They came in force to Alban (this name for north Britain, as distinct from Britannia, dates from the fifth century B.C.*) to found kingdoms of their own. Angus took Islay and Jura, and from him came the clan whose descendants six hundred years later were to produce Somerled, the kings of the Hebrides, and the Clan Donald Lords of the Isles. Fergus took south Argyll; and Lorn, the northern part of Argyll that still bears his name. All three petty kingdoms were later united. It is certain that by the middle of the sixth century the Scottish Dalriada stretched from the Firth of Clyde to Ardnamurchan, the northern boundary being ill-defined. An estimate of the Scots population at that time can be made if we accept the housing enumeration in *Chronicles of the Picts and Scots*:†

	Houses	*Armed muster*
Clan Angus, holding Islay and Jura	430	500 men
Clan Lorn, holding Lorn and Morvern	420	600
Clan Gabran (from Fergus), holding Kintyre, Knapdale, Cowal, Arran, Bute	560	300
	1,410	1,400

The houses were apparently grouped in settlements of twenty, for they had a sea-muster, assigning to each twenty houses fourteen benches for oarsmen. The armed musters give an average of one man to a house, suggesting a family unit whose size, if taken at five or six, would give a Dalriadan population of 7,000 to 8,000, excluding the native Picts.

The Scots and Picts were soon at war, while at the same time a battle for the Picts' minds was being fought by the Celtic Church. The great majority of northern Picts were pagan, the Scots Christian. When Columba conceived his mission to convert the northern Picts, Scottish Dalriada was ruled by his kinsman Conall (560–74). Columba was the son of Fedilmith mac Fergus, a great grandson of Niall of the Nine Hostages, who early in the fifth century had established the dynasty of Tara in Ulster.‡ His mother was Eithne, descended from kings of Leinster.

* Herodotus.
† 1867: Skene.
‡ 1961: Anderson.

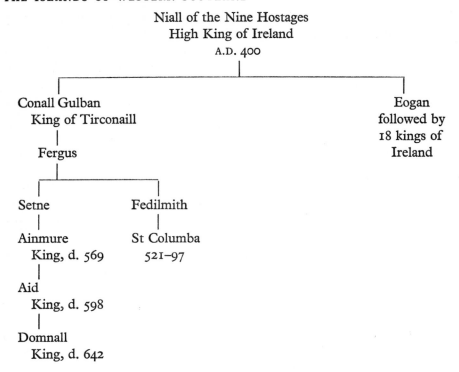

Niall of the Nine Hostages
High King of Ireland
A.D. 400

Conall Gulban
King of Tirconaill

Fergus

Setne

Ainmure
King, d. 569

Aid
King, d. 598

Domnall
King, d. 642

Fedilmith

St Columba
521–97

Eogan
followed by
18 kings of
Ireland

St Columba had been trained for the religious life from boyhood and given the Latin name for Dove, equivalent to the Gaelic Calman – a misnomer in point of character, which was ardent. While preparing his voyage to Iona he visited King Conall in Alban.* This meeting would be obligatory, for the occupation of an island by a company of monks would have to be negotiated with Dalriada's king, and the rights of its inhabitants discussed. It lay too on the northern frontier, where Mull was claimed by Scots and Picts alike. The meeting probably occurred in 562 at Dunadd, or (according to local tradition) at Caisteal Torr in Knapdale, and presumably concluded with Columba receiving authority to settle in Iona (then variously named Hii, Hia, Ioua – spellings used by Adomnan, Bede, and others. The name Iona came into general use in the eighteenth century, being changed from Ioua by typographical error). Bede says that Columba received Iona from the Picts after their conversion. This confirms their claim to the island, but possession lay with the Scots as shown by Adomnan, who wrote earlier and with more intimate knowledge.

* *c.*685: Adomnan.

Adomnan says of Columba's first voyage to Iona only that he sailed from Ireland to Britain with twelve disciples, when he was aged forty-two – that is, in 563. Later Irish chronicles have him sailing direct from Derry on Lough Foyle to reach Iona on Whitsun Eve, 12 May,* but for such detail there is no certain historical evidence. The course he probably followed, for it is the only safe and sensible course for a large currach with mast and lug-sail, would go up the west coast of Islay, thus avoiding the delays and labours of meeting adverse tides and winds in the Sound of Jura. (These points were demonstrated by experiment with a currach in 1963.) He is said to have taken the voyage in easy stages, landing on Islay and Oronsay.

Although apparently remote from the centres of power in Alban, Iona made a base well-chosen strategically for the conversion of the Picts. It lay only three days by sea from Ireland, and one or two from Crinan. Navigable waterways, requiring short portages, stretched by way of the Firth of Lorn and the Great Glen to Inverness at the heart of Pictland. Yet Iona was sufficiently isolated to give the monks the security their work needed. The Vikings were not yet rampant although their longships were probably using the outer isles.

Columba built his church and monastic houses of wood and wattle,† surrounded by an earthwork vallum to mark the bounds and keep out cattle. He obtained the shiploads of wattle from a landowner (presumably on Mull) in exchange for barley seed.‡ The Scots were the first architects in Alban to invent a way of squaring timber for large buildings,§ and it may be that the first church in Iona was thus built.|| The roof was thatched. The exact site of the monastery is not certainly known, but there is good reason to believe that the present abbey stands on it.

The smallest monasteries of the sixth century comprised 150 monks,¶ but the term *monach* or monk included lay brothers, who wore the skin sagum. Clerics wore coarse woollen garments of natural colour above a white tunic. Their heads were shaved in front of a line from ear to ear, leaving the hair at the back flowing down unchecked, as distinct from the Roman tonsure, in which the crown was shaved above a circular fringe. The original twelve disciples, who accompanied their founders to the first monastic sites in the Hebrides, were chosen for their

* 1876: Skene.
† Adomnan.
‡ Ibid.
§ Pownall: *Archaeologia* IX.
|| 1831: Logan.
¶ 1947: Carmichael.

crafts and trade skills. Their small numbers were rapidly augmented both locally and from Ireland. Converts became members of the *muinntir*, or Christian family. The monks built their own small cells, many scores to each site, from split hardwood, reeds, and turfs. A church, hospice for travellers, common-house, writing-house, refectory, kitchen, and others, were all built within the enclosure. Each monk had much work to do: in the fields where cattle were kept and crops sown, in fishing at sea, or in milling corn, rowing boats, milking cows, and copying the scriptures for use in preaching to the people of the country. Throughout such activity, foremost place was daily given to the divine office of prayer and worship. The people were told of the life and example of Christ and taught the corresponding code of thought and behaviour. The history of education in Alban began in the monasteries, where the children of the *muinntir* were given instruction, and their parents learned crafts or husbandry.*

Once established on Iona, Columba portaged a boat through the Great Glen to meet King Brude at a fortress near Inverness, perhaps Craig Phadrig. All that is known of that critical meeting is that Columba, in talking with the king and his chief Druid, required no interpreter and won access to Pictland for his monks with freedom to preach.† That this should have been achieved while the Picts and Scots were at war – the Picts had taken Dunadd in 560, although apparently not for long – says much for Columba's personality and diplomacy, and for the king's open-mindedness. Numerous monasteries and churches were subsequently established throughout the Highlands and Islands.

Nothing is known of the control of the islands in Columba's time. He had surprisingly little to do with the Outer Hebrides. It may be that Lewis had been settled by summering Vikings. Their presence in the Outer Hebrides would account for Columba's restriction of evangelism to the Picts of the inner isles and mainland, where his life's work lay. It is not evident from Adomnan's *Life* that Columba spent his time on missionary circuits. He did personally preach to the Picts of Alban, but devoted much time to spiritual exercises and monastic life. He held his monks to a strict discipline, and Bede says they went out from Iona to found many more monasteries and churches among the provinces of the Picts.

Attempts have been made to belittle Columba's work. Time, it is said, has exaggerated his example and achievements. That notion is refuted by Bede: 'Iona's monastery long held pre-eminence over most of the monasteries of the Scots, and over all the monasteries of the Picts, and was above them in com-

---

* 1947: Carmichael.
† Adomnan. 1961: Anderson.

munity rule.' Columba's work made possible the union of the several parts of Celtic civilization in Alban. From Fergus to James VI, sixty-three kings succeeded each other in 1,100 years, and forty-eight of these lie buried on Iona.* For a thousand years after Columba's death, his island was everywhere known as *I-Chaluim-cille*, the Island of St Calum. He, rather than Andrew, should have been Scotland's patron saint.

Several other men of spiritual power were active in the Hebrides in the sixth century. St Brendan of Clonfert had founded a small monastery on Eileach an Naoimh (Firth of Lorn) twenty-one years before Columba's arrival.† A third monastery was founded by St Moluag on Lismore between 561 and 564. This latter became a bishopric. Numerous island churches were founded by Columba and the Irish Picts Moluag, Findachan, and St Comgall, who had trained Moluag and founded the great Irish monastery of Bangor. After their death their work was consolidated by a succession of new island saints of the seventh century.

The Celtic Church of Erin and Alban was independent of Rome, which during the fourth and fifth centuries had been reduced to chaos while Huns, Goths, and Vandals overran the western empire. Rome itself had twice been sacked. Communications being thus severed, the Celtic Church had developed its own organization and administration, which in the Roman Church was diocesan and episcopal, but in the Celtic Church monastic and presbyterian: that is, church life was organized around the monastery, which was administered by a presbyter abbot, assisted by elders. A few bishops were appointed, but they held no precedence over the abbots.‡ The Celtic Church differed too from the Roman in its dating of Easter, in celebrating different masses, and in acknowledging only one head on earth, 'Our Lord'. Thus Columba, Brendan, Moluag, Comgall and others would not, we may assume, have accepted the Pope as the Vicar of Christ in Alban and Erin.

Early in the seventh century, Rome was again able to take interest in the Celtic Church. Many Irish and Scottish missionaries were then moving through Europe, and by their learning were helping to enrich the Catholic Church. Since they observed Easter on a different day from the Roman Church, Rome demanded conformity. The Celtic Church stood fast. Superficially, the dispute centred on the precise date of the Resurrection, but there was a more important issue at stake. The Celtic spokesman was St Columbanus of Bangor, who addressed to the Pope and his commission of inquiry two letters, which rejected

---

* 1549: Monro.
† See chapter 10, pp. 263–5.
‡ Bede, *Historia Ecclesiastica* (731).

the Bishop of Rome's claim to jurisdiction beyond the limits of the Roman Empire, and made counter-claim to the Celtic Church's right to follow its ancient customs.*

If the Celtic Church had held unitedly to this independent line, the Reformation of 1560, which had such injurious effects in the Hebrides, might not have occurred in Scotland. But divisions arose. At the Synod of Whitby in 664, the Celtic representative was persuaded to accept the Roman usages and authority. Iona reluctantly accepted the Roman Easter and tonsure but her subsidiary houses refused.† Divisions continued, and those who failed to conform were expelled from Pictland by King Nechtan in 717. The eastern districts were separated from Iona, where a schism occurred as refugees arrived from Pictish monasteries. The church was now in an unsettled and weakened state. It may have been in part the unhappiness thus caused that encouraged a strong development of asceticism in the seventh and eighth centuries, when men preferred to live apart from the monasteries on lonely islets and in wild places, trying to achieve the perfect life by a simple austerity with liberty of rule and conscience. Canons were passed to try – in vain – to bring the movement under control.

At Columba's death on Iona in 597, his main goal, the conversion of the Picts, had been won. New ideals had been presented to the peoples of Alban, and exemplified by the monks in their own lives. The high standards set were now, at the close of the eighth century, about to disappear, but they were never to be lost, for such standards once seen appear to draw men's aspirations even after long periods of lapse into their opposites.

The main factor in the first lapse was the descent of the Vikings in 794, when the Annals of Ulster state tersely, 'All coasts of Britain ravaged by the Gals'. Iona Abbey was destroyed in 795, was rebuilt and burned in 802, again levelled in 806, when the Vikings murdered sixty-eight monks at Martyr's Bay (two hundred yards south of the present jetty), yet again in 825, when they murdered the abbot and monks, and finally in 986, when they murdered the abbot and fifteen monks on the sands of the north point. The Vikings came to the Scottish coasts for plunder with seasonal regularity. In 807, the Iona community planned their escape to east Ireland and began to build a new monastery at Kells, which they completed in 814.‡ From this base they tried to re-staff Iona Abbey, and the persistent courage with which they did so commands admiration, for Kells itself

* 1876: Skene.
† 1961: Anderson.
‡ Ibid.

11. (*facing page*) The Stone Circle at Callernish, Lewis. Thirteen stones stand around the central monolith of 15 feet 7 inches.

12a. Double beehive cell on Eileach an Naoimh, the Isles of the Sea (Hinba).
It probably dates from the seventh century.

12b. The broch at Carloway, Lewis.

was seven times ravaged.* No relic of Columba and no chronicle of Iona has been preserved, although it may be that some were dispersed around Scotland or taken to Kells. It seems probable that the Book of Kells, a world masterpiece of MS illumination, and now in Trinity College, Dublin, had been started (if not completed) in Iona, since it can be dated to the eighth or early ninth century.†

Although the monasteries on the west coast and islands had to close down, the Celtic Church stayed alive. The monks went to earth, taking refuge in the eremitic life on small islands or in remote parts of big ones. They went as far out as the Flannan Isles, even to rock stacks like Luchruban (Pigmy Isle), a tidal islet eaten off the main cliff near the Butt of Lewis. An old stone cell still crouches on Luchruban's summit, thickly cushioned with sea-pinks, which even in high wind scent the June air. Its low walls form a narrow rectangle overlooking half a mile of riven coast to the Butt. Atlantic rollers seethe among the reefs, a score of black shags skim back and forth between cliffs and skerries, and hordes of gulls scream overhead. The site now is precisely as it was in the early ninth century, a fragment of land divorced from man and his works, but giving close communion with wild-life and the natural elements. Such retreat to the wilderness had already been fostered by general disgust at the Paschal quarrel with Rome, so that when the Vikings began their annual summer raids, the eremitic movement, formerly spiritually motivated, became for many a matter of practical politics. The anchorites made a numerous if scattered company, which by the mid-ninth century, when Scots and Picts were at last united, began to gather in communities known as Ceile De (or Culdees), the Companions of God. The Order, formed widely across Scotland and the Isles, founded churches, and for two hundred years nourished the light of ideals during an otherwise dark period.

The Vikings' devastation of Hebridean, Highland, and Irish coasts had been caused by a peculiar population explosion. Norway was divided into twenty-nine petty kingdoms or *fylker*, subject to indivisible succession under which, at a king's death, one male heir inherited all land while other sons and brothers were left without maintenance. But kingship itself resided less importantly in land and subjects than in possession of a *hird* or band of warriors. An economic crisis appears to have acted as a catalyst on the fylki warrior culture to precipitate huge, well-led bands set on piratical, land-raiding, and slave-trading expeditions, with

---

* Archdall's *Monasticon Hibernicum*.
† See below, p. 282.

the simple aim of improving their lot. This early cause was quite different from that of the later settlements.

The distance from Norway to Shetland is only two hundred miles, and to Lewis four hundred – no long voyage for the Vikings, who came to coasts already well known.* Their first tactics were to seize islands and use them as summer bases for mainland raids. All the monasteries of West Scotland were destroyed. Their next move, from bases on the Shetland and Orkney Islands, the Outer Hebrides, the Isle of Man, and Lambay Island in Dublin Bay, was to be the settlement of north Scotland and east Ireland during the ninth and following centuries.

The most important political effect of the Viking attack was the union of the Scots and Pictish Crowns. The Picts had thus far contained the Scots, Anglo-Saxons, and Britons, but the additional effort required to repel Norse invaders overtaxed their strength, and allowed Kenneth MacAlpin, King of Scots, to overthrow their power in 843 and unite the two kingdoms. In this he was aided by his descent from the Pictish royal house on his mother's side. Alban gradually became Scotland. Fortunately for the Scots, the Vikings, who had sacked Paris in 845, were dispersing their power all over western Europe. The Hebrides suffered deepest injury through the destruction of their cultural bridge with Ireland.

The Hebrides had so completely fallen to the Vikings, who by 850 had driven even Clan Angus out of Islay, that they were called by the Scots *Innsigal*, or Islands of the Foreigners. Norse settlement of the Hebrides was hastened from 872, when Harald Haarfager made himself the first king of all Norway. He introduced a feudal system deeply resented by the landowners, many of whom went into exile rather than accept vassalage. From their settlements on the Orkney and Shetland Islands, and the Hebrides, they so harassed the Norwegian coast† that Harald in 891 amassed a fleet and took the islands, which for the next 370 years were ruled by jarls, who although nominally viceroys usually acted independently of the Norwegian Crown – their people would not suffer feudalism. The greatest of these jarls was Godred Crovan, who ruled the Isle of Man and the Hebrides.

During his reign, a far-off battle at Hastings in the south of England was to have far-reaching effects on the welfare of the Hebridean people. Anglo-Norman infiltration of the Scottish court was in future years to undermine the unity of Lowland and Highland Scotland by splitting the nation's language, laws, and

* 1961: Arbman.
† Ari *Ynglinga Saga* (c.1100).

customs, and to subvert the clan system by feudalism. No ills of that kind came of the Norse occupation, for all its occasional ferocities.

Nothing is known of the Norse settlements in the Hebrides by direct evidence – there is not even a stone building that can be definitely attributed to Norsemen* – but much may be inferred by analogy from the structure of society in Man, the Orkneys and Shetlands, Iceland, Scandinavia, and from place-names and sagas.

Norse colonial society was organized in three classes: (1) the kings, whose varied functions were taken by Sea-kings ruling the fleets, Host-kings leading the warriors, Hérad and Fylki-kings governing on land, and Skatt-kings who were the lords of the Hebrides paying *skatt* or land-tax to Norway; (2) the *boendr*, who were the main body of land-holders; and (3) thralls, who in the Hebrides would at first be the Celts, for the Norse did not at once accept into their own free society a people subdued. Slavery was a recognized trade and captives were freely bought and sold. The fact of thralldom in the Hebrides is confirmed by a provision in the Treaty of Perth, which finally ceded the islands to Scotland, that the custom of enthralling a conquered race should not be applied to the Norse settlers.

Within their own free society, the Norsemen's political creed was fully democratic: government for the people by the people. Their land-tenure by allodial right (*odal* = ancestral possession) was the opposite of feudalism. It meant a holding by primal occupancy without a superior, bequeathable to children, and free of rent except for the giving of communal services. Real power lay with the *boendr*, who were the odallers, and long enjoyment of their freedom had made them vigorously individualistic, yet aware that strength lay in social unity, as shown by their readiness for self-sacrifice when the good of the community required it. They were competent farmers; as sailors, incomparable.

Each new settler had the right to water and wood, and to claim all land as far as he could throw his knife from the edge of the field around his home or *stadr*.†
His property had then to be fenced within the year. A *tun* or township had its *bolstadr* or principal farm with an inner field separated by dyke from an out-pasture or *saetr*. Houses were of wood.‡ The Norse settlement names, abbreviated or very slightly altered (*stadr* to sta, as in Tolsta; *bolstadr* to bost, as in Shawbost; *saetr* to shader, as in Grimshader) so abound in the Outer Hebrides that they give complete proof of permanent and widely-spread occupation. Norse place-names in Lewis are eighty per cent of the total, and sixty-six per cent in

* 1928: Royal Commission on Ancient Monuments.
† 1903: MacKenzie.
‡ 1928: Royal Commission on Ancient Monuments.

North Uist and Skye.* The people's rights on the common lands and fishing grounds were controlled by the *hérad*, or district, administered by a *hérsir* (whence the name of the Isle of Harris). Each homestead paid one penny as *skatt*. Measures of land – later continued by the Scots – were named and valued on a standard based on the weight of silver. Thus eighteen- or twenty-penny lands made an ounce land, and eight ounces made one merk or pound land.† (The term Penny Land survives in local names like Pennyghael in Mull, or Five Penny Borve in north-west Lewis.)

Government was by a system of council meetings called *Things*, which dealt with affairs great and small and were named for their purpose. The *Hus Thing* dealt with domestic business, the *Hof Thing* with religious, the *Log Thing* with law, and the *Leidar Thing* with war. An *Allsherjar Thing* (or *Al-Thing*), meaning the Thing of all the Hosts, was equivalent to a House of Commons. An arrow (later a cross) carried by runner summoned people to the *Things* for debate, when each freeman had one vote. The kings could be curbed by voting or withholding supplies, decisions for peace or war thus resting with the people. Rulers were elected and laws made. In course of time the laws were codified and the legislative function was transferred to the *Log Thing*, which became most important in peace.

The laws were surprisingly enlightened. Dishonesty in trade was punished by depriving the swindler of the law's protection, but a starving man or woman who stole food was excused punishment. Adulteration of food ranked as robbery. Injuries inflicted in private quarrels were punished by fine. Women had higher status than in Britain till the twentieth century. They held property in their own right, shared property acquired after marriage, and were protected by laws of divorce, which required that agreement to separate must be mutual, otherwise the offender lost his or her property. But a wife could procure divorce for proven ill-treatment, and the man for his wife's adultery. Marriage without sufficient means of support was forbidden. On betrothal, the couple were allowed to share the same bed, and a custom of 'bundling', without undressing, continued in the Outer Hebrides until the twentieth century.‡ The Norse protected bundling by imposing outlawry for breach of promise.

The Norsemen held traders in surprising respect. Their *kaupships* (merchant-men) carried no war-pennant at the masthead, no shields hung over the gunwales, and no dragons at the prow, and thus could be distinguished at a glance

* 1967: Simpson.
† 1250: Njals Saga.
‡ 1903: Mackenzie.

from warships. Even the Vikings, the professional pirates – and theirs was thought to be an honourable trade, like the cattle-rustling of the Gaelic clansmen – refrained from plundering *kaupships* at sea. Attack on an undefended boat was felt to be unworthy. Tales of relentless cruelty, of gross physical appetite, and of domineering personality, were told against them both by enemies and saga-writers, but such reports would undoubtedly exaggerate. The fact remains that they were readier in action than speech. They kept their sense of honour un-blunted, had a contempt for craftiness, and abhorrence of injustice. They accepted slavery as an institution while rejecting tyrannical government for themselves.

Their favourite sports were the same as the Celts: hunting, falconry, ball games, wrestling, swimming, and jumping. Their games included chess, riddles, and jugglery. In Lewis in 1831, seventy-seven walrus ivory chessmen were disclosed when a cow broke open a sand-dune on the south shore of Camus Uig. They have been dated to around A.D. 1200 and rank among the oldest chessmen in Europe. The pieces are exquisitely carved in two main sizes from several different sets. Each king, queen, bishop, and knight has been given individual character by a Norse craftsman allowing full play to imaginative expression – two knights, for example, are portrayed biting the tops of their shields in *berserkgangr*. The larger pieces are four or five inches high. Eleven specimens may be seen in the National Museum of Antiquities in Edinburgh, and sixty-six at the British Museum.*

The Norse were superb craftsmen and their ships, like their chessmen, things of beauty. Nor did they neglect the arts. Their music was played on the harp and an early form of violin, their *skalds* recited poetry, and saga-men told stories. Writing was known to them, if rarely practised, from the fourth century. They used the Runic script, adopting the Roman after their conversion to Christianity. A Runic Stone in the churchyard of Kilbar in Barra (now in the National Museum of Antiquities) is unique, for the Norse erected no sculptured stones elsewhere in the Hebrides.

Icelandic writers of the twelfth and thirteenth centuries record the religious beliefs of the Norsemen before their formal adoption of Christianity in the eleventh century. They shared with other Teutonic peoples belief in a pantheon of gods headed by Odin (the Anglo-Saxon Woden). They had a special regard for his son Thor. Sacrifices were offered in wooden temples, where the presiding priest was a chief, for there was no priestly class in the Scottish islands. At sacrificial feasts held in the spring, autumn, and mid-winter, the animals eaten

* Plate 216.

were horses, oxen, and boars. Human sacrifice was sometimes offered to Odin, but rarely to Thor. The Norsemen believed in a life after death, when the soul passed to the realm of Hel, who was the daughter of one of the lesser gods; but if the body were slain in battle the soul passed to Valhalla and dwelt with Odin. There feasting and fighting filled joyous days – but not in eternity. A most interesting facet of their thought was that not even the life of the gods would last for ever. A day far-distant was foreseen when Odin and Thor would fall and Valhalla be destroyed by fire. In their place, the gods of a younger generation would govern a better world.*

The form of burial practised in the Isles was chiefly inhumation. Ship burials were used for chiefs or rich merchants. These might be either by mounding or cremation. The rarity of Norse graves in the Hebrides – only four have been found in the outer isles – suggests that burning on a funeral pyre was more common. Ship burials have been found on Colonsay, Oronsay, and Canna. One on the sand dunes of Kiloran Bay in Colonsay contained skeletal remains of a man and horse, boat rivets, iron arrowheads, sword, spear, axe, and shield, and three coins, one dated 831–54. The man lay crouched with a pair of bronze scales between his chin and knees, which suggests that he may have been a merchant. Warriors favoured the funeral pyre, hoping from its purification for admission to Valhalla, together with possessions befitting their station – dogs, horses, falcons, and thralls – if these were burned with them. Ship cremations were generally on land, but the sagas occasionally tell of burning ships headed out to sea.

Christianity was accepted by the Norsemen of the Hebrides long before A.D. 1000, when it was legally established in Iceland. It is alleged of early converts that while they might pray to Christ in their *bolstadr*, they invoked Thor *in extremis*. Considering the Vikings' distaste for attack on defenceless *kaupships*, we might wonder at their sacking of churches, destruction of records, and repeated, merciless butchery of defenceless monks on Iona. A likely reason for this apparent malignity has been found in their reaction to Charlemagne's persecution – in the name of Christ – of the Teutonic people's religion.† The Emperor of the West had conceived for himself a religious mission in Europe. He invited the Saxons, who were allied to the Scandinavians and worshipped the same god, to choose between Christianity and death. To that end, he not only destroyed their temples but sowed hatred by putting 4,500 Saxon prisoners to the sword after the battle of Verden in 782. Until then, Norsemen had taken no action against the Christian Church. Thereafter, as fellow-followers of Odin, they hit back and

* 1899: Chadwick.
† 1903: Mackenzie.

spared no one. Once again, events far from the Hebrides, of which the islesmen were unaware, brought disaster.

After Godred Crovan's death on Islay in 1095, his successor took the title of King of Man and the Isles. The independent line taken by this jarldom, and the growing strength of the king of Scots, had been causing alarm to King Magnus III of Norway. Once already, in 1093, he had had to sail 'west over sea' to assert his suzerainty. Now, in 1098, he marshalled a great fleet and fell upon his Hebridean compatriots with intent to punish.

Western Europe was at this time enjoying a warm climate, which lasted two hundred years from around A.D. 1000. Temperatures were nearly 4°C. (7°F.) above former levels. If writers of the time report correctly, fig trees were growing on Lewis. An account written by Bjorn Cripplehand, a skald, reads as if he enjoyed the massacre from afar while basking aboard ship on a summer cruise. 'Fire played in the fig trees of Liodhus; it mounted up to heaven. Far and wide the people were driven to flight. The fire gushed out of their houses. The liberal king went with the fire over Ivist [Uist]. The boendr lost life and property. The king gained much gold.'* Again, 'The glad wolf reddened tooth and claw in many a mortal wound within Tiree . . . the people of Mull ran to exhaustion. Greenland's king caused maids to weep south in the islands.'†

Magnus devastated Lewis, Uist, Skye, Kintyre, and all the Argyll islands. Substantial woodlands had hitherto survived the fellings by peat and man, but Magnus's deliberate destruction of natural resources gave the trees of the outer isles and Skye a set-back from which they failed to recover before the population grew and the weather worsened.

He forced Edgar, King of Scots, to acknowledge his claim to the Hebrides, although not to the large Norse possessions on the mainland, which by now included almost the whole of Argyll and of north Scotland down to Inverness. Magnus, then aged twenty-five, was sufficiently pleased with the Scots to adopt their national dress, and to introduce the kilt to Norway, where it was worn for the next hundred years. This innovation earned him the nickname *Barfod*, or Bareleg. It is not certainly known how the Scots then wore the kilt. It probably differed from the Roman, Welsh, Manx, and Irish kilts in being a kilted plaid or striped blanket, belted round the waist and pinned at the breast, thus providing a covering for the trunk as well as the loins and thighs. It might less probably have been the short kilt (often wrongly said to be an eighteenth-century innovation),

---

* 1098: *Collectanea de Rebus Albanicus.*
† Sturla, *Magnus Saga* (c. 1280).

for that was worn by some Gaels at least as early as A.D. 1050, as clearly portrayed on five bronze figures at the shrine of St Manchan in Kings County,* and was worn in Scotland before 1124 by Alexander I, King of Scots, as shown on his seal.†

The Norse Kings of Man maintained their rule over the southern Hebrides only for another half century. Unawares they mothered their own conqueror. The rightful king of Argyll, Gillebride of Clan Angus, had married a daughter of the King of Man, but was forced into exile in Ireland. His Norse wife delivered a son, who was christened *Sumarlidi*, the Summer Traveller – a name commonly given by the Norse to Vikings, who voyaged in summer.‡ Around 1130, when Somerled had grown to manhood, he and his father returned to Scotland,§ raised the people of Morvern, and drove the Norsemen out of mainland Argyll. Established now as king of Argyll, Somerled made peace with Olav the Red, King of Man, whose sea-power appeared invincible, and married his daughter Ragnild. But when Olav was succeeded by his tyrannical son Godred in 1152, the island people turned to Somerled.

Somerled's sympathies naturally inclined to his Scots heritage, which had moulded his aspirations. He was a man of quick discernment, yet politically long-sighted, and knew how to wait without wasting time. His need was sea-power, without which he could be freed neither from the immediate Norse threat to his west flank nor the longer-term threat from the east, where Norman feudalism was developing at the heart of the Scots kingdom. More important than these, maybe, was the simple fact of his genius for sea-war and statecraft, and the need to give genius outlet. Providence offered, and Somerled seized.

Norse power was based on the dragon-prowed longships. These were clinker-built, up to $76\frac{1}{2}$ feet long, sharply pointed at both ends, narrow in the beam, but drawing less than three feet of water. They were easily managed by oar in creeks and bays. The oars were only sixteen feet long amidships, where the freeboard was under four feet high, but longer at the rising bow and stern. When the wind was abaft the beam the ships could be sailed under a large and heavy square-sail, which had the mast stepped on a keel-block over ten feet long to spread the strain. Ships of the Gokstad design had the keel a foot deeper amidships than at either end, so were able to beat against the wind at a wide angle (a facsimile was sailed across the Atlantic in 1893). Steering was by an oar, called a steerboard, on

* 1967: Donald (reproduction).
† 1831: Logan.
‡ 1971: Donald.
§ MacMhuirichs, *The Red and Black Books of Clanranald* (seventeenth century).

the 'starboard' or right-hand side of the stern, from which a tiller ran athwart the ship.

Longships varied widely in size and shape. The fastest were called *skutas*. The planking on the Gokstad ship was only one inch thick, having been reduced from three-inch timber to leave a series of projections to each side of the ship's ribs. The planks could thus be tied to the ribs with pine-roots. Nails and rivets were dispensed with, minimum weight being allied to maximum strength to give high performance. Not till the nineteenth century were racing machines made to such a standard of craftsmanship.* Slower and heavier ships were nailed and riveted, and a few were even sheathed with iron above the water-line.

Against contrary winds on long voyages, longships might have to be rowed night and day, therefore the likelihood is that they then carried three shifts of crew. The larger boats of ten oars a side thus carried a crew of sixty, of whom half would fight in battle. Some sagas may exaggerate when they cite ships of forty to sixty oars: in 896, two hundred men were carried in five ships, and twelve thousand men in 250, giving forty and forty-eight crewmen apiece. The crew hung their round shields, made of painted pine, along the gunwales of the outer bulwarks, and carried as arms a mail shirt, sword, axe, spear, javelin, and bows and arrows.

The Scots galley since the seventh century or earlier had been the *biorlinn* (Gaelic, short blade), a ship clinker-built of pine and oak on a long keel,† having the planks fastened by thongs. These were seaworthy vessels, but no match for the swifter, bigger, and stronger longships, which for the last three hundred years had given the Vikings complete supremacy at sea over all nations. Somerled knew that reconquest of the Hebrides could only be made by designing ships superior to the Norse in battle-effectiveness. Secretly, he then began to build a fleet of warships shorter than the Norse longships, but incorporating two new inventions, which gave them the advantages of quicker turn and more effective fire-power at close-quarters – the hinged rudder and a fighting-top at the mast-head. The design is given a clear portrayal on the Seal of Somerled on a charter given by his son Ragnall to Paisley Abbey in 1175.‡ The new ships were called *Naibheag* (pronounced Nyvaig), meaning Little Ship. They are said to have numbered fifty-eight,§ and could not have been of lesser number to match the full force of Godred's sea-power.

* 1961: Arbman.
† Adomnan.
‡ 1967: Donald.
§ Mackenzie, *History of the Outer Hebrides* (1903), gives the figure as eighty.

When news of the threat at last reached Godred in Man, he sailed for the Hebrides. On Epiphany, 6 January 1156, the two fleets engaged off the west coast of Islay. The battle raged till nightfall. Morning found the Norse battle-fleet broken – the only sea-fight lost in their history – but Somerled's crews were too exhausted to follow up to the Isle of Man. Somerled and Godred agreed to divide the Hebrides. Somerled took Bute and Arran under the nominal suzerainty of the Scottish Crown, and all the islands south of Ardnamurchan Point: Mull, Coll, Tiree, Jura, Islay, Colonsay, Gigha, and lesser isles – under the suzerainty of the Norwegian Crown, to whom he and his successors paid tribute. Godred retained Man, the Skye group, and the Outer Hebrides.

Somerled took up his seat in Islay. He berthed his fleet of Nyvaigs at Lagavulin Bay on the south coast, where Dunyvaig Castle was later built for their protection by his grandson, Donald I. Somerled's chief castle was Caisteal Claidh (Castle of the Trench) which he had built around 1154 on Fraoich Island to command the Sound of Islay. This was the first castle in the Hebrides built to square Norman design.

Malcolm IV, King of Scots, had reason to feel concerned at the great power of the king of Argyll, and asked Somerled for the surrender of his mainland territory. But Somerled had better reason to refuse than Malcolm to ask. The too large influx of Normans to the Scottish court was causing an alienation of the court from the Celtic people. This process had begun a hundred years earlier in the reign of Malcolm III, who (after defeating MacBeth) had married Margaret, sister of the English prince Edgar Aetheling. She had a pliant husband. Under her influence, the Celtic Church was supplanted by the Roman (she was later canonized), and Gaelic by English as the court language. English fugitives from Norman rule flocked to Scotland. The interests of the Celtic people were in consequence neglected. Margaret then sent her son David (aged thirteen) to the Norman court. He spent twenty years there and married a Norman widow, whose large possessions made him a vassal of the English Crown. When David succeeded to the Scottish throne in 1124, he brought back with him a thousand Anglo-Norman land-seekers, to whom he distributed estates. The Celtic owners were presumably dispossessed. Gaelic, which only fifty years earlier had been the language of all Scotland (except on Norse territory and along the English border), fell into disuse in the Lowlands. A triple cleavage, racial, linguistic, and political, was thus made between the Gaels of the Islands and Highlands and the English-speaking, feudalized Lowlands. Each came to think the other's tongue barbarous. The detestation in which feudalism was held by the Celtic islesmen, now well mixed with Norse blood, sprang from their long history of freedom and their natural rejection of the feudalistic stratification of society into classes. Somerled, half Norse, half Scots, might acknowledge the suzerainty of Scottish and Norwegian kings, but like his ancestors on both sides was not prepared to sacrifice the democratic polity nor to give up clan land to anyone. Thus when David I was succeeded by his son Malcolm IV in 1153, Somerled and other Celtic chiefs tried to approach him in order to break the Anglo-Norman grip on the Crown. This failing, they tried to force a treaty. Somerled in 1164 raised a fleet of 160 ships and sailed up the Clyde with ten thousand men gathered from Argyll, the Isles, and Ireland. He marched with half the force to Renfrew, where he camped and received the king's Breton steward, Walter Fitz Alan, the Baron of Renfrew. Early in the morning, Somerled was found assassinated in his tent.[*] This was, in a negative rather than a positive sense, a turning point in Hebridean history. Until then the Gaels had hope of halting the Anglo-Norman encroachment and of re-establishing a united Celtic kingdom. That hope and opportunity had now gone. The split between the Lowland and the Island and Highland Scots became wide and permanent. However much their leaders might cooperate from time to time to gain mutual objectives, as in the fourteenth-century war of independence, the Gaelic kingdom of the Hebrides now took its independent course.

Somerled's three sons divided the islands between them. Ragnall held Islay and Kintyre and the fleet of Nyvaigs. Dughall, the progenitor of Clan Dougall, held all the other isles of Argyll and the Lorn mainland. Angus held Arran and Bute. They felt no ties to the Scots Crown, whose court at Scone beyond forested and well-nigh roadless mountains was less accessible than Norway by sea. In this island triumvirate the House of Islay was dominant, and all of Somerled's first five successors there held rank as kings of the Isles.

The growing power of Scotland could not indefinitely tolerate Norse occupation of the mainland. In 1196, William the Lion wrested north Scotland from the Orkney jarldom. His grandson, Alexander III, instigated systematic attacks by the earl of Ross and other mainland chiefs on Skye and neighbouring islands, thus goading Hakon into his fatal expedition of 1263.

Norway's fleet of 120 ships sailed south through the Hebrides to the Firth of Clyde, where it anchored off Arran in late summer. Alexander, now aged twenty-two, had thought of everything. He had already contrived to take as hostage the son of Angus of Islay, King of the Isles, as safeguard against the latter's support of Hakon. He opened negotiations with Hakon and kept him talking for a month

[*] *Book of Clanranald.*

– waiting for the autumn gales. He kept patience while the hungry Vikings plundered the Clyde coast. His strategy won its reward.

On the night of 1 October a great gale sprang out of the west, driving many of the longships on to the leeshore at Largs.* Hakon, indecisive too long, promptly ordered a landing, but before this could be completed the Scots attacked at dawn. The battle lasted through the day of the 2nd while the storm at sea continued. Hakon was unable to reinforce his army with men or supplies from the fleet, which had in part been wrecked and widely scattered. He had to count himself lucky to escape at nightfall, and to be granted a truce to bury his dead and to withdraw seaward. His broken fleet sailed for the Orkneys, where Hakon died of fever. Alexander seized Skye and the Outer Hebrides. Three years later, Norway formally ceded the Hebrides at the treaty of Perth.

Alexander now confirmed Angus in his kingship – thus suggesting a feudal overlordship without obligation to prove it. Skye and the Outer Hebrides he granted to William, the earl of Ross, but confirmed Leod, son of Olav the Black (the former Norse king of Man) in his possession of lands in Skye and Lewis. When Alexander died by a fall from his horse in 1285, Scotland lost the most able of all her kings. His heir was his grand-daughter Margaret, the Maid of Norway. On her voyage to Scotland to take the throne, she too died. In the political skirmishing that followed, Edward I of England thought he saw his opportunity to annex the Scottish kingdom. Thus began the war of independence later won by Scotland at heavy cost.

Somerled's victory of 1156 had brought the Hebrides a hundred years of peace, and more to the isles of Argyll. Ragnall, better known as Reginald, plainly regarded the Christian Church as the principal power for good in the Hebrides, for he poured out money on it. He founded monasteries instead of building castles and rebuilt abbeys and chapels destroyed by the Vikings, including the Benedictine abbey of St Mary on Iona (1203), and also on Iona the nunnery of St Mary, which stands today as the most beautiful ruin of Scotland's west seaboard.

Donald I, succeeding in 1207, was a castle-builder, seeking strength for his realm without expansion. He led an expedition to Ireland to repel Norman invaders, as a consequence of which the House of Tara offered him the crown of Ireland. This he declined. He held to the Hebrides and gave his name to his clan, known thereafter as Clan Donald. (The name MacDonald, or Son of Donald, was not then a surname: it was a title for the chief alone.) All the kings of the

---

* 1383: Fordun, *Annalia*. 1876: Skene.

House of Islay had long reigns: one and all were either distinguished by wisdom or took good counsel. Their people prospered.

When war with England was about to begin, Clan Donald elected Angus Og (Young Angus) to rule the Isles. He was a personal friend of Robert the Bruce, who claimed the throne by descent from David I, but was now in extreme adversity. Angus buttressed his clan's fortunes by sheltering Bruce in his island and mainland castles, harrying the English warships with his fleet of Nyvaigs, and capturing their base on the Isle of Man prior to Bannockburn. To these services, which were already a major contribution to the Scottish victory, he added his own person and eighteen hundred men of Islay on the right wing of Bruce's battle array. In later years, his fleet supported the Scottish invasions of north England. A grateful king granted Angus Og the islands of Mull, Jura, Coll, and Tiree, which MacDougall of Lorn had forfeited by supporting the king's enemies. At the same time, Bruce caused consternation by asking the Island and Highland chiefs to show their charters. There had been no feudal kings to 'grant' their ancestors titles and charters when they had won and held their lands against Picts, Romans, Scots, or Vikings, as the case might be. A clan's land, they justly felt, could not be held by scraps of paper.

But the grants and charters continued to be issued – not to the clans, but to named chiefs in their own right. The chiefs accepted on these feudal terms. Bruce's son, David II, granted Angus Og's son, John MacDonald, the islands of Gigha, Scarba, Colonsay, Skye,* and Lewis-with-Harris,† to which John added by marriage to Amie of Garmoran the islands of Eigg, Rum, the Uists, Eriskay, and Barra, together with mainland Garmoran (Moidart, Knoydart, and Morvern). John now ruled the entire Hebrides. He made a second marriage to a daughter of Robert, the first Stewart king of Scots, and in deference to his father-in-law relinquished his title of king and assumed that of Lord of the Isles.

The Hebrides remained in fact a separate kingdom, whose MacDonald princes negotiated treaties with the kings of England, Ireland, France, and Scotland. Their vast territories were still further extended when John's grandson, Donald II, acquired the earldom of Ross, including not only Ross but much of Invernessshire. The Lords of the Isles now ruled the entire Atlantic seaboard from Assynt to the Mull of Kintyre, and from Lochaber to Rockall. Regional administration was based on four centres, on Islay, Mull, Skye, and Lewis.

---

* Grants by Edward Balliol, 1335, confirmed by David II. See *Acts of Parliament*, Vol. I, pp. 528–9.
† Ibid.

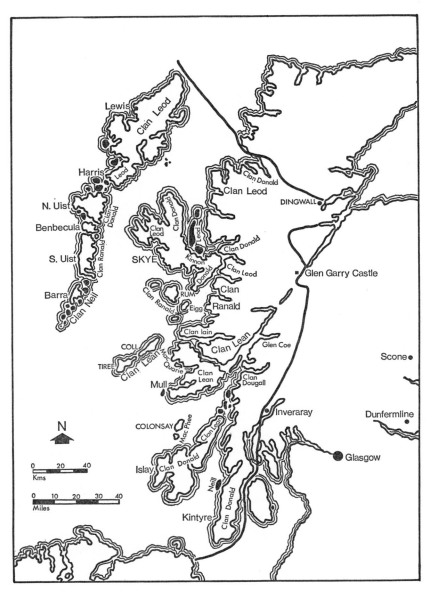

Map 18 *Lordship of the Isles AD 1420 and the Island Clans*

The Lords granted land to vassal clans of direct Donald descent and of other name. The principal clans of direct descent were:

Clan Ranald	of Moidart, Arisaig, Morar, Knoydart, the Small Isles, the Uists, Benbecula, Eriskay, Barra.
Clan Donald	of Sleat in Skye and of North Uist.
Clan Iain	of Ardnamurchan with lands in Islay, Jura, and Mull.
Clan Iain Mhor	of Islay.

The principal island clans not having direct male descent from Donald were:

Clan Gillean	of Mull, Coll, Tiree, Luing, Scarba, North Jura, the Isles of the Sea, Morvern, and Ardgour.
Clan Leod	of Lewis, Harris, west Skye, Raasay, Glenelg, Gairloch, and Assynt.
Clan Neil	of Barra.
Clan Neill	of Gigha.
Clan MacPhee	of Colonsay.
Clan MacKinnon	of central Skye and north Mull.
Clan MacQuarie	of Ulva and Gometra.

The Lords of the Isles are said to have conveyed land by a simple rhymed charter, which they confirmed by kneeling on the clan's stone of destiny. This sacred stone was always used for the inauguration of a chief of Clan Donald. In the days of the kingship the stone was kept on an islet of Loch Finlagan in Islay, but in 1380 was removed to Eigg, that being more central to the Kingdom. It differed from the *Lia Fail*, the stone of destiny on which the king of Scots sat to be crowned, in being a slab seven or eight feet long with a footprint cut on one side. At the ceremony of inauguration,* MacDonald stood with his bare left foot in the print – symbol of his oath to walk in the steps of his forefathers – while the bishop of the Isles or of Argyll offered him first a white wand and then a two-handed sword – symbols of his duties to defend justice and his people. He turned three times sunwise, three times brandished the great sword, and three times the chiefs and clansmen shouted *MacDhomhnuill*. Seven priests were normally in attendance and the ceremony ended with Mass. The new Lord of the Isles then feasted the company for a week.

* 1627: MacDonald. 1961: Munro.

The Lords were advised on Hebridean affairs by a council of fourteen chiefs which met on Eilean na Comhairle (Council Isle) at the north end of Loch Finlagan. A causeway gave access to the neighbouring island, Eilean Mor, where MacDonald's house stood with his great hall (sixty feet by twenty-nine), dining hall, chapel, guest house, servants' quarters, offices for clerics, and guardhouses. Finlagan was the administrative headquarters for the Hebrides.

Donald Monro, the Dean of the Isles (1549), gives membership of the council as 'four of the greatest nobles, four thanes of lesser estate, and four great men of the royal blood of Clan Donald'. The four nobles were MacLean of Duart, MacLean of Loch Buie, MacLeod of Harris, and MacLeod of Lewis. The four thanes were MacKinnon, MacNeill of Gigha, and MacNeil of Barra, with one other. The four men of royal blood were Clanranald, MacIain of Ardnamurchan, Clandonald of Kintyre, and Clan Alister Carryche of Lochaber. To these were added the Abbot of Icolmkill (Iona), and the Bishop of the Isles. The names and islands represented changed from one period to another; MacDonald himself was called by his islesmen *Buachaille nan Eileanan*, the Herdsman of the Isles.* And with reason. He gave them order, peace, wealth, and justice for nearly three hundred years† – peace being a relative term, but they had more of it than the mainland. Every large island had its own brieve and court of justice, and every clansman had right of appeal to the council at Finlagan.

The Council of the Isles had nothing like the status of the Norse *Things*. By the fifteenth century, the days when clansmen could choose a chief, or the chiefs their king, had vanished. There is no evidence that the Council dared to withhold supplies for ill-considered wars, nor did the negotiation of treaties and alliances fall within their province. They dealt with home affairs of the Atlantic principality, and were supreme on matters of law.‡

The chiefs are shown on carved effigies in chapels, and on grave slabs and crosses on their islands, as mostly if not always bearded, wearing a conical iron helmet, chain mail over the shoulders, and a saffron warcoat of quilted, thickly padded linen, which fell to knee-level. They carried the two-handed claymore, the pre-eminent weapon of the chief. The hilt had down-sloping cross-guards, the tips of which were ornamented with quartrefoils. The broad blades, two inches wide at the hilt and fifty inches long (they could be five feet eight inches over all), were tempered by highly skilled smiths, some of whom could shape

---

* 1952: Grant.
† 1549: Monro.
‡ 1627: MacDonald.

13a. Viking Longship.

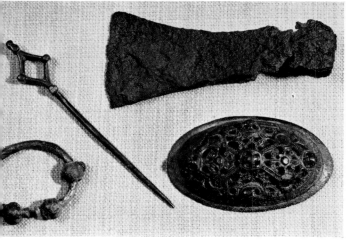

13b. Relics from a Viking grave on Colonsay at Kiloran Bay.

14a. Black house, Harris, built against sloping ground and fenced to keep cattle and sheep from grazing on the roof. 1955.

14b. Black house, Lewis, partially converted by giving it chimneys and one wall window (original windows set in the thatch).

15a. Tigh Geal, or white houses, North Uist, distinguished from black houses by mortared walls and the roof resting on the outer edge.

15b. The eye of a Tigh Geal, or white house, on Eriskay.

16a. An illicit still.

16b. Peat cutting, Lewis. The peats have been cut and cast up from the bank and now they are being set for the first stage in drying the fuel.

blades by rapid blows of a heavy hammer without aid of fire.* The Islay blades were celebrated throughout Scotland and much sought after. They were made by the family of MacEachern, who also created the famous Islay hilt. The site of their forge is three-quarters of a mile south-west of Kilchoman Church, behind a rock-face known as Creag Uinnsinn. A short way to its north, the Lords of the Isles had their summer palace on a grassy plateau. Other weapons displayed were a long-shafted battle-axe, a large dirk, and a bow and barbed arrows. The clansmen wore saffron tunic-shirts to knee-height and blue tartan plaids. Leather jerkins served for armour. Tartan was usually woven of two colours for the common clansmen and of more for richer men. Blue was fashionable.

The men of the Isles, of every rank, were not so much deeply religious as deeply reverential. They were easily led by the clergy, for their faith had the simplicity of a child's. This gave the Church much power to hold in check the chiefs' natural tendency to despotism as their feudal powers grew. They and their many relatives had a healthy fear of excommunication, and the clansmen of supernatural powers that a priest might invoke. The Church was thus able to have its decrees heard until the end of the fifteenth century, and to win the observance of Christian rites. But all was not well with the Church. The live spirit of the early Christian monks, centred on God, had become overlaid by formalism. Hence the Church had lost the reserves of strength needed to survive the political cataclysm now about to overtake the Hebrides. And when that came, the clergy relapsed into a self-centred apathy, unable any longer to speak or lead when that service was most needed by their people.

The downfall of the Lordship of the Isles had become inevitable (granted hind-sight) by the end of the fifteenth century. After their early rejection of feudal principle, the Lords had too readily accepted it. *De facto* monarchs of Atlantic Scotland, they commanded many thousands of well-armed fighting men, deployed hundreds of ships, sent their own ambassadors abroad, were courted by kings, granted lands to powerful clan chiefs in return for devotion to their royal dynasty, and were acknowledged by all Highland clans as the heads of the Gaelic race. They spoke, and their vassals obeyed. When they had first claimed the earldom of Ross in 1411, they were able to field an army of ten thousand men for the battle of Harlaw, one of such strength† that the safety and future 'independence' of the mainland could be seen to be under threat. They and the islesmen

---

* 1896: Drummond-Norie.
† The population of all Scotland would be less than 800,000 (an estimate from Sir John Sinclair's estimate of 600,000 in 1250).

were unable to feel allegiance to the kings of Scots, for which the latter were to blame, or to feel identity with the Lowlanders, who had become to them an alien race, not Scots, to be classed with the English as Sassenach. The Lords of the Isles' power had unluckily grown too great at the very time that they lost their former political acumen. Their statecraft became marked by brinkmanship. John II, the ninth prince of the House of Islay, and fourth Lord of the Isles, fell over the brink when he negotiated a treaty, dated 13 February 1462, with Edward IV of England for the dismemberment of Scotland.

His declaration of intent (to take the Highlands) was not followed by action, but the Scots Parliament got wind of the plot in 1476. They declared forfeit the land and titles of the Lord of the Isles and raised an army. This sobered John, who submitted, but his son Angus rebelled against his authority. Thrice in succession Angus defeated the mainland armies. Clan Donald loyalties were now split between father and son. For the first time in its long history, the House was divided, and fell. Angus engaged his father in the sea-battle of Bloody Bay off north Mull and won, but soon after was assassinated. Chaos ensued. The youthful King of Scots, James IV, now eighteen, had gained the energy and resources to bring John to trial in 1493 and break him. The Lordship was abolished.

Had James IV been more experienced, he might have let the Lordship stand, shorn of its mainland strength but strong enough to govern the Hebrides. His too drastic action brought the islesmen dire misfortune. He visited the Hebrides in person and granted charters to the chief land-holders, including members of the Council of the Isles. The king had strength of personality and in many wise acts displayed a generosity of mind that won allegiance. He was the last Scots king to speak Gaelic, and might have won the islesmen's hearts had he not, in a fit of impatience in 1499, thrown his gains away by granting the lieutenancy of the Isles to Campbell of Argyll – the one man whom the Hebridean and Highland chiefs could not accept. James's felling of the Donald Lordship, followed by his death at Flodden in 1514, left the Island chiefs and their clans destitute of a common head, a common policy, and of any object of loyalty. Thereafter it was every chief for himself and his own clan. The Scots kings and nobles were too divided and remote to enforce a rule of law, and the men to whom they delegated authority in the west too unprincipled to command respect. Before the sixteenth century was even half run, three full-scale rebellions and six clan feuds were raging through the Hebrides and mainland seaboard.

The political situation in the Hebrides at the opening of the sixteenth century might be summarized thus. The clan system had become permeated by the feudal principle that Somerled had foreseen and striven to reject. Unrestrained by the overlordship of his House of Islay, or by the religious institutions that his House had fostered, or by democratic controls, the clans inevitably fell into anarchy. Interminable feuds and piracy were the universal product.

Power had passed from the people at the granting of crown charters to persons. Most chiefs at first had been uncorrupted, but the clan system developed thereafter as a Celtic feudalism distinct from the Anglo-Norman. The democratic ideal of the earlier Gaelic and Norse peoples was strong enough to live on in the minds and hearts of the islesmen, for the patriarchal character of chiefship gave them an illusion of continuing freedom and independence long after these had ceased to be real. This Celtic feudalism drew elements of its character from the older Celtic, Norse, and Anglo-Norman systems, but evolved distinctive features, the most important of which was the absolutism of chiefs, which had basis neither in law nor in Celtic tradition. In essence it opposed a direct negative to the communal affirmation of the clan idea. Yet the patriarchal spirit had been so deeply implanted in the system over unnumbered centuries that it continued to move chiefs and islesmen alike until the late eighteenth century. There is much evidence that to this day it remains alive. But the clan system itself has perished, and the decline began when the divisive feudal principle was grafted on to it by kings of Scots against the will of their Gaelic people. The root-stock of clansmen failed to reject it – deceived perhaps by the very easiness of their relation with their chiefs, who betrayed them.

The chiefs' schizophrenic condition imparted to their clans a wasting disease. A first symptom was their clansmen's loss of unity. The warrior and farming classes were split apart in consequence of their chiefs' insatiable pugnacity. When the arts of war seemed constantly to be of weightier value than those of peace, the land-workers lost the respect of the fighting men, whose real duty should have been to protect the community, especially the farming community on whom the economic prosperity of all depended. With lost unity, both forfeited their communal rights to their lands and to liberty.* When supreme power lay in the chiefs' hands, the clan system was seen to imperil the security of the state. The chiefs' use of that power, uncurbed by their subjects, made calamitous history. During a hundred years of Hebridean anarchy, the arts, religion, commerce, all fell into abeyance. Modes of agriculture went unimproved till the nineteenth century. The elements of education were withheld till the eighteenth century. The final issue was to be the total disintegration of the clan system

* 1903: Mackenzie.

from around 1760 to 1800. And when that happened the people were to be left leaderless and voiceless, easy prey to new landowners who wore no patriarchal masks to sweeten tyrannical inflictions. No complaint came to Parliament from the common islesmen till late in the nineteenth century, for they had no franchise, and were not heard.

7

The Scots Settlements: 1500-1745

The conception that land, like sea and air, belongs to no person, but to all men, died in the Hebrides as a practical ideal when the early settlers had to begin defending the islands against aggressive incomers in the sixth or seventh centuries B.C. Tribal ownership certainly followed, if it did not precede these events. When the early Scots settlers arrived in the Hebrides, they held land for their clans. Since no one person, not even chief or king, could own land, the people annually divided arable land by lot, while holding pasture in common.* This system of allotment came to be called runrig, meaning strips of land on adjoining ridges or patches, each with a household responsible for its cultivation. The number of cattle that each man might graze on the common hill pasture was settled in proportion to the head of cattle he could fodder on his home farm in winter, and this rule was called souming and rouming.

The runrig system worked well when both arable and pasture were common lands and when all cooperated. Its weakness was the lack of incentive it gave a man to improve the soil, for the unfenced arable lots were overrun in winter by grazing animals, and a man who might think to improve his land was deterred from effort by the knowledge that his lot would be lost at the next draw. Inefficient as the common field system appears today, it was found suitable for the times, when common defence and coastal watching were essential, and close cooperation needed for herding, guarding crops by roster, and all work on land and sea.

* 1877: Skene.

Land cultivation was thus developed under clan ownership in townships. The Hebridean township, or community of smallholders, has been found through history to require a minimum of four households, that being the smallest functional unit for teamwork in clearing woodland, or reclaiming moorland, farming the land, and providing a boat's crew.* The early settlements or townships, like those of today, were for three reasons spread along the coastal strips rather than inland: first, because communication was by sea, largely on the sheltered east coasts; second, on the Inner Hebrides raised beaches and glacial deposits offered the best ground; third, on the Outer Hebrides (and some Inner) most of the best land lay on west coasts. From the earliest days until the nineteenth century, cattle-farming was universal, hence the hilly inland ground was much more fertile than it is today, with grassland running far into moorland pasture where now all is heather and rushes.† Even Jura, where all land away from the east coast is notoriously peat-bog or mountainous, had wide grazings and big herds of black cattle, which were exported by ferry from Lagg Bay to Keills in Knapdale. When I wander today over the lower moors I hear only curlews calling, or larks in their too short season. Snipe, plover, woodcock, and a few red grouse and blackcock, these find homes here. At the seaward fringe the rare chough breeds on lonely cliffs, and over the mountains a pair of golden eagles may be seen stooping or soaring. Deer are everywhere. Apart from these the land is empty. It is still delightful country; the warm moor scents and the stillness give welcome change from the unceasing breeze of the coast. An effort is needed to appreciate that here on Jura, as on other inner isles, notably Mull, the scene was once different, that all the shallow glens were green and thronged with cows and calves, and the moors dotted with shielings.

The early townships were not regarded as owning land in an exclusive sense – every man was aware that land was clan land, hence although the household lot can be seen to contain a germ of private ownership, the germ never developed. Even in later feudal times, private small-holdings subject to a superior were few and not recorded till 1664 in Skye.‡ This clan system of land distribution must have borne hard on the Norse settlers in 1266, when they had been so long accustomed to freehold tenure, but in compensation their younger sons had maintenance at home. Townships under Scots control were ensured a quicker spread.

* 1955: Darling.
† 1960: Budge.
‡ 1938: MacLeod.

Each chief allotted from his clan's land large farms to his near relatives, known as the *duinevasal* or gentlemen of the clan. They worked the land through sub-tenants – the islesmen for whom the chief was trustee. No formal leases were given for small-holdings, and only verbal grants for large estates. Rent was nominal and paid in kind: a few cows for a large farm – as late as 1408 MacKay paid Donald II of Islay a total of four cows yearly for eleven farms on the Mull of Oa* – or a sheep, grain, butter, cheese, and hens, for a small-holding.† The chief had mensal land, and no need of large rents. He had real need of men and services. The clansmen looked to their chief to lead, judge, and protect them, the chief to his clansmen for his safety and the dignity of his name. The real rent that he expected was well-fed fighting men, skilled in the use of arms and hardened to Hebridean sea and weather. The duty of his relatives was to see to it that he had them.

The principal crops grown in the sixteenth century, when records for the Isles became available, were oats and barley, with smaller amounts of flax, rye, hemp, and linseed. Then as now the most important cereal was oats, famous both for quality and abundance.‡ Grass was not grown for hay – its value for winter stock-feeding was not realized. The beasts required for winter food were slaughtered in autumn and the beef and mutton salted down. The rest of the beef cattle were turned out to fend for themselves, when they either lost all their fat or in bad winters died in large numbers through lack of fodder.§

Milk cows, if not kept in a byre, often shared the people's houses, and although confined to one end this was unpartitioned, for the islesmen, it is alleged, scrupled to shut out the cow from a view of the fire. The dung that accumulated on the floor in winter was carried in wickered creels to manure the fields, together with peat-ash from the hearth, old sooted thatch from the roof, and great quantities of seaweed from the beaches. Ash was found to be valuable and its method of spread bizarre. The woman of the house carried the heavy creel on her back while her husband, strolling behind, carrying nothing but a cudgel, struck the creel from side to side, sending out clouds of dust.‖

The arable land around the township or farm was usually divided into infield and outfield. All manure was laid on the infield, which was tilled. The outfield

---

* Charter, *General Register House*. 1895: Smith.
† See below, *Rents*, p. 211.
‡ 1549: Monro. 1938: MacLeod.
§ 1695: Martin.
‖ 1627: MacDonald.

was ploughable ground kept in grass and corn, and this was dunged by cattle folded there for the purpose. The hill pastures were ranged by cattle, sheep, and horses. Close beside the houses, grassy plots were kept as pasture for the working horse, for a few cows in summer, or sheep in winter months.* This pattern of land division is a natural one that has been followed on all the island farms from the sixteenth century till now, and it can be traced today even on small crofts like those of Iona, but not on the very small ones (four acres and a cow) so numerous on Lewis. Townships commonly held a pennyland, which varied greatly in size and pattern. Three pennylands in Mull around 1600 showed the following acreages:†

	Infield	Outfield	Green pasture	Hill pasture	Total
1.	64	16	19	497	596
2.	106	44	19	704	873
3.	68	27	29	872	996

A stone dyke (but often only an imaginary line) separated the arable from the hill pasture. The green pasture, so-called, was mostly ground too wet, or woody, or stony to be ploughed. On the bigger hill ranges and moors, which were deer forest, the people had shielings where they herded cows for six or seven weeks in summer.

There is no evidence that the hoe was ever much used for tillage in the Hebrides.‡ The tools in use from the sixteenth century onwards (and probably much earlier)§ were the *cas-chrom* (crooked foot), a special kind of foot-plough peculiar to the Hebrides, Shetlands, and North-west Scotland; the *cas-dhireach* (straight foot) or ordinary spade; two ploughs; and the harrow. The *cas-chrom* was superior to spade and plough: ground thus dug invariably gave a heavier crop, equal to ground twice ploughed; it could be used to cultivate either boggy ground or steep hill-slopes inaccessible to the plough; and it accomplished almost double the work of a spade with the same labour.‖

The *cas-chrom* had a six-foot shaft of oak or ash, which had the lower end, the 'head', naturally bent at an obtuse angle. Sometimes the head was a separate piece made fast to the shaft with iron hooks. It was approximately two feet

* 1880: Skene.
† Ibid.
‡ 1957: Jirlow and Whitaker.
§ 1831: Logan.
‖ Ibid. 1957: Jirlow and Whitaker.

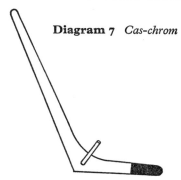

Diagram 7 *Cas-chrom*

six inches long, four or five inches wide, and shod with a six-inch tip. Between head and shaft, a strong wooden peg projected eight inches from the right-hand side. The worker placed his foot on the peg and drove the head tip-first down into the ground with two jerks. A sideways jerk on the shaft threw a clod of earth about ten inches wide to the left side. On stony ground, the lever was powerful enough to turn out boulders up to 200 lb. in weight. The *cas-chrom* worker moved backward, and twelve men working in line could dig an acre a day.

The islesmen were prejudiced against the plough, which even by the late eighteenth century was still a cumbersome wooden contraption requiring four men to the four-horse team – one man to walk backwards leading the team, another to guide the plough, and two more to dress the upturned soil to render it fit for seeding. Such ploughs if repeatedly used formed a pan under the top-soil, and this stopped the circulation of moisture. *Cas-chrom* work was free of that defect.

When light harrows were used in the sixteenth century, they were usually pulled by men and women wearing a breast-rope of grass or hair, or else were tied to the tail of a horse. Two rows of wooden teeth formed the harrow, with a big bundle of heather tied behind to smooth the earth.

The primitive ploughs used in the Middle Ages were the ard and ristle (*crann rusgaidh* and *crann ruslaidh*) both derived from Norwegian models. The ard had a curved beam drawn by a horse between shafts. The share was mortised to the beam, but since it lacked a coulter it could be used only with great difficulty on grassland, and not at all to break more heavily rooted ground. The ristle had only a sickle-shaped coulter, which made a ten-inch vertical cut, thus severing roots and allowing the ard to follow. The combination of these two ploughs was an important development, for large areas of outfield could

185

then be more speedily cultivated. But for infield and hill ground the *cas-chrom* was to remain in common use till the nineteenth century; on some islands, like Eriskay, it is occasionally used at the present day.

The *cas-dhireach*, which preceded the *cas-chrom*, was six feet long, with a single step. Ten or twelve men working as a team could dig two-thirds of an acre a day. Its more important use was for lazybedding. Great areas of moorland and hill-slope were thus made fertile. Lazybedding is widely practised to this day in the outer isles, although it has died out in most of the inner. Fed industriously with seaweed and tended for generations, the beds yielded luxuriant crops of oats and barley (and after the eighteenth century potatoes and hay).

The grain when ripe was uprooted by hand, not reaped by sickle (thus allowing the grain to fill out instead of shrinking). The women prepared it for milling in one of three ways. The common method with dry corn in the Highlands was to switch it from the ear with a stick, winnow it, then parch it slowly in a pot over the fire, while turning the grain with a wooden *speilag* or spatula. Another was to cut off the ears (but often they were left on the straw) and parch them in a kiln, then to set fire to them on the floor and winnow the blackened grain.* The method most popular in the Hebrides, because it gave more palatable bread, was named *graddan* (from *grad*, quick). The woman, sitting, took a sheaf of oats and set fire to the ears with a splinter of burning wood. Then she took a stick, and at the instant the husk was burnt beat off the grain, which fell on to a spread cloth or skin. The skill required a quick eye and exact timing (otherwise her resort was the kiln), and was a Highland and Island practice, lasting far into the eighteenth century.† The grain was parched in the pot and ground. Graddaning, which included firing after kiln-parching, was condemned by mainland observers for wasting straw, for lack of which cattle died in winter.

Grinding was a daily chore for women and querns were in every house. They were usually made of gneiss in two elliptical slabs, the upper having a convex face that fitted the concave lower face. Two women milled, one rotating the upper stone and the other feeding in the grain. Four hours were taken to grind a bushel, and the work had its own labour song. Normal daily milling was briefer. A man would carry home as much corn as might be wanted for supper and the next day's food, and this corn, it is recorded, would be reaped, dried, graddaned, ground, baked into bread, and eaten, all within two hours.‡

---

* 1771: Pennant.
† 1831: Logan. 1793: Statistical Account.
‡ 1695: Martin. 1831: Logan.

Since the islanders of the sixteenth century could supply almost all their own wants except wine from their own produce, import–export trade was negligible.* They reared large numbers of black cattle, a shaggy West Highland breed, probably aboriginal, which could live on the hills all the year round and thrive on coarse pasture. They were known as kyloes, and when cross-bred with mainland cows in the nineteenth century produced the tawny-red Highland cattle of today. They also kept poultry, horses, and numerous but small flocks of sheep like those of St Kilda,† of only twenty-five to thirty pounds' weight, but giving silky wool and excellent mutton. Pigs were not bred, for they were least able to live off island land.

Local fairs were organized on larger islands. From 1580 onwards, four-day fairs were held in Skye at Portree under crown licence. The products for sale in addition to livestock were wool, linen, hides, flour, butter, cheese, dried fish, and fresh salmon. Trade was by barter, rarely for money. An example of prices quoted was a milk cow, 50p, cheese, 5p a stone (then twenty-four pounds), and oatmeal $3\frac{1}{2}$p a stone.‡ At first strangers were few at the sales, but mainland traders were frequenting them before 1650. The cattle and horses sold were swum across to the mainland, or to other islands, where the sea-channels were narrow, as at Kyle Akin or Kyle Rhea. They were taken across at slack water in chains of five, tied jaw to tail with straw ropes. A four-oared boat led each chain, while a man at the stern held the first cow's rope. A hundred animals could thus be ferried in a day.§

Other exports to the mainland or abroad were mainly wool, hides, and fish. Coarse woollen plaiding went to Holland and Denmark, and wool in the fleece to manufacturers in East Scotland.

The great abundance of sea-fish was a harvest reaped by the islesmen of the sixteenth century, but again mainly for their own use, including part payment of teinds to the Church. Exports were small. The rich trade to be drawn from Hebridean seas was realized by Scots fishermen of the east coast around 1580, when they first came to the Minch, and from 1594 by the Dutch, who fished west of the Outer Isles. The Dutch, ironically, had been taught their skill by Scots settlers in Holland in 1429. A hundred years later the Dutch were out-fishing everyone, acknowledged superiors of the Scots and English in efficiency and enterprise. At the present time of European dispute about the six-mile

* 1906: Mackenzie. 1930: Nicolson.
† 1969: Darling.
‡ 1930: Nicolson. 1695: Martin.
§ 1695: Martin.

fishing limit around Britain, it is worth noting that James V (1513–42) gave the Dutch fishing busses (two-masted ships) verbal licence to fish Scottish waters only outwith twenty-eight miles, and when a too-greedy crew broke the bounds he had them beheaded, and their heads sent home in a barrel.*

The Dutch made huge profits in the seventeenth century. Four of their busses declared in 1628 a clear profit of £7,500 in three months, and reckoned that a thousand busses could be fully occupied. The local boats at this time numbered only a dozen based on Stornoway. These small numbers were not due, as in the Inner Hebrides, to lack of interest in commercial fishing, but to lack of opportunity. The foreign market was closed to them. They had no access, and no capital, for Stornoway was not a royal burgh. Only the freemen of royal burghs were allowed by statute to export home goods by sea or to import foreign, and this unjust monopoly stopped the growth of Hebridean fishing villages.

The Lowland market for island livestock in the sixteenth century, and in the first half of the seventeenth, had been equally restricted. This was due in part to racial antipathies, and to the political isolation of the Isles, hence the size of herds reared was limited to Hebridean needs. The only export market for surplus cattle was the royal burgh of Inverness, which had become the sole commercial centre for the North Highlands.

The export of black cattle to the mainland had begun in a small way before 1600. Its development into the foremost Hebridean industry was pioneered around 1650 by a warrior band from Skye, who escorted numerous droves to the great cattle trysts at Crieff and Falkirk.† A fighter escort was essential to deal with reivers, and the Skyemen's initiative in opening the routes established a trade that became the principal source of Hebridean wealth for nearly two centuries. The drive south was in autumn when the animals were in best condition. The new trade coincided with a dying away of clan warfare in the Isles, so that cattle could be reared safely in huge numbers. A boom set in. More money circulated, and the chiefs, who had held markedly aloof from trade, now engaged in it too. The value of land multiplied nearly forty times between 1600 and mid-century.‡ MacLeod's land of west Skye, Harris, and Glenelg, had been valued in the sixteenth century at only £40, for the chiefs' powers had not been based on high rentals. Now their demands grew excessive.

The trade had its ups and downs. Although the Hebrides were quiet in the

* 1919: Mackenzie.
† 1930: Nicolson.
‡ 1938: MacLeod.

latter half of the seventeenth century, not so the Highlands: many of the clansmen (islanders too) were then away for the royalist campaigns of Montrose, Charles II, and Dundee. The armed bands that roamed the glens following the break-up of armies despoiled the drovers of whole herds, but men with courage and wits were still able to win through to Crieff and Falkirk. The demand in the south for black cattle continued to grow – in 1723, thirty thousand were sold at a guinea a head to English dealers at the Crieff tryst.*

Donald Monro, the Dean of the Isles, wrote the first comprehensive description of the Hebrides in 1549. He gave little or no detail on the daily life of the people – for which we have to wait until 1695 for Martin Martin's *Description of the Western Islands* – but he shows clearly that despite incessant clan warfare and piracy the land was in good condition. Husbandry might be primitive, but the industry of the people compensated for lack of machines. The islands were much more heavily stocked than today, more intensively tilled, and fifty more were inhabited. There was no town like present-day Stornoway to concentrate people, who were spread more widely, even to cliff-bound islets like North Rona, forty-seven miles north of the Butt of Lewis.

Monro found almost everywhere that husbandry and peaceful pursuits and arts, not war, gave the common islesmen their chief interest and occupation. The most popular recreation was deer-hunting, not cattle-reiving. The people had abundance of barley and oats; the comment 'fertill and fruitfull of corne' appears on most of Monro's pages. It would thus appear that the most turbulent period of Hebridean political history coincided with a golden age in food production, when the land gave a greater yield in proportion to population than it has since.† Yet 150 years later, when the island clans had stopped warring, the economic state of the islands had greatly deteriorated. According to Martin, the fertility of the soil as declared by Monro had become a thing of the past.

In possible explanation of this anomaly, W. C. Mackenzie ascribes to Monro's survey a concern only for church lands, which were then extensive, free of rent and of burdens imposed by the chiefs, and more efficiently farmed under priestly control.‡ Monro's text when studied does not bear out that opinion. During the period 1550 to 1700 there occurred the second post-glacial oscillation of climate, called the Little Ice Age.§ The Arctic pack-ice returned to Iceland, the Hebrides were scourged by storm, cold summers, repeated failures of

---

* 1930: Nicolson.
† 1904: Hume Brown.
‡ 1919: Mackenzie.
§ See above, chapter 3.

harvest – and these very conditions were reported by Martin in accounting for the recurrent scarcity and destitution.

The worsening weather probably hastened the development of the Hebridean house-design named *Tigh Dubh* or Black House. On the mainland and the sheltered inmost isles, single-walled cottages with thatched roofs have often been called 'black houses' incorrectly, for the structure of the black house proper has seven distinctive features, four of which are definitive: the walls are drystone, they are double, the roof is thatch, and this roof is set upon the inner wall, not the outer. These features were combined only in the Hebrides and North Highlands, and are seen today only in Lewis, for example at Arnol, or Shawbost, or Valtos in Uig district, all on the west coast.

Diagram 8   *Black House*
(square-ended Black Houses were rare)

The design was evolved to withstand high wind. The double walls could be four to nine feet thick, and the space between was filled with peat, rubble, or earth. The placing of the roof on the inner wall – unique to the black house – served two purposes: no gale could lift the roof, for the outer wall became a baffle, shooting the blast up clear of the edge, and the tops of the outer walls gave a platform for running repairs on the straw thatch, and for re-thatching every few years, when the men would carefully separate the old outer layer from the soot-blackened inner layer. The latter was set aside for manure, and the former replaced as the new inner layer, on top of which they laid a new thatch with the roots upward to give anchorage. All was lashed down with ropes of woven heather or straw, weighted along the wall-tops with many boulders.

Other features of the black house were that the ends were rounded, not gabled; the roof had no chimney, for the hearth was set in the middle of the floor and vented smoke through a hole in the thatch; and one end of the house always appeared higher than the other, for both roof and floor sloped markedly, the reason being that man and beast wintered under the same roof and the low end was the cow's. The interior space could be fifty feet by twelve. Some, perhaps all in early days, were lit only by the door; later most had a few narrow windows, small and deep-sunk in the lowest thatch. In bad weather these were blocked with turf divots or bags of straw. A peat fire burned day and night so that all kept warm inside, and above the hearth a big iron pot hung by a chain from a beam. The hearth was set to one side of the roof-vent, lest heavy rain dampen the embers. Soot-smoke blackened the rafters, beams, and inner thatch, but the house was not named black house for this reason. The name *tigh dubh* meant dark house, for the drystone walls had a darker appearance than the cemented walls of the *tigh geal*, or white house,* which had the same smoke-vent and was just as black inside. Floors were of hard earth. An occasional sheep or goat often won access with the cow; and poultry, which in some islands abounded, were freely admitted at all seasons. The house was lit at night by cruisies. These were small iron lamps with an open bath of seal or whale oil. A wick of bullrush pith gave a smoky and smelly flame.

Not all houses were stone-built. Many were completely walled and roofed with divots. When the grass sprang they looked like green hillocks. They were sometimes built lean-to against crags, from which sheep and goats were able to graze the roofs. Cows are even known to have fallen through between the rafters.† Divot houses were still in use in Eriskay in 1935, and lean-to houses in South Uist in 1955.

The black-house structure was the best ever evolved in the Hebrides: so effective that sitting inside in a gale one could hear no wind. The buildings were not only much warmer‡ but of far better appearance than today's cement boxes. The shell, improved by damp-course and drainage, and bigger windows,

* 1949: Dwelly.
† 1930: Nicolson.
‡ Verbal report by islanders.

should have been perpetuated as an evolved design best fitting site and climate. The golden thatch on the low grey walls looked well against sea or moor, and they still do in parts of Lewis and Berneray, where some have been modernized – given chimneys, wooden floors and wall-panelling, running water, and electricity. The pity is that they are no longer built.

The chiefs and *duinevasal* – the latter becoming known in the seventeenth century as tacksmen (tenants of large farmlands) – lived in *tigh geal* and burned tallow candles. Their houses were partitioned, but even they housed cattle in winter. The greater chiefs had their castles, all built between the twelfth and sixteenth centuries: Finlagan, Claig, and Dunyvaig on Islay; Duart, Aros, and Moy, on Mull; Cairnburgh on the Treshnish Isles; Breacacha on Coll; Dunvegan, Duntulm, Camus, Maoil and Dun Sgathaich, on Skye; Kisimul off Barra; Stornoway, and a score of others, by which the Lords of the Isles, either directly or through their vassals, had held the Hebrides. But lesser chiefs and gentlemen of the clan were housed much like their own clansmen and went barelegged about their steadings.

Furniture was simple. The family slept in box beds in the eighteenth century. In the sixteenth, people slept on the ground on straw, or better on heather, which they laid on the floor stalk down and leaf up. Heather gave a refreshing scent. A contemporary Latin record says:

> This makes a pleasant bed, vying in softness with finest down . . . heath naturally absorbs moisture and restores strength to exhausted nerves, so that those who lie down weary at night arise in the morning alert and vigorous. They all have not only a contempt for pillows and blankets, but choose to cultivate hardiness . . . when they travel in other countries, they throw aside their host's bedclothes, fearing that these barbarian luxuries, as they call them, might affect their native hardness, and so wrapping themselves around with their plaids, go to sleep.*

The tartan plaid was the outdoor dress of both Islanders and Highlanders for at least eight centuries, counting from the tenth. In the Middle Ages they wore also the *leni-croich*, or saffron shirt. This 'shirt' (*leni*) dyed saffron was in reality a long linen robe reaching below the knees and belted like a kilt at the waist.† It was worn thus by the chief men of the Isles, and by the lesser orders in patchwork form. Early in the sixteenth century it went out of fashion, replaced

---

* 1582: Buchanan.
† 1695: Martin.

by short shirts of linen or wool. At the same time, blue and purple tartan plaids lost ground to brown hues, which gave better camouflage among the heather.* Many people wore *truis* or trews, especially when travelling on horse-back or aboard ship; these were skin-tight breeches, either tartan or coloured, fitting closely round the lower leg like a stocking. *Truis* were possibly older than the plaid, for they had been worn by the slaves of the Irish Gaels.† From the sixteenth century onward the kilted plaid became the national dress of the Highlands and Islands, whether worn over the saffron shirt, common shirt, or *truis*, but after the conquest of Lothian in 1018 it had also become common garb in the greater part of Scotland, including the Lowlands and Borders.

Known as *an breacan feilidh*, the chequered covering, the plaid was a piece of tartan cloth, closely woven of fine woollen thread, measuring six yards by two. When dressing, a man first laid his leather belt on the ground, or on a table or a grassy bank, laid the plaid on top, and then folded one end in pleats. (The word kilt is given in the early Irish records as *ceilt* – with hard c – meaning screening or concealment,‡ but was later used to mean 'to tuck in pleats'.) He lay on top and belted the kilted part round his waist. The pleats thus lay at the back from belt to knee. He finally arranged the upper part of the plaid in one of various ways, usually by drawing it up his back and over the front of the left shoulder, where he fastened it with a bodkin of bone or wood, or with a big silver brooch in which a cairngorm stone might be set. His sword arm was left unobstructed. The kilted part was worn shorter than is now the custom when wearing the short kilt or *feilidh beag* (little covering), so named because it rose no higher than the waist. This short modern kilt was introduced in the seventeenth century as two garments, a pleated kilt and upper plaid, but did not come into general use until the period 1715 to 1745.

The kilted plaid was a most practical garb for the times. It required no tailor to shape it, was much superior to trousers when traversing wet heather and fording burns, and its lightness and stretch allowed men to use their legs freely and to handle their arms with celerity. Its value during campaigns was repeatedly proven, for it enabled men to endure all weather without shelter. While others suffered from exposure, the clansmen could draw their plaids over head and shoulders, and when two or three slept together they had several folds under them and six on top. They could thus move long distances in storm and sleep

* 1582: Buchanan.
† 1925: McBride.
‡ 1967: Donald.

on snow* – in fact so accustomed were they to open-air sleep that during the rising of 1745 the clansmen were unwilling to use the tents provided. Their common practice before lying down was to dip the plaids in water and wring them out, for this swelled the thread, made them more windproof, and retained body-heat.†

Highland costume of today bears small resemblance to that of seventeenth-century clansmen. The men went barelegged. Shoes and stockings were not normally worn in summer, except by the gentry or on special occasions. Stockings were of cloth, usually of the same web as the plaid, and not knitted. Not till the seventeenth century were hide shoes cut to the shape of the feet. Neckties were not worn. The sporran, now usually an ornament, was, if worn at all, a simple pocket of goat's or badger's skin.

Accessories to the kilted plaid, such as short jackets left open in front, short doublets, and brogues, were worn mostly by the gentry and horsemen. But many men were wearing trews by 1695, and large round bonnets of thick cloth, blue, black, or grey, had become popular for Sunday wear. At this time breeches and waistcoats had come into general use, notably in Skye and Lewis, with the kilted plaid reserved for travel on foot, when it was easier on the limbs. Thus, while the kilt was in every islesman's possession, it was not, as in the Highlands, his daily wear.‡

Women's dress was the graceful *arisaid*, a white plaid (three yards by two) that fell from neck to heel. The cloth, pleated all round, was decorated with a few red, black, and blue stripes, each very thin. A high leather belt inlaid with silver had a plated end falling eighteen inches in front. Red coral or other stones were set in the metal, which was engraved. The *arisaid* was secured at the breast by a brass or silver brooch, which could be as big as a saucer and worth 100 merks (£5.55). At the raised centre a large crystal was ringed with finer stones, while the outer metal ring was closely engraved (animal and other devices). The women wore under the plaid, but with sleeves displayed outside it, a scarlet bodice flowing full at the arms but close-fitting at the wrists, where the sleeves were ringed with gold lace. Buttons were of plate set with stones. A big lock of hair hung down either cheek to the breast, where the lock was tied with ribbons. On the head, married women wore a linen kerchief, which tapered down the back, and maidens a snood (a ribbon). The women went barefoot in summer. On St Kilda they wore shoes of gannets necks, which were pulled on like socks

---

* 1582: Buchanan.
† 1831: Logan.
‡ Ibid.

and stitched at the front. These lasted only five days, but the supply was inexhaustible.*

The *arisaid* went out of full fashion in the late seventeenth century, when women of distinction took to mainland fashions, but the ordinary women of the Isles continued wearing it into the eighteenth century. Boys' dress in 1700 was the kilt, woollen shirt, sleeved waistcoat, and bare head and feet, winter and summer. A few older lads above ten years had rawhide brogues, but not for daily wear. The boys toughened themselves by bathing in cold water every morning.†

The full tartan *breacan feilidh* was thus worn only by the men. To remember and perpetuate the exact pattern, the women marked a piece of wood with the number of every thread of the stripes. Thus each island or region evolved a fixed sett, or tartan pattern of its own, and in consequence a glance at a man's plaid revealed where he came from, and therefore to what clan he belonged. In the seventeenth century, but not before, the clans began to appropriate to their families the tartans of their territories, and this transfer became significant as lands began to change hands, lost or gained by war or by economic and political change.

The process of dyeing the wool, spinning, weaving, and 'waulking' the cloth was the women's work. The dyes used were all vegetable – lichens, bog-myrtle, heather, roots, bark, and fruits – but the art of preparing them has long since been lost. The tartan cloth as it aged retained its colours unfaded.‡ When the wool had been carded and the yarn spun, dyed, woven, and steeped in urine, the cloth was waulked. This was the process of fulling – to cleanse the wool of oil and to thicken it – for which the women used a board ribbed lengthwise. It might be a long frame of wattled work, or even a door taken off its hinges. In St Kilda they used a mat of thick grass ropes. After the web had been washed, it was laid wet on the board in the open air. Four, six, eight, or up to fourteen women sat on straw bundles to each side and, applying their bare feet to the web, rubbed, pushed, and tumbled it, moving it rhythmically forward and sideways, and all the while sang a waulking song, which they would sometimes extemporize. The song slowly rose to a crescendo as the work neared the end.

Much of the hard work around the townships fell to the women. They not only spun, dyed, wove, and waulked, they made the family's clothing. They dug the soil along with the men, harrowed, reaped, gathered and stacked peats at

---

* 1695: Martin.
† Ibid. 1930: Nicolson.
‡ 1831: Logan.

the banks, bore the peats home in creels, cut grasses and heather for thatch or rope-making, carried the heavy bales long distances, collected seaweed, spread manure, milled grain, mended nets, and cooked and washed for large families. On top of all such work they bred and reared numerous children, of whom a large proportion died in the first two weeks after birth. Despite all the trials, they sang their way through life. They had songs for everything: as many milking songs as for waulking the cloth, quern songs, churning songs, reaping songs for cutting and binding, cradle songs, and even manure songs with a rhythm to match the spreading action. The men sang too, and their rowing songs, called *Iorram*, had a slow tempo to match the dip of oars – a famous example is the Mingulay boat-song. This prevalence of song and music throughout the Isles gave delight to visitors and quickened the musical talent of succeeding generations.

Mainlanders were frequent visitors to the Outer Hebrides, especially before the Little Ice Age cut down the standing crops, for the islanders were hospitable to a fault and this became widely known to men in need and to others still less scrupulous. A traveller was always made welcome, given a plaid for bedding, and never interrogated. Since there were no roads and many bogs, his feet were washed. There were no inns in the Outer Hebrides till the end of the seventeenth century, for the islesmen's natural hospitality made them superfluous. Strangers were drawn in particular to North Uist by its big barley crop. They asked, and therefore received free from the people, not only much grain but also horses, sheep, cows, wool, and other goods. Martin noted the presence of ten men in Uist, each with attendants, asking for free corn. All were entertained without charge and none sent away empty-handed. 'This,' he observes, 'is a great yet voluntary tax which has continued many ages.' It came to an end only through the increasing severity of climate. But the islanders continued to look after the poor. They had no organized welfare service for the sick and aged, but no man starved or lacked shelter so long as his chief and fellow clansmen could help him.

The great chiefs were no less hospitable than their own people. They kept open board. Strangers and clansmen could enter uninvited and take their place at table. A few of these chiefs, like the sixteenth-century MacNeil of Barra, might be professional buccaneers or worse, but whether of lofty or ignoble character all at their own tables were models of generosity. The islesmen had access to the gentlemen of the clan, could speak with them on terms of familiarity, and unconsciously adopted their manners, bearing, and style of speech; this would account at least in part for the islanders' well-known dignity of manner, and their superiority in that respect over Lowland and southern men of the same class.*

No men have spoken of their women more respectfully than Hebrideans.† The iniquitous circumstance under which men reared livestock, and, although they did other work, left the heavier burden of toil to their women, was a secondary product of the new feudalism, the primary being the splitting of the clansmen into two classes: the fighting men, who were excused labour and whose leisure occupation was hunting, and the field labourers, who were not allowed to leave their islands. The division was fixed before 1550.‡ This bred in both sexes a new attitude of mind towards work on the land: even in the women's eyes it seemed demeaning for men – yet not for women.

By 1578, the chiefship of clans had widely grown hereditary.§ This was not a firm date; different clans at different periods were able to reassert their elective powers, despite the universal granting of crown charters. But reassertions were temporary. The charters of lands were to chiefs and passed by inheritance to the male heirs by gavel-kind,‖ that is, to all sons equally, including illegitimates – a circumstance that allowed a degree of elective principle to persist where a chief's near relatives were strong enough to insist. But the land was in fact no longer the people's. They continued to regard it as theirs, and this illusion took a long time to die, being so deeply rooted in the past history of their race. On the chiefs' side, their sense of trusteeship likewise persisted; over-riding that came realization of their new powers. Gradually they were able to assert their ownership of the land by requiring payment of higher rents to pay for their wars and huge households. The *duinevasal* thus became tacksmen, receiving their land at a rent or tack. They disposed of the land both by sub-letting farms to tenants – usually on steelbow tenure under which stock was the tacksman's let with the land¶ – and by settling a large number of cottars, giving each a house with ground enough to sow a boll of oats (six bushels) and to keep a few cows. These people formed new townships with runrig arable and pasture. The tacksmen exacted from them all services under a feudal system still made easy by its patriarchal character.

At the same time (1550 to 1600), the chiefs succeeded in abolishing the brieveships and took to themselves full powers of heritable jurisdiction, including

---

* 1906: Mackenzie.
† 1695: Martin.
‡ 1549: Monro.
§ 1578: Leslie.
‖ 1919: Mackenzie.
¶ 1880: Skene.

the brieves' share of fines. They held the power of pit and gallows (the pit to drown women, the gallows for men). The Hebrides threw up a rich crop of chiefs powerful in personality, but of greatly varied moral character: a few, like the tenth MacLeod of Dunvegan, prodigiously evil, others enlightened. By and large, they seem to have administered justice impartially and without abusing their powers. The elders of each clan had regard to its good name and kept close watch on their chief's behaviour. As a general rule he took their counsel.

The chiefs themselves had become victims of circumstance under the hereditary system. Each young heir was expected to give proof of physical courage before his inauguration, and was made fit for it by training from early youth. He was surrounded by young men equally ambitious to prove themselves. If his time was too peaceful to provide an occasion, he had to make one by planning and leading a cattle raid on some neighbouring clan with whom relations had deteriorated. Such open raiding was universal clan custom, which the islanders did not think of as robbery with violence. What one clan lost it took in its turn, when its own chieftain was ready.*

The inauguration ceremonies for a chief continued as practised in the past.† The panegyrics delivered by the bard, extolling the courage, justice, generosity, wisdom, and power of the chief's family were not meant as flattery; they had the definite object of inciting him to acquire or imitate such virtues, for the good of all. His will would be law. His power would be absolute. His clansmen were devoted and their lives at his service.

The greater chiefs of the Isles were surrounded by considerable state and ceremony. Twenty or more household officers had the duty of attending them.‡ Each had clearly defined duties; some offices were personal to the holder, others hereditary. The Bard (or *Seanachaidh*) was the most important man in the clan's social life; poet, historian, genealogist, his mind was the clan's library. Many bards had considerable learning; some were creative poets; others, versed in literature, 'translatit in their awin toung mony craftis and science though they professit maist the science of medcinary and were richt excellent in it'.§ The father would train for office whichever of his sons showed most talent. The Harper and Piper both held high rank. The Seneschal or Steward had to know thoroughly the genealogy of every Island and Highland clan. The great families

---

* 1695: Martin.
† See Chapter 6.
‡ 1897: Lovat Fraser. 1695: Martin. 1831: Logan.
§ 1536: Bellenden.

required two: one at home to assign every man his place at table, which he indicated with a white rod, and no word spoken; the other to travel with the chief. The Quarter Master provided lodgings for all attendants at home and abroad. The Orator delivered speeches on public occasions, or to men of power, and harangued the clansmen before battle. The Armour Bearer carried the chief's claymore and target (later his gun), and attended his master night and day to prevent surprise. The Torch Bearer lighted the chief around castle or house and stood behind him at table. The Cup Bearer maintained the rounds in company or at table. A drinking party could last up to forty-eight hours, with barrow-men attending to wheel the fallen to bed. The Almoner cared for widows, orphans, and the aged. Besides these were the Physician, Master of Horse, Pursemaster, Standard Bearer, Jester, Bridleman, Porter (to carry the chief when fording rivers), Running Footman, Baggage Man, Piper's Man, and Forester – for the chiefs held mainland forests and many islands carried wood-land now vanished.

The Lords of the Isles had heralds, brieves, and many more officers, but after 1500 only the great chiefs kept so many as those listed, and the lesser around ten. They were attended too by several gentlemen of the House, being near relatives or favoured commoners, and by a bodyguard. The latter, picked from the clan's best families, were all young men trained to wrestling, swimming, putting the stone, jumping, and dancing; to skill in arms, mainly archery, the sword, and target; and to seamanship. Finally, the retinue when travelling was accompanied by a dozen lads who had no other business than to do their master's bidding. The formidable size and armed strength of a chief's 'tail' caused con-sternation to the citizens of Edinburgh and other towns when the chiefs passed through, whether to meetings of the Privy Council, or to Court, or on other visitations. In 1616 the Privy Council was moved to pass an Act pruning the length of the chief's tail according to his rank; MacLean of Duart's, for example, was cut to eight men, and MacLeod of Harris's to six.

A chief's progress through the Isles when he travelled to hold courts and inspect his land was like a royal regatta: a navy of galleys was required to transport the retainers, wine, and ale. Such magnificence could not be displayed cheaply, and provisioning came from a heavy burden placed on the islands' tenants. This was *Cuid Oidhche*, or night's portion, meaning as much food as the chief's company might eat, even if they numbered 600. The annual burden for Lewis, a forty-pound land, was 5,760 bolls of grain, 1,160 cows, 640 sheep, and a large quantity of fish and poultry. The merklands of Mull each paid yearly five bolls of barley, eight bolls of meal, twenty stones of cheese, four stones of butter, four milk cows, eight sheep, twenty-four hens, and two merks in silver.* The requisitioning of such supplies became known as sorning – a sorner being one who took hospitality uninvited. Other imposts of war could be levied by the chief at will.

The justice administered by the chiefs on their rounds might often have been rough, but their laws knew no delays. Strangely, the chiefs did not trouble to suppress piracy, which in the sixteenth century throve along the Scottish and English coasts. 'Broken men' who belonged to no clan – plainly, thieves and cut-throats from all parts of Scotland – made dens on inner islands, which then were well-wooded, such as Pabay, Raasay, and, notoriously, South Rona where their harbour was known as *Port nan Robaireann*. They preyed on sea-borne trade and menaced the fishing industry, which was growing prosperous. Their immunity from clan attack must certainly have meant that they plundered only Lowland, Dutch, and Flemish boats, with whom mercantile enterprise lay. The most enterprising of all the sea-rovers was the outer island chief, MacNeil of Barra. He sailed as far as west Ireland to make land-raids on Mayo or to prey on English, French, and Dutch ships. He and others were frequently 'put to the horn' (outlawed), but that held no terrors for an island chief ensconced in Kisimul Castle. Queen Elizabeth, outraged at shipping losses, demanded his head of James VI. James commissioned MacKenzie of Kintail to fetch him in. MacKenzie sailed to Barra, by a trick lured MacNeil aboard his galley, and shipped him back to Edinburgh. James was astonished to find that this terror of the seas was a friendly old man with a long grey beard. And MacNeil had the wit to remember that James was the son of Mary Queen of Scots: he claimed that his piracies, so called, had taken just toll of 'the woman who had killed your Majesty's mother'. James set him free. True, his estates were declared forfeit, but no one dared venture to try to take them.†

MacNeil was lucky to get away, for James VI was no friend to the Hebrides. Their affairs had too long been the scandal of his realm. He took a first step to their pacification by an Act of 1587 called the General Bond. It placed squarely on the chiefs' shoulders responsibility for their vassals' acts, and required from their purses large sums for a fund, from which innocent people suffering injury could claim compensation.

James, whose quick, shallow mind earned him the soubriquet 'the wisest fool in Christendom', followed the wisdom of his General Bond by the folly of

---

* 1577: An account for James VI.
† 1906: Mackenzie. 1938: MacLeod.

an openly attempted genocide in the Outer Hebrides. He needed money and promoted a company of Lowland gentlemen named the Fife Adventurers to plunder Lewis, which he declared to be 'inrychit with ane incredibill fertilitie of cornis and store of fischeings and utheris necessaris, surpassing far the plenty of any pairt of the inland'.* The premeditated rape of the island and murder of its people had first to be justified in terms loftier than financial gain to the king, therefore an Act of Parliament found that they were 'voyd of any knawledge of God or his religioun', had 'gavin thameselfis over to all kynd of barbaritie and inhumanitie', and this was held enough to warrant 'ruiting out the barbarous inhabitantis'.† No provision was made in the Act for the conversion to Christianity of these new-found heathens. Its declaration of intent was humbug. The Privy Council declared that no part of the Hebrides or Highlands should thenceforth be 'disponit in feu, tak, or utterways bot to Lowland men'.‡ It was openly avowed that the Lewis settlement would be followed by others.

The Fife Adventurers were headed by the King's cousin, the duke of Lennox. His commission authorized whatever 'slauchter, mutilation, fyre-raising, or utheris inconvenieties' the noble lord might choose for expelling the native people.§ As if this were not enough, the king later commissioned the Marquis of Huntly to seize the whole Outer Hebrides 'not be aggreement with the country people bot by extirpation of thame'.|| The first landings with six hundred mercenaries were made at Stornoway, then a township of fifty black houses, in November 1598, and two others in 1605 and 1609. All met the same fate – Neil MacLeod and his Lewismen sacked the camps, razed houses, carried off livestock, fired the stores, pirated ships in the Minch, twice took Stornoway Castle, and finally massacred the garrison. The Adventurers went bankrupt and did not come again. Had James been as successful in the Outer Hebrides as he was in Ulster at this time in supplanting the native people with Lowland and English colonists, the economic 'improvements' effected must have cost centuries of racial hatred. MacLeod's defence spared his people that evil legacy. It seems unjust that he lost Lewis in 1610, when James granted the island to MacKenzie of Kintail, who was strong enough to take and hold it.

The Hebrides had been so long aflame with wars that the king's law, as distinct from the chiefs', did not run. His Majesty's rents and taxes could not be

---

* 1598: Reg. of Privy Council.
† 1598: Acts of Parliament, Vol. IV, pp. 175–6.
‡ 1598: Reg. of Privy Council, Vol. V.
§ 1599: Ibid., Vol. VI, pp. 8–10.
|| 1605: Ibid., Vol. VII, pp. 360–2, and letter from James VI to Marquis of Huntly, 20 May 1607.

collected. The royal decrees were derided. The Crown's centuries-old policy of undermining Hebridean power by setting one chief against another had been a sowing of dragon's teeth. The general disorder had gained such notoriety that the king felt himself to be mocked. Discouraged by events from using force, James accepted advice from Andrew Knox, the Bishop of the Isles, that he try guile. But to win the chiefs' cooperation they had first to be gathered.

Lord Ochiltree was appointed king's sheep-dog. He called all Hebridean chiefs to a conference at Aros Castle in Mull. Confident in that island site and driven by curiosity, they came to a man. Ochiltree (Andrew Stewart) invited them to dine aboard his flagship *Moon*, where the Bishop of the Isles would preach a sermon. As if under spell, they accepted, were made prisoner, and taken to Edinburgh. They were set free on giving promise to attend a council on Iona, and there to ratify statutes to be drawn up by Bishop Knox.

In July 1609, on Iona, the chiefs approved nine statutes, which became a landmark of Hebridean history. The statutes helped greatly to improve the quality of life, and taken as a whole searched out causes of trouble. A précis reads thus:

1. The Church and clergy were to be maintained.
2. Inns were to be established to relieve the people of burdensome hospitality.
3. The chiefs' households were to be cut in size, to be supported by themselves, and not by tax on tenants; and no man was to live on the Isles without a trade or personal income.
4. Sorners were to be punished as thieves.
5. Islesmen in future were not to import wine, but might continue to brew their own ale.
6. Every man owning sixty cattle must send his eldest son to a Lowland school.
7. The use of firearms was forbidden.
8. Bards who glorified war were to be discouraged.
9. Enactments to enforce preceding acts.

This was the first time since the Lordship of the Isles that Hebridean chiefs had been invited to deal with island problems. They should have been asked a century earlier. As it was, fifty years were to pass before they took the statutes seriously. At first they ignored them. But a start had been made. The Privy Council kept reminding them of their duties, and adding to the statutes unwisely. Two Acts banned all tenants from the purchase or consumption of wine, and banned Gaelic as a language for use in schools. These were stupid and harmful regulations. A people cannot be made temperate by decree, and the education of children proceeds ill if not in their own tongue. Since the ban on wine was flouted, the Privy Council in 1622 imposed severe penalties on any shipmaster who carried wine to the Hebrides. The consequence was that whisky, which had not been drunk in quantity, was now distilled in every township. Smuggling became an honourable profession.

Sixteenth-century islesmen had not only been hard men, able to subsist for days on a campaign without food and shelter other than barley, cold water, and the plaid, but exceedingly abstemious. Their drinks were bland, made by fermenting whisked whey in wood, and ale from malted grain or heather-tops. Around 1550 a trade in wine had opened with France and Spain and become brisk as the century advanced. The Privy Council had cause for concern. The chiefs' carousels and feasts had become gastronomic feats, far beyond the capacities and constitution of modern man (Rory Mor's drinking horn at Dunvegan might be regarded as a symbol of the times – it held five pints of claret); and the example they set had affected the common clansmen, who, if the Bishop of the Isles spoke truly, had grown intemperate: 'For the insatiable desire whereof the said Islanders are so far possessed that, when there arrives any ship there with wines, they spend both days and nights in their excess of drinking, so long as there is any wine left; so that, being overcome with drink, there falls out many inconveniences among them, to the breach of His Majesty's peace.'*

Excesses died out by 1650. Ale was imported and wine consumption fell by two-thirds. Brandy and whisky were drunk by everyone 'to counteract the moist climate', but seventeenth-century 'whisky' should not be confused with the later, more famous product. Distilled from grain, usually oats, the spirit was variously named according to alcoholic content: *trestarig* if thrice distilled, and *usquebaugh* (from *uisge*, water, and *beatha*, life) if four times distilled.† Martin says that if any man exceeded two spoonfuls 'it would presently stop his breath, and endanger his life'.

The statutes also expressed concern for the state of the Church in the Hebrides – 'the great ignorance of the chiefs and their subjects, their neglect of all duty to God and the great growth of all kinds of vice' – but made no mention of the ill effects of the Reformation. Prior to the Reformation of around 1560 the clergy had become bogged in sloth, but the islesmen venerated the Church. Martin

* 1622: Reg. of Privy Council, Vol. XIII, pp. 20–21.
† 1695: Martin.

records that their habit was to kneel at first daily sight of a church building, however great the distance, and to say their Paternoster. Zeal for reformation was of mainland origin. But Island chiefs, like Lowland and Highland lords, seized the Church's lands and revenues and went unrebuked. With neither money nor influence, the Church in the Isles virtually ceased to exist.

While the Hebrides had not experienced the stimulating fervour of the Lowland Church, formalism had been at least a valuable prop and when that was kicked from under the Hebridean Church nothing was substituted. The mainland reformers were much too preoccupied with their own problems to spare a thought for the Hebrides. Their acts there were destructive. Valuable records, works of art and literature, were lost to posterity. In 1561 they stripped Iona Abbey and threw into the sea more than 350 carved crosses. The priceless library vanished. In remoter islands and districts, even the ceremonies of marriage and baptism now ended. The churches fell into disrepair. Wars, feuds, cruelties, piracies, bred an eye for an eye, tooth for a tooth doctrine – stony ground for Christian seed. The lack of any central authorities – religious, political, or economic – to impose restraints played equal part in the deterioration of human behaviour.

The Reformed Kirk on the mainland kept at first a balance between Presbyterian and Episcopalian parties. Most islanders were attached to the latter. When the Lowlands turned against 'Romish' practices, and the National Covenant was signed in 1638 to oust prelacy, the lords and chiefs who had seized Church lands gave it support for fear of losing property. In the civil war the islanders had to follow their chiefs, but unlike the Lowlanders they were free of bigotry – not out of broadminded charity, but from indifference. Hence Roman Catholics, Episcopalians, and Covenanting Presbyterians, could live in the Isles without fear for their lives. The changing fortunes of religious war ended with the triumph of Presbyterianism in 1688, but without disturbance to the minds or lives of Hebridean clergy and their flocks. They could conform to the new rules and find no change in essentials, which to them were the teachings of Christ. Whether the Church's administrators were labelled bishops or superintendents seemed to them a trifle, and they declined to be bothered about subtle differences in dogma. Exceptions were South Uist, Eriskay, Barra, and the Small Isles, which remained wholly Roman Catholic.

Tardy as the chiefs were in acting on the statutes, they were slowly trained to come to heel. Piracy continued off the Outer Hebrides,* where Clanranald's

* 1627: MacDonald.

galleys preyed on merchantmen until 1636, but by 1650 all pirates had been swept off the seas. The Privy Council frequently summoned the chiefs to Edinburgh, and they came. Their long tails had been shortened, but a modified sorning continued, for courts had to be held, and the rounds of the islands made with retinues. Clan feuds died away as disputes were settled by litigation. All this brought relief to the clansmen, but methods of agriculture and stock-raising went unimproved, for the chiefs did not give their minds to such matters, and were probably too pleased with the prosperity of their cattle trade.

By the close of the seventeenth century the chiefs had established orderly government. Relations between chief and clansmen were cordial and remained intimate. Even the least responsible chiefs, like MacNeil of Barra – who as late as 1675 greeted a King's Messenger, who was trying to serve a summons for debt at Kisimul Castle, with a volley of shots from the battlements fired from hagbutts, guns, and pistols* – even such as he were as fathers to their own people. The outlying Barra isles numbered a score, and were small and isolated; therefore when a tenant's wife died he would go to MacNeil, report his loss, and ask his chief to recommend a wife to him 'without which he cannot manage his affairs, nor beget followers to MacNeil, which would prove a public loss to him'.† MacNeil would then find a suitable match for the man, who would visit the woman with a bottle of whisky for the marriage ceremony, which was then consummated. When a tenant died, MacNeil would likewise find the widow a husband. If a tenant lost cows by misfortune, MacNeil made up the loss. When tenants grew too old to till the ground, MacNeil took them into his own family and gave them food and shelter.‡

The common practice of fosterage forged another strong bond. One of the chief's sons would be given to a clansman to be reared with his own children to the age of seventeen. The honour was coveted and the effect remarkable: Logan quotes a Highland saying, 'Affectionate to a man is a friend, but a foster brother is as the life-blood of the heart. No love in the world is comparable by many degrees to it.' Friendships were pledged, and the bond made sacred, by each drinking a drop of the other's blood drawn from the little finger. And this attachment was said to be indissoluble. The chief would promote his son's foster brother to high office near his person, and the lad's family would

---

* 1938: MacLeod.
† 1695: Martin.
‡ The need for a marriage agency persists to the present day – a service now given occasionally through the columns of the *Stornoway Gazette*.

receive a full reward on terms sometimes settled by deed.* The chief in turn would rear clansmen's sons with his own family, sometimes to the number of fifteen.

During the eclipse of the Church from 1500 to 1650, the rites of religion had fallen into disuse and required to be re-introduced by the reformed kirk. Until then, the marriage form had been handfasting. The couple clasped hands and agreed to live together for a year and a day. There was no other ceremony. The temporary marriage became permanent and binding in law if they continued in wedlock beyond the time prescribed. Until then they were free to part without reproach, but with duty laid on the man to maintain the children. When Church marriage was re-established in mid-century, handfasting died away. On the far-out islands, where the clergy could make only brief annual visits, simple marriage ceremonies were conducted by the laity. On St Kilda, which had two hundred inhabitants in 1700, a close scrutiny of the degrees of consanguinity was required before marriage. A girl was allowed to marry there at thirteen or fourteen years, 'though she have no other portion but a pound of horse-hair to make a gin to catch fowls'.† And a man would marry though he had only a couple of cows.

Despite dirty conditions in the black houses, children had a good expectation of life if they survived babyhood or later accident. Longevity was the rule and ages of eighty and ninety not uncommonly attained. The excellent state of general health, maintained without medical services, may be attributed in part to the natural environment of clean air and unpolluted earth; in part to clean living and simple diet. Martin records that mothers and wet nurses were abstemious and babies usually suckled till the end of the second year. They were bathed every morning and evening, some in warm water, some in cold. And the boys, incited no doubt by the great tales of the bards at ceilidhs, set out to make themselves hardy.

The diet of the people was largely vegetarian. 'There is no place so well stored with such great quantity of good beef and mutton,' wrote Martin, 'where so little of both is eaten.' Only persons of high rank ate meat daily, or had three meals. All others ate two meals. Their normal fare was *brochan* (oatmeal moistened with boiling water and butter), bread, butter, cheese, fish, eggs and milk. *Brochan* and bread were the staple diet in winter and spring – a diet not then stripped of its vitamin content by over-refinement of the grain before

* 1938: MacLeod.
† 1695: Martin.

milling. They drank no tea, coffee, or alcohol with their food, only pure water. The diet was ample and everyone had much exercise in the open air.

Martin makes no mention of eggs, of which a large quantity must have been eaten, for the *Book of Dunvegan* records nine thousand hens delivered in Skye as part-payment of rent to MacLeod each year (value, 1p a dozen).* Lewismen made annual expeditions twenty-seven miles west to the Flannan Isles and forty miles north to Sula Sgeir, to raid the auk and gannet colonies for eggs, birds, and feathers. In these days the herring shoals came into all the lochs, and were so abundant that in Stornoway a cran (750 fish) sold for 5p.† Gutted herring, tied in pairs by a rush through the gills and hung across a rope, were dried and preserved for eight months, without use of salt. The big mussel-beds were a valuable resource to poor families in bad years, when foul summers destroyed the harvest, and foul winters the livestock. In the Outer Hebrides, whale and seal meat gave seasonal additions to diet. Whales – and there were many kinds of different size – were a frequent nuisance to fishermen. Seals were taken in late October by clubbing them – as many as 320 young and old at one time on the skerries off North Uist – and by netting at narrow channels. The nets shaped to a purse-end were made of horse-hair rope.‡ On some islands fish were caught by stone dykes built across tidal waters, like Loch Bee in South Uist,§ or by heather dams built as thick nets across burns, as in Rum.‖ Edible seaweeds were much eaten, in particular dulse and caragheen. The latter was washed in fresh water, bleached, dried, then boiled in milk, when it formed a nutritious jelly.

Histories of Scotland usually record that the potato was first introduced from Ireland to the Hebrides by Clanranald in 1743. But Martin mentions it as a common food in 1695. Although widely grown it was not appreciated as a food of value, therefore not intensively cultivated. Plain fare and limited leisure brought their rewards. Not only was health generally good, but deformities of body and defects of mind were absent. In all his travels Martin saw no fat people nor any who looked starved. On the other hand, mainly because so little food was imported, the islands had no reserves to meet occasional famines when crops failed. In the notorious season of 1688, many people died of starvation in Skye.¶

* 1938: MacLeod.
† 1919: Mackenzie.
‡ 1695: Martin.
§ 1549: Monro. 1961: Munro.
‖ 1904: Geikie.
¶ 1793: Statistical Account.

Likewise, an occasional heavy toll was taken by epidemics. These were small-pox and 'fevers', the latter probably being typhus, to which bad sanitation contributed. They swept away whole townships, for remedies were primitive or superstitious. The people's very freedom from infections left them peculiarly prone by lack of immunization. On St Kilda, for example, the people were free of colds all the year round until the steward's annual visit with his retinue of forty to sixty men. Coughs and colds then invariably spread through the whole native community.

Herbal remedies were much used, and shock treatment was sometimes approved. A patient with jaundice would be laid on the floor face down, a black mark made on the eleventh vertebra, and this touched with redhot tongs. The sick man thus enlivened bolted out of doors 'till the pain be abated, which happens very speedily, and the patient recovers soon after'. The truth of the cure, we may think, was that no patient still with jaundice was prepared to admit as much to his doctors. Many of the remedies were purely superstitious, like touching an affected part with a healing stone.

When clan warfare ended early in the seventeenth century, peace was not accompanied by any notable increase in population, which Martin estimated as 40,000 in 1695, without saying how he arrived at the figure. A count in 1755 gave the same result.* The cull taken by infant mortality, smallpox, and typhus (but not emigration as yet) accounts for the failure of the population to rise.

The recreations contributing to health were the athletic sports previously mentioned, to which must be added horse-racing, golf, football, and shinty (played even on the sands of St Kilda with wooden clubs and a wooden ball†). Shinty had been brought by the Scots from Ireland, where it was played in the second century.‡ Horse-racing was a festive sport for the young on the North Uist machair. They rode bareback and barefoot, with whips of dried seaweed stalks and bridles of marram grass, which they threw on the horses' necks when racing began. Golf and football were popular in the lawless Hebrides, in spite of the Scots Parliament, which in 1457 had 'decreted and ordained that futeball and golf be utterly cryit doun and nocht usit', for golf led to neglect of archery, and football to riot.

Dice, cards, and draughts were the indoor games. Mental exercise was given at ceilidhs by proverbs and riddles, when each person in turn had to repeat a proverb or propound a riddle that had not been already mentioned, and more

---

* 1755: Webster.
† 1695: Martin.
‡ Reference in the will of the Irish King, Cathair Moir.

testingly – for the people had most retentive memories, being illiterate – by the composition of impromptu rhymed verse, to which all were expected to contribute. This latter was a favourite entertainment, and Martin, a Skyeman, testified of Lewismen that 'several are able to form a satire or a panegyric *ex tempore* without aid of stronger drink than water'.

The first proposals for a system of parish schools throughout Scotland had appeared in an Act of Council of 1616 inspired by the ideals of John Knox. His goal had been democracy in Church and State alike, and the means to it education, financed from the revenues of the old Church. The nobles' cupidity had defeated that end. In 1700, there was only one school in the Outer Hebrides, at Stornoway, and that for tacksmen's sons. Tacksmen of means engaged teachers of real ability, who inculcated a love of the classics (which a hundred years later drew amazed praise from Dr Johnson), but Gaelic continued as the exclusive tongue of the Isles into the nineteenth century. The Church of Scotland entered the field in 1709 by setting up the *Society for the Propagation of Christian Knowledge* with the Highlands and Islands as its sphere of activity. This was a vigorous organization, giving an elementary education with religious instruction. Its schools in the Isles were few and far between, could be held only in winter, and then usually in barns where the pupils sat on rushes spread on the floors. The teachers were paid, in 1690, only 50p a half year,* rising in 1717 to £8.33½ a year.† Yet they were imbued with enthusiasm (for learning). The pupils were much handicapped by the demand made on them to read only in English, for they repeated what they learned parrot-like without relating it to their daily life.‡ Organized education may thus be said to have taken its birth in the eighteenth century, but not till the nineteenth did it gain the means and strength from Church, State, and private bodies, to proliferate through the Hebrides in well-founded schools.

From 1609 to 1745 the Hebrides had enjoyed peace if not prosperity. In one warlike episode, Cromwell seized Lewis (unopposed) to deny its harbours to the Dutch fleet, and later the wars of the Restoration bedevilled the mainland, but the Island clans, unlike the Highland, felt little involvement, and held aloof. Their crops were no longer burned, nor their men's lives wasted. If they knew poverty, that was largely by comparison with material standards of the twentieth century, and was certainly not of spirit. Two independent observers of widely different backgrounds gave their opinions of Hebrideans at the close of the

* 1938: MacLeod.
† Accounts for Seaforth Estates, 1717. 1903: Mackenzie.
‡ 1919: Mackenzie.

seventeenth century. William Sacheverell, the English governor of Man (commissioned to salvage the Spanish galleon sunk in Tobermory Bay in Mull), wrote: 'They appear in all their actions to have a certain air of freedom and contempt of these trifles, luxury and ambition, which we so servilely creep after. They bind their appetites to their necessities, and their happiness consists, not in having much, but in coveting little.'

Martin Martin, summarizing his travels through the western isles, criticized the backward state of agriculture, the lack of trading opportunity, and of education, granted which the people might have had plenty of all things, and added: 'If any family reduced to low circumstances had a mind to retire to any of these isles, there is no part of the known world where they may have the products of sea and land cheaper, live more securely, or among a more tractable and mild people. And that the country in general is healthful, appears from the good state of health enjoyed by the inhabitants.'

Hebridean prices and wages, 1640–1740

The exchange of goods was almost exclusively by barter and services were paid for in kind. Prices were not often quoted in Hebridean records, and the examples noted below probably varied from one island to another.

	c. 1640	c. 1725
Black cattle	50p	£1
Hebridean sheep	11p	8½p
Horse	50p–£3.25	75p–£1.25
Hens p. dozen	1p	—
Herring p. barrel	£1	66½p
Beef & mutton p. pound	½p	½p
Barley & oats p. boll	2p	—
Meal p. stone	3½p	33½p
Butter p. stone	10p	16½p
Cheese p. stone	5p	8½p
Sugar p. pound	10p	5p
Linen shirt	1½p	—
Breeches	8½p–83½p	—
Plaid	30p	50p
Shoes p. pair	10p	—
Golf club and ball	6p	—
Tobacco p. pound	10p	10p–4p

	c. 1640	c. 1725
Wine p. gallon	—	44p
Beer p. gallon	—	8½p
Ale p. gallon	—	5½p
Usquebaugh p. gallon	—	20p
Brandy p. bottle	—	2½p
School teacher per annum		£8.33½
Minister per annum		£28–£56
Factor per annum		£33.33½–£50
Smith per annum		£2.60
Mason per annum		£12.50
Carpenter per annum		£12.50
Gamekeeper per annum		£5.50
Pipers per annum		£2.20
MacCrimmon per annum		£13.89

Estate Rentals between 1630 and 1724
(Chiefs' net money income)

Lewis	£1,000
St Kilda	£5.55
Harris	£600
West Skye	£1,000

Rents were paid in kind. The chiefs shipped the livestock and goods to Glasgow for conversion to cash.*

Rents, sixteenth century

SKYE: Rent for a pennyland (a township whose acreage of arable and pasture might vary from 600 acres to 1,000†):

6 stones meal, 6 stones cheese, 1 cow and 4/2d in money
(21p), of total value £1.21p.‡

MULL: Rent for a merkland (approximately 4 pennylands):

2 bolls meal, 2 bolls barley, 4 cows, 16 sheep, and 16
dozen poultry.§

* 1938: MacLeod.
† 1880: Skene.
‡ 1930: Nicolson.
§ 1577: An account for James VI.

8

The Recent Past:
1745-1900

Prince Charles Edward Stewart landed from France on Eriskay on 3 August 1745. He was not made welcome by Clanranald but in hope of winning the Highland chiefs sailed on to Arisaig. His reception 'there was equally cool. None of which was surprising. The Hebrides had been at peace for more than a hundred years, for the Jacobite risings of 1715 and 1719 had found little support from islesmen: they of all the people of Scotland having least cause to respect the word or wisdom of the House of Stewart. The prince came now to the Highlands, aged only twenty-five, without money, men, or arms. The mainland chiefs met and assessed him, and such was his personality that, spurning doubts, they raised the clans. On 18 September he was able to enter Edinburgh and proclaim his father, James Edward, king.

Only Clanranald, among the great chiefs holding islands (the Uists, Benbecula, and the Small Isles), had called out his island people, for they as Roman Catholics had real interest in the Jacobite cause. Seven months later, at Culloden, the Highland army was destroyed. It had been raised, and could only have been raised, under the system of Celtic feudalism, which Parliament now took apart by the enforcement of three Acts. These disarmed the clans, banned Highland dress, and abolished heritable jurisdictions. Parliament, forgetting that feudalism had originally been foisted by the Crown on an unwilling people, confused the feudal system with the clan system. The abolition of the chiefs' feudal powers should have revived and strengthened the clans, not destroyed them as Parliament planned. Yet so wide was the gap between Lowland thinking and Island and Highland realities that the Court of Session felt able to declare, 'When all military character, all feudal subordination, all heritable jurisdiction, all independent authority, of chiefs are extracted from what used to be called a clan, nothing remains of its essential character and peculiar features'.* This statement by men ignorant of history reversed the truth. It listed as though they were essentials the feudal growths that had in fact been sapping the clan system. Freed from these, the clans should have become vigorous social communities, capable of revitalizing Island and Highland life. That this opportunity was not taken was due to no Act of Parliament but to the choice of the chiefs. The feudal principle had lasted too long; the effort to kill it came too late and did not strike deep enough. It sprang up in another form. The Act of 1747 destroyed the Celtic form, but the chiefs substituted economic feudalism, and that choice abandoned the Islands and Highlands to an uncontrolled exploitation of resources, both of land and human life.

The choice made by the chiefs did not become apparent until nearly fifteen years after Culloden, during which time the clan system continued to function – and the demand in England for black cattle hugely rose. Prices soared from £1 a head to £2 or £3 between 1766 and 1769. Skye alone exported four thousand head annually,† and to sustain such exports huge island herds were reared. Everyone wanted more pasture. Tacksmen tried to oust smaller tenants by offering more rent, and the chiefs seized the chance to rack-rent the tacksmen. When the bad years came, and harvests failed, and stock died, and when finally the price of cattle fell, remissions of rent were given grudgingly if at all. Famine came to the Isles in 1768, 1769, 1772, and 1773. The poor roamed the beaches like Mesolithic man in search of shellfish and seaweed. But three-fifths of the chiefs were now absentee landowners, a new breed, educated at Eton, building new town and country mansions, and running up gambling and clothing debts in Edinburgh and London. They appointed factors, whose job it was to screw more money out of their estates. They still called themselves chiefs for the sake of the status it gave them, but they are better known as 'lairds'. They had rejected the patriarchal and trusteeship ideals as economic nonsense, meaning no more to them than to the Lowlanders to whom they had begun to sell the clans' land. Cattle were thus valued above men, rents were doubled and trebled,‡ estates were sold; and the tacksmen, plundered beyond their means to pay in recurrent lean years, were forced to emigrate to the American colonies. They took their sub-tenants with them. In the twelve years 1763–75, twenty thousand Highlanders and Islanders emigrated.§ A large (unrecorded) number

* 1906: Mackenzie, quoting a declaration of court, 1862.
† 1930: Nicolson.
‡ 1938: MacLeod. 1775: Pennant. 1775: Forbes. 1930: Nicolson. 1793: Statistical Accounts.
§ 1775: Forbes. 1793: Statistical Accounts. 1906: Mackenzie.

of islesmen, being destitute, had to bind themselves to export agents, who sold them like cattle at North American ports. This new form of slave-trade fostered fraudulent contracts and wholesale kidnappings. In 1774, seven slave-traders were cruising off the Inner and Outer Hebrides, entering every inhabited bay in search of human freight. The masters would cajole men, women, and children to emigrate under false promise, and where opportunity offered, or there was no official supervision, they kidnapped them to fill their ships to capacity.* One master, of the ship *Philadelphia*, felt free to kidnap boys off the beach in Stornoway harbour and to refuse the parents access before sailing, for Lewis had no chief, judge, or magistrate – only an absentee laird's factor, who had no power to raise anything but rents. Conditions aboard were no better than those of the African slave-traders† – gross overcrowding, bad and scarce water, and a high death-roll from typhus, cholera, smallpox, and dysentery. Since the ships and rigging were rotten, the emigrants were often landed too late to break or plant ground, had no tools to build houses, and starved if they did not indenture themselves as servants.

The Westminster government expressed concern at these losses in potential cannon-fodder, for the building of the British Empire had begun. They did not consider the slave-trade, or kidnappings, or Hebridean people, sufficiently important to demand despatch of a naval force to the Hebrides, but instead appointed a committee of inquiry, which eleven years later reported that Skye, Lewis, and Shetland should be made sheriffdoms (no action followed). When the American War of Independence broke out in 1775, government alarm grew at the past and present accession of Scottish fighting power to the rebels, but, as it happened, many were recruited to the British army and emigration decreased as new employment was given by a kelp boom, which had replaced the cattle boom.

The clan system may be said to have ended between 1763 and 1775. Its disintegration meant to islesmen the loss of the social system under which they and their forebears had lived in the Hebrides for at least 1,500 years. The emigrations of 1763 onwards had withdrawn many of the best families of the clans, the tacksmen of spirit, vigour, education, and of means – the men of weight who had formerly been able to mediate between people and chief. Their gradual disappearance deprived the people of leaders. The century and more of economic chaos that ensued proved to be far more disastrous to the quality

* *Home Office Papers*, 2 June 1774, pp. 219–20.
† 1963: Prebble – report to Colonial Secretary by Governor General of British North America.

of life in the Hebrides than the political chaos of the sixteenth century. It was accompanied by a population phenomenon, a great flood and ebb, each lasting approximately a hundred years. The high tide of 1841 came like the crisis of a fever, and did not (as many people have recently imagined) represent a healthy or prosperous state of society.

The great rise in population, despite the first heavy emigrations, had several different, interacting causes: the kelp industry, the potato crop, whisky distilling, fisheries, smallpox vaccination, and crofting.

The manufacture of kelp – an alkaline ash produced by the burning of sea-weed – started in North Uist in 1735. Knowledge of the method had been brought from Ireland to the Uists by MacDonald of Boisdale (Clanranald),* who later introduced large-scale potato planting. The product was used in the manufacture of glass, soap, and linen. The large quantities of soda-ash required for these industries in Britain came in the form of barilla, imported from Spain and the Canary Isles, France, Italy and Sicily. Hebridean beginnings were therefore modest. Kelp-making spread to Harris, Lewis, Skye, and Mull, where in 1750 it fetched £1 a ton, rising to £3.50 a ton in 1755. Kelpers earned $7\frac{1}{2}$p a week, which then was a fair wage.

The seaweeds harvested were principally the deep-sea tangle *Laminaria digitata* and *L. saccharina*, these being drift-weeds cast up on west coasts in enormous quantity after storms; and the wrack-weeds growing within the tidal range mainly on east coasts, *Fucus nodosus*, *F. serratus*, and *F. vesiculosus*, or knobbed, black, and bladder wracks. The weeds were gathered at low water both from boats and by wading, cut by sickles and long hooks, carried in creels and carts to the foreshore for drying in the sun, then to shallow pits where they were burned to a slag, which was broken up while hot by a sprinkling of water. The production of good quality kelp was skilled work at the firing stage. A ton could be won from twenty-two tons of wet weed. Its composition was potassium chloride 17%–25%, sodium chloride (common salt) 14%, potassium sulphate 10%–14%, sodium carbonate 4%–5%, iodine 1%–6%, a little magnesium salt, and much insoluble ash.

When Britain entered the Seven Years War in 1756 against France and her allies, and seized her colonial possessions in America and India, supplies of barilla dwindled and were cut off. The price of kelp steadily rose to £20 a ton, reaching a maximum of £22 during the American War of Independence (1775–83) when Britain was opposed by all Europe. Although the price fell thereafter,

* 1906: Mackenzie.

215

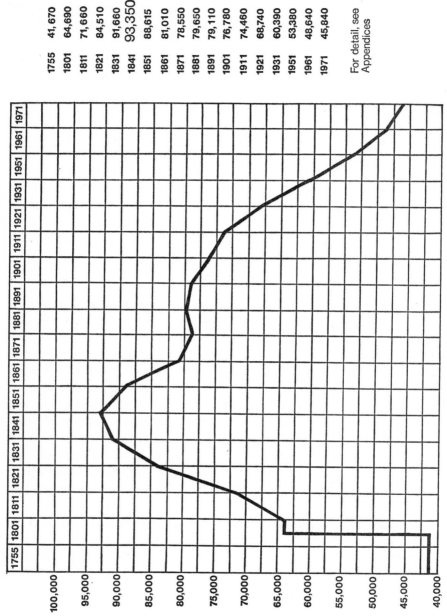

1755	41,670	
1801	64,690	
1811	71,660	
1821	84,510	
1831	91,660	
1841	93,350	
1851	88,615	
1861	81,010	
1871	78,550	
1881	79,650	
1891	79,110	
1901	76,780	
1911	74,460	
1921	68,740	
1931	60,390	
1951	53,380	
1961	48,640	
1971	45,840	

For detail, see
Appendices

Diagram 9 *Population of the Hebrides*

the Napoleonic wars and their aftermath held it to £10 a ton until 1822. For sixty-six years the Hebrides thus enjoyed a bonanza, in which the tacksmen, lairds, and remaining chiefs all shared. The kelp revenue for the owner of North Uist reached a peak of £14,000 a year, for Lewis £8,000, for Harris £2,180, and for Mull £15,000. Kelper-teams earned £4 a ton. A kelper on Mull could earn £8 a year. In regard to labour, the lairds had performed a *volte face*. People had become valuable – except on some inner islands, where owners were replacing men with sheep. Otherwise emigration had ended. The possession of any kind of house or hovel by the coast assured an income and justified early marriage, so that the population of the Isles more than doubled between 1755 and 1821.

The lairds raised their rents to the tacksmen, who passed on the impost, to the deep resentment of smallholders who felt that kelp was manna from the sea, not a land crop, profits coming from their own hard labour (the work was exacting) while the landowner contributed nothing. The conservative islesmen were becoming radical. In the previous rush for cattle-land, too many people without means either to pay exorbitant rent or to emigrate had been pushed out into poverty-stricken communities by the shores. They now lived in relative comfort, but the landowners' rapacity in taking a double toll, both in kelp profit and higher rents, incensed them, more especially when the rentals were quickly spent in the capital cities, and not reinvested in the Hebrides.

There were exceptions to the rule. MacLeod between 1811 and 1829 paid £15,000 for the first roads to be made in Skye (the government giving £25,000 and the crofters free labour). Against this, MacLeod and the Long Island owners trebled their rents for the second time in 1811. The tenants were unable to pay and everywhere threatened to emigrate. Many did so.* Arrears mounted. The chiefs realized that land without tenants would be valueless, and granted remissions.

The battle of Waterloo came as bad news to the Hebrides. The duties on salt and barilla were lowered in 1817 and 1822. This depressed the market for kelp, but when shortly afterwards the huge deposits of sulphate of potash at Strassfurt in Germany were exploited, and a cheaper means found for producing soda from salt, the price of kelp dropped to £2 a ton. The bubble had burst and ruin faced everyone. Farming and fishing had been allowed to fall into long-lasting neglect. The landowners' improvidency now caused the sale of every Outer Hebridean

---

* 1938: MacLeod. 1947: Carmichael.

island without exception. Only a few of the Inner Isles remained in the hands of the old chiefs' families.

It was not only the landowners, but all classes, who had at first ignored and then forgotten that kelp profits were subject to a continuing state of war and to vagaries of politics, and therefore were not a genuine, lasting product of land or sea.

The swollen population of the Isles, which by 1831 had reached 92,000, had been made possible less by kelp itself than by the introduction of the potato and crofting. Further aid had been given by a remarkable growth in whisky distilling as a cottage industry.

Large potato plantings had first been made on Uist in 1743 by order of MacDonald against the wish of his people, who declared potatoes worthless.* The crop spread to Lewis and Skye and before 1780 had become the staple food of all the Hebrides. Oats eaten as brochan and bannocks came second. An example from one parish in Skye should suffice: in the period 1801–41 the population increased from 2,555 to 3,625; the grain product (oats and barley, 1,600 bolls) did not increase; but the potato crop jumped from 5,000 barrels to 32,000.† The people had become fully dependent on one crop for half the year, while kelp work and whisky distilling gave them purchasing power to tide over the period between one crop and the next. Such was the position on all islands.

Powerful aid from distilling developed in the 1780s. Whisky distilled mainly from barley had been the universal beverage of the Isles from the mid-eighteenth century. The advent of the potato released for distilling large quantities of barley that had previously been required for food. The rise of the island's export trade in whisky was caused first by rack-renting and second by short-sighted legislation. Mainland grain shortages during the American and Napoleonic wars prompted the Commissioners of Supply to conserve grain by prohibiting whisky distilling in 1782, 1795, and 1797. Their policy vacillated, for in other years they restricted legal distilling by a heavy licence duty of £9 on each gallon of still-capacity. Illicit distilling and smuggling throve on such bans and obstructions, developing into a domestic industry of economic importance.‡ The island farms and townships all had stills for home consumption; in order to pay rents these were now turned to the export trade.

* 1919: Mackenzie.
† 1880: Skene.
‡ 1970: Glen. 1772: Pennant. 1811: Macdonald. 1824: MacCulloch. 1845: Statistical Account, Vol. VII.

Tiree alone exported up to three thousand gallons a year. Landowners and factors either approved or promoted private distilling to get rents from the proceeds. By 1800, illicit distilling and smuggling in the Hebrides had a growth unparalleled in the rest of the kingdom. As operators gained skill in separating out the best of the distillate, illicit whisky became superior to the legal product. Legal distillers, faced with tax on stills, duty on spirit, and competition from a superior product, either went bankrupt or entered the illicit business.*

Copper stills of ten gallons' capacity could be bought complete with worm, arm, and head for under £5 from Campbeltown in Kintyre.† Since distillation took nearly a month, cooperative work – largely left to the women – was required among the families of a township. Again this encouraged early marriage. Many widows and spinsters distilled for themselves, or gave this service to men of substance, but cooperation was more convenient, for if one operator was caught by an exciseman all shared the payment of the fine, and stills when confiscated could be promptly replaced. The net profits were around 50p a week for each still. In 1822, the price of whisky was 50p a gallon at 20% above proof (a 'proof' spirit is 57% pure alcohol), but prices could vary from 50p to 380p a gallon according to the scarcity or otherwise of grain and the quality of the product.

The smugglers, whose task was to ship the whisky to the mainland coast, and direct to Glasgow, were the crofter–fishermen, who organized themselves in small bands. Both they and the still operators, if brought to court, could rely on having sympathy and some protection from the magistrates, who were the landowners. The excisemen in the Isles had an impossible task. They were not Gaelic speakers, and were usually without local knowledge of the sea channels. The land was roadless except for narrow bridle-tracks, which had no signposts. Thus they were easily misdirected and confounded. They were not always safe in encounters with still operators, and were liable to receive rough treatment from smugglers. The men they arrested were sometimes freed by force.‡ On the seizure of one Revenue boat by smugglers, its crew were set adrift in their own boat without tackle and oars.§ In such general conditions many of the excisemen came to terms with the distillers. In Lewis, when an officer was offered a glass, it was customary to ask if he preferred 'Coll' or 'Gress', these

* 1845: Statistical Account, Vol. VII.
† 1970: Glen.
‡ 1947: Carmichael.
§ 1845: Statistical Account.

being the townships (a few miles to the north of Stornoway) where the most celebrated whiskies were distilled.*

Galled at the loss of revenue, the government tried every way to end the trade except the right one. They charged a heavy licence fee on stills, they prohibited stills of under five hundred gallons' capacity, they imposed a high duty of 47p a gallon – always failure. Light dawned. In 1822, they asked only a licence fee of £10 and cut the duty to a modest sum. They had found the answer. Many illicit distillers now took out licences. Smuggling began to die away, and had disappeared even from the Argyll islands by mid-century.

The year 1823 thus saw the birth of the Scotch Whisky industry, but the loss of the cottage industry embarrassed both islesmen and lairds, more especially in coinciding with the failure of kelp. Distilling had helped to maintain an over-large population when help was most needed to meet rack-renting. The trade had gone but the need remained. The trebling of rents in 1810 had seemed, in the eyes of the landowners, to be justified not only by kelp prosperity but by the increase of land-values following the introduction of large sheep-flocks.

As early as 1750, a demand for Scottish wool had sprung up in England and Europe. During the next ten years the flockmasters of the Southern Uplands had begun to exploit Highland pastures, for which they could offer high rents and be sure of a good return on ground hitherto uncropped by sheep. The flocks they brought in were the blackface breed, which by 1790 had ousted the smaller indigenous sheep in the southern Highlands. The Hebridean land-owners were at first unmoved by this development, for black cattle ranching was at the peak of prosperity in 1770, and although it waned thereafter it kept a high level of profit to the start of the nineteenth century.† Meantime the American and Napoleonic wars intensified the demand for home-grown wool and mutton. By 1810 the price of Hebridean sheep, which had been 20–30p in 1770, had quadrupled.‡ When it was suddenly discovered that Cheviot sheep did not require to be folded at night and could withstand the West Highland winter, the island landowners performed their second *volte face* to stock and people. Cattle herds were cut down. Small farms were amalgamated. In most islands the beef and dairy industries disappeared. By the early years of the nineteenth century, sheep had become the main stock, and cottars a nuisance.§

The landowners' problem was what to do with men formerly employed on

---

* 1919: Mackenzie.
† Islay was exporting 3,000 head annually (Feolin ferry records, 1801–7).
‡ 1938: MacLeod.
§ Ibid.

cattle. In the 1770s the tenant of a farm paying £50 rent would employ up to twenty farm servants,* for large-scale dairying was the rule, apart from herding and droving, and the great quantities of butter and cheese produced went towards part-payment of rent; but now (c. 1810) a single shepherd sufficed for farm work. The men could not all be employed on kelp. MacLeod of Dunvegan's summary of the three possible solutions reveals the origin of the crofting system: (1) clearance and emigration, (2) fisheries, (3) the distribution of land as crofts.

Clearance had already begun on the mainland, where a Yorkshireman, George Leveson-Gower, had married the countess of Sutherland and was now 'improving' her land for sheep by evicting 15,000 men, women, and children, and burning their homes. But the Isles were still in the hands of the chiefs' families, who were revolted at the very notion of such methods.

The establishment of fisheries had already been tried unsuccessfully by several companies and chiefs. The British Fisheries Society, established in 1786, had set up stations on Skye, Mull, the Long Isle, and mainland coast, with the object of creating a reserve of men for the Royal Navy. England was then most fully aware of the importance of naval power. The stations were each built with houses, store, and quay, and every family settling was allotted a small croft of its own with grazing for one or two cows. The project failed for two reasons. First, the price of salt was exorbitant at 50p a barrel (a barrel of cured herring sold for 95p) and could often not be had at the very time that the big shoals entered the lochs.† Second, the people of the Inner Hebrides and some of the Outer could not be persuaded to specialize in commercial fishing. The sea teemed with herring, cod, ling, and others, but only Lewis at that time engaged in the industry, having 100 boats employing 500 men in 1765 (North Uist, which in the seventeenth century had 400 boats using Lochmaddy, had now given up herring fishing). Between 1800 and 1810, exports brought Stornoway £10,400 a year for fish and £2,000 for oil. MacDonald of Skye, perhaps inspired by the Lewis example, spent much money building fishing boats and engaging east-coast fishermen to train the Skyemen, but his efforts were wasted. Yet inner islanders were good seamen; all owned boats and all fished for subsistence, but in happy-go-lucky style. Prodigious shoals came into the lochs, when 'People are instantly afloat with every species of seaworthy craft . . . they press forward with utmost eagerness to the field of slaughter – sloops, schooners,

---

* 1772: Pennant.
† 1793: Statistical Account.

wherries, boats of all sizes, are seen constantly flying on the wings of the wind from creek to creek, and from loch to loch, according as the varying reports of men, or the noisy flights of birds, or tumbling and spouting of whales and porpoises attract them'.* MacLeod tried to form a big fishing station near Dunvegan when kelp failed, but still the men hung back. The truth seems to be, as MacLeod concluded, 'Fishing never appealed to Inner Islesmen or Highlanders'.

Having rejected clearance, and failed with fisheries, the landowners decided to provide maintenance for their people by giving them crofts.

The principle of crofting, as distinguished from the runrig system of arable held in common, was one man to one holding. The arable was divided permanently between the joint tenants as separate 'crofts', only the pasture now being held in common. A few crofts of this kind had been first introduced to Skye by MacLeod in 1664, and again in 1718 by MacDonald and some of the tacksmen. Rent was paid in kind and services, the latter becoming so onerous that the men had only two days a week to work their own allotments. Cultivation had to be done by the women – and was done so well that every available patch grew a crop of barley or oats.† The British Fisheries Society had provided two-acre crofts. Apart from such deviations, runrig prevailed throughout the Hebrides until 1811, when the large-scale institution of crofting began. The ancient clachans, each a cluster of black houses huddled alongside the runrig arable,‡ now tended to break up, replaced by a more dispersed pattern of settlement.§ The new townships, formed to relieve congestion on the old, took a linear pattern with each croft-strip bearing its own house. Very good examples can be seen on the north-west coast of Lewis. (Runrig did not entirely disappear, but in modified forms with longer terms of allotment was often integrated with crofting and can be found in outer isles at the present day.)

Crofting made for improvement in the cultivation of land, but other factors of the time worked against its success. The principle of lease-holding had been established by an Act of 1753, and that brought great gains to the larger farms by soil-improvement and enclosure of land (hitherto not done to avoid increase of rent), but the Act did not extend to small-holdings. In the absence of leases, crofters could be removed at will, but now that they were free of joint tenancies there was nothing to prevent them sub-dividing their land among cottars. They

---

* 1793: Statistical Account.
† 1730: Burt.
‡ 1845: Statistical Account.
§ 1961: Moisley.

did this to excess while crofting played a secondary role to kelp-production, the cottars giving labour as rent. The amalgamation of cattle farms to form sheep farms added to their number, and the emigration of larger tenants and tacksmen when rents trebled threw still more displaced cottars on to the croft-land, which was now occupied by a population far greater than it could naturally bear, because the tenants would not see their relatives and friends in distress. There followed intensive cultivation of one or two crops, which impoverished the soil, for the lots were too small to allow proper rotation of crops. Scantier yields then gave inadequate support to a family even in good years, and now there were two families at least to a croft. And still the population mounted. For example,* one township of Skye was held by twenty-two families of crofters, on whom lived a parasitical growth of twenty-five families of cottars (called squatters), giving a total population of 250 people – double the number the ground could maintain. A parish of 46,000 acres, comprising 5,000 acres of arable and 41,000 of pasture, held four large farms on which twenty-five families of cottars squatted, and thirty-seven townships held by 334 crofter-families, on whom three hundred squatter-families were imposed. Everywhere in the Isles the pattern was the same. Only two pillars supported this dangerous social structure: the kelp trade and the potato crop.

The first island to be cleared was Rum, in 1828. MacLean of Coll, who owned the island, shipped all 443 of his cottars and crofters to America, replacing them with one flockmaster, a few shepherds, and 8,000 sheep.† Whatever misery may lie hidden behind these bare facts, the lot of his people seems easy compared with events on other islands twenty years later.

The kelp trade had virtually ended by 1825; around 1830, the herring shoals disappeared from the sea-lochs of the inner isles; and in 1835 the first potato blight struck the Hebrides. The effect was immediate destitution. Yet the population continued to rise for six years, reaching its peak of 93,000 in 1841. Few landowners found strength to face the human disaster. MacDonald of Skye spent large sums of money helping a thousand of his poorer clansmen to emigrate to Australia and America. MacLean of Coll, who had impoverished himself buying food for nearly 1,500 of his people on Coll, resolved to clear the island, not this time for sheep, but in the best interest of all. Half the people were transported and crofts laid out as larger farms. His clearance of 1841 was too sharp and sudden, even if well-intended. But worse was coming. Potato

---

* 1847–50: Report of Board for the Relief of Highland Destitution.
† 1874: Miller.

blight returned in the successive years 1846–8 and yet again in 1850. There was no longer enough seed for planting. Destitution changed to famine on a vast scale, beyond all local control or remedy – a situation that would nowadays be declared a national emergency. The Westminster government refused funds, but set up a Colonial Land and Emigration Department to compile statistics. The granaries of the southern shipping ports were full,* yet the government gave no direction for the distribution of grain. The people affected had neither voting rights nor representation in Parliament. As late as 1850, at the worst of the famines, the Free Church was still appealing to the Secretary of State for aid. Apart from starvation, the people were suffering cold from lack of clothing. They had no change of clothes day or night, were using meal bags for under- and outer-garments, and all went barefoot in winter.

MacLeod of Dunvegan gave out of his own pocket £225 a week towards relief. His effort to help his people, who had supported his family for six hundred years, ruined him, and when warned of that coming event he answered that he would not let men die. He was one of the few landowners to retain a moral conscience. Another was Lord MacDonald. Both, apparently with full deliberation, chose ruin. The decision, which must have been agonizing, turned out to be unavailing, for their affairs had to be placed in the hands of trustees, who appointed ruthless factors. The evictions that followed were to prove more terrible than starvation. MacLeod did what else he could. He founded relief committees in Glasgow and Edinburgh, which in three years raised £209,000.† The funds were administered by two Destitution Boards, which gave relief in return for work, mostly on road-building. No productive industry could be devised to give permanent employment. Emigration was the only solution to gross over-population and its consequent evils of abused land and famine. In 1851 a private Emigration Society was formed in Skye, and grew rapidly into a national organization, gaining belated help from the Emigration Department, which supplied transport ships, leaving the Society (now with its headquarters in London) to find the passage-money by public appeal. A solution to the Hebridean problem was thus presented to the lairds. A few were themselves in desperate straits: most were absentees, and Lowlanders; yet the haste in which they acted was despicable. One Robert Chalmers had spoken their mind: 'Of late years the landlords have very properly done all they could to substitute a population of sheep for the innumerable hordes of useless human beings who

* *Inverness Courier*, January 1847.
† 1938: MacLeod.

17a. Spinning, at Scalpay
Island, 1962.

17b. Weaving Harris tweed
on Lewis.

18a. Herring fleet off Kisimul Castle, Castlebay, Barra, *circa* 1900.

18b. Fishing boats in Stornoway harbour, Lewis, *circa* 1965.

formerly vegetated upon a soil that seemed barren of everything else.'* The substitution was called improvement. The idea that a landowner had the right to do with his property and tenants as he saw fit had supplanted the clan ideal of trusteeship, and bore the most poisonous fruit ever grown on the Atlantic seaboard. Emigration had become essential, but the way chosen for forcing it was barbarous. The islanders loved their homelands, were reluctant to leave, and were evicted.

Men no longer found army service an acceptable escape. From 1760 onwards, many islanders had joined the Highland regiments raised for service in the first American wars by the former chiefs, who – where they had held to their patriarchal character – had no difficulty in raising recruits. The steady flow of islanders to army and navy had been maintained through the Napoleonic wars. In the forty years ended 1837, Skye alone contributed to the British army 21 lieutenant-generals and major-generals, 45 colonels, 600 commissioned officers, and 10,000 soldiers.† Behind such splendid figures some ugly truths lay hidden. Men were at first driven out of the Isles to the army by famine and rack-renting during the cattle boom, then by the landowners' change to sheep-farming, when they recruited men ostensibly for patriotic reasons but in reality to thin out the population. There is evidence that men joined up under threat of losing their land, on which they had no leases;‡ that they were persuaded by promise of leases to their fathers, who instead were evicted; and that men were press-ganged. Recruitment of any kind came to a dead stop at mid-century. When Lord Napier interrogated crofters at Portree in 1883, and asked why, if poor and unemployed, they did not join the army, he was answered, 'Why should we fight for our kingdom when we see so much poverty and neglect by our sovereign and legislators? That is the idea which has sunk in the minds of Skyemen so very much'.§

Lewis escaped more lightly than other islands. It had been bought in 1844 by Sir James Matheson, an East India merchant, who spent £240,000 on improvements, and paid for the emigration of 1,800 people to Canada. A great lobster fishery had sprung up at Loch Roag, where the agent of a London company was paying out nearly £4,000 a year in wages (40,000 lobsters were said to have been exported in one week),‖ despite which, more than 11,000 of Lewis's 19,000

---

* 1827: Chalmers.
† 1845: Statistical Account. 1856: Ross.
‡ 1800: Garnett. 1963: Prebble.
§ 1884: Royal Commission, Minutes of Evidence.
‖ 1903: Mackenzie.

people had to get relief from the Destitution Fund. There were no evictions. Everywhere else in the Hebrides, forced clearance was in full swing. Troops and police were freely used when resistance was offered.

The new landowners were Lowlanders who knew nothing of Hebridean life. The prejudice felt against them by the islesmen was at once justified. Colonel John Gordon, who had bought South Uist and Barra, offered Barra (for which he had paid £38,050) to the nation as a convict station. The government declined to buy but made him a transportation grant. He brought in the ship *Admiral*, landed police, bailiffs, and press gangs, and ordered the people to meet, under penalty of fine, to hear the solution of their problems. When the people gathered they were seized and dragged aboard. Men who resisted were felled with truncheons and handcuffed; those who escaped, including some who swam ashore from the ship, were chased by the police and press gangs. The latter were directed by the Reverend Henry Beatson, a Presbyterian minister of whom an eye-witness reported, 'He may be seen in Castlebay directing his men like a gamekeeper with hounds,' and likened the scene to a slave hunt on the African coast.* Cart loads of bound men were brought south from Benbecula, followed by their weeping women and children. Every crofter on Barra was evicted, and everything their families possessed of stock and property confiscated. About eight hundred people were cleared from the Barra Isles and double that number from South Uist. The *Quebec Times* of 1851 to 1852 reported that they were landed on the Canadian coast and left starving. Once famous in history for their hospitality, the helpless, shrunken women, with children on their backs, were later begging for bread around the homesteads of Hamilton and Toronto. Families who escaped the transport ships found shelter throughout the Hebrides in caves or turf huts by the shores and lived on shellfish. Some were given a few acres on small islands like Eriskay, which were thought too bare and exposed for profit from sheep; others were dispersed on the offshore islets or granted deserts like east Harris. On Harris, which had been bought by the earl of Dunmore and Sir Edward Scott, the people cleared from the fertile west coast to the rock-bound east had not enough soil to bury their dead.† They created a new type of lazybed by building up snake-like platforms of peat on the rock hollows, spreading these with seaweed, and planting potatoes and oats. Long sustained industry made them fertile. The rocky bays gave harbour for their boats and the sea was kinder than man.

* 1857: MacLeod.
† 1966: Murray.

The improvers' defence, briefly stated, was that prices were rising and sheep not paying as well as expected.* The land in winter would not carry its full summer stock, so that large flocks had to be wintered in the low country at high rents. Great numbers of sheep brought to the islands died before they acclimatized. Tenants taking over sheep farms were therefore required to pay an acclimatization fee on stock, and this added-value tax had risen by 1845 to 50%. The fee had been injurious to landowners because many tenants after paying were unable to meet the rents, and if landowners called in the leases they were bound under the terms to take over stock at added-value prices. The sheep too were seriously impoverishing the land. They did not, like cattle, enrich it with manure. Cattle had given life to finer grass by cropping the coarser; sheep nibbled too close. Great tracts of fertile land were being thickly covered in bracken, for the sheep carried in the seeds in their wool. Sheep would not eat the bent grass, which covered much island ground on which cattle had fed. At the very time that land was thus deteriorating, the price of wool was falling as a consequence of the industrial revolution and peace with the United States, resulting in mass production of cheap cotton garments. As if this were not enough (said the landowners), the Disruption of the Church in 1843 had moved the government to transfer care of the poor from the Church to Parochial Boards. By the Poor Law Act of 1845, proprietors were required to contribute money to support the poor in their parishes. In years of mass famine this was too heavy a burden. They could think of only two answers: extend the sheep ranges and clear the fertile ground of people.

The work of eviction in the Hebrides continued over thirty years. Gruesome tales abound – more especially where resistance was offered – of houses razed, thatch fired, of people returning to die of exposure by the blackened walls of their homes; but all were accompanied by the kind of scene witnessed by Sir Archibald Geikie when he was a lad of seventeen in Skye:

> One afternoon [1852] as I was returning from my ramble, a strange wailing sound reached my ears at intervals on the breeze from the west. On gaining the top of a hill on the south side of the valley, I could see a long and motley procession wending along the road that led from Suishnish. . . . It was a miscellaneous gathering of at least three generations of crofters. There were old men and women, too feeble to walk, who were placed in carts, the younger members of the community on foot were carrying their bundles of clothes and household effects, while the children, with looks of alarm, walked

---

* 1884: Royal Commission. 1938: MacLeod.

alongside. .... Everyone was in tears ... a cry of grief went up to heaven; the long plaintive wail like a funeral coronach was resumed; and after the last of the emigrants had disappeared behind the hill, the sound seemed to re-echo through the whole wide valley of Strath in one prolonged note of desolation. .... I have often wandered since then over the solitary ground of Suishnish. Not a soul is to be seen there now; but the greener patches of field, and the crumbling walls, mark where an active and happy community once lived.*

The landowners' lot improved in the 1860s. The American Civil War again made sheep-farming profitable. Improved communications and the industrial revolution greatly raised the value of deer forests. New roads had been made in the Highlands and Islands. Inverness was now linked to the south by stage coaches, and by a railway started in 1846; to the west by the Caledonian canal (1822). The first steamboat service from Skye (1830) plied weekly to Glasgow by 1840, calling at other islands on the way. Oban had steamships by 1850 (and a railway by 1880). Stornoway, now with a population of 2,500 (1861), had a regular packet service running thrice weekly to the mainland at Poolewe. These and other transport services encouraged rich English industrialists to rent deer forests and grouse moors. In 1851, MacLeod's estate had received £200 for the shootings; by 1870, the Harris forest alone was valued at £3,000. But no attempt was made to mitigate the evil lot of the crofters by reduction of rent, by kindlier treatment, or by leaving their holdings intact. To the contrary, the landowners' behaviour was characterized by the most narrow self-interest and inhumanity.

Emigration from the Isles on the great scale known as the Clearances had ended by the close of the 1860s, although the clearances themselves continued, causing appalling congestion on the crofts. Holdings and grazings were being continually cut to extend farms and sheep- and deer-ranges. Ten or twelve families would be removed to give one shepherd a new range. The people thus dispossessed were settled on crofts against the will of the crofters, who were sometimes evicted for voicing protest.† The crofts were of two to fourteen acres (most of two to six). It was reckoned that a man needed seven acres to keep a cow, horse, pig, and potato ground.† There were far too many people to far too small crofts. The ground was overworked and exhausted. Cows were able to calve only once in three years, and then had too little milk to nourish their

* 1904: Geikie.
† 1884: Royal Commission, Evidence.

calves.* Cattle were bled to nourish humans. The birth rate did not drop, and this may be attributed in great part to vaccination against smallpox, which in previous centuries had been one of the principal killers in the Isles. Congestion now became the dominant human problem.

The lairds and factors could afford to be, and therefore were, tyrannical. Without security of tenure the people would submit to anything rather than lose their holdings. If dispossessed, they received no compensation for improvements made, and land reclaimed from the moor was often wrested from them without acknowledgement.* Ingoing tenants were obliged to pay the arrears of those evicted,* and having paid for possession, they would find their grazings taken for the laird's sheep or deer without reduction of rent.* The lairds after 1850 were getting large rents for stalking, so would not allow crofters to protect their holdings from deer.* Crops were thus eaten down year by year, and if crofters kept a dog to guard the crops it would be shot by the laird's gamekeeper.* The house roofs were everywhere dilapidated, because lairds would not allow crofters to disturb grouse by taking rushes or heather from the hills.* On some estates, the crofters were not allowed to keep a horse, and so had to carry the heaviest loads on their own backs.* Few dared to protest, and fewer still to bring complaints before magistrates, for these were the lairds.*

That revolt was slow in coming need not be thought surprising. Earlier revolts had been easily crushed by the constables' ash batons, for the destruction of the clan system had been recent, the Clearances chaotic and sweeping, leaving the people leaderless with police, army, press, public opinion, and even churchmen arrayed against them (the latter sided with their patrons, the lairds). The Lowland Scots and English had been quite without understanding. An entire social structure had disintegrated, depriving men of traditional focusing points for living, for standards, for judgement. Thus they felt lost and bewildered and were broken in spirit. A most tragic sign of that breaking occurred in mid-century. Whatever their trials might have been in the past, and they had often been severe, always they had kept gaiety of heart, an exuberance of spirit that from end to end of the Hebrides found expression in song for every labour of the day, and for any leisure left at night. The pipes or fiddle were in every house, and the dance was joyfully boisterous. At mid-century, an almost universal silence fell upon the Hebrides. The people sang and danced no more.

Renaissance of spirit had to wait for a new generation of men. By 1875 the

* Ibid.

young of 1850 had grown to manhood and action was not delayed. Most of the cottars and crofters had become largely (some entirely) dependent for subsistence on their earnings as fishermen. Few owned boats. They served as hired hands on the herring fleets operating from Barra and Stornoway in May and June, and then on the east coast from July to September.* Many had taken service on the two Kintyre fleets fishing on the Irish Sea out of Campbeltown and Carradale. They earned good wages and large numbers returned to the Isles for winter fishing, married young, and needed small-holdings. They had not inherited their fathers' conservatism. They felt no respect for landowners; they no longer attributed suffering to the will of God; they questioned the justice of continuing clearances, of filched pasture, of insecurity of tenure, of the valuation of deer above human life, of rack-renting, and of tyranny. As if by miracle, they had grown up unimpaired in spirit. Revolt burst out first in riots in Lewis in 1874. It spread to other islands. In Skye, men put out their stock to pasture, defied interdict, and went to prison for it. A healthy militancy was abroad, interpreted as an ugly lawlessness by local and legal authorities.

The honour of defeating the new tyranny by winning national recognition and reform went to the men and women of Skye in the Battle of the Braes.

At Braes, the district bordering the Narrows of Raasay, the crofters had been deprived of their grazings on Ben Lee. They offered higher rent than the tenant when his lease ran out, but were refused by the landowner. They withheld rent and released their sheep on the hill.* The factor, Ballingall, ordered eviction and sent out a sheriff's officer with two men from Portree to serve notice. The women of Braes intercepted them on the road and forced them to burn the papers. The Sheriff of Invernessshire felt such outrage that he called for a strong force of Glasgow police to move in and serve summonses. The men of Braes prepared to resist and posted sentinels. The Sheriff and Chief Constable had resort to a legal trick. They made no move until the legal period for serving a summons had expired, by which time (early April 1882) most of the young crofters had gone off to join the Kintyre fleets (their absence was later to be seen as providential). One mid-April morning, sixty policemen under two sheriffs and their officers entered Braes at sunrise in pouring rain. The people were taken by surprise, but a hundred men and women from the townships of Balmeanach and Peinchorrain tumbled out of bed to confront the invaders. The police seized half a dozen men and hustled them on to the north-going road

* Ibid.

230

towards Portree. The people hurled a volley of stones and attacked with flails. The police won their way to the gorge of Allt nan Gobhlaig, where they were mobbed on both flanks, but gathered and made a baton charge. The crofters did not fall back, but the diversion allowed the sheriffs and prisoner-squad to get across the river. A few hundred yards farther, the road crossed the face of a sea-cliff, on the top of which the crofters had earlier built a big ammunition dump of boulders. They now ran to the top and sent down such a heavy bombardment that the police were stopped. Several fell seriously injured, and all the while crofter-reinforcements could be seen streaming on to the cliff-top. Realizing that their lives might be lost, the police saved themselves by a disciplined rush to open ground where the people closed with them. Hand-to-hand fighting ensued. Heads were split. The women joined in and many were badly hurt. During that running battle towards Portree it was only by chance that no men were killed, as certainly they would have been had the real fighting strength of the townships been present. The police in sorry state finally gained Portree with five prisoners, who went to trial at Inverness.

All Skye was now seething with rage. No man of position could any longer feel secure. Worse events seemed likely to follow, so the Inverness court played safe by letting the men go on payment of fines, which were immediately subscribed by the public. The government took alarm. Warships were despatched to Skye and troops landed, but the crofters were not overawed as intended. Gladstone, who was then Prime Minister, began to sense the truth – that since 1746 there had been a gross dereliction of responsible government, both local and central. In 1883 he appointed a Royal Commission of six men under a Scotsman, Lord Napier, who ten years earlier had been Governor General of India. Their report when presented to Parliament within the year disclosed 'a state of misery, of wrong-doing, and of patient long-suffering, without parallel in the history of our country'.

This time Parliament acted promptly, for the tide of public opinion had changed in the last forty years. There was strong and vocal national feeling that no men should have power from unjust laws to inflict such cruelties. The result was the Magna Carta of the Hebrides: the Crofters Holding Act of 1886. It gave all tenants who paid rent of less than £30 a year (later £50) fixity of tenure, and established a Crofters Commission to take over from landowners the entire management of their crofting estates with power to fix fair rents. A crofter might leave at will, and if so he surrendered his croft to the landlord, who was compelled to accept the house standing on it at valuation – which effectively stopped landowners from contriving large emigrations. If the crofter stayed on,

231

his croft descended to his heir; and his house, which was free of rates, could not be seized for debt.

When the commissioners came to assess fair rentals, they further exposed the landowners' injustices and made reductions of fifty per cent. Arrears were written off to seventy per cent. A public demand then grew for the break-up of sheep farms and deer forests. This finally led Parliament to pass the Congested Districts (Scotland) Act of 1897, which created a board with money and power to put crofters on land and to provide stock, fencing, seed, and houses. The crofting system thus devised for the Hebrides had faults, but more important than any of these was the removal of injustice. The crofters' poverty was at least lessened, and the benefit seen in better housing, improvements to the land, for which there was now real incentive, and the changed bearing of men freed from economic slavery.

Apart from the institution of crofting, the changes in livestock, and the introduction of turnips, hay, and potatoes, the actual methods of agriculture had changed little in three centuries; nor had the manner of rural life. The wooden plough had been discarded in 1820, but the *cas-chrom* and lazybeds remained in general use. A glimpse into township life in the Long Isle could appear in 1880 like 1580, as shown by this excerpt from a contemporary account* (which I have abbreviated):

Having finished their tillage, the people go early in June to the hill grazings with their flocks. This is a busy day in the townships. Like bees about to swarm, the families bring their herds together and drive them away. The sheep lead, the cattle next, and horses follow. The men carry burdens of sticks, heather, ropes, spades, etc. to repair the summer huts [*sgitheil bothain*] or shielings. The women carry bedding, meal, dairy and cooking utensils. Round below their waists is a thick woollen cord or leather strap, underneath which their skirts are drawn up to enable them to walk easily over the moors. Barefooted, bare-headed boys and girls with dogs flit hither and thither, keeping the herds together, and now and then having a neck and neck race with some perverse animal that tries to get away. There is much noise. Men several at a time direct and scold. Women knit, sing, talk, and walk as free and erect as if there were no burdens on their backs, nor in their hearts. Above this din, sheep bleat, cows low, and mares neigh. All who meet them on the way bless the trial, as it is called, and wish it a good flitting day.

* 1880: Carmichael.

When the shieling has been reached and burdens laid down, the huts are repaired, fires kindled, and food prepared. The people bring forward every man's stock separately, and as they are driven into an enclosure, the constable and one other on either side of the gate see that only the proper souming has been brought. Then the cattle are turned out to graze.

The feast that follows is simple, chiefly cheese, which every housewife provides from last year's produce. They say grace, and every head is uncovered, and every knee bowed, as they dedicate themselves and their flocks to Christ. . . . The walls of shieling huts are of turf, the roofs of sticks covered with divots. Usually two huts are together, the larger being the dwelling, the smaller the dairy.

This style of hut (*sgithiol*) is distinguished from the *both cloiche* or stone beehive:

Diagram 10 *Beehive Houses*

233

This is entirely of stone, the roof tapering to a cone. The apex is capped with a flag, holed like a millstone for egress of smoke. In the walls of the hut, two or three feet from the floor, are recesses for utensils, while along the thick walls, low near the ground, are the beds. The entrance to these beds in the walls is slightly raised above the floor – a small hole only big enough for a person to creep through. This sleeping bunk is called a *crupa* [from *crupadh*, to crouch]. It was a special feature of St Kildan houses, the houses themselves being called crupa from the feature. These beehive houses are still the shielings of the Lewis people. Invariably two or three strong, healthy girls share the same shieling. Here they remain making butter and cheese till the corn is ripe for reaping, when they and the cattle return home. The people enjoy this life at the hill pasture and many of the best lyric songs in their language are in praise of the loved summer shielings.

Completely intact beehives, built within the last eighty years, may be seen today on the Lewis moors in the Uig district.

Township buildings were almost all black houses. Late in the nineteenth century many were given separate doors for cows and humans, and further improved by partitioning the interior to wall-height. White houses (with lime-cemented walls) were almost entirely in the hands of tacksmen during the eighteenth century. They had boarded floors, glass windows, and thatched roofs. Most had small libraries in more languages than one. On larger islands, white houses increased in number during the nineteenth century, but only in favoured places and they were still far outnumbered by the black.

The abolition of Highland dress in 1746 had been deeply resented, so that when the 'Unclothing Act' was repealed in 1782 the kilt and plaid returned to full favour in the Isles.* Fashion swung to such an extreme – even curtains and chair-covers were made of tartan – that reaction swiftly followed and the wearing of national dress died out before 1800. A revival came on the publication of Sir Walter Scott's verse and novels, but this again died by mid-century. People dressed as elsewhere: jacket and trousers for men, and for women dark gowns, worn with frilled muslin caps. Women's hair was drawn back from the forehead and pinned in a bun at the crown.† For work in the windy fields they wore three skirts, the first of red flannel, the second black, often with thin red stripes, the third of tweed made voluminous to be pulled over the head and shoulders in rain.‡

* 1793: Statistical Account.
† 1930: Nicolson.
‡ 1966: Murray.

While life in the inland parts remained unaltered, at least in its general tenor, the nineteenth century had brought great changes at ports. Between 1800 and 1860, Stornoway had built up a thriving export trade in cattle and fish, and owned forty-four ships trading with France, Holland, the Baltic, Sweden, Norway, and Ireland.* The ousting of sail by steam after 1860 ended the shipping enterprise, but fishing prospered with landings valued at £105,000.† By the close of the century, Stornoway had become a busy town of nearly 3,500 inhabitants. A fleet of several hundred wherries – twin-masted boats with lug-sails – packed the harbour throughout the year.‡ When heading out for the Minch at nightfall, their huge brown sails filled all the sky. At Barra, the Castle-bay fleet and fishery were likewise expanding. Tobermory had a population of nearly two thousand in 1875, when it was created a burgh, but although graced by an excellent harbour, where seventy ships had formerly been seen at anchor, it could not compete with Oban as a fishing port, its decline becoming final after the opening of the Oban railway in 1880. A steamboat service had been organized for the Argyll islands from 1830 by David Hutcheson, prior to which a voyage from the Clyde to Skye took ten to fifteen days under sail, for piers were few and the packets made detours into numerous lochs to load and unload sheep and cattle.§ After 1830 steamers so multiplied that by 1890 as many as eleven were entering Loch Dunvegan in one week.|| Presumably more called at Portree, and still more at the numerous ports of Islay (some of which were also fishing villages) – Port Ellen, Bowmore, Port Askaig, and others. The new opportunities given by steamer, rail, and road transport encouraged the tide of emigration, which had slackened (almost halted) around 1880, to flow once again, and to that movement further impetus was given in the last decade of the century by the spread of education.

Educational progress under the Church had got off to a slow start after Culloden, for although the SPCK was then broadening its base to include spinning, knitting, sewing, and elementary education, the Presbyterian clergy were much preoccupied with the persecution of Episcopalians for their Stewart sympathies (mainland and Inner Hebrides only), with presiding at Kirk Sessions where they laid down the moral law and could make defaulters suffer, and with farming. They were no longer slothful, but were too heavily engaged with

* 1919: Mackenzie.
† 1900: Crofters Commission.
‡ 1949: MacGregor.
§ 1904: Geikie.
|| 1938: MacLeod.

affairs to give time to parishioners' education. As the powers of the chiefs declined, so theirs increased. In the process of becoming parish lairds, they lost touch with the people. Like the tacksmen of the time they were men of much culture. Dr Johnson was no man to flatter anyone, yet he declared the Hebridean clergy to be able men, possessed of a high order of learning and scholarship. He found conversation in Latin to be not uncommon if tacksmen did not want their servants to overhear, and says of Skye, 'One of the remarkable things is that there are so many books in it. . . . Without is the rough ocean and the rocky land. . . . Within is plenty and elegance, beauty and gaiety . . . more gentleness of manners or a more pleasing appearance of domestic society is not found in the most polished countries. . . . Their conversation is decent and inoffensive.' And finally (of their hospitality), 'I know not how we shall get away.'*

Johnson was speaking of the upper echelons of Hebridean society. Pennant says of the lower, 'They have in themselves a natural politeness and address that flows from the meanest when least expected.'† And when they had been reduced by sixty continuous years of clearance and eviction, Lord Napier could still write in his Report to Parliament, 'The habitations of the people are of a character that would imply physical and moral degradation in the eyes of those who do not know how much decency, courtesy, virtue, and even mental refinement, survive amid the sordid surroundings of a Highland hovel.' This was rich ground for the seed of education, but apart from the SPCK that seed was never sown in the eighteenth century. The spirit of the people, frustrated at every turn, suddenly found expression in extreme religious fervour.

Evangelism began in Skye in 1805 when an illiterate preacher, John Farquarson, converted a blind fiddler named Donald Munro. Munro preached a new puritanism – a renunciation of all recreation of body and mind, of lay music, games and sports, dancing, story-telling, tobacco, alcohol – and spoke with such force that wherever he was heard a religious revival followed. All Skye was converted. The people even brought their bagpipes and fiddles to be burned on a great public bonfire at the head of Loch Snizort. Zeal mounted to a gale that swept the Hebrides – the Catholic isles alone escaping the storm – and tore away much of the oral literature and knowledge of musical arts that had been built up over the last millennium. The majority of the clergy, on the other hand, were already moving in the opposite direction, away from austerity of thought and deed and from Knox's democratic ideas.

---

* 1775: Johnson. 1930: Nicolson.
† 1775: Pennant.

In the 1830s, a sharp controversy arose in the Church of Scotland on patronage and the liberty of congregations to reject ministers presented to livings by landowners. When that liberty was denied by the courts, 474 ministers seceded from the Church in 1843 and formed the Free Church of Scotland. In the Islands and Highlands, three-quarters of the people went out with their dissenting ministers. In the Hebrides, the Disruption came as a welcome chance of protest at the laxity (as it was conceived) of the established clergy, their remoteness from the people, and their apparently callous acceptance of evictions, clearances, and oppression. The mainland clearances had been proceeding for thirty years without condemnation from the Church. The clergy had betrayed their trust as surely as the earlier chiefs. They had observed on their own livings the crucifixion of their people and had not spoken out. With few exceptions, they had given aid to factors and owners in gathering crofters and cottars for transportation, or in deceiving them in the owners' interest. Some had threatened the rebellious with damnation. Their rewards were new manses, a few acres of pasture, and a continued living.* Seen thus to be in their patrons' pockets, the clergy had forfeited respect. By natural reaction, dissenting ministers won such a fervent following in the Hebrides that their power grew over-great and their zeal extreme. They led their parishioners in renewed denunciation of traditional customs and the normal delights of healthy men. The most innocent entertainments came under ban: piping was damned as frivolity, story as untruth, and song as vanity. Dancing became a temptation of the devil. Expressions of joy in life were held to be inconsistent with devoutness – an attitude strong in Lewis, where the high standards of Cromwell's Puritans, who had spent a decade on the island, were remembered and revived. The ministers of the Free Church held in the nineteenth century a dictatorial authority, and were able, by their uttered word, to banish from the isles men who gave them offence. The islanders' traditional hospitality went unimpaired, but the clergy were unconsciously mutilating their lives. In the more relaxed society of the Catholic isles, the clergy thought the ceilidh and musical arts to be life-nourishing, so that South Uist took over Skye's position as the centre of island piping, and became with Barra the richest source of folk-tale and saga.

An excellent result of the Disruption was competition between the Free and Established Churches in founding schools. In 1825, the number of people unable to read in the Hebrides was seventy per cent of those above eight years of age† (the same as the figure for England in the late eighteenth century). The

---

* 1963: Prebble.
† 1825: Moral Statistics of the Highlands and Islands. (The Highland figure was 40%.)

publication of these statistics stimulated the clergy to meet the educational needs of the time. Their famous discipline of 'catechism and cane' proved most effective, for by 1866 the figure for illiteracy was down to 26·5% in the Outer Hebrides, which then had a hundred schools.* The Church rule instilled learning, turned out large numbers of famous men, and directed island pupils towards the Church and professions as the main goals for bright minds. A notable feature of the system was the extent to which parish schools gave pupils a higher education.

The Education (Scotland) Act of 1872 brought long-overdue intervention by the State. Elected School Boards then replaced clerical administration. Attendance at school was made compulsory to the age of thirteen, secondary schools were designated to give the link between primary schools and the universities, and the boards made responsible for accommodation. Thus, when the tide of emigration again flowed at the close of the nineteenth century, it was for the first time a healthy flow, not force by landowners nor imposed by economic disaster, but chosen by people whose horizons had been widened by education. The islands had become too small to contain them all. They seized the new opportunities offered by mechanical transport. There were also economic pressures, for the standard of living was rising, and that too was good. It has been a great mistake, made by many men writing of the Hebrides, to regard reduction of population as an evil. The evil in nineteenth-century reduction lay in the way it was done – the good end used to justify bad means – not in reduction itself. The islands had become so grossly over-populated, and the land so abused, that men could live no better than their grazing animals, and they suffered more.

The lessons to be learned from such events are numerous, but in essence simple. A unique contribution had been made by the Celts to Hebridean life – and to British – in their thousand-year demonstration of a practical ideal, that land was vested in the people to be managed for them by men elected by them. They were original democrats, owing nothing to the Greek city-states. Depopulation need not have gone so far as it did in the eighteenth and nineteenth centuries and would have been accomplished by totally different methods, had clan chiefs held to their role as trustees for their people's land. And one thing appears certain from the most recent events, as from past history, that the islands will never know just government where 'owners' so-called, public or private, depart from that first social principle.

* 1866: Sheriff Nicholson.

Hebridean prices and wages, 1750-1890

	c. 1750	c. 1790	c. 1850	c. 1890
Cattle	£2.35	£2.20	£7-£10	£7-£14
Hebridean Sheep	12p-18p	20p-80p	—	—
Blackface ewe	—	—	35p-48p	£1.25
Blackface wedder	—	—	50p-60p	£2
Cheviot ewe	—	—	£1	£1.60
Cheviot wedder	—	—	—	£2.65
Horse	£2	—	£7	—
Hens p. dozen	15p	—	—	—
Beef & mutton p. lb.	1½p	—	—	—
Herring p. barrel	—	95p	—	—
Barley & oats p. boll	—	85p	—	—
Meal p. stone	33½p-45p	55p-75p	80p	—
Butter p. stone	25p	43p	—	—
Cheese p. stone	12½p	18p	—	—
Tea p. lb.	90p-£1.20	—	—	—
Sugar p. lb.	4p-7½p	—	—	—
Salt p. barrel	—	50p	—	—
Plaid	60p-70p	—	—	—
Shoes p. pair	—	12½p	—	—
Tobacco p. lb.	30p	—	—	—
Claret p. bottle	6½p-17½p	—	—	—
Sherry p. bottle	7½p	—	—	—
Brandy p. bottle	22p	—	—	—
Whisky p. bottle	5p	5p	6p-48p	—
Whisky p. gallon	—	40p-60p	—	—
School teacher p.a.	£18	£20	£23-30	£92
Minister p.a.	£60	£100	£150-£271	—
Smith p.a.	—	—	£23.40	—
Carpenter p.a.	—	£16.90	—	—
Mason p. day	—	4p-7p	12½p-15p	—
Tailor, itinerant p. day	—	2½p-3½p	—	—

	c. 1750	c. 1790	c. 1850	c. 1890
Casual labourer p. day	—	3½p*	5p	—
Casual woman labourer p. day	—	1½p	5p	10p–15p
Labourer p.a.	—	£1.40–£1.55	£5–£10	—
Labourer, woman p.a.	—	40p	£3–£4	—
Ploughman p.a.	—	—	—	£24
Forester p.a.	—	—	—	£40
Gamekeeper p.a.	—	—	—	£45
Cattle herd p.a.	—	£2	—	—
Dairywoman p.a.	—	75p–40p	—	25p a week
Maid servant p.a.	—	40p–£1	—	—
Man servant p.a.	—	£2–£3.50	—	—
Kelper, skilled p.a.	—	£6.50	—	—
Kelper, p. week	—	7½p–15p	—	—

Note: People in the eighteenth century were normally paid in kind, or in part money and part kind, and this continued into the nineteenth century.

Rentals, 1750–1900

	c. 1760	c. 1840	c. 1900
Lewis	£1,200	£9,800	£32,768
Harris	—	—	£5,145
North Uist	£1,300	—	£5,301
South Uist	£500	£5,635 in 1861	—
West Skye (MacLeod)	£1,100	—	£24,000

* This high rate for male labour was caused by recruitment to the army and an exodus to Lowland harvesting.

9

The Recent Past:
1900-1972

At the opening of the twentieth century many island districts remained congested. Landowners and crofters held different views on that problem. It was the landowners' opinion (1920) that a comfortable living could be made on a holding rented at £50 a year, but not on one of £10 (the average West Highland rent), and that in many isles rents were close to £3. MacLeod cited the township of Fjorlig in Skye which made a profit of £900 on six hundred sheep. While this might have been big money for a sheep farmer, it brought twenty-seven crofters only £33 each. Their total annual income was not above £50. 'There is here poverty,' said he, 'that no juggling with land can cure. The only thing to make people prosper is to remove half to other lands.' As the cost of living rose, larger farms could then pay higher rents to the landowners. (MacLeod's estate was earning £20,000 a year on a capital investment of £80,000, which he thought a small return.*)

The crofters' view was that they had no wish to emigrate, that further clearance was unnecessary, and that the population of the Hebrides had already dropped to 75,000, for whom there was enough land if made available. The trouble was that the Congested Districts Board under a Conservative government was not making it available.

Both parties spoke good sense: the crofters in saying that landowners held for profit or pleasure too much land, which if differently managed could support larger numbers of islesmen; the landowners in saying that population was still too large to allow each family a living commensurate with rising standards, even though more land was granted. History was to prove each right in marked degree.

* 1938: MacLeod.

The balance of rightness must have tipped more heavily to the islesmen's side had land-resources not been mismanaged and squandered in past centuries. The islands' earlier wealth had been too far depleted by man's ignorance, greed, passion, and neglect – not all of it Hebridean – to nourish a population of 75,000. The Conservative party, in power from 1886–1905, could support neither solution – it naturally abhorred the dispossession of landowners, while clearance, in the form of organized emigration imposed 'for the good of all', was no longer practical politics.

Government inaction caused trouble to flare up again in the Barra Isles, where the landless survivors of the clearances were growing in number. Lady Gordon Cathcart had succeeded as owner, but visited her islands only once in fifty-four years. When the hungry cottars appealed for a grant of land they received no reply. Then, perhaps recalling that times were changing, she made a tiny grant at the north tip of Barra. The men of Mingulay and Castlebay, becoming desperate, raided her island of Vatersay, which was run as one farm, built wooden huts, and stayed as squatters. Two strokes of providence helped them to better fortune: a Liberal government took office that year under Campbell Bannerman, a Glasgow Scot; and Lady Gordon Cathcart tried to evict the Vatersay raiders. Ten of the men arrested were sentenced at Edinburgh to six months in Calton jail. This caused such a storm of public protest that sentences were quartered and the government formulated a new land policy for the Highlands and Islands. In 1909 the secretary of state bought Vatersay for £6,250 and the squatters became crofters: in 1911 a Scottish Land Court took over the work of the Crofters' Commission; and in 1912 the work of the Congested Districts Board was transferred to a Scottish Board of Agriculture, but with added powers to force landowners to sell estates and to break large farms into small-holdings.

The new Board had no sooner set hand to plough than war broke out with Germany. The islesmen returned home in 1918 from the Royal Navy and Highland regiments in no mood to go cap in hand to landowners begging for a few acres. In 1918, the men of South Uist seized Lady Gordon Cathcart's farms, and fortunately the Board of Agriculture was there to confirm them in the tenure of crofts. Thus spurred by ex-servicemen, the board set to work with a will. Large territories were bought in Skye and Tiree, which became the most heavily crofted areas of west Scotland. The big farms were divided and the very small crofts enlarged; preservation of game for shooting on these islands virtually ceased; and all this allowed the retention of large native communities.

The landowners attacked government policy for endeavouring to keep in the country people for whom there was no remunerative employment. Despite the prognostications of doom, crofting continued to grow, for the landowners (and other opposition) had overlooked two essential points: firstly, that where crofting was not economically viable in itself it could be an acceptable way of life if the crofter had other money-earning employment, and such ancillary industries were available, or being made available on most large islands; and, secondly, the islesmen had a love of the land implanted deep in their beings. They were prepared to live frugally if only they had land, and were not willing to give up a small croft to work full-time in a more profitable trade. This last point has given much pain to the orderly minds of economists.

Outer Hebridean society was (and is) unique in Britain for the wide range of men's skills. The crofters were (and are) fishermen, builders, weavers, mechanics, and much more. Obviously specialization would bring higher earnings from increased efficiency and output. Crofts could be enlarged into farms and made more productive. But this logic failed from its false premise – that the islesman's primary need was money. It would appear that what he wanted first was land. Even a little would do if he could not have much. He needed money too to give him a standard of living matching that of the mainland, but that was not yet his basic need. It was certainly not so in the 1920s. It has also been argued that where specialization is modified life is more varied, interesting and refreshing, therefore perhaps happier. But the point was academic. The people loved their land and that was the hard fact on which Improvers, old and new, banged their heads in vain.

Crofting is central to island life.

As standards of living rose in the new century, the crofter had to develop his means of supply beyond a purely subsistence husbandry to pay for imports by exports. Exports could come from only four sources – the natural resources of the land, the products of the croft, which meant cattle and sheep rather than crops, the sea, and the sale of labour to industries at home or abroad while the croft was retained. Since by its nature crofting could not rise much above subsistence level except in favoured places, part-time work in ancillary industries became a vital requisite of island life. This sale of labour also became a vexing problem when it led to men abandoning their homes and leaving the land under-populated.

The chief ancillary occupations were part-time fishing, weaving, seafaring, coastal transport services, the building trade, and road-making. In the outer isles, the most important of these was the fishing.

Stornoway by 1912 had developed into the main centre of the Scottish herring industry. A fleet of a thousand boats brought the town a prosperity that lasted through seventeen years of competition with East Coast steam drifters. In Barra and Harris also, the people were stimulated by the mainland boats coming in to Castlebay and Scalpay. The men went off to the East Coast fishing in autumn, and their women to the herring curing as far south as Yarmouth and Lowestoft.* The men began to get boats of their own. At the full development, several hundred boats were out nightly. When in harbour, packed gunwale to gunwale, they formed a pontoon on which it was allegedly possible to cross from Castlebay to Vatersay (1½ miles, so presumably in seeming only). Thus the populations of Lewis, Harris, and Barra rose to their maxima in 1911.† Their quays were the busiest of the west seaboard. Stornoway, Scalpay, and Castlebay resounded to the chatter, song, and laughter of girls gutting and curing herring for export, to the screaming of gulls, to the clatter of cargo boats loading and unloading, and to the smack of coopers' hammers on barrels. After a heavy catch the work went on day and night. The two principal markets were Germany and Russia.

When the war broke out in 1914 the overseas markets were lost and the Barra fishery closed down, but the reduced Stornoway fleet stayed in action. It fared well, since other fishing activity died away round the British coasts. The Hebrides gave more men to the Navy and Army, in proportion to population, than any other region of the United Kingdom or Commonwealth. But whereas Lewis could give six thousand men (nearly a fifth of its population) in four years‡ and still find fishermen, other islands like Barra and Scalpay had not enough people. War casualties were heavy, and when the men returned the quays and laid-up boats had gone derelict. Having no capital for repair and replacement, many chose a career in the Merchant Navy. Women who had worked in munition factories or national service jobs now chose domestic service on the mainland. Families began to emigrate to Canada, and everywhere depopulation restarted.§

In 1918, Lord Leverhulme bought Lewis-with-Harris. He was the founder of the Port Sunlight soap-factory in Cheshire. A most long-sighted businessman, Leverhulme appreciated the potential wealth of Hebridean waters, foresaw that the market for cured herring would die as national taste changed, and proposed instead to develop the herring fishery with a large canning factory at

---

* *Stornoway Gazette*, 14 November 1964.
† Appendix, population table.
‡ Lewis Association Report, No. 6.
§ *Stornoway Gazette*, 14 November 1964.

Stornoway. On the mainland he opened numerous retail shops (MacFisheries) to assure an outlet. His plans, otherwise excellent, were in advance of his time.

The fishermen of the Outer Hebrides, if they were to compete with the steam drifters and trawlers, required expensive modern boats and new harbour facilities. They had no capital to provide these, but Leverhulme did. His arrival on the islands seemed, on the face of it, a heaven-sent chance for a basic reconstitution of the industry. But expensive boats could be made to pay only if they were kept continually at sea to supply a factory manned full-time. This new situation was incompatible with crofting. Using lug-sail boats, Lewismen had been able to combine their fishing with crofting, and were not yet prepared to change their traditional way of life to meet the radical change in the character of the fishing industry.[*] On top of their lack of support, Leverhulme had trouble with the Board of Agriculture, which led him to transfer developments from Lewis to Harris, where he found cooperation. At the township of Obbe on the south coast (re-named Leverburgh), he built piers, kippering sheds, houses, and new roads. The first landings from his fleet of trawlers in 1924 were so big that men had to be brought from the mainland to help in curing and packing. He died in 1925. His executors abandoned all and sold the island as several estates. Large areas tenanted by mainland farmers were made croftland, which allowed the native people to return to the west coast, from which they had been so long debarred.

Lewismen continued with traditional fishing practice, every active man and woman playing a part ashore and afloat. They so prospered that some had ventured to get motor-boats when the notorious depression of 1929 curtailed the European market. Then, as Lord Leverhulme had foreseen, there occurred at home and abroad changes in public taste and politics, which closed all doors.

Cured herring were no longer wanted on the mainland in former bulk. Fresh herring from Hebridean ports could not be fetched quickly enough to market to compete with catches by mainland drifters sailing under power direct to rail- and road-heads at Mallaig, Gairloch, Ullapool, and Oban. In 1933, the new German policy of self-sufficiency and the new economic policy of Russia closed the biggest foreign markets. The British government delivered the *coup de grâce* by adopting a cheap food policy that sanctioned the dumping of Norwegian herring at East Coast ports. The Hebridean curing stations had to close down. The fleets dwindled to negligible size.

---

[*] 1964: Blake.

THE ISLANDS OF WESTERN SCOTLAND

Numbers of Crofter Fishermen*

	1913	1924	1939	1944
Lewis-with-Harris	4066	2981	1700	1024
Barra–Uist	998	817	416	390
	5064	3798	2116	1414

The outbreak of the Second World War completed the disaster. Vigorous young men were again drained away in disproportion to the size of the islands. Lack of money after the armistice again checked revival of the herring fishery. White fishing collapsed as East Coast and foreign trawlers over-fished the Hebridean seas, poached within legal limits, swept the inshore banks and from Gigha to Lewis destroyed the gear of local line fishermen. The men had to beach their boats. Between 1930 and 1960 the decline was so great that latterly there were only twenty-five boats of forty-foot length or more based on island harbours. Lewis-with-Harris had only eleven full-time crews, and only a couple of hundred men fished for the mainland market.† Islesmen continued to fish for themselves, but even on Lewis the people came to depend for part of the year on supplies from mainland fishing boats.

Islesmen may seem slow to change, since they will not accept hustle. They have never lacked a resilient courage. As fishing failed after the war, the Lewis-men developed the tweed-weaving industry, which originated in Harris before the Clearances. Lewis-with-Harris has no more grazing and arable land than the Uists and Barra, which have only a third of its land area, yet has more than thrice their population. Clearance patterns only partly explain the anomaly. It would seem that Lewismen, facing a sharper challenge than the men of the south islands, whose machair had given them an easier agricultural life, were repeatedly forced to find ways of livelihood other than in land, and rose so well to the challenge that their island carries a far larger population than crofting could possibly maintain. When the earl of Dunmore bought Harris in 1834, his wife organized the sale of the first Harris tweeds in London. The crofters' weaving skill had long been famous, but they produced the cloth only for their own backs or the local market. The countess's energetic promotion of sales caused the early development of the industry. In 1877, commercial weaving of tweed spread to South Uist and Barra, then north in 1881 to Lochs in Lewis, finally to Uig, the whole west coast, and to Stornoway.‡

* 1955: Darling, from Fishery Board returns.
† 1964: Blake.
‡ 1964: Patent Office.

246

The industry flourished exceedingly after 1946. Spinning and finishing became centred at five Stornoway mills, which delivered yarn daily to crofter–weavers in the villages of Lewis and Harris, where much capital was invested in modern domestic looms. By the 1960s the annual production had grown to six million yards, worth nearly £4 million, three-quarters of which was exported, much of it to the United States. The fame of Harris Tweed had for many years encouraged mainland producers to market their own cloth under the same name, when only the weaving had been done in the Outer Hebrides. This ended in a Court of Session action of 1964, when Lord Hunter gave judgement for the island producers. A tweed wins the distinctive orb trade mark of Harris Tweed only if it meets the legal definition: 'A tweed made from pure virgin wool, produced in Scotland, spun, dyed, and finished in the Outer Hebrides, and hand-woven by the islanders at their own homes in the islands of Lewis, Harris, Uist, Barra, and their several appurtenancies, and all known as the Outer Hebrides.'

The industry was then consuming a third of the Scottish wool clip. The Stornoway mills employed 1,000 workers and distributed yarn to 1,500 landward weavers. A man could weave in a week 2½ tweeds (a tweed is 80 yards by 28½ inches), earning approximately £7 a tweed. The exclusion of mainland producers after 1964 was expected to bring a further expansion of trade, but the industry had in fact reached its peak in the decade 1960–70. Competition with man-made fibres and changes of fashion caused a recession, which after 1970 became a slump. Weavers in 1972 were getting £10 a tweed, but more than twenty per cent were unemployed. Distribution of yarn landwards fell off to an issue at intervals of two or three weeks. Recruits were no longer joining the industry, for the crofter–weavers' employment, and the security of their investment, had become uncertain. They were not eligible for unemployment benefit (being self-employed), and this had become a great hardship for some, a cause for anxiety to all, and manifestly unjust. They might have been enrolled as employees of the mills, so many weavers to each, but many of the crofters, like the fishermen before them, wanted to retain their independence. There is hope for the future: fashions will change again. The tailors demand double-width tweeds, which lessen production cost, therefore plans are being laid to re-equip the weavers with new looms at a cost of approximately £500,000.

When fishing had failed, many islesmen had preferred seafaring as a way of life to weaving, which had to be done standing or sitting day-long in a shed and was tiring on the eyes. In the old days, when they had sold their labour to Dutch, mainland, or Orkney fleets, the work could be readily fitted in with crofting, but that became difficult when they entered the Merchant Navy. All

247

islands lost a large number of their young men in this way. Their inborn skill in seamanship made Hebridean deckhands and masters respected all over the world. Islay suffered heavily through proximity to the Clyde and lack of crofting strength. So many of her men attained officer-rank that the island became known as 'the captains' nursery'. They had no crofts to hold their families to Islay and therefore settled on the mainland; whereas in the Outer Isles the men went home between voyages and helped their wives on the crofts. Much employment at sea and ashore has been given by cargo and passenger steamers plying to the islands from West Loch Tarbert, Oban, Fort William, Mallaig, Kyle of Lochalsh, and the Clyde. To these have been added MacBrayne's car-ferries, introduced in the 1960s (with inefficient, outdated side-loading) to capture tourist traffic.

Construction industry (road- and house-building, etc.) now employs large numbers – more than sixteen per cent of all industries in Lewis, for example, or more than thirteen per cent in Skye.* All islands have good road surfaces, except where roads end at townships that lack a tourist attraction – for the great improvement in Island and Highland roads has not been made for the benefit of inhabitants (despite protestations to the contrary by local politicians) but to get summer tourist trade. The crofters benefit in spare-time work. During this century the outer islanders have been re-housed. Black houses have almost entirely disappeared except in Lewis, where they are retained only as weaving sheds and byres, or converted to white houses. The new and old stand incongruously together along the west coast of Lewis, the old in tumble-down state, and the new with ugly, grey-cemented walls of two storeys, roofed in corrugated iron, or composite slate, or tarred felt. Huge peat stacks beside each house make a useful wind-break and the air is scented with the reek of the fires. On all other islands the houses are well painted and more pleasing to the eye.

Other industries that together employ a thousand men and women are knitwear on the outer isles, whisky distilling on the inner isles, the alginate industry of the Uists, Lewis, and Tiree, Forestry Commission plantations on Mull and Skye, the processing of shellfish on Lewis, Grimsay, and Islay, and casual labour on airfields.

Outer island women are famous for their knitting, and much help in marketing the product from Eriskay and the Uists has been given by Highland Home Industries Ltd. Stornoway has a factory where Harris yarn sweaters, knitted in Harris by the women in their own houses, are brought for finishing.

Whisky distilleries might be thought to be large employers, with barley grown

* 1972: Russell.

248

as a cash-crop alongside, but this is not so. Barley of the required quantity and quality has to be imported and the bigger distilleries employ only around thirty men each (those of Jura and Mull much fewer). Thus Islay has eight distilleries paying annual tax of £20 million, but they employ only two hundred men. The old method of malting barley by spreading it on the heated floor of a 'barn' has been replaced in Skye and Jura by the import of already malted barley from the mainland, hence peat-cutters and carters and grain-spreaders are no longer required.

An industry of greater value to crofters is the collection of seaweed for the factories of Alginate Industries Ltd on South Uist, North Uist, and Lewis. The weed is dried over coal or oil furnaces, milled to a fine grain, and sent to the mainland for processing. The final product is a chemical whose properties are jelling, thickening, and stabilizing, for use in a wide range of industries, principally food (puddings, jellies, cocktail cherries, etc.), textiles, paper, ceramics, and welding. Exports valued at over £2 million are made annually from Scotland to 131 countries around the world.* When the first factory was opened at Boisdale, South Uist, in 1943, the crofters, remembering the collapse of the kelp trade, were naturally doubtful of the new enterprise. But they cooperated, to their lasting profit.

The crofters turn out as they find time to cut rockweed (ascophyllum) from May to August on the east coast, and to collect tangle (laminaria) from October to March on the west coast. Thus the work is seasonal, for not many can collect both. They cut the rockweed with sickles, working from motor-boats, and tow the weed back to collecting points in 'rafts', which are immense flat masses held together by a floating rope-loop. These are hauled into shallow water, and when the tide ebbs are pitch-forked into lorries. Four tons of wet weed make a ton of dry, and the men are paid £3 a wet ton. Some cutters will bring in four or five tons in a day, but tide and weather forbid daily work and average earnings are not high. A team of two men can average twenty tons in a good week when conditions are unusually favourable. The bulk of the weed for processing is tangle, priced at £9 for an air-dried ton. The number of men employed in the Uists and Lewis is around sixty full-time in three factories (Lochboisdale, Lochmaddy, and Keose), with about 450 part-time collectors. The industry brings to the islands £130,000 a year in wages.

The Foresty Commission since 1925 has planted in the Hebrides 28,000 acres, giving full-time employment to ninety-three workers.†

* Report from Alginate Industries Ltd, 1972.
† Report from the Forestry Commission, 1972.

	Acreage	Men (full-time)	Outturn (1972)
Mull	14,169	50	7,960 cu. m.
Skye	9,112	33	3,850
Lewis	1,779	5	
Jura	1,351	2	in care and
Islay	987	1	maintenance
Raasay	589	2	stage
Uist	18	–	research plot
	28,005	93	11,810 cu. m.

Forestry employs few men in the Hebrides, and no crofters – unless when a few Skyemen may be used for contract thinning or haulage. The whole of the Skye production and eighty per cent of Mull's goes to the pulp mill at Fort William. Mull farmers say that the Commission is gobbling up too much grazing ground. They want forestry, but not to the detriment of a balanced economy.

Such were the principal industries, some growing, some ailing, which, with much larger service industries that included tourism, distributive trades, and transport, supported the crofting economy around 1960, when government departments resolved to invest in islesmen. The first expression of a new, positive policy was the promotion of an Outer Hebrides Fishery Training Scheme by the Department of Agriculture and Fisheries, the White Fish Authority, and the Herring Industry Board, during the years 1959–63. The second was by an Act of Parliament in 1965 forming the Highlands and Islands Development Board to assist the people to improve their economic and social conditions. During the preceding thirty years' decline, islesmen had virtually ceased to be fishermen,* although part-time lobster fishing was flourishing in a small way. This absurd situation, in which island seas could be harvested by fleets from Europe and the mainland while islanders were obliged to remain onlookers, was now ending.

The Fishery Training Scheme provided twelve boats to form the nucleus of a new fleet, and gave the men essential training in handling modern equipment. Each boat cost £15,000, the fishermen repaying seventy per cent over twenty years. Stornoway had ten of the new boats, and the fish landings there in 1964 were valued at herring £72,000, white fish £25,600, and prawns £74,000.

* 1969: HIDB.

Such figures are largely meaningless in themselves, for they include landings from boats from other ports, and do not include the big landings made by Stornoway boats at mainland ports, but they serve to reveal the extraordinary new growth of prawn trawling in the Minch. They also made islanders aware that Stornoway's modest landings could be greatly increased only if a processing factory were added to its deep-freeze plant and cold-storage depot, thus offering fishermen an island market, and providing jobs ashore on a ratio of one or two to each man afloat. The islanders had at last accepted Lord Leverhulme's original idea, with its full-time implications. Their demand for further development grew enthusiastic.

The HIDB in its first year reinforced success by launching a scheme to provide twenty-five new boats (54-foot stern trawlers, equipped also for herring ringing or seining) at a cost of £750,000. These boats went mainly to Lewis and Scalpay. The policy was again successful beyond expectation. The Board could not meet the demand for boats. A further ten had to be added to the list, second-hand boats bought, smaller boats built for shellfishing (especially lobstering), and for sea-angling, and the whole scheme extended to the north and west Highlands and Islands. A processing factory was established at Stornoway with skinning and filleting machines and a kippering kiln. Another was set up at Grimsay (North Uist) to process lobsters, giving fifty local fishermen continuity of work for the first time. The Long Isle, taking principal share of the west-coast lobster catch, had big storage ponds at Stornoway, Bernera, Harris, and Uist. Prawn and lobster fishing so boomed from 1963 that west-coast landings in 1968 exceeded the value of herring (herring £1.573 m., shellfish £1.688 m., white fish £2.372 m.). By December 1971, the Board had invested £2.6 m. in fisheries, had commissioned thirty-five new boats (twenty-one to the Long Isle), and approved 122 applications for second-hand boats and seventy-five for smaller shellfish boats (up to thirty-nine feet). This investment paid a dividend to the national economy, for the value of landings more than doubled in seven years, rising from £4.25 m. in 1964 to £10.3 m. in 1971.* A total fleet of 960 island and West Highland boats was now in action. In all, assistance had been approved for 235 boats employing 850 men. Of these boats 172 were then fishing and their landings worth £1.75 m. The Outer Hebrides' share was fifty-two boats with thirty-two fishing. The value of landings there (only a portion of the whole) had been raised from £168,000 in 1966 to £484,000 in 1970. The presence of numerous klondykers at Storno-

---

* HIDB report, 1971. Part of the rise is due to inflation of the currency.

way had attracted more fishing boats and given the factory a larger choice for processing.*

The Board's investment in fishing has thus transformed the Highland and Island industry out of recognition. The renewal of life and activity is seen in good second-hand boats continually entering the area, new boats being launched, more and more men receiving training in the latest equipment and methods, 1,400 jobs created or saved, and income of £1.3 m. generated (average income £1,000 a man). The fishermen have new confidence and have shown that given the chance islesmen are as vigorous and capable fishermen as any in Scotland.† Already the extended scheme is felt to be insufficient to meet the demand and further extension is yet again required. Such an upsurge of enthusiasm, sense of purpose, and profit, could not have been engendered in the Isles by any comparable investment in tourism, which is not, like seawork, the islesman's *métier*.

The most interesting results have appeared on two small islands that have specialized in fishing – Scalpay (population 444) and Eriskay (population 206) – where more than sixty per cent of the working males get their living from fishing, and most of the rest from the Merchant Navy.‡ Scalpay now has a fleet of twelve, and Eriskay six (plus two lobster boats), both having doubled their fleets with help from the Board. Under good island leadership, a high level of prosperity has been reached, with boys entering the fleet direct from school and each crew member from skipper to boy getting an equal share of earnings. This division of spoil on a basis of ideal communism is not repeated on the mainland, and is a powerful influence in attacting recruits not only from the schools but the Merchant Navy. Both men and women who had hitherto been seeking employment elsewhere are now tending to return to the islands.

In his 1972 report to the HIDB, William Russell points out that Stornoway is far from realizing its potential as a port for fish-landings and processing, because Minch boats find their most economic delivery points at mainland ports for mainland markets; therefore he advocates an expansion of fishing west of Lewis, which would make Stornoway a natural market between fishing grounds and the mainland. This would mean the development of a west-coast port, say at Breasclete, from which fish would go east by road to Stornoway, be processed at expanded plants, and shipped to Ullapool by the new ferry. Stornoway could have a promising future as a fishing port instead of a base for

* 1972: Russell.
† 1969: HIDB, Report on Fisheries.
‡ 1972: Russell.

local boats. Barra at the south end of the Long Isle would be equally well placed for development as a second large-scale processing centre.

The future of Hebridean fishing, which appears so bright, has been clouded by the fishing regulations of the European Economic Community. Islanders are concerned not only at the withdrawal of fishing limits from twelve miles to six between the Butt of Lewis and Barra Head, but also at market price-fixing. In the UK, prices vary across the country according to transport costs, but under EEC regulations prices are made uniform by imposing a period-average taken at central markets, and a minimum price is fixed below which fish may not be sold for the table. Since island prices are lower than Scottish averages, and Scottish minima are well below EEC minima, it follows that much of the island landings will be priced out of the market.

Again, when the twelve-mile limit was imposed in 1964, fish-yields greatly increased during the next six years. The UK fish-catch was £29 m. in 1970, of which £17 m. was calculated to come from within the six-mile limit. And that high proportion is claimed as the benefit gradually accruing to the six-mile belt from the protection afforded to the six- to twelve-mile belt. Thus during the ten years' grace before the regulations are applied, the fishermen's anxiety will mount and confidence ebb, undermining alike his preparedness to invest in boats and gear, and the businessman's plans for development ashore.* The government seems unlikely to resolve such vital issues, for the truth is that no one is sure how the regulations will work in practice, so that conflicting opinion may bring a wait-and-see policy.

A still worse threat might yet arise from the extension of oil-exploitation from the North Sea to Atlantic waters, accompanied by oil-leakage from the sea-bed resulting in large-scale pollution of the fishing grounds. Primary food resources should never thus be put in jeopardy. Test borings are now being made.

The Board's promotion-policy in the Isles goes much further than fisheries. Its first chairman, Professor Sir Robert Grieve, grasped the essential point that although crofting could not support the crofter full-time, it gave him deep satisfaction. He wrote, 'If one had to look now for a way of life which would keep that number of people in such relatively intractable territory, it would be difficult to contrive a better system. Its future continuance depends on other employment support.'† Therefore the Board's policy has been to promote a

* 1972: Russell.
† 1966: HIDB report.

253

variety of industrial growth points. The industries aided include the Tobermory distillery; Alginate Industries, who were enabled to build ten boats for seaweed collectors; shellfish processing at Port Ellen in Islay and Grimsay in Uist, from which escallops and lobsters are flown to Paris and London; and factories on Barra manufacturing perfume, spectacle-frames, and thermostat components. At Kyles Paible and Balimore in North Uist, the Board in 1967 initiated a bulb-production scheme, which proved so successful on the first twenty-six acres planted (crocuses gave a hundred per cent yield, tulips and daffodils fifty per cent, comparing favourably with Netherland yields) that the Board planned to reclaim for bulb-growing 1,500 acres of tidal strand at Vallay. In order to compensate for heavy freight charges, plantations had to be large, concentrated on one area, and not dispersed.* The plan, after scrutiny by a technical committee, was turned down in 1972 on grounds of expense.

The Board's formidable tasks have been made feasible by the earlier introduction of widespread telephone links, electric power, and air and sea services. Granted such communications, the Board's main effort apart from fisheries has been directed to helping tourism, a principal deterrent to which had been lack of accommodation. Skye, Islay, Barra, and Tiree have many boarding houses and several good hotels, notably Skye, but most are converted houses, not purpose-built. The Board has therefore planned to spend £1 m. building five luxury hotels in the Highlands and Islands. The first (sixty-two bedrooms) opened at Craignure in Mull in 1971, and the second (thirty to forty bedrooms) is now being built at Tangusdale in Barra. These will earn money for mainland investors rather than help crofters. The tourist brings much money into some islands – more than a quarter of a million passengers and a hundred thousand cars annually cross the south ferries to Skye. Lewis at the other extreme has few, for the sea-passage is long and the crofter feels able neither to let his house in summer nor to accept loans for building tourist chalets. The outer isles have much to offer the summer holiday-maker in miles of sandy beaches, sea-cliffs and seascapes, lower rainfall and more sunshine than the West Highlands, but this often at a sacrifice of comfort and convenience, for the beaches are windswept and accommodation less sophisticated than on the mainland. The Isles will always be more enjoyed by visitors who are vigorous and disposed to activity in the open air than by the majority who prefer daytime sunbathing and night-time entertainment. The islands thus draw more tourers than residential holidaymakers – an example is the summer-long flood of day-visitors to Iona

* 1969: HIDB report.

from Oban. The inner isles have greater development potential for tourism than the outer. But work is seasonal, the season short, and income from it less than it seems when much money is spent on imports to meet tourist taste. Even in Skye, the Board has been criticized for preoccupation with tourism to the neglect of fishery there.* The Skyemen's concern for fishery may sound odd in light of past history. In 1970, a Skyeman observed that Uig on the north-west coast offered the shortest turn-around trip for herring boats fishing the Minch. Only four boats were then prawn-fishing out of Uig. He opened a buying and selling agency, and a year later fourteen or sixteen boats were calling at Uig daily, others clustering round klondykers anchored offshore to receive their herring catches, loaded lorries were leaving the pier, and up to forty men were being employed. The herring landings were then valued at £316,655 and the pier had to be enlarged at a cost of £100,000 to cope with the traffic. The Skyeman's initiative in contriving this development without help from the Board is the best sign of changed times.

Industries old and new and efforts to help them have been undermined by the present level of freight charges. The Isles, once the cheapest place to live in the United Kingdom, are now the dearest, despite subsidies given to steamer services. Freight charges have pushed up the cost of living to a frightening degree. Life and work are crippled. Freight on the Minch varies from six to twenty-four times higher per ton mile than lorry freight on the mainland.† In this serious situation, the Board made a study of northern Norway, where topography and economic conditions resemble those of the Highlands and Islands. The Norwegian government were controlling freight and fares by deliberately using subsidy of the transport system to achieve development. Short take-off aircraft, used in a network of feeder services, were giving passenger traffic a growth rate of twenty-five per cent a year, thus side-stepping the expensive alternatives of road-links and ferry-delays. Car-ferry charges were close to those that the Board had been urging on the Secretary of State.

The Board have repeatedly stated the truth that shipping charges are an intolerable burden on island life, should be held closer to the level of mainland freight, and that this end could be achieved by classifying water-crossings as extensions of mainland roads. Despite the Board's representations, freight and fares have continually risen, and enterprises been stifled or thwarted, and closed down. Depopulation, while abating, has shown no sign of ending.

* 1972: Russell.
† 1967: HIDB report.

Transport services on the remote frontiers of a country are inevitably expensive to run, but that does not mean such regions are uneconomic to hold except on a superficial consideration. When a frontier region like the Hebrides is not held, then a new frontier has to be formed farther back, which in turn will become 'uneconomic' to hold, and so reason for retreat will become repetitive.* Whereas, if the outer fringe is held, and communications are supported by subsidy as in Norway, the regenerated activity of the fringe imparts real benefit also to the communities on the inner lines of transport service. The whole mainland sea-board can benefit from the proposed reduction of island freight. It is in the national interest that this decision should be taken.

The government in 1972 rejected the plea to increase present levels of subsidy. They proposed instead to exploit road-haulage through an introduction of roll-on/roll-off vessels that would charge by reference to wheeled length irrespective of weight, and operate from purpose-built terminals on the shortest practicable sea-crossings. They accepted increased capital investment but not subsidy.

Some mainlanders would reject financial aid whether for transport or island agriculture as unjustified by their future prospects. Islanders have replied that the Treasury takes more than £20 m. a year in tax on Islay whisky, and could wisely plough back more of these whisky millions into land development and transport. Since 1956, nearly 40,000 acres of moorland have been reclaimed in the Highlands and Islands.† Scores of thousands of acres – more than 20,000 on Mull alone – could be reclaimed for farming and crofting at a third of the cost of tree-planting, resulting in large increases of cattle and lamb production.‡

Crofting agriculture has been widely criticized as anachronistic, its units being too small and its tenure so rigid that the system has become fossilized, meaning that crofting communities have been unable to adjust to change.§ A crofter's security of tenure applies only to his continuing use of the land for agriculture, thus he cannot share in any increased value arising from a change in land use, and is therefore without incentive either to initiate or cooperate in development other than agricultural.|| Since he does not own the land, he cannot use his own house (even though he built it himself) as security for a loan. Building grants and loans have therefore been given by the government (Crofters

---

* 1972: Russell.
† 1971: Crofters Commission.
‡ Campbell Finlay, Mull.
§ 1971: Turnock. 1968: Gillanders.
|| 1968: Crofters Commission.

19a. Scalpay harbour, Harris.

19b. Stornoway.

20a. St Mary's Abbey, Iona. Founded in 1203 by Ragnall, King of the Isles, on the site of St Columba's monastery, and rebuilt between 1480 and 1500. The plan of the church is a Greek cross from which the square tower rises 70 feet at the centre. To the south (right) of the cloister stands the nave, to the north the refectory, to the east the chapter house and dormitory with the north transept to their right, and to the west the former kitchens, now offices.

20b. Iona abbey church. The sacristy doorway of 1500 in the chancel is carved from Carsaig freestone.

Act 1955), but these are not available to sons, daughters, or others, who could find work near the family holding, but are obliged to wait for a house until their parents die – by which time they are committed to living elsewhere. The Crofters Commission (formed in 1955) regarded this restriction of aid to one house per croft as the greatest single barrier to the development of townships and the real cause there of high average age levels.*

To overcome these various difficulties, the Commission asked in 1968 for new legislation to convert crofting tenure into owner-occupation, and to extend grants and loans to others of like economic status on a basis of need instead of tenure, arguing that these measures would release initiative. In August 1972, the Secretary of State accepted the Commission's advice on owner-occupancy, which he modified in proposals to allow the crofter an option either to remain as tenant or to buy his house and inbye land, but not common grazing unless that had already in part been apportioned to him. To avoid a communal loss of winter grazing, the township would have pre-emption on the land (but not the house). The housing assistance available to tenants would extend to an owner up to a limit of seven years. Should the crofter elect to continue as tenant, he would have three new rights: (1) title to the site of his house and garden; (2) to acquire inbye land for non-agricultural development in agreement with his landlord, failing which a right to apply to the Land Court for an order; and (3) a share in the development-value of land that had been resumed for development by the landlord.

Critics of the proposals declare that owner-occupation, while welcome, is not in itself a solution to crofting problems.† It can lead to fragmentation of an estate with consequent deterioration in both management and agriculture, and with lost opportunity for development since amalgamation of crofts will be more difficult. The proposals have not removed the principal handicap to crofting life by allowing grants for more than one house to a croft. While the State may feel reluctant to create such a precedent, an encouraging fact is that the cost to the State of providing a croft house has proved to be only half that of a council house of the same size in the same area.‡ Apart from that money-saving aspect, the social benefit has been important, for the crofters are given a feeling of independence through not having to wait passively on local authority action while townships disintegrate. Hence the Commission's recommendation, if accepted, could be an effective instrument of regional development. Norway

* 1971: Crofters Commission.
† Scottish Landowners Federation, *Scotsman*, 5 August 1972.
‡ 1968: Grant.

has shown that that policy may be the only stimulant required to assure the survival of numerous communities.*

The quest for croft-land has become intense. In 1971, the Commission received six hundred applications – many from people south of the Border seeking holiday homes or 'a more satisfying way of life'.† A free market in crofts under owner-occupation could destroy crofting. The large-scale purchase of crofts for holiday homes by townspeople and Lowlanders, or by estate agencies on their behalf, could in time reduce active townships to ghost villages through the native people's inability to compete in the property market. Already in the Highlands and Islands the process has begun. House prices in remote country of high scenic quality have become inflated by the pressure of population, traffic, work, and development farther south. Conditions have become ripe for speculation in land of an antisocial kind. This is already happening and would flare up on the creation of a multitude of small landowners, unless the new legislation includes safeguards.

Forecasts that there can be no future in crofting have been made from time to time during the last century by reporters from universities and government commissions. The massive aid required would be unjustified, they say, because the possession of land by crofters is much less important than the profitable use of land, which almost everywhere is being used to poor advantage.‡

This opinion seems unbalanced. It fails to take account of human need, of social benefit, and of all the field evidence. Croft farming, if not the mainstay of island economy, has a gross product worth several million pounds a year.§ More than 18,000 crofts survive in the Highlands and Islands because the system, in spite of faults, has worked well in holding people to the land, and holding communities together with such strength that townships have survived to the present day while other industries, on which they originally depended, have waxed and waned, changed or died. The new Improvers, who would solve the need for changes in crofting by amalgamating the small 'non-viable' units, have paid no heed to island history, which shows that such a process does not retain the labour force and is socially disastrous. Clearance of small-holders from Mull and Coll in favour of larger farms has provided salutary lessons. Coll is not unprosperous, but under stock-farming its population has dwindled to 120 (mostly Lowlanders) with decay of social life and loss of facilities, whereas

* 1971: Fraser.
† 1971: Crofters Commission.
‡ 1968: Gillanders.
§ 1971: Fraser.

its sister island of Tiree, strong in crofting, retains a vigorous Gaelic-speaking people. Likewise, Skye has more than thrice the population of Mull, although Mull has better land (some of the best in the Highlands*). Amalgamation does have its place, where it can be applied to larger crofts with all-round gain, but is inappropriate to the smaller, part-time crofts in the Isles, where living costs are high and crofting is both a useful source of income and a secure base for fishermen, seamen, seaweed collectors, roadmen, weavers, builders, and others, whose time and energy are not used up by the work that gives their principal earnings. The economic value of crofts to crofters will grow, not diminish, as food prices rise on Britain's entry to the E E C. Crofting's social value is not in dispute. The astonishing feat of this island people in holding their land and keeping their racial characteristics and culture through two hundred years of recurrent famine, emigration, clearance, poverty, persecution, war, neglect, and intolerance, was made possible by the communal strength of the crofting town-ships.† They survived because always they were able to adapt to harsh, changing conditions. Granted the stimulus of sensible legislation, they should not fail in the future.

Depopulation has not yet been stemmed, for the cause has not been removed. Since Munro wrote in 1549 more than a hundred islands have been deserted (including islands that were settled after his time), but desertion should not be confused with depopulation. When the pattern of desertion is examined,‡ it appears that only forty-four isles held more than twenty people at the time of abandonment, only nine held more than a hundred, and that several of the latter islands carried their larger number from passing causes – evictions, or congestion, or the manning of industries that failed. Most were very small, but only a few could be classified as remote by Hebridean standards. The deciding factors in abandonment were usually social rather than economic; due not to poverty but to a growing sense of isolation from social facilities developing else-where. Until late in the nineteenth century, insularity did not imply isolation, for the Highlands and Islands had few roads, so that many mainland townships were more isolated than island townships where people could go by boat to market, to church, or even to their shielings with livestock. Isolation by distance mattered little, for the need of regular communication was rarely felt. The vigorous St Kildans, for example, built no sea-going boat to give access to Harris. But a sense of isolation, where none had been before, came with the development

* 1955: Darling.
† 1971: Fraser.
‡ 1966: Moisley.

of roads and steam engines. People grew aware that economic progress could bring them educational, medical, and other services, which they wanted.

Thus an island with a population of less than one hundred is in danger, for it supports with increasing difficulty the social facilities that make life tolerable. It is small islands that are prone to desertion, and for each community there is a critical size below which desertion becomes inevitable. But there is no hard and fast rule; minimum figures vary according to site and circumstance. A community must be big enough (like Coll) to support an elementary school and a district nurse, or else (like Iona) have daily access to such services. Where there can be no daily access and numbers fail, then the point at which a local government declines to provide an essential service can be as much a matter of politics as finance. Some three thousand people have been dispersed from islands on their desertion* – a minute figure compared to the great emigrations – and those who left usually went to other islands, not to the mainland, for they were trying to escape isolation not insularity. Hence desertion of islands has been a negligible factor in depopulation and has not meant abandonment of good land, for almost all are grazed and probably more productive than when they were congested.

People everywhere tend to seek better social facilities. Stornoway grows while rural Lewis and every other island (except Islay) diminishes. Emigration is bound to continue as a feature of Hebridean society until such time as unemployment levels and average incomes more closely match those of the mainland, where price levels are much lower.

Average gross earnings (male)†

	1965	1968	1970
Highlands and Islands	£870	£1,044	£1,166
Scotland	£892	£1,089	£1,258
UK	£995	£1,192	£1,368

Unemployment: percentage of working population in 1971

Lewis	24%	Scotland	5.6%
Skye	9%	UK	3.5%
Islay	22% (approx.)	Highlands	8.6%

A matter of real concern, as noted earlier, is that men and women who leave for the mainland are often those of enterprising character and bright mind, so

* 1966: Moisley.
† Scottish Abstract of Statistics, 1971.

that potential leaders are lost. That truth is not the whole truth, for while the islands have given much to the wider world, they have also received much. There is two-way traffic. And there is a sense in which not even the Hebrides are islands. Likewise, a United Kingdom that neglects to nourish outer limbs inflicts self-injury, is far from united, and loses more of value to its life than ever it gains. In practical terms, this means that industries need to be set up and fostered, so that opportunities for employment retain in the Isles a sufficient number of young people to sustain leadership and all social facilities for a full life. Some of the ways in which this end might be won have been seen and pointed out to central government by their own advisers. A few of these ways have recently been followed. They would be overbold islesmen who on that account would start counting chickens. Westminster is remote from Hebridean realities. But at least they have reason to feel confidence in themselves. Hebrideans are survivors – tough, resilient, and resourceful. They could not otherwise have held the Hebrides. The mould of the islesmen's future is in their own hands, if those hands can be made young hands.

10

Architecture of Church and Castle

Buildings that at one and the same time are skilfully planned to their purpose, built soundly, and delight the beholder's eye, are in the Hebrides either ruinous or, if still intact, few. The art of the master mason would be gone too were it not for recent work on the restoration of Iona Abbey and several castles. The new work done by architects for local and central government has given little pleasure to man's aesthetic faculty, and some of it (at Village Bay in St Kilda, for example) is downright ugly. There are several beautiful villages in the Hebrides – Dervaig in Mull, Edinbain in Skye, Cornaigmore (modern) in Tiree – but they are examples of good house-building on good sites rather than architecture. The patrons of the latter have been mainly the Church and the Chiefs.

A considerable architectural art was displayed by the broch-builders from the first century B.C.* The Scots when they came built their houses, as distinct from their dry-stone forts, in wood, and continued the practice till the twelfth century.† The monasteries too were of wood, and the earliest stone buildings to survive from the Christian era are on Eileach an Naoimh in the Isles of the Sea (the Garvellachs), built on the site of St Brendan of Clonfert's foundation of the sixth century. They merit examination as prototypes of early monastic ruins found on other islands, and have peculiar interest as standing on Columba's Hinba.

The Celtic monastic system encouraged monks to seek occasional retreat to

* See chapter 5.
† 1896: MacGibbon and Ross.

262

solitary places, which they called 'deserts'. Rocky and uninhabited islands were a favourite choice. Adomnan constantly refers to an island named Hinba, to the monastery on which Columba used to withdraw for contemplation, and which he came to love as dearly as Iona. The total destruction of records during the Viking invasions caused the identity of Hinba to be lost, but Adomnan helps by siting it 'in Muirbulc-mar', which means in a great arm of the sea. This well describes the position of Eileach an Naoimh within the long arm of the Firth of Lorn. He makes it clear that Hinba was within easy reach of Iona, and says that when Brendan (at the age of almost ninety) sailed from Ireland to visit Columba he found him at Hinba unexpectedly. The one place at which Brendan would certainly call on his voyage would be his own foundation on the Isles of the Sea.

W. J. Watson[*] confused the issue by choosing to regard the monastery, not the island, as sited *in Muirbulc-mar*, thus excluding Eileach an Naoimh. But when Adomnan's text is examined it gives no ground for Watson's restriction of meaning.[†] Equally important, the Gaelic translation of Hinba (pronounced Eenba) must be taken from old, not modern Gaelic. Dwelly records *In* as island, and the now obsolete *Ba* as sea, giving Isle of the Sea. The unpronounced H indicates a plural. The original name would be *Na Hinba*, but the definite article is usually dropped, leaving *Hinba*, the Isles of the Sea. This in fact has been their name from time immemorial. Bartholomew's maps give it, but OS maps give only Garvellachs, from *Garbh Eileach*, or Rough Rock, a relatively new name. Perhaps both maps should revert to Hinba. That Eileach an Naoimh is Columba's Hinba is agreed by all authorities from Reeves (1857) and Skene (1876) to the 1930 report by the Glasgow Archaeological Society and the 1953 paper by Simpson.

Eileach an Naoimh, one mile long, is the southmost of four small islands that stretch four miles in line astern, each sloping up from the south-east to present bold cliffs to the open sea. They are uninhabited. Seen from a distance, Eileach an Naoimh looks like a bare skerry, but its south end is sheltered by a hill of 252 feet, which gives secluded glens and grassy hollows on the east side, in contrast to the Atlantic shore. The rock is limestone and calcareous slate (Dalradian), and the island therefore so full of flowers that in the course of an hour's walk I have noted more than fifty species. In May and June, cuckoos and corncrakes call from the low ground and larks from the hillside above. The

[*] In 1926.
[†] W. Douglas Simpson (1955) concurs.

monastic ruins lie in a wide green hollow above the narrow creek of the landing-place. Only low, crumbled walls remain, but the site is spacious with a vallum, chapel, monastery, church, barn, kiln, and beehive cells. Adjoining the monastery is a walled herb-garden and graveyard with ancient upended slabs. Until last century the latter included ornamented slabs and crosses carved with ships, arms, and cognizances of Clan Donald, Gillean, Fingon, and others, but all have since been removed by thieves.

The ruins are of varied date and none is contemporary with St Brendan. His original chapel of the sixth century would certainly be of wood, and since not even Iona was rebuilt in stone before the ninth century, no earlier date can be assigned to the chapel on Eileach an Naoimh.* In size, 21 feet 6 inches by 12 feet, it is identical with the other monastic chapels of the Inner Hebrides – Islay, Tiree, Skye – which all had low thatched roofs. W. D. Simpson suggests that the monastery so-called was in reality the monks' farmhouse with a byre at the north angle, access to the house through the byre giving a sheltered entrance. The evidence suggests that the building was not a monastery but a monastic outpost of Iona Abbey, built later than the chapel and before the church, which had mortared walls and a chancel. The kiln, with its stone oven built above a fireplace and flue would be used for parching corn.

A two-cell beehive, ninety yards east of the church, is built as a figure-of-eight with diameters of fourteen and thirteen feet – larger than the usual, which were six to ten feet. The two outer doors and one inner are four feet high. In 1937, the Ministry of Works partially restored one of the cells, which now stands more than ten feet high with the roof complete in half-section.† Beehive construction had been devised in Neolithic times, and many of the small stone circles on islands could be the lowest courses of beehive houses. The low courses were laid vertically, while the upper were given an inward overlap until they met in beehive shape at the copestone. A square vent in the roof formed a small window, widely splayed inside. The solitaries of the Celtic Church adopted beehives from the native builders and occupied them as cells on skerries as remote as Sula Sgeir and on islets like the Flannans. Beehives were associated also with monasteries, such as the nunnery on Canna, and the Annait monastery at Dunvegan in Skye. The best examples are those of Eileach an Naoimh, where one of the two compartments was probably an oratory. Beehive construction, using a round, oval, or four-sided plan was developed in clachans of the Outer Hebrides, and continued to be used there in summer shielings until this

* 1955: Simpson.
† Plate 12a.

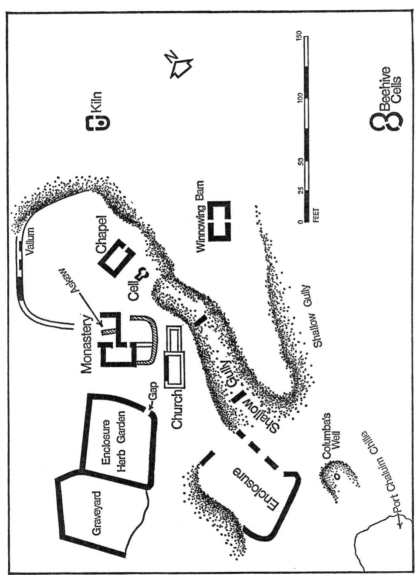

Diagram 11 *Plan of the Ninth-century Monastic Settlement of Eileach an Naoimh*

265

century. Completely intact beehives built within the last eighty years may still be seen on the Lewis moors.

The Norse invasion stopped any development of an architectural art, which was introduced to the Hebrides on the Norman conquest of England. Queen Margaret in 1074 built the first Norman chapel of St Oran on Iona. Fifty years later, the arrival of Normans in Scotland in large numbers caused Somerled to use their skills in building Castle Sween in Knapdale. Celtic forts had been dry-stone, built circular to give strength against battering-rams. The Norman castles, being mortared, could be made square and yet be stronger than the circular. The first of Somerled's Hebridean castles built to Norman plan was Claig on Fraoch Eilean in the Sound of Islay, *c.* 1154. The next three hundred years became the castle-building era for the defence of the Lordship of the Isles.

The ancient Celtic vallum of rock and earth was thus replaced by the great wall of enceinte, built thirty to fifty feet high and up to ten feet thick. Behind this curtain wall, the chief's long hall was at first built in stone like a big black house with a chimneyless thatched roof.* The wall of enceinte was then found to give insufficient security, and the Norman keep-tower was added, made square or rectangular with a gabled roof whose ridge never rose above the height of a five-foot, crenellated parapet.† Nearly thirty such castles eventually protected the Atlantic principality, twenty-three of them on the inner isles, and more than half of these around Mull and Skye, which were most vulnerable. They are now all reduced to picturesque ruins, with four exceptions – Dunvegan, Kisimul, Duart, and Breacacha on Coll, which survive intact. In light of recent Hebridean history, it seems astonishing that these four are still inhabited by members of the families that built them or took early possession. The MacLeods have lived for seven hundred years without break at Dunvegan, which is thus the longest-inhabited castle of Scotland. Kisimul was restored between 1938 and 1959 by its 45th MacNeil chief; Duart in 1912 by Sir Fitzroy MacLean; and Breacacha from 1966 by Colonel MacLean Bristol. Dunvegan and Duart are open to the public.

Dunvegan and Duart have been greatly altered since they were first built, Kisimul less so, and while these three are the most imposing in size and site, the one I choose for description is Breacacha, for it is the most interesting of all architecturally. All the castles differed widely in size, shape, and detail – masons were expert in tailoring each to fit the underlying crags – but Breacacha,

* W. D. Simpson in 1967: Moncrieff.
† 1896: MacGibbon and Ross.

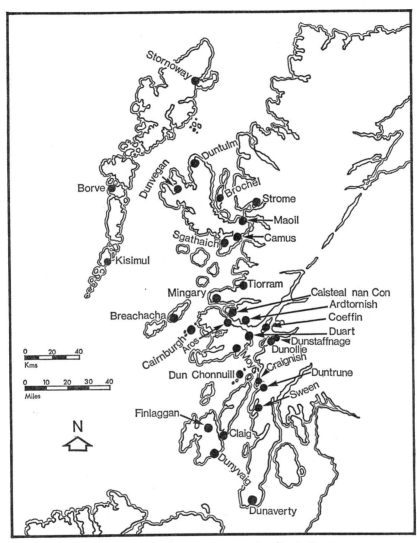

Map 19 *Castles of the Atlantic Principality*
(**12th – 15th century**)

although relatively small, is the least altered medieval castle of the Hebrides.*

It stands close by the shore of a bay on south Coll. Behind it stretch the wide flats of Breacacha, the Speckled Field, named from the huge spread of wild flowers on its grassland, where cattle graze in large herds. The castle has wide views to the Treshnish Isles and the hills of Mull, and to the distant Paps of Jura. There is no record of its building. Simpson, MacGibbon, and Ross all agree in assigning it to the early fourteenth century, when it was most probably built by Angus Og of Islay, King of the Isles, when he received Coll on Mac-Dougall's forfeiture around 1314. The MacDonalds had always been able to command the best-informed master-masons, and the one sent to supervise the the erection of Breacacha knew every latest device used in the defensive and

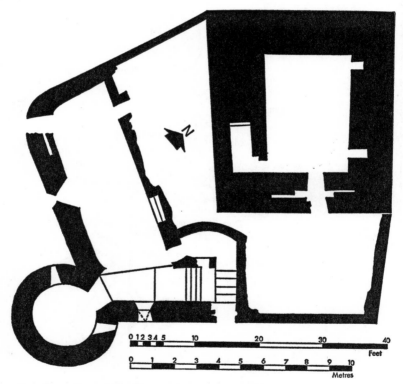

From Transactions of The Glasgow Archaelogical Society, Vol. X 1941

Diagram 12 *Breacacha Castle, Coll.*
(**14th century**)

* 1939: Simpson.

domestic planning of the great mainland castles. At Breacacha he reproduced in miniature the most advanced conceptions of his time, although clearly with local men, for the masonry was crudely worked.*

The curtain walls are trapezoidal (no two are parallel), about eighteen feet high and four and a half thick. A square keep is set in the north angle, and a round tower extrudes beyond the south angle. A most unusual feature is that the yard thus enclosed (forty-three feet at widest) is in two parts, the north part from which the keep rises being nearly ten feet higher than the south yard, which contained a hall-house later destroyed, its debris probably being used to raise the north platform. The keep stands fifty feet including its five-foot parapet, on a base of thirty-two feet by twenty-eight, within which the walls are seven feet thick. Its north and west sides are ringed by a second curtain. Originally there was a third and outermost wall of earth and timber, which has now vanished.† The keep is much the same size as Kisimul's, but with four storeys instead of three. The round tower stands thirty feet on a sixteen-foot external diameter. Its second storey is entered from the wall-walk of the curtain and lit by loopholes. One window gives a view to the bay. The upper room has a barrel-vault roof, topped for defence by a platform.

The overall plan is defensively excellent and makes full use of the stratagems of the time, which are executed with economy of space and material. The keep has its main entrance on the first floor, its wall-walk is ample, the parapet wall and south turret are corbelled out to give a better field of fire to base, crosslet loopholes pierce the main fabric, and the door to the parapet opens inward to halt an enemy rush. The curtain walls have a wall-walk, and their south and east gateways are given double protection both from the flank by the round tower and from above by square wall-turrets projecting on corbels, which have machicolated floors for dropping stone or fire on to enemy heads. The round tower's flat roof gave an ammunition platform with embrasured parapets. These and various other points of interest are nowhere else in the Hebrides all brought together in one castle, for the others if not ruined have been partially adapted to their new role as mansion houses.

The most heavily defended seaways were those around Mull and the Lorn coast, which commanded the entrance to the Great Glen – the chiefs of Clan Donald and their many allies had vast mainland possessions. Thus Somerled's son, Dughall, took Dunollie Castle for his seat as Lord of Lorn in the twelfth

---

* Ibid.
† 1867: Skene, Vol. 3.

century. In the thirteenth, Ewen of Lorn built Dunstaffnage at the mouth of Loch Etive, while the kings of the Isles built Mingary on Ardnamurchan, and Duart and Aros on Mull. Several others were added in the fourteenth century. They were mightier castles by far than Breacacha. Duart, Dunollie, and Aros were set on precipitous crags, and Duart's keep alone (sixty-three feet by forty-six, with walls fifteen feet thick) enclosed more ground than Breacacha's outer curtain. They were units in a defensive system for the Lorn coast: beacon signals could be relayed thirty-five miles down the Sound of Mull from Mingary to Dunollie by way of Caisteal nan Con, Aros, Ardtornish, and Duart. Mac-Dougall could know within half an hour if his north frontier was threatened, or by reverse signal summon force to the centre.

The Norse were not builders in stone, and much of the best architectural work in the Isles was done by the Scots on ecclesiastical buildings within a hundred years of their departure. Somerled's son Ragnall rebuilt Iona Abbey in 1203, and while no paper record of its plan survives, all Hebridean monasteries of the time were planned somewhat alike – an open cloister-garth surrounded by a covered walk, flanked on one side by the church, and on the opposite side by refectory and kitchen. On the east or west side of the transept (or else of the cloister) lay the chapter house and sacristy, with the dormitory and library above. Other apartments and stores were fitted in according to the site. The abbey's appearance may be gauged from the extraordinary beauty of the Nunnery of St Mary, which Ragnall built on Iona at the same time (appointing his sister Beatrice prioress). Although ruinous – the low walls of the cloister, chapter house, and refectory have become a rock-garden around cut-grass floors – much of the outer wall still stands and the stone is pink granite quarried from the Ross of Mull, dappled with blocks of black schist and lined with creamy sandstone from Carsaig at windows, arches, doorways, and all outer corners.

Ragnall built the nunnery for the Benedictine Order, and the Vatican still has the deed of confirmation dated 1203.* The buildings occupy a sixty-eight-foot quadrangle with the church, fifty-eight feet by twenty, at the north side and the refectory at the south. The refectory's two gables and south wall remain at full height; its upper storey was probably the dormitory. The church has nave, choir, a north aisle, and sacristy, but is not cruciform. The nave is lit from its west gable by two round-headed narrow windows, widely splayed in sandstone on both inner and outer sides, while the north aisle has been given

* 1896: MacGibbon and Ross.

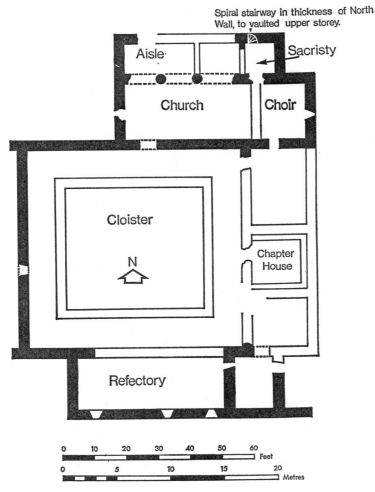

Diagram 13 *Nunnery of St Mary, Iona. Thirteenth century*

three moulded sandstone arches resting on stout piers. These arches at some late date have been walled to half their height. The sacristy fills the angle between choir and aisle. In the thickness of its north wall a spiral stairway (intact) leads to a vaulted upper storey.

The largest monastic building to survive in the Hebrides, after Iona's abbey and nunnery, is the Priory of Oronsay, built around 1360 by John of Islay,

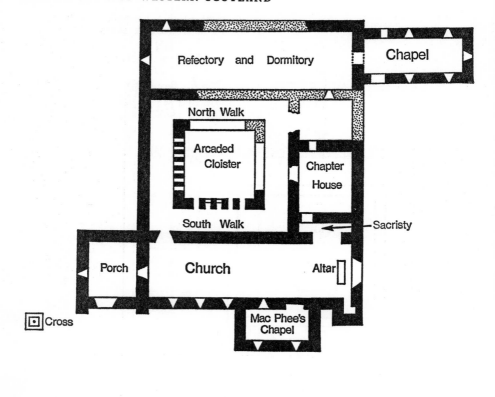

Diagram 14 *Oronsay Priory. Fourteenth century*

sixth King of the Isles. He probably built the priory at the same time as his chapel of Cill Daltain on Islay, for the shape of their lancet windows is almost identical, and both were donated to the Church in exchange for a bill of divorcement, which allowed him to marry the daughter of the king of Scots, Margaret Stewart.*

Oronsay is a tidal island at the south end of Colonsay. Measuring less than

* 1967: Donald.

21a. Beaker from a chambered cairn
at Rudh an Dunain, Skye.

21c. Fifteenth-century clarsach.

21b. Norse chessmen carved from walrus ivory, dated AD 1200, discovered in
1831 within a sand dune at Ardroil, Camus Uig, Lewis.

22a. The Book of Kells.
The monogram page,
Matthew 1.18.

22b. Grave slab of Murdoch MacPhee of Colonsay,
dated 1539, in Oronsay Priory. The great sword
and the galley were Clan Donald's emblem of
power over land and sea, and could only have been
used by MacPhee after the fall of the Lordship
of the Isles.

23. (*facing page*) The Kildalton Cross, Islay. This is the
most beautiful cross ever raised in Scotland. Opinions
on the date range from the eighth to fourteenth
centuries. The cross stands 9 feet and the whole
has been cut in one piece.

24. Herring girl, Castlebay, Barra.

three miles by two, it bears a conical hill of 304 feet, which has the priory set at the foot of its south-west slope. The priory was built on the site of a sixth-century monastery, thought to have been a dependency of Kiloran Abbey on Colonsay. That much-favoured island has traceable remains of ten old churches and Oronsay of two, in addition to the abbey, which by oral tradition Columba is said to have founded and dedicated to St Oran. The abbey has vanished, for its stones were taken by Malcolm MacNeil, who had bought the island from Campbell of Argyll, to build Colonsay House in 1722.* The priory was likewise plundered to build Oronsay farmhouse, but although roofless and ruinous, the walls are in fair condition.

The ground plan, eight-five feet by sixty-five, differs from that of Iona's nunnery in that church and refectory have changed sides and taken the full length of the north and south walls, while two small chapels project north-east and south. The rooms seem tiny and the cloister small. The church to the south side is sixty-five feet by eighteen, with entry through a porch to its west. It had extensive wooden stalls, of which a few traces remain, and an organ gallery to which access was given by a stone stair on the south wall. A schist doorway in the south wall gives entry to the mortuary chapel of MacPhee, which has been recently re-roofed to house twenty-seven tombstone slabs, each six feet long, on which are carved armed warriors, long swords, monks, a bishop, and an old woman, all framed with floral designs. Much of the art-work is of high quality. The abbey and old chapels of west Argyll – Iona, Oronsay, Inch Kenneth, Islay, Keills and Kilmory in Knapdale, Kilmartin in Lorn, and others, contain the world's most valuable collection of late Celtic stone carving.† On the north wall of the church, a schist doorway leads to the cloister, forty-one feet square. The walk is seven feet wide with arcades around the garth that have been most beautifully shaped in a style required by the peculiar kind of schist slabs used in the Hebrides for tombstones and crosses. The south arcade, unlike the others, has five round-headed arches, each long and narrow, neatly turned on thin slabs without freestone. The other three arcades, only one of which survives by a restoration of 1883,‡ were built on shafts two feet ten inches high by one foot broad but only two or three inches thick. They were placed thirty inches apart and given moulded caps and bases. Lancet arches were set on top by resting straight slabs against each other in reversed V-shape, each with ends cut to meet exactly. Martin Martin reported in 1695 that all arcades were complete.

* 1935: Loder.
† 1964: Richardson.
‡ 1896: MacGibbon and Ross.

A century later three had gone, but in 1883 fragments found scattered through the priory proved sufficient to allow a restoration of the west arcade, which is now the only example of its kind in the Hebrides.

Outside the priory to its south-west, a fine cross stands twelve feet high, carved in scroll-work and foliage not distinctively Celtic. The site is sunny if exposed, remote at the edge of the ocean. To its south-west an apron of skerries spreads around Eilean nan Ron (Seals' Island), where the colony of Atlantic seals is one thousand strong in September. The natural beauty of the priory's site is greatly marred by the farm buildings, which are set too close.

The Hebrides' only ancient church not ruinous, apart from Iona's, is the priory church of St Clement at Rodil in south Harris. By oral tradition the priory had been founded from Iona and destroyed by the Vikings. If so, it had probably been wooden: no trace of any domestic buildings survive. The existing church was first mentioned by Dean Monro in 1549, but no one knows who built it, or who was St Clement. Rodil had long been MacLeod's burial ground, so the likely builder would be an early chief. The church was certainly restored (if not built) by Alexander MacLeod (Alasdair Crotach), the seventh chief, around 1500.* Architectural features suggest that he used masons who had worked at that time on the restoration of Iona Abbey. During the last two centuries it has been four times repaired.

The church is small, cruciform, and made of local gneiss with sandstone dressings from Carsaig. The plan is a Latin cross with nave, transepts, and miniature choir. The top of the cross is to the east, while the west end bears a square, crenellated tower fifty-six feet high. The outer walls are undecorated, uncluttered by outbuildings, and of pleasing simplicity. The well-proportioned interior has been much praised for its decoration by three tombs in the nave and choir, each bearing the recumbent effigy of a warrior chief sculpted from a jet black schist that glitters with quartz granules.

The outstanding tomb is that of Alasdair Crotach in the choir.† Its form is unique in the Isles, for the only one like it – a recessed tomb with its back sculpted in panels in St Donan's chapel in Eigg – is ruinous and was never of comparable quality.

MacLeod's tomb has the arched recess entirely enclosed by a gable-shaped moulding. The outer face of the arch has for its keystone a sculpture of the Holy Trinity supported by the four evangelists, and below them eight other

---

* 1793: Statistical Account. 1884: Ross.
† Its description properly belongs to chapter 11, but I deal with it here for convenience.

arch-stones carved with haloed apostles and censing angels. All these are formal and not so distinctively engraved as the twelve panels on the inner face of the recess. The panelling of flat surfaces was typical of Celtic decoration, except that here the customary foliage is absent. The panels are in three horizontal rows. The top row depicts at centre the Sun in Glory flanked by trumpeting angels, with an angel to either side holding a lighted candle. The second row shows in the central panels the Virgin seated, crowned, and canopied, her right hand holding a lily and the other supporting the child. She is flanked by canopied niches containing a benedictory bishop and St Clement (so named on his plinth) holding a skull. The two outside panels portray a galley and castle towers. The bottom row has an armed chief setting off for the hunt accompanied by two gillies each with two hounds on the leash; three stags; St Michael and Satan weighing souls in the balance; and a last panel cut in raised Gothic script, recording in Latin that the tomb was prepared by Alexander MacLeod of Dunvegan, son of William MacLeod, in 1528. On the slab under the arch lies MacLeod's effigy in plate armour, wearing a bascinet and camail.* His head rests on a cushion and his feet on a mythical monster. His claymore, with pear-shaped pommel and straight quillons ending in trefoils, rests between his legs. The tomb as a whole is unpretentious, yet richly sculptured to a good design.

A few incidental carvings decorate the walls of the tower: on the west side a canopied bishop, with two men set on the cant below; on the east, two fishermen in a boat, with a horse below; on the north a bull's head – MacLeod's emblem. The south wall bears a rarity, a *sheela-na-gig*, or roughly hewn small man holding his erect penis. The Celtic churches of Ireland have at least thirty-six of these fertility figures, but the only other in Scotland, on the west wall of Iona's nunnery, has recently disappeared. The chips knocked off this otherwise excellent Rodil specimen were caused by the countess of Dunmore, who ordered her gillie to fire his gun at it.†

Iona Abbey is the Hebrides' most splendid building. Ragnall, King of the Isles, founded it as a Benedictine abbey dedicated to Mary, and built on the site of St Columba's monastery. Although his abbey fell to ruin three hundred years later, it gave the foundations and part of the wall and pillar structure of the present abbey when that was rebuilt between 1480 and 1500. A bishopric of the Isles had been created in 1430, and the abbey on its completion in 1500 was raised to a cathedral. The Reformation of 1560 made any monastery or a

---

* The battle headdress of noblemen from the late fourteenth century: the bascinet was a light steel helmet, open at the front, with a mail hood (or camail) attached.
† 1969: Moncrieffe.

church of that size equally useless to the diminished Church of the Isles. Iona was seized by MacLean of Duart in 1574, then by Campbell of Argyll in 1688. Argyll still owns it, but the eighth duke gave the roofless buildings in 1899 to the Iona Trustees of the Church of Scotland, who restored the church during the eight years ended 1910, and the cloisters, refectory, chapter house, infirmary, and Michael Chapel, during the twenty-seven years ended 1965.

The abbey stands on a meadow close under Dun I (pronounced Doon Ee), a hill of 332 feet near Iona's east shore. Its stone is a rosy granite quarried from Tormore on the Ross of Mull, and seen from that shore the abbey merges unobtrusively into the crags of Dun I. Seen close, its pink mass might have seemed too heavy in colour had it not, through the builder's foresight, been relieved with dark green and black schist, Torridonian flags, and creamy sandstone. The granite is further lightened by the sparkle of its own quartz and mica, getting more sun to that good end than Mull. The abbey is a very much better work of architectural art than might appear at first sight. No tall spires amaze the eye. It has no flying buttresses, no lofty dome, no glories of stained glass or multiple vaults. These would have looked inappropriate on a small island site, to which the abbey has instead been perfectly proportioned, the granite rough-hewn to match the crags of shore and hill, the ornamentation kept simple and the walls made stout to harmonize with the natural features of a windy coast.

The ground taken by the abbey is roughly two hundred feet square. The church on its south side is planned as a Greek cross, from which a square tower lifts seventy feet above the crossing. The main doorway faces west and dates from 1500. In front of it stands St Martin's Cross, with a concrete replica of St John's Cross alongside. The latter, made for the Iona Trustees at a cost of £5,000 and erected in 1970, is an exact reproduction, but looks so obviously fake that it does injury to the abbey's appearance.

Within the church there is much to appreciate, and detailed information is available on site, or in books published by the Iona Community. I give here only points of first interest. Porch, nave, and chancel, which together measure (internally) 147 feet by 23, are crossed at centre by transepts seventy feet long from north to south. All floors are flagstoned, and the nave has been given a flat wooden ceiling that in the Middle Ages extended over the now vaulted choir and transepts. The stones of the walls display such a variety of natural colour that they give to the church a better decoration than tapestries. At the crossing, the arches and piers to north and west are Ragnall's of the thirteenth century, as also a small part of the east wall in the north transept. On the latter hangs

Le Maitre's oil-painting of the crucifixion, remarkable for its successful angularities of form. The choir dates from the early sixteenth century, but the stalls are modern. To its south side, an arched aisle leading back to the transept has pillars of 1500 with Celtic carvings on the capitals, showing an angel trying to weigh souls while a devil tips the scales, a dove, a chief on horseback, crucifixion scenes, and grotesque figures. Identical slab carvings formerly in St Oran's Chapel bear the date 1489.* On the north side of the chancel, a superb sacristy doorway of 1500 has three massive arches of Carsaig sandstone recessed one behind the other in Romanesque style. The altar (now a communion table) below the big east window is made of slabs of Iona marble veined with green serpentine, quarried from a bay on the south-east coast.

Two doors in the north wall of the nave lead to the cloister, seventy-three feet by sixty-five. The walk is ten feet wide with sandstone arcades around a grassed garth. Only two arches of the original arcade survive in the north-west corner, but all were restored by 1959. Their slim, smooth lines contrast with the rough-granite, and the capitals of the shafts are being beautifully engraved in the leaves, fruits, and flowers of many nations. The work, by Douglas Bisset and Christopher Hall, continues. At the garth's centre a modern bronze sculpture by Jacob Lipchitz was erected in 1959, and has caused much controversy. It is in my own opinion excellent. The statue, squat and heavy, represents the descent of the Spirit through the Virgin, who is shown enveloped by a heart-shaped stream that issues from the beak of a dove poised above her hollow skull.

The abbey's domestic buildings were restored by the Iona Community founded and led by the Reverend George MacLeod (now Lord MacLeod of Fiunary). His Church of Scotland brotherhood of ministers and laymen have the task of maintaining the abbey, sharing a common life of worship and work, and of service in parishes.

There are many other buildings of lesser but historic interest in the Isles, like the ancient chapels of Kildalton on Islay, St Donan's on Eigg, Inch Kenneth off Mull, where Highland chiefs were buried when the sea was too wild for a crossing to Iona; the well-preserved fourteenth-century castle of Moy in Mull; the eighteenth-century round church of Bowmore in Islay; or, as an example of nineteenth-century building done by islesmen during the first potato famine (1835), St Mary's church at Bornish on the west coast of South Uist. The stone exterior at Bornish is as plain as any bit of island crag. Inside, the splendid gneiss and wooden pews have both been left bare. High up on the walls, arched

* 1896: MacGibbon and Ross, Vol. III.

windows add loftiness to the vaulted roof. There is nowhere any architectural decoration, yet the effect is powerful, for emphasis was given to simplicity by a renovation of 1956–58. Behind the altar, one huge green drapery falls from roof to floor. The nailed Christ is borne high on that wall on a great wooden cross. The stark dignity of this interior is quite unusual. I should not be surprised if it were unique in Scotland.

The very best of the Hebridean buildings demonstrate that their architecture is good art, not depending for effect on ornament, but relying primarily on the creative powers of the builder's mind and imagination, as limited by site, material, and funds, and by the ideas and opportunities of the changing times.

II

Celtic Arts of the Hebrides

Zoomorphic and symbolic figures carved on stone are the earliest Celtic art in the Hebrides. They belong to the Pictish period and cannot be dated more precisely. Zoomorphics are simple figures of mammals, birds, and reptiles, represented by deliberate invention of non-existent forms, although all limbs are correctly related. They are incised on otherwise undecorated stone with a skill and verve demonstrating that true copies of nature would have presented no difficulty. The best of Pictish carvings are said to be unparalleled in Dark Age art.* Man is never carved, nor is plant life, hence the zoomorphic forms, which are spread widely across Europe, seem to show that the imitation of nature was forbidden, perhaps because the creation of living things was the prerogative of deity, and too close an imitation by man presumptuous.† Whatever the reason, the Celtic artists of Ireland, Alban, and the Hebrides confined themselves to zoomorphics, which they used also to decorate wood, bone, ivory, and metal, and to very numerous abstract designs, almost certainly druidic. These include the crescent with V-rod and the forked lightning on mirrors, as shown below.‡ Floral carvings were not introduced until the start of the Christian era.

Later designs, which became distinctive to Celtic art in its Pictish and Gaelic schools, were elaborate spiral patterns and interlacings based on the craft of plaited basketry. Most races had used them for carvings – spiral key-patterns had been carved on mammoth ivories in Russia around 20,000 to 15,000 B.C.§

---

* 1954: Stevenson.
† 1944: Bain.
‡ For interpretation, see 1964: Donald, pp. 67–71; and 1970: Stevenson.
§ 1944: Bain.

1. TIREE

2. CANNA

3. S. RONALDSAY

4. CANNA

5. S. RONALDSAY

6. S. RONALDSAY

7. TIREE

8. INVERURY

Diagram 15 *Pictish Zoomorphics and Symbols*

– but the Irish and Pictish Celts developed them to a fine art early in the Christian period. Knotwork interlacing appears on Pictish slabs probably of the ninth century,[*] when these stones are for the first time not rough but dressed, and not incised but carved on both sides in relief. The Hebridean carvings reached fullest development in the Argyll islands of Islay, Oronsay, Iona, and Mull during the thirteenth to sixteenth centuries. Islay alone has more than a hundred examples,[†] many so weathered that only a trace of design is left, others well-preserved works of great character, like the crosses at Kildalton and Kilchoman. These, with the St Martin's and St John's crosses of Iona are the most beautiful of the Hebrides. Some are like panels from an Irish illuminated MS. Ranking with them, not in beauty of overall shape but in refinement of carving, I would place the MacPhee slab (1539) from Oronsay, and the tomb of Rodil.

Hebridean carving owed everything to the Irish masters, and to the Scots who brought them. All arts in the Hebrides depended for development on the leisure that patronage alone could provide, and this was dispensed by the clan chiefs and the Celtic church. On Islay, the Kings and Lords of the Isles appointed an Irish family as hereditary master-carvers[‡] (together with bards, harpers, and others). They were creative artists able to break with the older school by making original designs of scroll-work and foliage, which appear on their crosses at Kilchoman and Oronsay. The Kildalton Cross, the most famous of all, is most probably theirs too, for although like St John's Cross it is generally dated to the ninth century, there seems to be small justification for dates so early. The Isles were then overrun by Vikings who were ruthless in destroying every Christian trace. The Kildalton Cross was probably made for John I, when he built Cill Dalltain chapel in 1360 at the same time as Oronsay Priory.[§] The chapel in south Islay lies off the road on a site sheltered by birch and hazel. The cross to its side stands nine feet high, the whole cut in one piece with an open circle quartered by four arms, which like the shaft are elaborately carved. The arms do not form a perfect right-angle with the shaft, an irregularity in no way detracting from the moving grace of the whole form, which is enhanced by its green patina.

The scheme of decoration bears out the later date. Prior to the twelfth century the schemes usually favoured ornamental designs that excluded figures.[||] On

---

* 1896: MacGibbon and Ross.
† 1895: Graham.
‡ 1970: Donald.
§ Ibid.
|| 1895: Graham.

the Kildalton Cross, figures feature on all four arms front and back. The shaft is carved in spiral work and small bosses, the centre of the head (front) in a large raised boss of zoomorphics ringed by interlaced-work, and (back) a plain boss ringed by seven smaller bosses on a background of serpents. On the front of the arms are two angels, David grasping a lion by its open jaws, a sheep, two birds feeding on grapes, a virgin and child flanked by two winged angels, the sacrifice of Isaac by Abraham, and other figures. On the back are five beasts ringed by serpents, spirals, interlacings, and bosses. The same arguments on dating apply to St Martin's Cross, whose whinstone shaft is carved with Daniel and the lion, David playing before Saul, the virgin and child, and others.

Islay has seventeen crosses, Iona only three of note, for more than 360 were thrown into the sea by the reformers of 1561. From Islay to Lewis, numerous tomb-slabs survived, for they less often bore the crucifixion, being carved instead with chiefs in armour, swords, shears, leafage, fish, foxes, otters, wolves, hounds, stags, cats, birds, galleys, and the like. After the seventeenth century, the carvings show a marked decadence, for the Lordship had gone and the islands become impoverished on every plane.

The early enthusiasm of the Celtic Church, which had sped missionaries across Europe between Iceland and Rome, overflowed in works of art, literature, and chronicles. The monks' dedication gave them a vitality with which they were able to invest even the meticulously drawn complexities of MS illumination. They gave to it unflagging thought and imaginative invention, which transformed what might have been dull, burdensome work into marvels of design, colour, and calligraphy. Nowhere else in art is an infinite capacity for taking pains so distinctly a mark of genius. It attained its apogee in the Books of Durrow, Lindisfarne, and Kells – all three made at monasteries founded either by St Columba or by monks from Iona. The Book of Kells (the Gospels in Latin) is acknowledged by all as the most beautiful book in the world. It was probably illuminated in Iona,* where the scriptorium had been devoted to MS work for two centuries. Whether it was completed there or at Kells when the monks evacuated the island in 807-14, is unlikely now to be known. The MS has been dated to the late eighth or early ninth centuries. It and others of the kind powerfully influenced the work of Irish stone-carvers in the Hebrides, just as earlier three-dimensional work had given themes to the illuminers.†

The Celtic MS illuminations are the most extraordinary phenomena in

---

* 1970: Stevenson. 1964: Richardson. 1968: Grimble.
† 1944: Bain, but on this latter point a contrary opinion is well-expressed in 1970: Stevenson.

Europe's medieval art. They appear without certain source, without a fore-running development in MSS at home or abroad, suddenly an art in its climax, from which further work is deterioration.* The Norse invasions made continued dedication to the work impossible. Dedication is the appropriate word. Initial letters grow and spread over the pages in a richness of decoration hitherto un-attempted, often in work of such minuteness that it could not be appraised by contemporary human eyes, for which it was not made (optical glass dates from the eighteenth century). Professor J. O. Westwood reports from the Book of Armagh, 'In a space of quarter of an inch I counted with a magnifying glass no less than 158 interlacements of a slender ribbon pattern formed of white lines edged with black ones upon a black ground. No wonder that tradition should allege that these unerring lines should have been traced by angels.' In the Book of Kells, the monogram page of St Matthew (I. 18) includes a panel three-eighths of an inch square on which I have counted two hundred interlacements. The tools and aids to eyesight used by the monks to draw so exactly beyond the ability of modern artists is not known.† The Book of Kells would be distin-guished from all other of the world's MSS even by its smaller illuminated initials. Every verse throughout the Gospels begins with one, no two are alike; their profusion seems infinite in variety of original design, and so brings one to a sense of awe. The larger concepts of design have a grace no less marvellous, when one judges by the best of the work.

On the restoration of Scots rule in the Hebrides in 1156 and 1266, the arts again flourished, especially on Islay and the isles of Argyll. Islay had a privileged position in its nearness to Lough Foyle on the Ulster coast. Poets, minstrels, and stone or metal workers in circuit between Ireland and the Highland and Island courts naturally used the Islay route by way of Loch Indaal, more especially during the Lordship when Islay was the capital, but also long after. The Dewar MSS report that the traffic gave the people of Islay a wider outlook and a character unique in the Highlands and Islands, 'more cultured, perhaps shrewder and sharper than those whose home is in more retired places'. Before the Norse invasion the chief musical instrument had been the *chruit* or lyre, to which Iona's monks sang like the Druids before them.‡ It was ousted there-after by the Celtic harp or *clarsach*, which had a curved forepillar about three feet high, thirty-two metal strings, and a sound box hollowed out of solid wood. By the twelfth century the Scots harpers were renowned. Giraldus Cambriensis

* 1905: Haselof.
† 1944: Bain.
‡ 1932: Galpin.

(the Welsh historian), after praising the wonderful skill of the Irish harpists, whose music 'is not slow and solemn as in the instrumental music of Britain . . . but the sounds are rapid and articulate yet at the same time sweet and pleasing', adds that the Scots far surpassed the Irish harpists 'inasmuch as it is to that country that they now resort, as to the genuine source of the art'. The island harpists were held in great veneration and their names have come down to us: MacKerral, harpist to the Lords of the Isles, Roderick Morrison of Lewis, harpist to MacLeod, and others. Most were bards as well as musicians. George Buchanan (tutor to Mary Queen of Scots) wrote of the islesmen in 1565: 'They are exceedingly fond of music and employ harps of a peculiar kind, some are strung with brass and some with catgut. In playing, they strike the wires with a quill, or with their nails grown long for the purpose; but their strong fancy is to adorn their harps with silver and gems, those who are too poor substituting crystals instead.'

Early in the sixteenth century bagpipes had become a rival to the harp. There has been much dispute how and with whom the bagpipes came to Scotland. They were known in Mesopotamia and Greece in 700 and 400 B.C., in Rome in A.D. 54 (as shown on a coin of Nero), and therefore were certain to be known to the Celts. The Picts had them in the first century A.D.,* and the Scots brought them to the Hebrides from Ireland. Pipes were found better than 'buglis blawand hiddeous' at frighting an enemy, to which end they were used by Clan Donald at Bannockburn. The hereditary pipers to the Lords of the Isles were the MacArthurs of Skye, who founded in Islay (at Proaig) a school as famous in its day as the MacCrimmons in Skye. The MacCrimmons became hereditary pipers to MacLeod of Dunvegan from 1540, when Alasdair Crotach granted them land at Boreraig. Here, for nearly 250 years, their school won national fame. And that was not a reputation won easily in Scotland, where piping had become universally popular from the fifteenth century. The royal court had pipers from 1362,† kings played them, most Lowland burghs kept hereditary pipers, and Edinburgh fined citizens who refused pipers a billet.‡ The clan chiefs sent their pipers to the island schools for seven or eight years' training, and a good piper could memorize two hundred pibrochs.

The main parts of the Highland bagpipe are the windbag inflated by blowpipe, an oboe chanter with a compass of nine notes, and clarinet drones. The third drone or Great Pipe was added in the eighteenth century. The key is

* Quintilianus, and 1949: Sachs.
† Exchequer Rolls.
‡ 1947: Farmer.

A major with a natural G and sharp C and F, giving a scale unique to the Highland pipe. The same note is not easily repeated on the chanter without the interpolation of grace-notes called warblers, and these, originally used to hide a difficulty, are reckoned one of the beauties of pipe music, brilliance in warblers being the mark of a skilful player.

Ordinary pipe tunes – songs, ballads, reels, and marches – have three parts, each played twice before the next is begun. The classic music of the pipes, named *Ceol Mor*, or Great Music, is the pibroch, a uniquely Scottish art form that cannot be played on any other instrument. Basically it is an air with variations for laments, salutes, and gatherings, but is otherwise not simple, for the music is as highly stylized as a sonata. Nothing is haphazard, everything is strictly ordered. There are four main sections: the tune or *urlar*, *siubhal* or *dithis*, *taorluath*, and *Crunluath*. The *Ceol Mor* proceeds on a regular *urlar*, each of its sections (ten in all) being trebled (varied), some in free melodic style and others in a prescribed pattern of grace-notes becoming more and more complicated, and finishing with a repeat of the *urlar*.

The Scots pipers were taught verbally by *canntaireachd*,* a system of vocables each with specific meaning. A short excerpt from MacCrimmon's system goss thus:

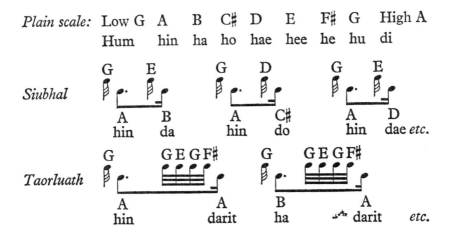

Popular as the bagpipes were, they were not appreciated in Lewis, where the violin became the favourite instrument in the seventeenth century. At the

* 1966: Collinson.

same time the trump or Jew's harp began to displace the *clarsach*. Music and all arts suffered a series of severe set-backs after the '45: the pipes were temporarily proscribed as a clan instrument, harp music died out, the chiefs withdrew patronage, the Church disrupted, famine and the clearances swept communities away. Even MacLeod withdrew his patronage of the MacCrimmons in 1770 – land values had soared and he wanted their Boreraig farm. Several hundred of the old pibrochs have survived through the piping families, who committed *canntaireachd* to paper. During this century pipe music has revived again, notably in South Uist and Skye, and indeed throughout the world. (But the college of piping is now in Glasgow.)

Much of the instrumental music of the Isles was generated by the Establishment – the hereditary musicians and their schools – rather than down at islefolk level, but that situation was reversed in song. The songs of the Hebrides show an outstanding range of expression. They are based on eleven different scales, including the major, Old minor, and the pentatonic. The latter (which corresponds with the five black keys of the piano) is one of the world's oldest, once used in tuning lyres. Most of the music is based on a melodic line with little harmony or counterpoint as we know it. Like much of Europe's music it developed from western Asia through the ancient Mediterranean world, and this influence still shows in a droning sound decorated with grace-notes, not unlike Indian music of today. Thus, after the Reformation, when the old psalters were destroyed, new tunes composed by Lowlanders substituted, and new verses in English sent out to the Hebrides without music, the islesmen had to learn the foreign tunes orally, and naturally decorated them with grace-notes, sometimes lengthening each syllable by as many as ten notes.* Furthermore, the precentor preceded each line with a 'reading', when he sang Asian-sounding cantillations having nothing to do with the tunes, which became known as 'Long Tunes'. Abbreviated versions are still sung in this way by congregations in the outer isles, each singer improvising grace-notes that weave an intricate pattern round the ground notes of the tune.

Hebridean songs cover every aspect of life; love and labour, war and religion, birth and death, sea and land, the odyssey and the dance. But the influence of the sea has been most pronounced of all. Something of its rhythm is always there. The best of the songs share an astringent purity of expression that associates in my own mind with wave-swept rock. 'There are melodies among these songs,' wrote Ernest Newman, 'that are as perfect as any melody could

* 1966: Collinson.

be. Schubert himself never wrote a more perfect melody than *Seagull of the Land-under-Waves.*'*

FAOLEAG TIRE-FO-THUINN

Old Skye air

Andante con moto ♩ = 78

Ho rionn ei - le   o   o hibh   o   o - i   ri_

bho   o-a   ho   ho__ rionn ei - le   o   ho-i - o

- ho   Fhaoileig bhig   is   fhaoileig   mhara   Ho rionn
(Little gulls and white wave-crests)

ei - le   o   O-ibh   o   o - i - ri - bho

o   a   ho   ho   rionn ei - le   o   ho-i - o

ho   Fhaoileig a' chuain na   ceil t'ealaidh
(Gulls of the ocean hide not your song)

The complete version has a slightly varied second half and has four verses.

The islesmen's vocal music often expresses emotion in purely musical terms by arrangement of vowels and syllables that need have no meaning save the musical. This is obvious even in *puirt-a-beul* or mouth-music, sung for dancing (in the absence of pipe or fiddle) in a repetitive, tongue-twisting rapid rhythm, similar to the pipes. Its recurring vowel-sound *u = oo* gives the mouth-music

* Recorded by Fraser and MacLeod, *Songs of the Hebrides*, 1909.

a live quality superior to an instrument, or certainly more passionate. Even in labour songs, like the best of the waulking songs, the singers can be carried away by the strong rhythm as they work to a crescendo. Many of the songs can be thought of as motifs open to elaboration, sung in a free style. Some are in rondo form, a chorus with verses framed for repetition without boredom. Rhythms, though strong, are sometimes irregular, like a milking song in seven-beat time, or a waulking song with five beats against three. Bards chanted long tales in metre, thus in several songs the music fits around words in phrases rather than bar-lines.

This long oral tradition (virtually nothing was written down) could not have survived last century's social catastrophe had not many of the songs been rescued by Marjory Kennedy Fraser and others. She learned to play the *clarsach* and to speak Gaelic, then with the help of the Reverend Dr Kenneth MacLeod (Skye and Eigg) collected *The Songs of the Hebrides* in three volumes. They began on Eriskay in 1905. 'In a little over twenty-four hours,' wrote Mrs Fraser, 'I had sailed, I felt, out of the twentieth century back at least to the 1600s.' One of the first songs they collected was *An Eriskay Love Lilt :*

> Bheir mi o ro bhan o,
> Bheir mi o ro bhan i;
> Bheir mi o ru o ho,
> Sad am I without thee
> Thou'rt the music of my heart,
> Harp of joy, oh! *chruit mo chridhe**
> Moon of guidance by night,
> Strength and light thou'rt to me.

Their work was invaluable, not only for the splendid collection they saved for posterity, but for the inspiration they gave to others to do likewise, and perhaps do it better. They have been justly criticized for their arrangement of the songs,† many of which were falsified in character to give popular settings. More scholarly work on Gaelic music has been done by Frances Tolmie, Margaret Fay Shaw, and Francis Collinson. Dr J. L. Campbell of Canna has recorded some 1,300 songs since 1937. The Provincial and National Mods organized by *An Comunn Gaidhealach,* and the BBC broadcasts, help to keep the traditional music and song alive. On hearing performances I feel an urgent need for new,

* Harp of my heart.
† 1966: Collinson.

288

creative composition. Fine as the traditional work may be – and while some is dull stuff the best deserves an international appreciation that meantime it does not have – it can remain a fully live tradition only if new work grows out of it, as it does out of Gaelic poetry.

The earliest Hebridean literature was the Irish transmitted by the bards orally in three cycles: ancient myths, the Cuchullin romances, and the Ossianic tales of Fionn and his son Ossian. To these were added much religious and secular poetry, panegyrics on the ruling families, and the clan wars. Fragments of these survive in the *Book of the Dean of Lismore*, written down in 1512–26 by James MacGregor; in the *Red and Black Book of Clan Ranald* by the Mac-Mhuirichs of Clan Donald, who flourished for five hundred years, serving first the Lords of the Isles and later Clanranald, from whom they held lands in South Uist; and in Irish MSS. Another famous bardic family was the O'Muirgheasains under MacLeod of Harris and Skye. Much of the bards' work has perished, but much would no doubt be caught in the net of the *ceilidh*.

The social life of the Gael found its most happy expression through the *ceilidh*, an institution that profoundly influenced the minds and lives of the island people. It was not as now a formal occasion or concert. Both the early and crofting townships were extremely communalistic, the people sociable to a degree no longer possible. After the day's cooperative work, when night fell, the houses were not places of private retreat. The people of a township strolled around visiting each other, passing the time in conversations (*ceilidh*) from which stories and song arose spontaneously. They would gather round the peat fires in each other's black houses to hear music and poetry and enjoy the sagas of the race. They sang their own songs and spoke their own poetry. No men were more respected than the bards, who would retell the ancient tales and folklore to eager listeners, and add their own compositions. Successive generations were thus imbued with a love of poetry and music, often passionate, both sexes developing gifts of expression and a quick ear for good work. A correct and fluent speech was encouraged, for this won praise.

A limit was put on the cultivation of arts by estrangement from the Lowlands, the lack of wide commercial intercourse, and the unremitting work that required every man to turn his hand to a wide variety of skills. Such conditions developed in men great resourcefulness, and gave them a range of interest that made for happiness at the expense of leisure. Thus Martin Martin, remarking on their genius for expressive as well as pragmatic arts, made this criticism in 1695: 'The unhappiness of their education and their want of converse with foreign nations, deprives them of the opportunity to cultivate and beautify their genius, which seems to have been formed for great attainments.'

Bishop Knox's *Regulations for Chiefs* of 1616 banned bards as sorners to be punished in the stocks, and decreed that the Gaelic language be abolished. He was of course ignored. The bards, in the absence of books, were a vital means of transmitting knowledge. They were also, in the absence of a Church that had deserted its station, not without moral force in praising generosity, kindness to the weak, courage, fortitude, and honour. But they eulogized the heroics of war, which drew the Privy Council's censure.

As if to mock the Council, a Celtic renaissance started in the seventeenth century, when Scottish Gaels began to transform the poetry of Ireland and Scotland.* The passing centuries had shown few signs of originality until Mary MacLeod of Bernera found new rhythms and stressed metres, at a time when new Highland bards were arising, like Iain (Lom) MacDonald (who was made Poet Laureate to Charles II). The aftermath of the '45 threw up a new and more gifted succession of lyric poets, men of greater art and loftier thought: in the Highlands, Alexander MacDonald, whose masterpiece was the *Birlinn of Clanranald* (the longest in the language, describing a voyage from South Uist to Ireland),† Duncan Ban MacIntyre, Robb Donn, and Dugald Buchanan (whose published verse ran to forty editions); in the Islands, John MacCodrum of North Uist (bard to MacDonald of Sleat). Their themes were natural beauty, love, elegies, satires, and the Jacobite cause. They sang in joy and sorrow, which even in translation shows their vivid imagery and depth of feeling.

These men re-created the Gaelic tradition, which numerous successors like Neil MacLeod and Mairi Mhor nan Oran in Skye continued, but the ban on Gaelic in schools, imposed by ignorant politicians to try to 'civilize' the Hebrides and Highlands by emasculating their culture, began to take effect. The education of the chiefs' sons in the Lowlands helped to transform them into an alien class of landowners. Bardship ended as a clan office. Patronage was stopped. At the start of the nineteenth century every Island and Highland district still had its own bard. A century later, when the Clearances had come and gone, Gaeldom had no poet of known reputation.

But the love and knowledge of Gaelic literature remained stored in men's minds. Some of the bards could still command more than a thousand stories, songs, and verses. The creativity killed out in one generation sprang up in the next. Local bards were at work as always, and their talent continues through

---

* 1904: Maclean.
† 1961: Campbell.

to the present in the verse of Donald MacIntyre (Domhnall Ruadh)* of South Uist and Angus Campbell (Am Puilean)† in Lewis.

A new base for the generation of literature became established in the universities. In Lewis especially, the number of both sexes who, through the Nicolson Institute at Stornoway, graduate at mainland universities, is higher in proportion to population than anywhere else in Britain. Portree High School is likewise an important nursery. The twentieth-century renaissance (1930 onwards) is largely the work of Lewis and Skye men, with communication by paper replacing the oral. Among its heralds were three Lewismen, John Munro and Murdo Murray, two First World War poets who broke with traditional metre and rhythm to express new experience, and after them the poet and essayist James Thomson. They prepared the way for the most distinguished poet of the century, Sorley MacLean of Raasay and Skye.

With MacLean the renaissance was seen to have arrived. His principal works (1930–50) used traditional metre in wide-ranging thought and sympathies new to Gaelic poetry.‡ His first collected works, *Dain do Eimhir*, appeared in 1943, and he is still writing. In the front rank of Gaelic poets today§ stands Derick Thomson of Lewis (son of James Thomson), whose verse to date has been published in three volumes: *An Dealbh Briste* (The Broken Picture) 1951; *Eadar Samhradh is Foghar* (Between Summer and Autumn) 1967; and *An Rathad Cian* (The Far Road) in 1970. The magazine *Gairm*, under his editorship, publishes a perennial stream of new poets, most notably Donald MacAulay of Lewis. Another of Lewis's foremost poets is Iain Crichton Smith, who writes verse in both English and Gaelic, short stories, plays, and essays in Gaelic, and novels in English. All those mentioned are from the academic field, and although the two schools meet in the work of Angus Campbell of Ness, the best-known poets are no longer living in townships. Although in one sense sad, this has none the less been good for their poetry: it has freed thought and emotion from the bounds imposed by the small social group, opened doors to let in a fresh, critical air, and led to great variety in style, form, and technique. The bards are keenly aware of the crisis in Gaelic culture and have managed to keep strong ties with their native life and Celtic tradition. Gaelic poetry and prose, although a relatively small stream, still flows with a steady pulse, for the Hebrides remain the heart-land, while the writers' township has become all the world.

* Collected Verse, *Sporan Dhomhnaill*, 1968.
† Collected Verse, *Moll is Cruithneachd*, 1972. Autobiography, 1972.
‡ 1968: Thomson.
§ *Glasgow Review*, 1965, Iain Crichton Smith.

It is not possible (as it once might have been) to cite any Gaelic verse as typifying contemporary work. But I offer a short poem from *Eadar Samhradh is Foghar* by Derick Thomson as an example of quality. The English translation is also his:

CLANN NIGHEAN AN SGADAIN

An gàire mar chraiteachan salainn
ga fhroiseadh bho 'm bial,
an sàl 's am picil air an teanga,
's na meuran cruinne, goirid a dheanadh giullachd,
no a thogadh leanabh gu socair, cuimir,
seasgair, fallain,
gun mhearachd,
's na sùilean cho domhainn ri fèath.

B'e bun-os-cionn na h-eachdraidh a dh'fhàg iad
'nan tràillean aig ciùrairean cutach,
thall 's a-bhos air Galldachd 's an Sasuinn.
Bu shaillte an duais a thàrr iad
ás na mìltean bharaillean ud,
gaoth na mara geur air an craiceann,
is eallach a' bhochdainn 'nan ciste,
is mara b'e an gàire
shaoileadh tu gu robh an teud briste.

Ach bha craiteachan uaille air an cridhe,
ga chumail fallain,
is bheireadh cutag an teanga
slisinn á fanaid nan Gall –
agus bha obair rompa fhathast
nuair gheibheadh iad dhachaidh,
ged nach biodh maoin ac':
air oidhche robach gheamhraidh,
ma bha sud an dàn dhaibh,
dheanadh iad daoine.

THE HERRING GIRLS

Their laughter like a sprinkling of salt
showered from their lips,
brine and pickle on their tongues,
and the stubby short fingers that could handle fish,
or lift a child gently, neatly,
safely, wholesomely,
unerringly,
and the eyes that were as deep as a calm.

The topsy-turvy of history had made them
slaves to short-arsed curers,
here and there in the Lowlands, in England.
Salt the reward they won
from those thousands of barrels,
the sea-wind sharp on their skins,
and the burden of poverty in their kists,
and were it not for their laughter
you might think the harp-string was broken.

But there was a sprinkling of pride in their hearts,
keeping them sound,
and their tongues' gutting-knife
would tear a strip from the Lowlanders' mockery ·
and there was work awaiting them
when they got home,
though they had no wealth:
on a wild winter's night,
if that were their lot,
they would make men.

Conclusion

The inhabited Hebrides, like mainland Britain, may have no wilderness country in the strict sense (unaltered by man), but in the broader sense their share of wild land is a huge one, for their industries have not been of a kind that mar natural beauty, even when causing change. Their land and life show extremes of contrast. Under lowering skies the isles appear as Britain's last frontier, bleak hill-spines half submerged on the world's edge. They are blasted by gales, and yet Scotland has no other coastland where spring and summer flowers grow so luxuriantly – the sea-air is scented and the eye dazzled. Miles of shell-sand beaches stretch alongside water so clear that the surface blues are underlaid by the bottom colours, by the sandy greens and seaweed mauves that glow through in the underwater light. In early summer the dark cliffs become alive with screaming sea-birds, while all along the machair larks sing and cuckoos call from dawn till midnight. Stark islands, where heather barely clings to naked rock, have green crofts with fields of yellow corn hidden among their many folds, or lazybeds where the ditches and burns are yellowed by massed irises. Palm trees grow in sight of quartzite mountain tops, and magnolias near seal-skerries.

The Hebrides are an asset to Britain. Their Atlantic scene and site have unique beauty and scientific interest. The islesmen are a distinctive people whose immensely valuable services to Britain and the Commonwealth have won small reward. Can their beauty of environment and way of life be maintained, and the isles held peopled and prosperous? In a country where degradation of the natural environment and concentration of people in conurbations proceeds apace, it is important that an affirmative answer should be found. It can only be found if the lessons taught by history are learned. I have picked out six of these lessons.

(1) The first requires acceptance of a paradox. In the islands, emigration is not necessarily an evil. Their natural resources have a natural limit. They can never retain all their young. Emigration of any surplus population is inevitable and desirable, for overpopulation impairs both the land and its people. At the same time, since depopulation in most islands has gone too far, every effort must be made to retain a people as large in number and as well-balanced in age and sex as possible, by conservation of land and resources, and by a deliberate central government policy of support for the nation's periphery.

(2) The conservation of land and resources by the preservation of dunes and marram, which has been much neglected, by reclamation or re-seeding of moor-land, in which the islesmen of Lewis have excelled, by tree-planting to give shelter-belts, and by conservation of fish stocks (at present inefficient) – all these are works that the islanders can accomplish for themselves given more autonomy, but with means and help from the mainland. The conservation of land and human stock go together, elementary moves in maintaining a way of life that gives deep satisfactions.

(3) The best way for central government to support the periphery has been shown by Norway. The very high cost of living in the Isles and the drain on industries caused by too heavy freight should be reduced by transport subsidy to equality with the mainland level, and by tax concessions. The tolerable prosperity of the Isles would be shed inwards to the mainland coastal regions. The whole country would share some of the advantage.

(4) The retention of young people in the Isles is of primary importance. The revival of industries no longer suppressed by excessive freight, which at present makes a double tax on their products, would obviously create more jobs for the young. But still more basically, the lack of secondary or high school education on islands, requiring the children's long absence at mainland schools and subjecting them to awkward, uncertain weekend travel, has had the effect of depleting the Isles both of young people who are wooed away, and of parents who would otherwise live there. The islands have far too few secondary schools. They should be given all they need, as a basic human right. The sum involved would be trifling compared to the cost of the rocket range on South Uist (£28 m.). It would be life-encouraging.

(5) I have tried to bring out of the recent history of the Isles an important fact, that the islesmen's survival has been due to the natural strength of the crofting and township system, which held them to the land when all else had failed. It alone was able to give the close communal work, the friendship, the sense of trust and constant sharing, that could bind people and give them

strength in face of a social disaster without parallel in Britain's recent history. They would be ill-advised ever to let outside planners talk them off their land or degrade their environment, or enlist them as rats in the money-race.

(6) Life and conditions in the Isles are so different from the mainland that proper government cannot be achieved by remote control. On the one hand, the support of central government is necessary; on the other, the efficient administration of the means should be left to the islanders in a greater measure than has yet been envisaged since they lost self-government in the fifteenth century. They have suffered continually through distance from the centre of power in Edinburgh and London, where ignorance of the island people, their life and land and working conditions, has been abysmal. Edinburgh when a capital city was more arrogant and less enlightened than London. It was the Scots, not the English, who tried in the seventeenth century to uproot the Gaelic language and culture, an act of mental darkness confirmed, ironically, by the Education Act of 1872. More pragmatically, a third of the landward houses in the Outer Hebrides had no piped water in 1972, although central government had approved a large swimming pool for the rocket range. Misgovernment by neglect and by misconceived legislation has afflicted the Hebrides for nearly five hundred years, and been due largely to the islands' remoteness and lack of adequate representation either on national councils or in parliament. The creation now of a regional authority for the Western Isles may be only half the answer. A lesson may be learned from the Faeroe Islands. Granted self-government by Denmark in 1948, they have since prospered exceedingly, for the release of initiative and enterprise that ensued, directed by men who knew the needs of their own land and people, gave the opportunity, hitherto lacking, for fulfilment. Given a like chance, the people and industries of the Hebrides could blossom as surprisingly as their own machair land in summer.

Bibliography

Bibliography

Geology and natural history: Chapters 2, 3 and 4

1865 GEIKIE, A., *Scenery of Scotland*.

1888 HARVEY-BROWN and BUCKLEY, *Vertebrate Fauna of Scotland*.

1897 GEIKIE, A., *Geology*.

1929 HARMER, S. F., *Cetacea. Encyclopedia Britannica*.

1941 HARKER, A., *The West Highlands and the Hebrides*.

1948 PHEMISTER, J., *The Northern Highlands, British Regional Geology* (HMSO).

1949 TANSLEY, A. G., *The British Islands and their Vegetation*.

1952 MANLEY, GORDON, *Climate and the British Scene*.

1956 CHARLESWORTH, J. D., *Late Glacial History of the Highlands and Islands of Scotland, Transactions of Royal Society of Edinburgh*, Vol. LXII, Part III, No. 19, 1954–55 (Oliver and Boyd, 1956).

1956 DURNO, S. E., *Pollen analysis of peat deposits in Scotland, Scottish Geographical Magazine*, May 1972.

1957 FORD, E. B., *Butterflies*.

1957 MACCULLOCH, DONALD, B. *The Wondrous Isle of Staffa* (3rd edn).

1960 MAXWELL, GAVIN, *Ring of Bright Water*.

1961 MCVEAN, D. N., *Flora and vegetation on the islands of St Kilda and North Rona, Journal of Ecology*, No. 49.

1962 ENGEL, L., *The Sea*.

1962 MCVEAN, D. N. and D. A. RATCLIFFE, *Plant Communities of The Scottish Highlands*, Monograph of the Nature Conservancy (HMSO).

1964 BEISER, ARTHUR, *The Earth*.

1964 BULLARD, E. C., *Continental Drift, Journal of the Geological Society*, London, 120.

1964 BURNETT, J. H., *Vegetation of Scotland*.

1964 MACVEAN, D., *Prehistory and Ecological History*, in *Vegetation of Scotland*, Chapter 16.

1964   RICHEY, J. E., *Scotland: The Tertiary Volcanic Districts, British Regional Geology*, third edn, revised (HMSO).
1964   SMITH, MALCOLM, *British Amphibians and Reptiles*.
1964   STEPHEN, DAVID, *Scottish Wild Life*.
1965   CRAIG, G. E., Editor, *The Geology of Scotland*.
1966   LAMB, H. H., *Changing Climate*.
1967   FITTER, R., *Penguin Dictionary of British Natural History*.
1967   RAYNER, DOROTHY H., *The Stratigraphy of the British Isles*.
1967   SISSONS, J. B., *The Evolution of Scotland's Scenery*.
1968   MATTHEWS, HARRISON, *British Mammals*.
1969   DARLING, J. FRASER and J. MORTON BOYD, *The Highlands and Islands*.
1969   FITTER, R., Editor, *Book of British Birds*.
1969   PENNINGTON, W., *History of British Vegetation*.
1970   RITCHIE, W. and A. MATHER, *The Beaches of Lewis and Harris*, Dept. of Geography, Univ. of Aberdeen, for the Countryside Commission for Scotland.
1971   RITCHIE, W., *The Beaches of Barra and the Uists*. As above.
1972   FORD, E. B., *Moths* (3rd edn).

Prehistory: Chapter 5

*c.*685   ADOMNAN, *Life of St Columba*, Edited A. O. Anderson and M. O. Anderson (Nelson, 1961).
1876–80 SKENE, W. F., *Celtic Scotland*, 3 vols.
1903   ALLEN, J. ROMILLY, *Early Christian Monuments of Scotland*.
1912   SOMERVILLE, BOYLE, *Callernish, Journal of the Anthropological Institute of Great Britain and Ireland*, Vol. xlii.
1922   ANDERSON, A. O., *Early Sources of Scottish History*.
1923   PERRY, W. J., *Children of the Sun*.
1924   PERRY, W. J., *Growth of Civilization*.
1928   ROYAL COMMISSION on Ancient and Historical Monuments, Scotland, *The Outer Hebrides, Skye, and the Small Isles*.
1931–32 SOCIETY OF ANTIQUARIES OF SCOTLAND. (1) *Excavation Report on wheelhouse of Bac Mhic Connain, North Uist*. (2) *Ogham*. Proc. Soc. Ant. Scot. LXVI.
1935   CHILDE, V. GORDON, *The Prehistory of Scotland*.
1940   SIMPSON, W. DOUGLAS, *St Ninian and the Origins of the Christian Church in Scotland*.
1946   CHILDE, V. GORDON, *Scotland before the Scots*.
1949   PIGOTT, STUART, *British Prehistory*.
1954   LACAILLE, A. D., *The Stone Age in Scotland*.
1954   WAINWRIGHT, F. T., *The Problem of the Picts*.
1955   CHADWICK, NORA K., *The Name Pict, Scottish Gaelic Studies*, Vol. 8, 146–76, Celtic Dept., Univ. of Aberdeen.
1957   BIBBY, GEOFFREY, *Testimony of the Spade*.
1957   SIMPSON, W. DOUGLAS, *The Historical St Columba*.

1958 PIGOTT, STUART, *Scotland before History.*
1962 ATKINSON, R. J. C., *Fishermen and Farmers,* in *Prehistoric Peoples of Scotland.*
1962 PIGOTT, STUART, Editor, *The Prehistoric Peoples of Scotland.*
1962 WAINWRIGHT, F. T., Editor, *The Northern Isles.*
1963 FEACHEM, R. W., *A Guide to Prehistoric Scotland.*
1964–70 DOMHNULL GRUAMACH, *The Foundations of Islay,* 2 vols, Graham Donald, Islay.
1964 MACKIE, EUAN W., *Monamore Neolithic Cairn, Arran, Antiquity,* March 1964.
1965 MACKIE, EUAN W., *Brochs and the Hebridean Iron Age, Antiquity,* 39, pp. 266–78.
      ——, *Dun Mor Vaul Broch. Antiquity,* December.
      ——, *The origin and development of the broch and wheelhouse building cultures of the Scottish Iron Age, Proc. Prehist. Soc.,* xxxi.
1966 RIVET, A. L. F., Editor, *The Iron Age in Northern Britain.*
1967–72 COUNCIL FOR BRITISH ARCHAEOLOGY, Scottish Regional Group, *Discovery and Excavation.*
1967 HENDERSON, ISOBEL, *The Picts.*
1967 THOM, A., *Megalithic Sites in Britain.*
1968 THOM, A., *Cup and ring marks,* in *Systematics,* VI, No. 173.
1969 CASE, HUMPHREY, *Neolithic Explanations, Antiquity,* XLIII, No. 171.
1969 MACKIE, EUAN W., *The Historical Context of the Origin of the Brochs, Scot. Archaeological Forum.*
      ——, *Radiocarbon Dates and the Scottish Iron Age, Antiquity,* XLIII, No. 169.
1970 HAMILTON, JOHN, *The Brochs of Mousa and Clickhimin* (HMSO).
1970 MACKIE, EUAN W., *The Scottish Iron Age, Scottish Historical Review,* XLIX, No. 147.
1972 HENSHALL, AUDREY S., *The Chambered Tombs of Scotland,* Vol. 2.

Historical and general: Chapters 1 and 6 to 9

1536 BELLENDEN, JOHN, *Chroniklis of Scotland* (a free translation of Boece's *Historia Gentis Scotorum*).
1549 MONRO, DONALD, *A Description of the Western Islands of Scotland.*
1566 CARSWELL, JOHN, *Liturgy.*
1578 LESLIE, JOHN, *De Origine, Moribus, et Rebus Gestis Scotorum.* (See E. G. Cody's edn of 1888–95.)
1582 BUCHANAN, GEORGE, *Rerum Scoticorum Historia,* 4 vols, trans. James Aikman, 1827.
1588 *State Papers of Scotland.*
1595 ANONYMOUS, *Description of the Isles of Scotland.* (Written between 1577 and 1595, probably for James VI.)
1598 *Acts of Parliament,* Vol. IV.
1598 *Register of the Privy Council.*
1627–28 MACDONALD, HUGH, *The History of Clan Donald.* (An MS history by the Sennachie of Sleat.)
1630 KEATINGS, G., *History of Ireland.*

1695   MARTIN MARTIN, *Description of the Western Islands of Scotland.*

c. 1730   BURT, CAPTAIN, *Letters from the North of Scotland.*

1746–75   FORBES, ROBERT, *The Lyon in Mourning, Scottish History Society*, 3 vols, 1894–96, ed. Henry Paton.

1755   WEBSTER, A., *An account of the number of people in Scotland in 1755*, MS in National Library, Edinburgh.

1771–5   PENNANT, T., *A Tour in Scotland and the Western Isles*, 2 vols.

1771–85   CREGEEN, E. R., Editor, *Argyll Estate Instructions, Mull, Morvern, Tiree, Scottish Historical Society*, Vol. I. (Constable.)

1774   *Home Office Papers*, 2 June.

1775   JOHNSON, SAMUEL, *Journey to the Western Islands of Scotland.*

1782   FLATEGAN and FRISIAN MSS, *Haco's Expedition against Scotland*, 1263.

1785   BOSWELL, JAMES, *A Journal of a Tour to the Hebrides with Samuel Johnson.*

1787   KNOX, JOHN, *A Tour through the Highlands of Scotland and the Hebride Isles in 1776.*

1791–98   SINCLAIR, JOHN, *The Statistical Account of Scotland*, 21 Vols.

1793   STATISTICAL ACCOUNT OF SCOTLAND, *Argyll, Invernessshire, Ross and Cromarty. Sutherland.*

1800   GARNETT, T., *Tour through the Highlands.*

1808   WALKER, J., *An Economic History of the Hebrides and Highlands of Scotland.*

1811   MACDONALD, J., *General View of the Agriculture of the Hebrides.*

1813   GRANT, PATRICK, *Decisions of the Court of Session.* (Collected by Grant of Elchies and ed. W. M. Morison.)

1819   MACCULLOCH, J., *Description of the Western Islands of Scotland.*

1824   MACCULLOCH, J., *Highlands and Western Isles of Scotland*, 4 Vols.

1825   *Moral Statistics of the Highlands and Islands of Scotland.*

1826   SINCLAIR, JOHN, *Analysis of the Statistical Account of Scotland*, p. 148.

1827   CHALMERS, ROBERT, *Picture of Scotland.*

1831   LOGAN, JAMES, *The Scottish Gael.*

1845   NEW STATISTICAL ACCOUNT OF SCOTLAND, *Argyll, Invernessshire, Ross and Cromarty. Sutherland.*

1847   *Collectanea de Rebus Albanicus*, Iona Club, Edinburgh.

1856   ROSS, DONALD, *Letters on the Depopulation of the Highlands.*

1857   MACLEOD, DONALD, *Gloomy Memories in the Highlands of Scotland.*

1857   REEVES, WILLIAM, Editor, *Adomnan's Life of St Columba, Irish Archaeological and Celtic Society*, Dublin.

1865   GEIKIE, A., *Scenery of Scotland.*

1866   NICHOLSON, Sheriff, *Report on Education in the Hebrides.*

1867   SKENE, W. F., *Chronicles of the Picts and Scots* (including *Tract of the Scots of Dalriada*, c.498, MS in Trinity College, Dublin. Other versions in Book of Ballimote and Book of Lecain.) Pub. by authority of the Lord Commissioner of HM Treasury and the Lord Clerk Register of Scotland.

1874   MILLER, HUGH, *Cruise of the Betsy*, 1846.

1874   WALCOTT, M. E. C., *Scoti-Monasticum.*

1876–80   SKENE, W. F., *Celtic Scotland*, 3 Vols.

1880 CARMICHAEL, A., *Grazing and Agrestic Customs of the Outer Hebrides.* Contributed to Skene's *Celtic Scotland*, 1880, and to Appendix A of Report by Royal Commission on the Highlands and Islands, 1884.

1881 GREGORY, D., *History of the Western Highlands and Isles of Scotland.*

1884 ROYAL COMMISSION, *Report on the Highlands and Islands and Evidence taken by H.M. Commissioners of Inquiry into the condition of Crofters and Cottars in the Highlands and Islands, 1883,* 5 Vols.

1887 ATKINSON, E. R., Editor, *Book of Ballymote* (giving first key to Ogham script).

1887 HENNESSY, W. M., Editor, *The Annals of Ulster* (original MS in Trinity College, Dublin).

1892 MACBAIN, *Ptolemy's Geography of Scotland.*

1895 SMITH, G. GREGORY, *The Book of Islay* (reprints of old charters).

1895–97 STOKES, WHITLEY, Editor, *The Annals of Tigernach* (original MS in Bodleian library).

1896 DRUMMOND-NORIE, W., *The Highland Sword, Celtic Monthly,* June, August, September, October.

1896 MURPHY, D., Editor, *The Annals of Clonmacnoise.*

1897 FRASER, J. A. LOVAT, *The Highland Chief, Celtic Monthly,* Vol. 5, No. 4.

1897 MACDONALD, DAVID, *The National Dress, Celtic Monthly,* Vol. 5, No. 9.

1899 CHADWICK, H. M., *The Cult of Othin.*

1900 CROFTERS COMMISSION, *Report.*

1901 PEEL, C. V. A., *Wild Sport in the Outer Hebrides.*

1903 JOYCE, P. W., *A Social History of Ancient Ireland,* 2 vols.

1903 MACKENZIE, W. C., *History of the Outer Hebrides.*

1904 BROWN, P. HUME, *Scotland in the Time of Queen Mary.*

1904 GEIKIE, A., *Scottish Reminiscences.*

1906 MACKENZIE, W. C., *Short History of the Scottish Highlands.*

1908–26 HASTINGS, J., *Teutonic Religion, Encyclopedia of Religion and Ethics.*

1909 BROWN, P. HUME, *History of Scotland,* 3 Vols.

1910 HENDERSON, G., *The Norse Influence on Celtic Scotland.*

1916 MACKENZIE, W. C., *Races of Ireland and Scotland.*

1919 MACKENZIE, W. C., *The Book of the Lews.*

1922 ANDERSON, A. O., *Early Sources of Scottish History.*

1922 ANDERSON, J. G. C., Editor, *Tacitus : Agricola.*

1923 MACCORMICK, JOHN, *Island of Mull.*

1924 MACBAIN, ALEXANDER, *Place-names of the Highlands and Islands of Scotland.*

1925 MCBRIDE, MCKENZIE, *Highland Dress, Harmsworth's Encyclopedia.*

1925 PRESS, M. A. C., *Laxdaela Saga.*

1926 WATSON, W. J., *History of the Celtic Place Names of Scotland.*

1927 SIMPSON, W. DOUGLAS, *The Historical St Columba.*

1929 KELLETT, E. E., Editor, *Northern Saga.*

1930 NICOLSON, A., *History of Skye.*

1932 LAING, S., Editor, *Heimskringla* (the Norse King Saga).

1933 MILLS, S. M., Editor, *The Saga of Hrolf Kraki.*

1935 JONES, G., Editor, *Four Icelandic Sagas.*

1935   LODER, J. de VERE, *Colonsay and Oronsay.*

1936   ROYAL SCOTTISH GEOGRAPHICAL SOCIETY, *The Early Maps of Scotland* (revised edn).

1938   MACLEOD OF MACLEOD, *The Book of Dunvegan,* 2 Vols, 1340–1920 (Spalding Club, Aberdeen).

1938   TAYLOR, A. B., Editor, *Orkneyinga Saga.*

1940   SIMPSON, W. DOUGLAS, *St Ninian and the Origins of the Christian Church in Scotland.*

1942   CUBBON, N. and B. R. S. MEGAW, *The Western Isles and Growth of the Manx Parliament, Journal of the Manx Museum,* Vol. V, June.

1943   MCLINTOCK, H. F., *Old Irish and Highland Dress.*

1944–50 LEWIS ASSOCIATION, *Reports on Harris Tweed, Fishing Industry, Western Isles,* etc., undated.

1947   CARMICHAEL, IAN, *Lismore in Alba.*

1949   ATKINSON, R., *Island Going.*

1949   DWELLY, EDWARD, *Illustrated Gaelic Dictionary* (preferred here to any other dictionary – records 100,000 words to which it gives more meanings than others, including the obsolete, as against 70,000 words in the most comprehensive Irish Gaelic glossary).

1949   KNOX, JOHN, *History of the Reformation in Scotland,* Ed. W. Croft Dickinson, 2 Vols.

1949   MACGREGOR, A. A., *The Western Isles.*

1949   SALAMAN, R. W., *History and Social Influence of the Potato.*

1950   KINVIG, R. H., *A History of the Isle of Man.*

1952   GRANT, I. F., *The Clan Donald.*

1953   MACGREGOR, A. A., *Skye and the Inner Hebrides.*

1953–59 MURCHISTON, T. M., *Deserted Hebridean Isles, Transactions of the Gaelic Society of Inverness,* 42, 283–343.

1954   TAYLOR, Principal, *Commission of Inquiry into Crofting.*

1955   CHADWICK, N. K., *Pictish and Celtic Marriage, Scottish Gaelic Studies,* Celtic Dept., Univ. of Aberdeen.

1955   DARLING, F. FRASER, *West Highland Survey.*

1955   GEDDES, A., *Isle of Lewis and Harris.*

1957   JIRLOW, RAGNAR, and IAN WHITAKER, *The Plough in Scotland, Scottish Studies,* Vol. I, Univ. of Edinburgh.

1957   DASENT, G. W., Editor, *Njal's Saga* (*c.*1250).

1957   SIMPSON, W. DOUGLAS, *The Historical St Columba.*

1960   BUDGE, DONALD, *Jura.*

1961   ANDERSON, A. O. and M. O. ANDERSON, Editors, *Adomnan's Life of St Columba.*

1961   ARBMAN, HOLGER, *The Vikings,* trans. and edited by Alan Binns.

1961   MOISLEY, H. A., *North Uist in 1799, Scot. Geog. Mag.,* Vol. 7.

1961   MUNRO, R. W., *Monro's Western Isles of Scotland.*

1961   SCOTT MONCRIEFF, GEORGE, *The Scottish Islands.*

1962   COULL, J. R., *The Island of Tiree, Scot. Geog. Mag.,* Vol. 78.

1962   O'DELL, A. C. and KENNETH WATSON, *The Highlands and Islands of Scotland.*

1963   PREBBLE, JOHN, *The Highland Clearances.*

1964   BLAKE, JOHN L., *Report on the Outer Hebrides Fishery Training Scheme, Scottish Studies,* Vol. 8, Univ. of Edinburgh.

1964   DOMHNULL GRUAMACH, *Foundations of Islay,* Vol. 1, Graham Donald, Isle of Islay.

1964   GILLANDERS, F., *The Highland Economy, Glasgow Herald,* 16 and 18 December.

1964   MARTECH CONSULTANTS LTD, *Highland Opportunity, Report for Scottish Vigilantes Assoc.* (Invergordon).

1964   PATENT OFFICE, *Report on Patent Design, and Trade Mark Case No. 16, Harris Tweed,* pp. 477–591.

1964   THIRD STATISTICAL ACCOUNT, *Argyll.*

1965–71   HIGHLANDS AND ISLANDS DEVELOPMENT BOARD, *Annual Reports,* Nos 1–6.

1965   SERGEANT, MAURICE, *Mull Survey,* School of Town and Country Planning, Edinburgh College of Art.

1965   STEELE, TOM, *Life and Death of St Kilda.*

1966   MOISLEY, H. A., *The Deserted Hebrides, Scottish Studies,* Vol. 10, Univ. of Edinburgh.

1966   MURRAY, W. H., *The Hebrides.*

1967   DOMHNULL GRUAMACH, *The House of Islay* (second edn), Graham Donald, Isle of Islay.

1967   MONCRIEFFE OF THAT ILK, *The Highland Clans.*

1967   ROSS, ANN, *Pagan Celtic Britain.*

1967   SIMPSON, W. DOUGLAS, *Portrait of Skye and the Outer Isles.*

1968   CROFTERS COMMISSION, *Recommendations for the Modernisation of Crofting,* Report to the Secretary of State.

1968   GILLANDERS, F., *The Economic Life of Gaelic Scotland Today,* in *Future of the Highlands.*

1968   GRANT, J. S., *A Prospect for Highland Initiative, Scotsman,* 24 and 25 October.

1968   THOMSON, DERICK S. and IAN, GRIMBLE, Editors, *The Future of the Highlands.*

1968   SMALL, A., *Historical Geography of the Norse and Viking Colonization of the Scottish Highlands, Norsk Geografisk Tidsskrift,* 22.

1969   HIGHLANDS AND ISLANDS DEVELOPMENT BOARD, *Special Report No. 2, Development of Fisheries.*

1970   CAMERON, LORD, *Report by Scottish Inshore Fisheries Committee.*

1970   DOMHNULL GRUAMACH, *Foundations of Islay,* Vol. 2, Graham Donald, Isle of Islay.

1970   GLEN, I. A., *Illicit Stills, Scottish Studies,* Vol. 14, Univ. of Edinburgh.

1970   THOMAS, C., *The Early Christian Archaeology of North Britain.*

1970   TURNOCK, DAVID, *Patterns of Highland Development.*

1971   CROFTERS COMMISSION, *Annual Report.*

1971   FRASER, A., *Crofting's Role in the Survival of the Highlands, Scotsman,* 7 August,

1972   GREIG, M. A., *A Study of the economic impact of the Highlands and Islands Development Board's investment in Fisheries* (HIDB, Inverness).

1972   HARDINGE, LESLIE, *The Celtic Church in Britain.*

1972   RUSSELL, W., *In Great Waters*, Special Report No. 7 on Fisheries (HIDB, Inverness).

Architecture and the Arts: Chapters 10 and 11

1856–67 STUART, JOHN, Editor, *The Ancient Sculptured Stones of Scotland*, The Spalding Club.

1862   MACLAUCHLAN, T., Editor, *The Book of the Dean of Lismore*.

1881   DRUMMOND, J., *Sculptured Stones of Iona and the West Highlands*, Soc. of *Antiq. of Scotland*.

1884–8 ROSS, ALEXANDER, *St Clement's Church, Harris*, Proc. of Soc. of Antiq. of *Scotland*, p. 118.

1886–90 SKENE, W. F., *Celtic Scotland*, 3 Vols.

1887–92 MACGIBBON, DAVID and THOMAS ROSS, *The Castellated and Domestic Architecture of Scotland*, 12th–18th centuries, 5 Vols.

1891   MACPHERSON, MARY (Mairi Mhor nan Orain), *Dain Agus Orain Ghaidlig* (Inverness).

1895   GRAHAM, ROBERT C., *The Carved Stones of Islay*.

1896   MACGIBBON, DAVID and THOMAS ROSS, *The Ecclesiastical Architecture of Scotland*, to the 17th century, 3 Vols.

1902   MACLEAN, MAGNUS, *The Literature of the Celts*.

1903   ALLEN, J. ROMILLY, *The Early Christian Monuments of Scotland*, Soc. of Antiq. of Scotland.

1904   ARMSTRONG, R. G., *The Irish and Highland Harps*.

1904   MACLEAN, MAGNUS, *The Literature of the Highlands*.

1905   HASELOF, A., *Histoire de l'art* (edited A. Michel, Paris).

1907   MACKENZIE, JOHN, *The Beauties of Gaelic Poetry*.

1909–22 FRASER, MARJORY KENNEDY and KENNETH MACLEOD, *Songs of the Hebrides*, 3 Vols.

1911   FLOOD, W. H. GRATTAN, *The Bagpipe*.

1911   MACDONALD, ANGUS and ARCHIBALD MACDONALD, *The MacDonald Collection of Gaelic Poetry* (from the Lordship of the Isles).

1920   SULLIVAN, EDWARD, *The Book of Kells* (reproductions of pages).

1924   MACDONALD, A., *Poems of Alexander MacDonald* (MacMhaigstir Alasdair).

1928–54 CARMICHAEL, ALEXANDER, *Carmina Gadelica*, 5 Vols.

1932   GALPIN, FRANCIS W., *Old English Instruments of Music*.

1937   GALPIN, FRANCIS W., *European Musical Instruments*.

1938   MATHESON, WILLIAM, *The Songs of John MacCodrum*.

1939   ROSS, NEIL, Editor, *Heroic Poetry from the Book of the Dean of Lismore*.

1941   SIMPSON, W. DOUGLAS, *Breacacha Castle*, Trans. of Glasgow Archaeological Society, Vol. X.

1942   SACHS, CURT, *A History of Musical Instruments*.

1943   MACLEAN, SORLEY, *Dain do Eimhir* (Wm. Maclellan, Glasgow).

1946   HALIDAY, T. S. and G. BRUCE, *Scottish Sculpture* (Findlay, Dundee).

1947   FARMER, HENRY G., *A History of Music in Scotland*.

1949   DONINGTON, ROBERT, *The Instruments of Music*.

1949   SACHS, CURT, *A Short History of World Music.*

1951   THOMSON, DERICK, *An Dealbh Briste* (Gaelic poems with some translations, Serif Books, Edinburgh).

1952–72 *Gairm*, Gaelic quarterly, 227 Bath Street, Glasgow, C2.

1954   STEVENSON, R. B. K., *Pictish Art*, in *Problem of the Picts.*

1955   SHAW, MARGARET FAY, *Folksongs and Folklore of South Uist.*

1955   SIMPSON, W. DOUGLAS, *Eileach an Naoimh, Scottish Gaelic Studies*, Vol. 9, Celtic Dept., Univ. of Aberdeen.

1958–61 THOMSON, DERICK, *Gaelic Poets of the Eighteenth Century, An Gaidheal.*

1959   BAIN, GEORGE, *Celtic Art.*

1959   SIMPSON, W. DOUGLAS, *Scottish Castles* (HMSO).

1961   CAMPBELL, J. L., *Birlinn of Chlann Raghnaill by Alexander MacDonald, Royal Irish Academy Text, Scottish Gaelic Studies*, Vol. 9, Celtic Dept., Univ. of Aberdeen. (See also translation by Sheriff Nicolson, *An Gaidheal*, I, 60.)

1963   CRUDEN, STUART, *The Scottish Castle.*

1964   RICHARDSON, JAMES, *The Medieval Stone Carver in Scotland.*

1965   SIMPSON, W. DOUGLAS, *The Ancient Stones of Scotland.*

1966   COLLINSON, FRANCIS, *The Traditional and National Music of Scotland.*

1966   MACAULAY, DONALD, *On some aspects of the appreciation of modern Gaelic poetry, Scottish Gaelic Studies*, Vol. 11, Celtic Dept., Univ. of Aberdeen.

1966   THOMSON, DERICK, *The MacMhuirich Bardic Family, trans.* of the Gaelic Society of Inverness, Vol. 43.

1968   GRIMBLE, IAN, *Unsceptred Isles*, in *Future of the Highlands.*

1968   THOMSON, DERICK, *Literature and the Arts* in *Future of the Highlands.*

1970   SCHOLES, PERCY A., Editor, *Oxford Companion to Music.*

1970   STEVENSON, R. B. K., *Sculpture in Scotland in the 6th–9th Centuries A.D., Kolloquium über spätantike und fruhmittelalterliche skulptur*, Band II, Heidelberg Academy of Science.

1973   THOMSON, DERICK, *Introduction to Gaelic Poetry* (Gollancz).

Appendix

Population of the principal island groups

	[2]1755	1801	1811	1821	1831	1841	1851	1861
Islay[1]	5,344	8,364	10,035	12,171	**14,992**	13,582	12,315	10,348
Gigha	514	556	511	**573**	534	550	547	464
Colonsay	439	805	786	904	893	**979**	837	598
Jura	658	1,202	1,157	1,264	1,312	**1,320**	1,064	1,038
Mull	5,287	8,539	9,383	**10,612**	10,538	10,054	8,369	7,240
Lismore	900	[5]1,030	1,323	1,638	**1,790**	1,399	[6]1,305	853
Coll	1,193	1,162	1,277	1,264	1,316	**1,442**	1,109	779
Tiree	1,509	4,001	4,142	4,181	**4,453**	4,391	3,709	3,204
Small Isles	943	1,543	1,547	**1,620**	1,005	993	916	567
Skye	11,252	15,788	17,029	20,827	22,796	**23,074**	22,536	19,591
Lewis	6,386	9,168	10,092	12,231	14,541	17,016	19,694	21,032
Stornoway[7]						1,333	2,374	2,587
Harris	1,969	2,996	3,569	3,909	3,900	4,429	4,250	4,178
North Uist	1,909	3,010	3,863	**4,971**	4,603	4,428	3,918	3,910
South Uist	2,209	4,595	4,825	6,038	6,890	**7,327**	6,173	5,346
Barra	1,150	1,925	2,114	2,303	2,097	2,363	1,873	1,853
	41,662	64,684	71,653	84,506	91,660	**93,347**	88,615	81,001

(1) The enumeration for outliers is included in each group-figure, as Cara with Gigha, Oronsay with Colonsay, etc.

(2) Enumeration by parish ministers collected by Rev. A. Webster, DD.

(3) Enumeration taken in June, increased by visitors.

(4) Detail for Colonsay, Jura, Small Is., Coll, Tiree, and Lismore not yet released by Census Office.

1871	1881	1891	1901	1911	[3]1921	1931	1951	1961	[4]1971
8,131	7,527	7,319	6,839	6,283	5,727	4,958	4,269	3,869	3,875
390	376	382	368	324	264	243	190	163	140
456	395	381	313	273	282	238	233	166 }	381
943	931	717	625	570	460	376	263	254 }	
6,335	5,529	5,029	4,557	4,082	3,707	3,149	2,625	2,330	2,170
705	619	556	494	407	350	280	191	155	120
723	643	522	432	389	383	322	209	147 }	1,054
2,837	2,733	2,452	2,195	1,825	1,716	1,451	1,200	996 }	
522	541	433	455	386	355	281	215	170	150
18,114	17,680	16,478	14,561	13,282	11,584	10,345	8,537	7,772	7,481
23,446	25,421	27,490	28,760	29,532	28,245	25,079	23,595	21,937	20,739
2,498	2,627	3,287	3,711	3,735	3,946	3,644	4,817	5,229	5,279
4,095	4,784	4,980	5,249	5,427	5,255	4,468	3,977	3,285	2,963
4,107	4,264	4,187	3,891	3,677	3,223	2,817	2,220	1,925	1,807
5,749	6,063	5,821	5,490	5,383	4,839	4,236	3,765	[8]3,995	3,799
1,997	2,141	2,359	2,545	2,620	2,345	2,140	1,884	1,467	1,159
78,550	79,647	79,106	76,774	74,460	68,735	60,383	53,373	48,631	[9]45,838

(5) Estimates from Webster and Carmichael's *Lismore in Alba*.
(6) Estimate by Carmichael.
(7) Stornoway figures are included in those for Lewis.

(8) Increase caused by opening of rocket range.
(9) Census totals are only approximate, for the Hebrides have a large floating population.

Index

Index